2000 BIENNALE OF SYDNEY 2000

VENUES:

ART GALLERY OF NEW SOUTH WALES

MUSEUM OF CONTEMPORARY ART

ARTSPACE

OBJECT GALLERIES

CUSTOMS HOUSE

GOVERNMENT HOUSE

SYDNEY OPERA HOUSE

SYDNEY FILM FESTIVAL

CITY OF SYDNEY

BIENNALE OF

12TH
BIENNALE
OF SYDNEY
26 MAY – 30 JULY 2000

SYDNEY 2000

SELECTION PANEL:

FUMIO NANJO

LOUISE NERI

HETTI PERKINS

SIR NICHOLAS SEROTA

ROBERT STORR

HARALD SZEEMANN

NICK WATERLOW OAM

Catalogue compilation:
Ewen McDonald & Rilka Oakley
Editor: Ewen McDonald
Copy Editor: Jo Wodak
Catalogue Manager: Rilka Oakley
Catalogue Consultant: David Ell
Design: Harry Williamson Design Partnership
Production Design: Andrew Davies
Print Production: Netprint Pty Ltd, Sydney
Scanning, Pre-press & Printing:
D&D Printing Pty Ltd, Melbourne,
using CristalRaster CTP technology
Printing plates supplied by Agfa Australia

All dimensions are stated in centimetres in
order of height, width, depth.

Biennale of Sydney 2000

ISBN: 0 9596619 9 9

1. Art, Modern – 20th century – Exhibitions.
2. Art, Modern – 20th century. 3. Art – New
South Wales – Sydney – Exhibitions.
4. Biennale of Sydney 2000 – Catalogs.
I. McDonald, Ewen. II. Biennale of Sydney.

700.7499441

Contents

Chairman's Foreword
Guido Belgiorno-Nettis

The 12th Biennale of Sydney is special, not just because it is poised on the brink of a new millennium, but also because it marks the commencement of our second quarter century of operation, an important milestone in the history of the Biennale.

From the very beginning when the first exhibition premiered at the newly opened Opera House in 1973, our aim was to bring to Australia the latest developments in contemporary art from around the world. Since then, eleven exhibitions have shown the work of over 1,000 artists from almost 60 countries. Participating artists, curators and critics as well as dealers and collectors have also given talks, lectures and workshops. This rich and steady diet of innovative art and stimulating artists has had an enormously positive impact on the visual arts in Australia. The dynamic program for international visitors has not only introduced fresh ideas and perspectives to the Australian scene, it has forged institutional and personal international relationships of lasting benefit. Dialogue is now firmly established,

along with robust cultural links which would otherwise not exist today.

The *Biennale of Sydney 2000* continues this outstanding tradition with a special international selection panel invited by the Board to bring their vision and expertise to bear on the challenging task of choosing the artists. Our distinguished panel members are Hetti Perkins, Fumio Nanjo, Louise Neri, Sir Nicholas Serota, Robert Storr and Harald Szeemann. Under the chairmanship of Nick Waterlow, they have shaped an exhibition specifically intended to mark the end of an era by concentrating on fewer artists whose work and ideas have stood the test of time. The result is a remarkable range of artists distinguished by their radical thinking and their innovative practice. Spanning a number of decades, the exhibition aims to demonstrate the continuity of work and ideas at the end of our century.

First and foremost I would like to thank the artists for it is their imagination and vitality which makes this exhibition possible. We are

particularly grateful to the generosity of lenders in many countries — both private and public — who have kindly agreed to lend works from their collections. Without their cooperation and flexibility this exhibition could not have been realised. We have acknowledged them individually elsewhere in this publication.

I would also like to thank our venue partners in this enterprise, the Art Gallery of New South Wales — the traditional home of the Biennale — as well as the Museum of Contemporary Art, which is participating for the second time and has dedicated its entire facility to this event. We thank both institutions for their commitment and infrastructural support. Thanks are also due to their staff who have worked in close collaboration with Biennale staff to realise this ambitious exhibition. We are also appreciative of the support and creative collaboration of our participating venues, Artspace, Government House and the Historic Houses Trust of New South Wales, the Sydney Opera House, the Sydney Film Festival, as well as Object

Galleries and Customs House. Without their participation we would not be able to present an exhibition of such colour and depth.

The support of the New South Wales Government Ministry for the Arts and the Australia Council for the Arts provides the backbone of our Australian public funding, and we are grateful for their contribution at a number of levels. This exhibition could not have taken place without the support of the New South Wales Government Exhibitions Indemnity Scheme, for it is their support which provides the crucial insurance cover.

We also acknowledge the generosity of this year's principal corporate sponsors, Tempo Services Limited and Transfield Pty Limited, as well as the continuing principal sponsorship of the City of Sydney, which has made an unprecedented commitment of support over three Biennale exhibitions.

I would like to acknowledge the generosity of many foreign governments through their cultural and foreign ministries, as well as their various individual arts agencies and cultural organisations. Their continuing assistance allows us to bring the world's most challenging contemporary art to Australia and to continue to offer programs which increase the vital cultural exchange of people and ideas.

Our debt to many supporting sponsors and companies who provided substantial sponsorship and valuable support in kind is acknowledged elsewhere in this exhibition catalogue. I would particularly like to acknowledge ABN AMRO, Accor, A.T. Kearney, Beyond Online, Issues & Images, J C Decaux, Lowndes Lambert and News Limited through the Daily Telegraph in addition to Toshiba International and Shisedo Co. Ltd. I would also like to extend a very warm thank you to our individual donors, Ann Lewis and David Coe, whose financial contribution is in addition to their substantial personal commitment as Board members. The assistance of Gene and Brian Sherman is also much appreciated and has helped to make possible the presentation of Cai Guo-Qiang.

Our dedicated Board of Directors and the commitment of the resourceful staff of the Biennale led by our dynamic General Manager, Paula Latos-Valier, have made possible the realisation of this 12th Biennale within a tight time and budget framework. Thanks are due to them all for their exceptional dedication and skill which brought the *Biennale of Sydney 2000* to fruition. We are particularly grateful to Nick Waterlow, who chaired and guided the deliberations of the international panel and worked so consistently to realise their curatorial vision.

Presenting and promoting Australian art for over a quarter of a century has been inspirational, not just to Australian artists but to Australian art as a whole. As we stand at the start of a new century, the Biennale of Sydney acknowledges the success of the past through the contribution and achievement of many dedicated organisations and individuals, and looks with enthusiasm to the possibilities of the future.

Second Nature
David Malouf

When Patrick White was awarded the Nobel Prize for Literature in 1973 he was honoured by the Swedish Academy for having, like a navigator or explorer, added a fifth and previously unknown continent to the map of literature; for having opened up to view the contours, the colours, the natural and social history of a New World that had till then been hidden and which had at last come into a being so actual and immediate that readers in the world at large could now enter and move in it as if they had known it all their lives.

The Academy was speaking metaphorically of course, but the metaphor was a strong one. The body of White's work, that fifth continent of fictional event and character, of evocative and sometimes exotic landscapes, was a product of mind and imagination but had a real counterpart of which White's version was a living reflection.

The notion of a new continent of the imagination, to be discovered and opened up to the scrutiny but also to the delectation of observers, is a useful one for all the arts, but especially perhaps for the visual arts, since there is always, in that case, an original that can be used as a gauge both of the accuracy of the artist's eye and the power of his transforming vision. It has always been the business of the plastic arts to render reality and at the same time, by recreating it in a different space, to bring into the world a new object, one that can be observed and even handled but which belongs as well to mind and consciousness, and speaks, through the visible, of what is there but cannot, until the artist has laid it bare and structured our way of seeing, be seen.

In fact 1973 was a late moment in the history of Australian 'making'. Our fifth continent had for millennia existed in the mind of indigenous Australians; its physical reality had been remade there as myth, song, body and rock art, and in story-maps in the sand. Long before White, others, novelists and poets, had found existential terror or comfort in its vastness and given a voice to the experience, both shared and private, of its people. Painters with an eye, an inner eye, for what is local and primary had already 'taken in' what was new and commandingly challenging in it, the expanse of its horizons and its soaring skies, the way its topography and vegetation are animated by the special qualities of its light and air. By 1973 the land had been remade in the consciousness of Australians as a second nature — nature domesticated, nature as Pastoral (one thinks of the imaginary temples that John Glover set down in a remote corner of real Tasmania, or the sketches the young Lloyd Rees made of his native Brisbane transformed to a classical city in the style of Poussin), nature in its wilder aspects as antipodean Sublime. All this was as much the product of rich imagination as of the recording eye, a world reconstructed in each artist and in each new work by a particular way of seeing, by many ways of seeing, since the land presents itself, from one part of the continent to another, in many lights and under many aspects, and to each observer in a different guise and with a different secret to reveal, as something both unique and ordinary, both familiar and new.

To see how all this works out in artists as various yet 'typical' as Von Guérard, Streeton, the Nolan of the early Wimmera paintings, Margaret Preston, the Boyd of the Shoalhaven landscapes, Fred Williams, John Wolseley, John Olsen, William Robinson, or to observe the use to which Ken Unsworth puts river stones or Rosalie Gascoigne the thistle sticks or a goose-feather that she translates from one landscape world to another, is to recognise the astonishing diversity of the scene and the multiple histories that are embedded in it. It is also to be brought up hard against what each artist brings to the scene: the different way each artist gets what he has grasped into shape, into the frame — or, in the case of photographers like Tracey Moffatt or Bill Henson, into the camera frame.

All this is a work of re-creation, of works made in the spirit of recreation or play, but sacred play, since what it seeks finally is a made place where world and mind, object and subject, are one.

And this is the point where two great and once widely divergent traditions cross: one the Western tradition of landscape thinking, and shaping and rendering, that goes back at least to the Renaissance, the other an indigenous tradition that reaches back millennia but has only recently, under European influence, found a way of achieving a more permanent form. By taking on Western materials and techniques, one of the world's most ancient forms of making has remade itself by attempting what might, till now, have seemed antithetical to everything it stood for: the fitting of its uncontained vision into the dimensions of a frame, the fitting in Time of what belonged originally, of its very nature, to the timeless and ephemeral, a map in the sand.

There are lessons here for every kind of making. The variety of what indigenous artists like the late Mick Namarari Tjapaltjarri or John Mawurndjul or Ginger Riley Munduwalawala create and have to show tells us much about how large a part the individual hand may play even in works where the subject is fixed and the role of the artist determined by strict customs. And in the commitment of indigenous artists to the sacred duty of recreating in apprehensible form their natural history and all its world of ritual and belief, we see in an open way what in other places has been obscured, that such work has its origins in a deep human need: to take the places we inhabit into our consciousness; to make them places of the mind, and by re-imagining them as objects that are graspable, to possess the world we live in as a part of our selves, a second nature where we are at last fully at home.

Tracey Moffatt
Something More No. 1 1989
photograph
90 x 150 cm
courtesy Roslyn Oxley9 Gallery, Sydney

Bruce Nauman
*Left or Standing, Standing or Left
Standing* 1971-1999
wallboard, yellow fluorescent lights,
text, video text "standing"
courtesy Sperone Westwater,
New York

Introduction
Nick Waterlow

Every word, every line, every thought is prompted by the age we live in, with all its circumstances, its ties, its efforts, its past and present. It is impossible to act or think independently and arbitrarily. This is comforting in a way. To the individual, the collective experience of the age represents a bond — and also, in a sense, security; there will always be possibilities even in disaster. — Gerhard Richter, *Notizen*, 1962

The Biennale of Sydney in the year 2000 differs from its predecessors in several ways. The most noticeable alteration is that for the second time in its 27 year history no single artistic director has been in charge. The inaugural Biennale, held at the Opera House in 1973 and opened by Prime Minister Gough Whitlam, was chosen by a committee. This, the twelfth, is selected by a panel of six curators and museum specialists from different parts of the world.

In 1998 the Board of the Biennale formed a think-tank, charged with the task of conceiving an exhibition that would make a clear mark in a year crowded with significant events, each clamouring for public attention both internationally and nationally. One thought was that, in this instance, several good minds might be better than one and that a group of well-informed people around the world might produce an exhibition of greater breadth with easier access to both artists and their work than might otherwise be the case. A second thought was that there needed to be a balance between existing and new work, as well as between painting, sculpture and other more traditional mediums and installation, electronic, film and video based work. A third thought was that the exhibition should bring together a multi-generational group of artists whose vision has effected change, from a local to a global extent; and that the Biennale should draw attention to the continuity of vision linking the two centuries.

The Biennale Board accepted all these recommendations and proceeded to invite six key people to join an international selection panel. Each one enthusiastically agreed to participate, which speaks well of the esteem in which the Biennale of Sydney is held. They were Fumio Nanjo (Tokyo), Louise Neri (New York), Hetti Perkins (Sydney), Sir Nicholas Serota (London), Robert Storr (New York) and Harald Szeemann (Zurich). I was asked to chair the panel and to act as a link between the Board and the selection process. Authority without responsibility seemed an ideal position but any such dream role was dispelled rather quickly. Working with this group of colleagues has been demanding yet rewarding — much time and effort has been devoted to the exhibition despite hectic individual schedules.

The original brief to the selection panel, which I paraphrase, suggested 'the exhibition concentrate on a select number of living artists whose work has had the most lasting impact and has challenged the status quo over the past fifteen to twenty years. Many will have been outstanding and individual thinkers of this age, whose work has created controversy and caused attitudes to change. They could all be defined as change agents.'

Each member was asked to think globally and put forward a number of artists. Deliberation took place over several months and culminated in two key meetings of the selection panel which took place in Venice in June 1999, to coincide with the opening of Harald Szeemann's Biennale. Murphy's Law (if anything can go wrong it always will) intervened and to my disappointment, at the last minute, I was unable to attend. However Paula Latos-Valier, General Manager of the Biennale of Sydney, was present, Nick Serota agreed to hold the reins, and I was in touch via telephone conference calls. The result was a preliminary list of artists, an outline of works, and a working title Agents of Change. From this solid base the 12th Biennale of Sydney evolved.

The panel nominated a number of key artists as foundation stones — Louise Bourgeois, Ilya and Emilia Kabakov, Bruce Nauman, Sigmar Polke, Gerhard Richter and Richard Serra. A group was established around the notion of Chaos Theory, centred on Dieter Roth who, though no longer alive, remains influential along with the late Martin Kippenberger, Franz West and Paul McCarthy. Attention was then turned to significant artists from Asia even though some are now based in New York. These include Cai Guo-Qiang, Yayoi Kusama, Mariko Mori, Xu Bing, Yun Suknam, the Philippines collective Sanggawa and Yoko Ono. Artists from Europe and the Americas were added — Doug Aitken, Matthew Barney, Vanessa Beecroft, Sophie Calle, Marlene Dumas, Andreas Gursky, Boris Mikhailov, Juan Muñoz, Chris Ofili, Pipilotti Rist, Luc Tuymans, Gillian Wearing, Stan Douglas, Gary Hill, Adriana Varejão and Jeff Wall. These artists were considered to be innovators in their respective fields.

Alongside these groupings African-based Seydou Keïta and Bodys Isek Kingelez and Iranian-born Shirin Neshat were selected, each of whom has introduced new knowledge through their practice. To complete the survey Australian and New Zealand artists were selected, including a number of important indigenous artists from both countries.

The process of creating an exhibition, particularly one of this complexity and with six curators based in different parts of the world, requires flexibility, durability and ingenuity, as well as openness and trust. This was necessary because several artists on the original list, including Maurizio Cattelan, David Hammons, Gabriel Orozco, Doris Salcedo, Sigmar Polke and Richard Serra, were for a variety of reasons unable to participate and because the global focus and generational balance as well as a range of different practices had to be maintained. Robert Storr described the outcome as "an assorted assortment — or curatorial readymade — but a lively group in the end". Nick Serota comments in his interview that: "when you bring together a group of people with very diverse backgrounds you can have a much more interesting conversation, and hopefully that will be reflected in the experience of the visitor at the Biennale; that is to say that you get a much richer show. I think one of the great strengths of the exhibition in 2000 will be its diversity." There is certainly remarkable painting, sculpture and photography as well as electronic media.

As the exhibition took shape it became obvious that the working title Agents of Change was no longer appropriate for the range of artists and projects selected — especially as some of the younger artists included in the show have had as yet little international exposure. As a title the directness of Biennale of Sydney 2000 became more appealing — it epitomises the broad range of ideas and concerns included in the exhibition unhindered by any particular curatorial impediment. This Biennale looks at the work of one millennium as a way of moving forward to the next.

Since its inauguration in 1973 over 1000 of the world's most remarkable artists have been represented in twelve Biennale exhibitions. Much important work would never otherwise have been seen in Australia. The Biennale has been instrumental in creating both a critical awareness and an informed understanding of the minds and motivations of contemporary artists. One way this has been achieved is through lectures, workshops and discussions with visiting and local artists, curators, writers and museum specialists. This Biennale features a number of talks involving luminaries outside the visual arts but in related creative fields such as film, food, architecture and design, and the sciences.

One of the most remarkable manifestations of the past quarter century has been the emergence of Aboriginal art into the international arena. The first time that Aboriginal artists were included in an international exhibition was in the 1979 Biennale of Sydney. Subsequent Biennales have also included their work, a highlight being the *Aboriginal Memorial* in the 1988 exhibition. This consisted of 200 hollow log bone coffins which are now in the collection of the National Gallery of Australia.

The Biennale of Sydney 2000 includes the work of Aboriginal artists from both rural and urban settings, from the bark painting of John Mawurndjal to the photographic and film imagery of Destiny Deacon. Australian representation alongside this work includes Ken Unsworth, whose river stone sculptures made such an impact at the 1978 Venice Biennale; disquieting photographic sequences by Bill Henson; Fiona Hall's *Gene Pool* garden which reunites species from Gondwanaland; bronze and wax sculptures and woodcuts by Mike Parr; and Gwyn Hanssen Pigott's delicate ceramic forms. New Zealand representation includes a body of work by the late, much lamented Rosalie Gascoigne; Lisa Reihana's video installation *Native Portraits* and a range of congruent objects; the performance group The Pacific Sisters; and Bill Hammond with a series of iconic paintings often representing upright bird-like sentinels guarding a lost world.

The international selection panel has chosen artists from most parts of the globe, many disciplines and several generations, as well as a number of artists being seen in Australia for the first time, as should always be the case. These include Luc Tuymans from Belgium with a range of enigmatic and powerful paintings, Adriana Varejaõ from Brazil whose post-colonial two-dimensional surfaces literally burst at the seams, and from the United States Doug Aitken with a haunting signature video piece *Eraser* and Paul McCarthy with the remarkable new baroque setting for his multimedia installation *Painter*. Others who are prominent elsewhere but seldom seen in Australia include Yoko Ono, Matthew Barney, Gary Hill, Marlene Dumas and Jeff Wall. Ground-breaking electronic media artists including Matthew Barney, Stan Douglas, Gary Hill, Shirin Neshat and Pipilotti Rist are also represented.

This Biennale highlights a remarkable range of different painting styles in the work of Gordon Bennett, Marlene Dumas, Bill Hammond, John Mawurndjul, Chris Ofili, Gerhard Richter, Ginger Riley, Sanggawa, Mick Namarari Tjapaltjarri, Luc Tuymans and Adriana Varejão. Luc Tuymans explains these differences, in relation to portraiture, in a recent interview (*Modern Painters*, Autumn 1999): "If I were to paint you, your face would be longer. It's unavoidable. I might try to go against that, but still in the end there would be distortion. And that's what painting is: in a sense it is distortion. So it's as

inadequate as any other form of memory. But the strange thing is that it is memorised differently, because it is rendered in paint, and also through a person. For that reason people will always react completely differently to a painting than to a photograph or a film, or any other medium."

The continuity of art is one of the themes explored by the Biennale's selection panel as relevant to the new millennium. Bryan Robertson, who produced the memorable *Australian Painters* exhibition in 1961 when director of London's Whitechapel Art Gallery, comments on this premise in his introduction to his *Critic's Choice* exhibition at Cambridge's Fitzwilliam Museum: "ancient art, classical or medieval art is for me not remote or dead but totally alive forever, making a continuous whole with the best of art made yesterday or today. All great art lives in a continuous present." There are now only artificial divides between robust contemporary art and that of the past. The last century thrived on the ideology of progress and hierarchy, with one movement succeeding another and one centre dominating the periphery. That will not be the case in the new century. The Biennale of Sydney 2000 presents, in the words of Gerhard Richter, "the collective experience of the age" through the vision of a number of artists, so necessary as an antidote to existing hegemonies.

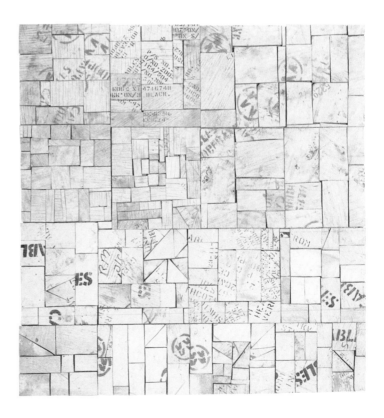

Rosalie Gascoigne
White City 1993-1994
synthetic polymer paint on sawn wood
on composition board
110.5 x 108 cm
collection: the artist's estate
courtesy Roslyn Oxley9 Gallery, Sydney

Stealing time
Hetti Perkins

Let none tell me the past is wholly gone.
Now is so small a part of time, so small a part
Of all the race years that have moulded me.[1]

Indigenous Australian art has undergone change more radical and profound in a mere two hundred or so years than possibly in any of the preceding thousands, even hundreds of thousands, of years that place it as the world's oldest continuous art tradition. While evidence exists of innovation prior to colonisation, it is irrefutable that all post-colonial indigenous artists are the harbingers of immense change. The Aboriginal and Torres Strait Islander artists in the *Biennale of Sydney 2000* are representatives of an historic and fundamental transformation of indigenous art in Australia. And still indigenous culture, of which art is the artefact, remains immutable as an essence that permeates the life of every indigenous person. It is the diverse revelations of this spirit that characterise indigenous art now.

Within this climate of change, the last few decades of the twentieth century witnessed a revolutionary shift in indigenous arts: in film, literature, dance, performance and, of course, the visual arts. This sudden emergence was all the more extraordinary considered in the context of Australia's colonial past and the active suppression of our cultural heritage. With few exceptions, those in positions of authority over indigenous people — from the government to the church, mission managers to pastoralists — made determined efforts to undermine the fundamental links that connect the individual to culture through language, country and family.

Paradoxically, it was precisely this external pressure that triggered a virtual implosion of indigenous culture. Such a radical shift in the visibility of indigenous art cannot be seen as some kind of gradual 'evolution'. Nor can the motive for such an outpouring of cultural expression be simply and cynically reduced to

Mick Namarari Tjapaltjarri
Untitled 1989
polymer paint on canvas
149 x 35 cm
collection: Anthony &
Beverly Knight, Melbourne

Destiny Deacon (opposite)
The Fashion Parade 1991
colour photocopy
21 x 29.7 cm
courtesy the artist

mere financial impetus, as Aboriginal artists laboured for too many years with little or no economic benefit. Rather, indigenous arts were forged in the aftershock of the cataclysmic act of invasion, experienced by successive Aboriginal communities as the colonial frontier swept through the country. The result was a critical transformation of Aboriginal art through the work of contemporary indigenous artists who have, in turn, transformed Australia's cultural landscape.

Yet the fact that this revolutionary art movement remains firmly rooted in a distinctive cultural tradition has seen it largely excluded from the contemporary arts arena. The western dialectic of traditional and contemporary fails to accommodate change within indigenous art practice, whether it be the innovative potential of bark

 painting or the metamorphoses of rock and sandpainting. Artists using introduced media are accommodated by being aligned with or assimilated into western art. However, it is also often those artists using the tools of the avant-garde who are the most vehement critics of the self-invested centres of political and artworld power.

The scepticism with which change in indigenous art is received is ironic considering the positive connotations allied with the notion of progress in the western context. When applied to Aboriginal art it is seen as a negative, an arbiter of the end — a modern day echo of the dying race theories that preceded the assimilationist policies of the mid-20th century. And, indeed, when considered in the context of land loss, trauma and poverty it could appear a reasonable assumption. Yet there is another side that speaks of cultural maintenance and resilience.

The phenomenon of Papunya Tula painting, which heralded the Western Desert art movement, is one of the most remarkable stories in Australian art history. It began in the early 1970s in a small government-established settlement several hours by dirt road west of Alice Springs. It was in Papunya that hundreds of Aboriginal people of differing language groups from surrounding country converged in accordance

with the government's centralising policy of the day. Faced with land loss, high mortality rates and endemic poverty, Papunya was a dismal and depressing community presenting few opportunities for its indigenous inhabitants. On the flip side of the social burden were extreme cultural tensions created by the proximity of different language groups and their limited ability to maintain their cultural obligations.

Mick Namarari Tjapaltjarri, who passed away in late 1998, was one of a group of men who began painting in Papunya encouraged by the arrival of schoolteacher Geoff Bardon in the early 1970s. Tjapaltjarri proceeded to maintain a 'consistently brilliant' presence in the movement's history.[2] An innovator even in the earliest days of the movement, Tjapaltjarri continued to reinvent his style and interpretation of his Tjukurrpa (dreaming stories). The influence of Tjapaltjarri's subtle graduations of dashes, undulating stripes and billowing clouds of bright coloured dots can be seen in the works of his peers in the late 1980s, yet the origins of these apparently unorthodox images lie in his archetypal works created at the genesis of the Papunya Tula movement. A senior Pintupi man, Tjapaltjarri extended the classic iconic references to his country and its stories to encompass an interpretative visual narrative that conveyed his own affinity with country.

Particularly over the past decade, Eastern Kunwinjku artist John Mawurndjul has developed an inventive and distinctive painting style that centres on experimentation with rarrk (cross hatching infill) as a creative feature in his bark paintings. Dispersed among the intersecting planes of rarrk are repeating patterns that have literal meanings. Circular symbols representing sacred waterholes float across the surface of the rarrk, which at times assumes the transformative power of Ngalyod (the rainbow serpent), evolving into the writhing body of the serpent or becoming flayed, landscape-like, over the bark's surface. In recent times, this innovative treatment of rarrk has extended to the point where it dominates almost the entire surface of the bark, overwhelming the figurative elements. In these later works the formidable authority of Ngalyod and the sacredness of the Mardayin ceremonies are implicit in this 'abstract' expression of ancestral power.

Mawurndjul's artistic lineage may be traced back to the late Peter Marralwanga and Yirawala, artistic contemporaries and friends in their time. Demonstrating an aptitude as a painter early in his life, Mawurndjul was greatly encouraged by Marralwanga who, like Yirawala (once dubbed the Picasso of Arnhem Land!), was a respected cultural leader recognised by many as a pioneer in bark painting. While Marralwanga was ritually responsible for Mawurndjul's cultural upbringing, he was also a key influence in the realisation of Mawurndjul's artistic potential.[3] Yirawala and

southeastern Arnhem Land. This single-minded dedication is reminiscent of the late Rosalie Gascoigne, both artists assembling idiosyncratic constructions of familiar landscapes. Comprising a series of recurring elements, Riley's paintings exploit fantastic colour and compositional combinations to brilliant effect. His blazing sunsets and bright skyscapes are often framed

Marralwanga painted regularly from the early 1970s after having established the outstation at Marrkolidjban southwest of Maningrida. Many Aboriginal families, like Tjapaltjarri's, moved back to their traditional lands following the implementation of land rights in the Northern Territory. Subsequently, regional art centres were set up by Aboriginal communities to service the artists of the area, such as Maningrida Arts and Culture in central Arnhem Land. Maningrida artists, including England Banggala, James Iyuna (Mawurndjul's younger brother) and Crusoe Kuningbal, are noted for their sculptures of towering spirit beings, conveying their ongoing presence and influence. Mawurndjul and his family also established an outstation in the early 1990s at Milmilngkan, in country whose natural and supernatural features continue to emerge in his paintings. "Sometimes that Ngalyod gets inside my head and makes me go mad."[4]

"My mind is all over the place — here, there, over there."[5] Since emerging as a dynamic new force in contemporary indigenous arts ten years ago, Ginger Riley Munduwalawala has relentlessly pursued an idiosyncratic vision of his country, saying "I do not look backward. I look forward." Riley's fascination for painting was inspired by an encounter with Albert Namatjira in the late 1950s. Like Namatjira, Riley is now renowned for his panoramic visions of his 'mother country', around Limmen Bight River in

by the triangular body markings of the Mara people, while the idiosyncratic flattened foregrounding of the landscape is embellished by stippled pastel hues. Ngak Ngak, the sea eagle, dominates the Riley landscape. Whether impressively perched on the Four Archers or swooping vengefully out of the sky, its iconic status testifies the respect Riley accords this significant ancestral being.

In recent works a new theme has emerged, following Riley's inheritance of the right to paint the Ruined City. The Ruined City, depicted as a group of oddly shaped rocky outcrops, is an imaginary landscape painted, he says, "with his mind, his soul, his third eye". Riley explains that he has never visited this site in his grandfather's country: "In the Dreamtime there is a Ruined City, but I have never seen that city, although they used to tell." But even in this new landscape the omnipresent Ngak Ngak watches over Ginger Riley, who is "just a painter — I can do what I like — I like to paint".

"Why can't I be an artist? Everyone else is!" In Destiny Deacon's collaborative video with Michael Riley, for *Australian Perspecta 1999*, Destiny's alter ego Delores bemoans the fact that her draughtsmanship skills (or lack thereof) preclude her from enrolling in a fictional TAFE Aboriginal art class. Through the mediums of photography and video (and, in this video,

Ginger Riley
Munduwalawala
*Ngak Ngak and the
owl at night* 1997
synthetic polymer
paint on canvas
57 x 123 cm
courtesy the artist
& Alcaston Gallery,
Melbourne

Delores herself, who moonlights as a fortune teller), Destiny parodies stereotypes of contemporary indigenous life based on her experiences as a Koori woman living in inner city Melbourne — a community Marcia Langton has described as the "survivors of Australia's colonial wars now exiled in the Housing Commission 'burbs".[6] In complete contrast to the previously favoured 'native' stereotype of the 'noble savage', Destiny brilliantly satirises the new trope of the welfare dependant — the single mother, the un-employed, etc. — engaging empathy with these 'victims' of colonisation, as much as she does with the kitsch representations of indigenous people as garden gnomes, dollies and golliwogs.

Recently, Murri theatre director and writer Wesley Enoch described the role of indigenous arts as giving "an emotional voice to political ideas".[7] And indeed, indigenous artists working today, by virtue of their historicity, give resonance to a history that would otherwise be "drained of everything but the language to say it in".[8] This 'emotional voice' often emerges in the work of indigenous artists as frankly autobiographical, its polemic expressed through a connection to country or drawing on the contemporary experiences of the artists themselves. In one of her earliest photographic works, Deacon juxtaposed an image of herself against a book cover image of a young black woman bearing the title 'Venus Half-Caste'. In a much later work she appears again, this time in a setting and pose suggestive of Frida Kahlo with a little white dolly sitting alongside. Both works are reminis-cent of Tracey Moffatt's *Something More*, where Moffatt casts herself as the protagonist in a narrative that ends with her premature demise on the road to fame and fortune — somewhat un-autobiographical in fact! This Hollywood-style drama leaves the question open as to who (or what) has to be sacrificed for stardom.

While Moffatt's *Scarred for Life* series dwells on the particular childhood experiences of anony-mous individuals, the work of all the artists throws into harsh relief the scars on Australia's psyche. Filtering through the work of Deacon, Moffatt and Gordon Bennett is an undercurrent of cruelty that gives it its incisive edge. Bennett's paintings, installation and performance works interrogate the positioning of Aboriginal people historically and in contemporary Australian society. In his paintings, Bennett appropriates the icons of western art history — from Van Gogh to Pollock to Mondrian — to contextualise archival images of exploration, occupation and conflict from our colonial past. This process Bennett

describes as "a strategy of intervention and disturbance in the field of representation".[9] Bennett's own experience makes the link between the past and the present in that his discovery as a young man of his Aboriginal identity becomes an analogy for the white-washing of Australia's history. Taking this further, Bennett uses his own body in performance as a metaphor for the colonisation of Aboriginality by western culture and by appropriating in response the celebrated images of western culture.

Aboriginal and Torres Strait Islander artists have replaced the much loved turn-of-the-century nationalistic renderings of Australia's landscape — that indigenous people were conveniently absent from — with a new vision of Australia's cultural and political landscape. This vision spans the continent from Melbourne to Maningrida, from suburban Brisbane to the Western Desert. Most significantly, it also spans time, remaining contained within a cultural continuum that has only recently intersected with other worlds. In Enoch's postwar stage musical *The Sunshine Club*, returned Aboriginal soldier Frank Doyle is finally thwarted by the racism of a small town and told by his aunty, "This is not your time". Upon this, the cast turns to the audience and asks, "If not now, then when?" The way ahead from the crossroads where we now find ourselves is in our hands.

Let no one say the past is dead.
The past is all about us and within.
Haunted by tribal memories, I know
This little now, this accidental present,
Is not the all of me, whose long making
Is so much of the past.[10]

1 Oodgeroo Noonuccal, 'The Past', in Kevin Gilbert (ed.) *Inside Black Australia: An Anthology of Aboriginal Poetry*, Penguin, 1988

2 John Kean, *East to West: Land in Papunya Painting*, exhibition catalogue, Tandanya Aboriginal Cultural Institute, Adelaide, 1990

3 Luke Taylor, 'John Mawurndjul: Weaver in Ochre', in *In Place, Out of Time*, exhibition catalogue, Museum of Modern Art, Oxford, 1997

4 John Mawurndjul, quoted in Murray Garde, 'Ngalyod in my head: The Art of John Mawurndjul', in *Mawurndjul/Bulunbulun*, exhibition catalogue, Annandale Galleries, Sydney, 1997

5 All quotes from Ginger Riley in Judith Ryan, *Ginger Riley*, exhibition catalogue, National Gallery of Victoria, Melbourne, 1997

6 Marcia Langton, 'The Valley of the Dolls: Black humour in the art of Destiny Deacon', *Art & Australia*, Vol. 35 No. 1, 1997

7 Wesley Enoch speaking at the annual Lottie Lyle lecture as part of the National Performance Conference, 21 January 2000, Sydney Opera House

8 Toni Morrison, *Jazz*, Chatto & Windus, London, 1992

9 Gordon Bennett, 'The Manifest Toe', in Gordon Bennett and Ian McLean, *The Art of Gordon Bennett*, Craftsman House, Sydney, 1996, p. 33

10 Oodgeroo Noonuccal, op cit

The author wishes to thank Deborah Edwards, Hannah Fink, Judith Ryan and Luke Taylor. Sydney, February 2000

Thoughts on the year 2000 Reflections of a time traveller

Harald Szeemann

Once again I was on a plane, going to a biennale. This time southern Brazil had jumped at the chance, in opposition to and/or complementing the male-dominated event in São Paolo. And in Porto Alegre it was truly a joy to see all female curators in action, on the water, in warehouses and in an empty power plant. While there were a great many objects and pictures, they were pointedly feminist and also anticlerical. Just problems of this continent — not a trace of globalisation.

In most countries, the Y2K bug did not do the damage that the eternal pessimists expected and hoped for, so that they could say, shrugging their shoulders self-righteously, "Nothing happened, thanks to us". Not without raking in billions beforehand. However, in Italy, the bug attacked the judicial system. Prisoners were suddenly 100 years older and harmless. Leave had to be cancelled because the biographical details were no longer correct. And we read: "We had to go back to the old handwritten cards to get things more or less sorted out."

Unlike the incarcerated, to those of us who live with art and artists this news was balm, honey, music of the spheres. Anyone from the world of art who lives in contact with the individual imagination which, even if it strikes abruptly, is always continuity — 'steady stream' — never believes in the drastic impact of a date. For time is also steady stream. One can swim with it or against it, try to outsmart it from one dose of jet lag to the next, escape it in moments of timelessness or lose it in moments of shock, but it does not allow itself to be fixed consciously and in the Gregorian way to twelve strokes of the bell, during which everything is damn well supposed to

happen and eventuate. The storms Lothar and Martin, raging, killing and devastating a few days earlier, were far more accurate harbingers of the next era than the billions' worth of fireworks, talk shows and entertainment offered on New Years Eve along the lines of "Everything will be trotted out, ranging from dancing natives to sophisticated events".

Of course there were beautiful 'Views' or 'Sights', to be expected when we're constantly told how expensive it is to provide a spectrum of culture from island to urban. Among the usual globalised mixture, the Eiffel Tower, with its caressing, entwining, structure-emphasising, exploding and ejaculating dance of rockets and fireworks, was certainly *the* spectacle, both controlled and over the top. And London and Sydney provided magnificent explosions of glowing gardens. But it was all gone the next morning, while *The 2000 Sculpture* by Walter De Maria in the Kunsthaus Zurich continued to radiate its energy quietly, visible only in daylight, stimulating both meditation and introspection — a real counterpoint to all the hurly-burly. In spite of the controlled use of standardised energy bars made of fragile plaster, the rising-falling-rising-falling herring-bone arrangement generated from the number of sides (5 7 9) constantly offered new patterns, sometimes architectural, sometimes musical, sometimes forming fields — a physical presence of 2000 sculptures. By suggesting timelessness, it stopped time and made it more precious, creating pockets of time in the flow of time.

What I like about artists today is their desire for permeability in the network of the representation; one is constantly present at micro-macro elucidations. Previously, one would have said that the individual obsession contains a reference to the universal; it must be rooted in the (auto)biographical.

We find this rootedness not only in the art of the indigenous peoples but also in a great many artists who are represented in Sydney as well as in those who, for one reason or another, are absent. Naturally it has found stronger expression in artists who came from the periphery into the 'centre'. Ilya Kabakov has monumentalised

Doug Aitken
eraser 1998
production still
courtesy the artist & 303 Gallery, New York

the clash of two plights, one social and one ideological, and does not tire of converting the ridiculous transformations of the 'correct' utopia of the classless society, in a way that is sometimes tragic, sometimes funny and sometimes sad-poetic, into impressive spaces: habitat, indoctrination room, psychiatric institution and dachas of past eras where time has stood still. Just as Kabakov draws energies from the tension between the authoritarian and dissidents, a western artist such as Martin Kippenberger took his bold and true paradoxes from the artistic climate in Germany. While Franz West, as an individual, embodies everything that contemporary Austria, a small country, once a great power of innovation and spirituality, still retains of the vision of a happy apocalypse. A whole generation derives from Brancusi via Franz West; they call themselves 'the giving artists'. Jason Rhoades, who took his father's vegetable garden as the theme for his last large installation in Hamburg, belongs to it, as does his somewhat older Californian colleague Paul McCarthy. In their art there is a complex fusion of formal elements and processes — processual, innovative,

regressive, deteriorised, constructivist, kinetically non-classifiable, difficult to read, yet directly communicating a somewhat crazy energy.

In the immediate post-war period, heroism mutated into the Internet from visualised levels of meaning fed by the most varied roots (parental home, childhood, process, effort, intentional incomprehensibility as a new non-style medium, individual mythology threatening controlled, precise uses, experiments with materials, integrated loved objects — with sketches and notes a never completely understood common thread). The result has been something like a collective memory seen as a system branching in all directions and staged from the ground up, which finally drives the institution to the brink of its possibilities once again. Of course, there are nasty, well-meaning people who say that all the trash of the 50s and 60s is being revived, but fail to see that concepts have been expanded, that concept and interventionist push have become a visualised and shaped system. After all, for a long time now we have accepted that the intensity of intention finds its own medium.

Richard Serra, who was invited but unfortunately couldn't participate, with fantastic singlemindedness, continually demands that iron, steel and weight stretch further, thus arriving at magnificent, new, concentrated, sculptural, plastic solutions driven by the qualities of the material. His latest achievement, *Torqued Ellipses,* is a superb representative of the latest revolution in the fine arts. He multiplied the views and the focal points. The young artists of today prefer the multiplication of points of view in space more than the blurring of individual points of view; they let the pendulum swing between structure and accumulation and thus remove the basis for the ambivalent to polyvalent object character of work fostered throughout the century; they destabilise the ready-made. One no longer circles *around,* one loses oneself *in*. Brancusi's studio is an early example of this. The character of the event overwhelms the specificity of the location. Narration is spread out, behaviour is directly presented, the constantly changing image is preferred to concentrated, weighty unambiguity.

This includes the preference for the moving image, and thus for film and the electronic media when frontality is still being sought. The cut replaces the composition, like the opening up of pictorial space previously did in paintings. Rapid change as in Pipilotti Rist's early pieces; the multiplied facets of everyday life as in the video wall with 128 monitors by Dieter Roth, who records himself in all life's situations, demodulating Le Corbusier's *Modules*, or places the medium of the television among wanderers like Christian Jankowski who, armed with five questions on achievement, reception and success, infiltrates the tangled web of Italian TV channels in order to make, with pretended naivete, the 'art' of successful fortune-tellers' programs into his own art. Intention and association are always running away from traditional ways of looking at art to forms of expression in which the element of play, the ludic, is greater. None of them are afraid of leaving the 'white cube', of being theatrical and playful, of locating themselves between Beckett and the musical or of using obsessions temporarily.

There are parallels here with the last decade of the 19th century. During the Paris 'fin de siècle mousseux' the Les Nabis group advanced, still from the self-chosen centre of the easel picture, to Christian mysticism and to Strindberg's and Ibsen's emancipation tragedies, but also to burlesque marionette theatre, to such eccentric creators as Alfred Jarry, and to the homo erotic love songs of Verlaine. These were taken as pretext and content for art and their intensity as increasing the quality of life.

What is different in art today? There are far more women, who have loosened and enriched the themes and content of contemporary art by direct expression of feelings about the body, new body experiences, giving life, dissolving concepts into qualities, crying out against taboos and discrimination, and by double strategies — not like the Chinese artists who want to change 'something' in the totalitarian state but at the same time take on the parameters of western aesthetics for themselves — but rather as defining qualities of a majority still kept in a minority's ghetto. Yet women are in a better position in art than in society at large, with all of its pressures.

More and more regions are emerging which use their museum and exhibition structures for networking, thus offering artists opportunities to make their mark. More and more biennales are coming into being, suggesting a trend towards globalisation or perhaps a growing together of the arts of this world. There has been a displacement of the concentrations of energy — look at the continents of Asia, Africa, Australia and Latin America. Former strongholds such as Paris and, more recently, New York are losing their significance, because the standards and judgements set there on what's current, innovative or out-of-date have become obsolete. This has changed abruptly in the last few years. What is truly local can be linked more easily to the universal demand, loving one another mutually and poetically and no longer remaining in the aesthetic and dialectic contra. Biennales are more open than ever, but they don't work without roots.

Robert Storr
interviewed by Nick Waterlow

What knowledge did you have of this part of the world and the Sydney Biennale when you were asked to become a member of the International Selection Committee?
Less than I should, I have to say. I know a certain number of Australian curators, Australian artists, I know something about what's been done in previous Biennales but I don't have intimate knowledge of it. And I more or less approached the problem as something in the present tense, not so much about its history but about what is going on now and what curators coming from other worlds can possibly contribute to it. All of these things are improvisatory, I think, and they are about the moment that they happen, and the job of the curators who are resident in the country is to sort out all those suggestions in terms of what's needed and what's known where they live. I think the job of the outside curator is to brainstorm with their colleagues and make what one hopes will be useful proposals.

How many Australian artists, whose work you remember vividly, have you seen in New York? Tracey Moffatt, for example.
Certainly, and Mike Parr and there are a number of people from different generations as well. There was a show at PS1, sometime in the 80s. They introduced a number of Australian artists and certainly younger artists have come to the fore recently.

And there was the 1984 show at the Guggenheim that introduced Bill Henson and others.
Actually, I met Bill in New York through a friend of mine, Michael Heyward, who was the editor of *Scripsi*, and who lived in Brooklyn near me. So I first became acquainted with him and his work through a very local grapevine.

Do you remember the Asia Society Exhibition of Indigenous Art from Australia?
I don't, I must confess. Indigenous art, as a general phenomenon, is very well known in this

country, but the individual artists are not so well known in detail. There is still a lot of work to be done, I think, on that front. I saw the exhibition at the Venice Biennale two years ago with three Australian Aboriginal artists and gained some real grasp of what they were doing. But for many Americans or other people not close to the situation, it's all new. The rhythms of careers and the differences of styles are things that must be much more precisely defined.

You're right that a good number of Australian artists are known in other parts of the world but when people come to Sydney to see a Biennale they expect to see artists from this part of the world that they mightn't have seen in other places. That's the idea. There are several functions for biennales in general. One is to bring art that is otherwise not sufficiently represented by galleries to the places where they are organised, and they tend to thrive where the public is eager for such periodic injections of the 'now'. In such places, the event of the biennale draws energy, draws loan clout, draws all kinds of things to that situation, but it also has to do with the migratory population of people who go to biennales, as opposed to the population in the immediate hinterland before this takes place, and it's their chance to discover worlds that they've heard about or seen a few things from but don't know really very well. And it's getting to be rather taxing now because you have to travel around the world several times every couple of years to do it, but it's worth the effort.

Bill Henson
Untitled 1983/84
detail, centre panel
of triptych
type c photography
100 x 80 cm
courtesy Roslyn Oxley9
Gallery, Sydney

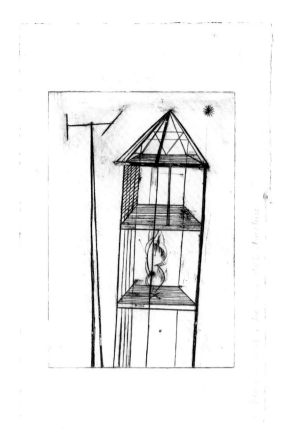

The initial selection process was a meeting of six people from different parts of the world, different backgrounds. How did you feel it worked?
I think it is in the nature of things that people come with what they want and what they expect, and in some cases they are simply argued out of their positions and in other cases they are awakened to things they didn't imagine. But there was enough give and take, and enough change of heart all round the table, that we came up with a much stronger list. If it was simply diplomatic trade-offs, where you negotiated treaties rather than actually organising shows, they wouldn't be any fun at all. What's fun is when people with strong convictions come together and say, if I have my person and you have your person it still doesn't make a show, so let's start over again, remake the list and put it together in a way that makes an exhibition.

Nick Serota was saying in London recently that there are certain loose groupings that will give it a particular structure and those structures will open out . One he was talking about was honouring senior artists and he talked about a group that included Louise Bourgeois, Gerhard Richter, Bruce Nauman, Sigmar Polke, Ilya and Emilia Kabakov and Richard Serra. Unfortunately Serra and Polke are not in the show but the others all will be. Did you also feel it was important to honour a few senior artists in the context of this Biennale?

I have never thought that the division according to generation was the most fruitful way to think about things, I don't mean in this context, but in any context. Take Louise for example. Louise is more surprising, more contemporary than 50 percent of the artists who are a third of her age, partly because she is aware of those younger artists and damned if she is going to be left in their dust. Gerhard Richter is an artist who has worked very steadily and very carefully for a long period of time, but he has established a very broad position, as has Polke. To treat them in terms of their age group, when they entered the scene, seems to me to make less sense than to treat them in terms of what they now represent to a really alert audience. And Bruce Nauman is the same. Bruce is one of the people who has broken definitively the notion that what an artist does is develop a single identity and a single style. Gerhard has as well. And this is only possible in the careers of artists who have spent a lot of time at it, who have been able to do one thing and then make the change and survive the often negative response to that change, and who make it clear that the next thing that they did was real — and then who do it again all over. Almost by definition, such people have to be so-called senior or established artists, but I don't think any of them would like the connotation that the terms might imply.

Thinking of a younger generation, it's always important that the Biennale in Sydney brings people to these shores never seen here before. Luc Tuymans is of course one of those. Where did you first see his work?
I first saw his work in *documenta IX* in Kassel. Actually, I first met him at that time, which was in 1990. It was the *documenta* where he was in this marvellous pavilion — which Gerhard was also in actually — this marvellous pavilion in a park down near a river, and he had a small number of paintings that have now become almost iconic. He was a very nervous young guy and these were terrific pictures, and it's interesting he should have been in the same area as Gerhard because they are doing things that are related, and clearly Tuymans has learned a lot from Richter but he is not doing Richters. He is not the second team, he is his own man, but it is a transmission of ideas and ambivalences really, you know, from one generation to the next and it's resulted in very, very strong work.

Another grouping that Nick Serota discussed was around the notion of Chaos, which would include artists like McCarthy, Kippenberger,

Franz West and Dieter Roth. Can you recall any of the thinking involved here, because there are elements that link their work?

There are. All these people have experimented with, but are not involved in, the appearance of rebellion or in simple obvious stylistic ways of looking messy. They're interested in creating work that cannot be put back together comfortably, which is a different thing because you can be more or less messy in appearance. The question is whether you create a situation where the viewer has to look very hard to create a whole out of it, and if they are able to do so, it is always made clear by the intrinsic qualities of the situation, environment, installation, whatever it is, that this is a contingent whole, it's not a fixed entity. And there are quite a lot of artists now who are kind of seduced by the idea that putting a bunch of junk on the floor represents the same thing, and it doesn't, any more than bad gestural painting in the 1950s was the equal of good gestural painting in the 1950s.

To quote you from your fax: "The final list has arrived. It is an assorted assortment — or curatorial readymade — but a lively group in the end. The best part of the final version is the increase in the number of Australians and New Zealanders. Few are familiar to me except as names or single images. I really look forward to seeing their work." I think that's one of the real purposes of this Biennale in Sydney.
It should be.

Do you feel there is anything that is going to emerge in the next few years that will alter the notion of the biennale as we now know it?
I think the great danger is that the proliferation of them and the patterns of making them will become familiar to all concerned, to the point that the necessary friction and the necessary frustration will evaporate. Each exhibition type has a form; monographic shows, survey shows, all of these things have a form. The biennale is a form. The minute these things become fixed and the procedures for them become known, they tend to go stale. On the other hand, you can't entirely reinvent the form every time either. So you have to understand that you're working within a kind of a tradition, but you have to make it fresh. I think there was a tendency, for example, within recent years, to simply increase the number of artists exponentially, to make it exciting that way. And we had some biennales or the equivalent of biennales that were so large that no-one looked good and the thrill of exposure to new things quickly turned into exhaustion. I think biennales that are made more tightly, that are narrower than some of those before, open up a way, if you will, to operate within the convention but to operate in such a way that nonetheless creates rigour.

Are there any final points you would like to make?
I don't want to mention a particular artist but one never knows just how these things are going to come out. The most important thing is that they really do have to happen. Exhibitions are not something you can guarantee and the minute one tries to do that, that's the surest sign that they'll be predictable. So I look forward to this one, saying I'm not sure where it's going to be at, even though I'm part of it. I'm an eager visitor, as well as somebody who had a piece of it.

Louise Bourgeois (opposite)
He disappeared into complete silence 1947
plate 6: line engraving on paper
collection: National Gallery of Australia, Canberra

Luc Tuymans (left)
Illegitimate II 1997
oil on canvas
113 x 77.5 cm
private collection, Belgium
courtesy Zeno X Gallery, Antwerp
photography: Felix Tirry

Sir Nicholas Serota
interviewed by Nick Waterlow

What were your early experiences of Australian art of the modernist period?
I didn't see the great exhibition that Bryan Robertson did at the Whitechapel Art Gallery in 1961 but in the 70s and early 80s I became aware of what artists like Mike Parr, Imants Tillers and others were doing, principally through exhibitions seen here that were round up or survey shows, and then of course by the Australian presence at the Venice Biennale.

Going back to your visit in 1996, what particular memories do you have of being in Australia?
I think I was struck by the incredible energy, especially in Sydney, and the sense of a country that was reorienting itself culturally from a European/American direction towards an Asian/Pacific interest. Of course when I came in 96 it coincided with an opportunity to see the second APT.

The second Asia-Pacific Triennial.
That visit certainly helped me to look at the world in a different way.

Did you have any particular prior knowledge of the Biennale of Sydney?
No, sadly I've never seen one of the Biennales other than obviously having looked pretty closely at some of the catalogues and records of the shows, and I remember having quite a long discussion with both Lynne Cooke and Jonathan Watkins about the 1996 and 1998 shows.

Do you see the function of the Biennale of Sydney differing in any way from the other biennales?
I think it has become a show which can have a different outlook from a number of the biennales; especially the 2000 show, which has this somewhat retrospective character, in part at least. It gives a very interesting overview of the way in which art has developed over the last fifteen or twenty years.

With a considerable indigenous representation it will cover every area of Aboriginal art too, which has been a quite remarkable revelation over the last quarter of a century.
When we were discussing the selection last European summer, it seemed to us important that there should be a very strong component from Australia and New Zealand, not simply because the exhibition was taking place in Sydney but also because there seemed to have been some very, very interesting work made in Australia in recent years. In 1996 I was most struck by a new generation of younger Australian artists, such as Fiona Hall and others, and equally there was this very strong Aboriginal strand in the contemporary culture.

There are a number of advantages, we think, in bringing together an international panel who can consolidate their broad knowledge, and hopefully create an event, that might be quite difficult for one person to do here. What particular advantages do you think people like yourself can bring to this situation?
I think that when you bring together a group of people with very diverse backgrounds you can have a much more interesting conversation, and hopefully that will be reflected in the experience of the visitor at the Biennale; that is to say that you get a much richer show. I think one of the great strengths of the exhibition in 2000 will be its diversity. I think that both Jonathan and Lynne would accept that the shows that they did in 1996 and 1998 deliberately dealt with one or two particular strands within the discourse of contemporary art. What they were not trying to do was to sum up the state-of-play, in a given year. I hope that this year's Biennale will do that for visitors. I think that does develop directly from the kind of conversations within the advisory panel meetings.

Looking though the examples of work coming through the Biennale office, we're recognising that the variety will be considerable …
And I do think one of the strengths of a show of this kind is that it should try and set art from Australia and New Zealand in an international context; so this Biennale ought to be a different biennale from one that is done in Istanbul or Johannesburg or elsewhere, not least by virtue of the fact that it provides a context for working Australian artists.

That was the original purpose of the Sydney Biennale and I think it will fulfil it again in May 2000. The selection process seemed to work effectively in Venice. How did you feel about it?

Bill Hammond
Hokey Pokey 1998 (detail)
acrylic on canvas on stretchers
200 x 500 cm
private collection, Auckland
photography: Julia Brooke-White

One of the things we set out to do in our first meeting was to try and establish some parameters for the show, by looking at those older artists whose work continued to be interesting but which had set directions for younger artists. The first choices we made were artists like Bruce Nauman, Gerhard Richter, Louise Bourgeois, Dieter Roth, and from there we worked out into a number of different areas; each of those artists could be regarded as father-figure/mother-figure for a number of other artists in the exhibition, not directly perhaps but in terms of a sphere of influence.

Are there any particular artists who will bring something specific to Australia that we haven't seen here before?
I don't think Dieter Roth has been seen in Australia in a significant way, nor Martin Kippenberger, who died in the late 90s. Both of those artists in a sense reflect a certain tendency which is, in sensibility, a very long way from minimalism and conceptualism although it has a strong intellectual foundation. The nature of the work is much more chaotic and I think that kind of work seen in Australia will give a new impetus to a different way of thinking.

Somebody else we've never seen here before is Adriana Varejão, who I thought looked strong in the Liverpool Tate as part of the first Liverpool Biennial.
Yes, and I've seen other work of hers in the course of the past year which has been very strong. I think it's a very good moment to be showing her. The Sydney Biennale has often shown the work of women artists but I think that this year the grouping is very strong, including Marlene Dumas, Vanessa Beecroft, Tracey Moffatt and Pipilotti Rist. With the exception of Dumas who is slightly older, these are all artists who have come to the fore in the last four or five years and I think it's striking that they're making a very distinctive contribution.

Are there any final points you would like to make on the whole process?
The purpose of these large exhibitions is to foster exchange and to stimulate discussion and occasionally controversy. The success of the Sydney Biennale in its history has been that it has helped to bring Australian artists into an international discussion, but equally it's given visitors in Australia a chance to see some of the more exciting things that are happening elsewhere in the world. It reduces distance and it promotes discussion.

On that point I was thinking of the Aboriginal Memorial, *the 200 hollow logs that were first shown in the 1988 Biennale of Sydney, which are now on display in St Petersburg.*
I saw them in Hanover recently ... It was clear that a German audience was deeply interested. So that's just one element from a previous Biennale bringing the world closer together.

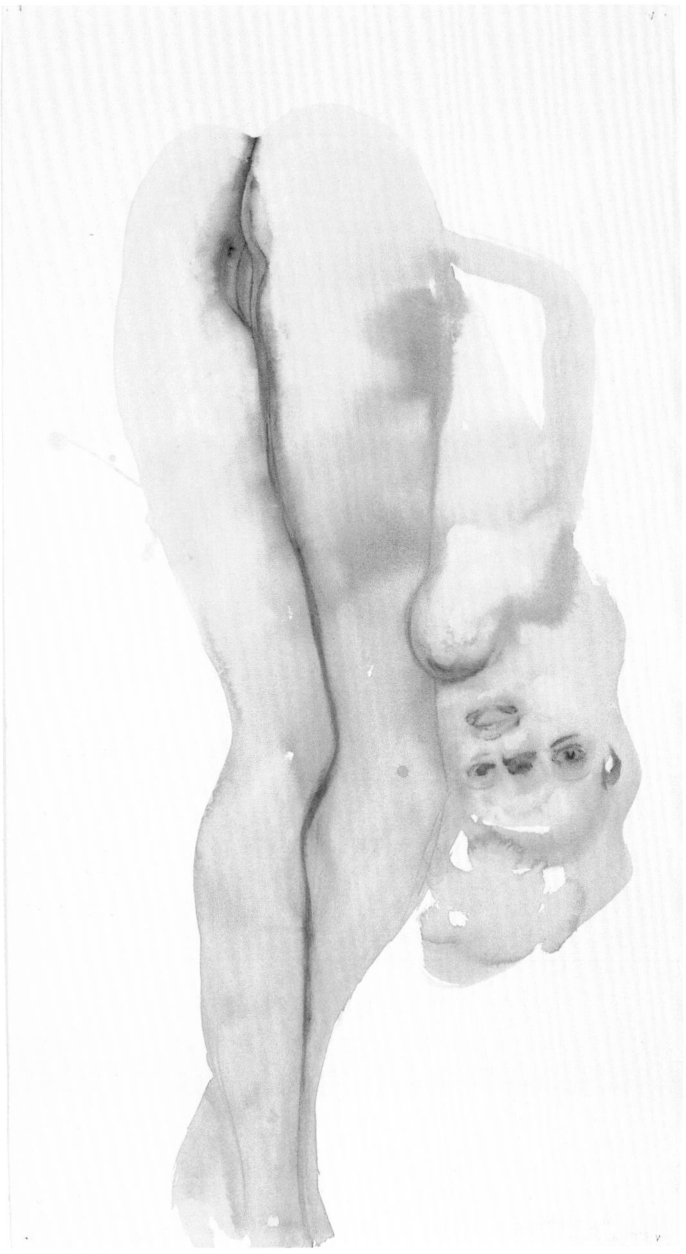

Marlene Dumas
Dorothy D-Lite 1998
ink and acrylic on paper
125 x 70 cm
courtesy the artist
photography: Gent Yan Uah Rouij

Change
Fumio Nanjo

Mariko Mori
Burning Desire 1997-1998
glass photo interlay
5 panels
courtesy Deitch Projects,
New York

In western thinking change can be fundamental and revolutionary. It occurs as a leap from a steady state that dominates up until that very moment. Its transformation appears as a 'paradigm shift', Thomas Kuhn's term for a replacement of the basic scientific frame. Kuhn uses the term 'paradigm' in relation to scientific assumptions about the world that are thought to be universal, that give scientists a set of conditions for a certain period of time. This is called 'normal science', science which is supported by a fixed paradigm or framework that grants legitimacy to scientific endeavour. Kuhn proposes that one paradigm can be replaced by another, not in a linear manner but in a dis-continuous and revolutionary way. He argues that a scientific revolution, upsetting this tradition, leads to a new world view with a fresh framework.

Science provides a view of our world, of nature and culture, which affects how we observe the universe in a way not based on logic alone. Galileo knew this. He posits the 'universe' or 'nature' as a great book to be endlessly read by human beings. Scientists must tell their discoveries as a story by interpreting 'nature' as a text. Thus 'truth' is not discovered but invented. Astronomy developed by Copernicus, Kepler and Galileo transformed the geometric view of Ptolemaic theory to a heliocentric theory, through a combination of logic, meticulous observations and mathematical formulae. This scientific revolution was completed by Newton in the 17th century. The next important transformation was brought about by Darwin's theory of evolution. With Darwinism, the idea that humans were created by God as special beings at the centre of the universe was shattered. The new paradigm, in which human beings are thought accidental developments in the course of evolution, leads to the denial of God.

Now a third conversion is happening, which owes much to modern technology. Technology has become so powerful that the earth cannot limitlessly support human activities and desires. The earth is like a spaceship, a physically limited entity. In fact, due to space travel technology, we can now see the earth as an image in limitless space.

More change is now taking place, brought about by the information explosion as computers take a bigger role in the development of science and technology. The 'net' is changing our lifestyles, by altering our sense of size and distance in the world. But the information revolution is merely a sign of a larger scale transformation. The image of the universe in which we reside is being re-drawn, because of the integration of macro and micro visions through a combination of the theories relating to elementary particles and cosmogony. However, the most fundamental change for humans will be caused by genetic engineering, which will enable us to control and manipulate our own lives. We will again have to ask about the meaning of life. The question cannot be answered by the linear history of mechanical technology, but a new understanding of the world may result from the development of science and technology.

In Asian thinking, on the other hand, very little attention has been paid to the notion of 'change'. This is due to the idea that there is always an unchangeable universality behind everything, even transmutation. This idea creates peace of mind; its realisation is achieved by spiritual awakening. The oldest Japanese historical novel, *Heike Monogatari*, begins with the well-known passage: "The sound of the Gion Shoja bells echoes the impermanence of all things."[1] It tells us about the emptiness of historical truth, that nothing is permanent, and observes the collapse of the prosperous 'samurai' caste. In other words, there is an eastern tradition that recognises the meaninglessness of change.

Dualism is part of a premise of recognition. The Japanese verb 'wakaru' (to understand) derives from 'wakeru' (to divide); it means sorting a thing out by dividing it into two, so learning begins with classification. Western thinking is also based on the division of one from another, on distinctions between notions such as here and there, right and wrong, good and bad, beauty and ugliness, life and death. Dualism lies behind Hegel's dialectics. Dichotomy creates the issue of identity because identification insists on difference. Zhuangzi and Zen Buddhism, on the other hand, seek to avoid falling into this dichotomy.

In eastern thought the phenomena of nature and the universe cannot be classified, but they can be reduced to one total vision. Eastern thinkers try to transcend difference to maintain a holistic vision. Zhuangzi calls the idea of the sameness of all things 'oneness' (Issha) or 'chaos'. It is the essence of reality, he argues, which cannot be expressed in a language that divides things into two categories. Thus, in the east, an enlightened one doesn't use words, but remains silent. Wittgenstein, after studying mysticism, expressed a similar idea.

A recent scientific achievement has been 'chaos' theory — the idea that irregular unpredictable patterns are generated from fixed non-linear systems. Repeated calculations on a computer generate complex irregularities from simple algebraic formula. However, understanding the flow of a system does not mean control of the system itself. And most systems in nature are non-linear, and thus contain chaos within. This means that future events are not pre-determined but accidental, and thus humans are free from the yoke of destiny. At the end of *Die Zeit des Weltbildes*, Heidegger argues that when the calculable world leaps from quantity to quality, incalculable things such as invisible shadows (*unsichtbare Schatten*) will cover all things on earth. This suggests the disappearance of any possibility that humans can understand and control the world. When trying to understand reality, humans cannot recognise anything without an agent or medium. Recognition, which relies on sensory organs such as eyes and ears, is not reliable. Linguistic understanding is also uncertain. Humans can understand reality only as a shadow. The computer's repeated calculations are the only way to prove an insight, not the imperfect human. The recent movie *Matrix* seems true because its story is metaphorically already real.

Art expresses our intuitive vision of the world. Changes in the subject expressed do exist, but change itself does not. Basho, a 17th century 'haiku' master, wrote of 'Immutability and Fashion' (*Fueki Ryukuo*), suggesting that immutability is hidden in the changes of fashion. Fashion may represent the Zeitgeist, but it also expresses the spirit of universality. Basho could see the universality of change. Art is based on an aesthetic intuition; it can appear ahead of world change, or embody the spirit of the times. Its vision follows the same course as science, which is to say a new and unique vision can appear in the works of a genius.

The participants in the *Biennale of Sydney 2000* are artists who express and question their vision of reality in works which embrace change and the possibility of change.

[1] Trans. Helen Craig McCullough, *Genji & Heike: Selections from The Tale of Genji and The Tale of the Heike*, Stanford Uni.versity Press, Stanford, 1994

Yayoi Kusama
Dots Obsession 1999
installation view
mixed media,
nine balloons
courtesy the artist
photography:
Norihiro Ueno

Artists / Biennale of Sydney 2000

Doug Aitken

Matthew Barney

Vanessa Beecroft

Gordon Bennett

Louise Bourgeois

Cai Guo-Qiang

Sophie Calle

Destiny Deacon

Stan Douglas

Marlene Dumas

Rosalie Gascoigne

Andreas Gursky

Fiona Hall

Bill Hammond

Gwyn Hanssen Pigott

Bill Henson

Gary Hill

Ilya & Emilia Kabakov

Seydou Keïta

Bodys Isek Kingelez

Martin Kippenberger

Yayoi Kusama

John Mawurndjul
& Maningrida Sculpture

Paul McCarthy

Boris Mikhailov

Tracey Moffatt

Mariko Mori

Juan Muñoz

Bruce Nauman

Shirin Neshat

Chris Ofili

Yoko Ono

Mike Parr

Lisa Reihana
& The Pacific Sisters

Gerhard Richter

Ginger Riley

Pipilotti Rist

Dieter Roth

Sanggawa

Mick Namarari Tjapaltjarri

Luc Tuymans

Ken Unsworth

Adriana Varejão

Jeff Wall

Gillian Wearing

Franz West

Xu Bing

Yun Suknam

Doug Aitken

I believe in communication. Contemporary art must use the most clear, pertinent, and precise means available. If communication is the nucleus, the areas of art making and pop culture can be free to follow their respective paths. Paths that are at times infinitely separate and other times collide ...

On one level Eraser *attempts to lose the distancing between the viewer and the content of the work. The work is linear in structure, but I don't believe this means the viewer necessarily needs to encounter it passively. There is an area of immersion that can be created without sacrificing content. A twilight of perception where ideas and iconography flicker and reinvent themselves.*
— Doug Aitken

Whatever may be the first generation of video's ultimate accomplishments and short-comings, the 1990s have seen a new generation of artists arise who have gone beyond the traditional borders of 'art' video in search of a new way to engage with the medium. Rather than taking their cues from the self-reflexive obsessions of minimalism and its attempts to do away with illusion, they are turning to cinema and television to borrow their visual and technical means. And one of the most prominent has been Doug Aitken, the young American artist who won the international prize at the 1999 Venice Biennale for his video installation *Electric Earth*.

Since the early 1990s, he has been cross-pollinating the styles of film, music video, documentary and com-mercials into his own unique brand of visual narrative. The first time I saw his work, I was immediately struck by the fact that what I was viewing was neither video art, nor cinema, nor television, but a hybrid concoction of all film genres. Aitken himself, I learned later, has his own term for it: pure communication.

On one level, the notion of pure communication is a licence for him to embrace all the formal possibilities of film and video, all its gestures, techniques and visual strategies. "The more you move through the culture, the more these boundaries [between art, commerce, film, etc.] just become limitations. The question I ask is what are the tools you need for the content you want to put forth?" says Aitken. Obviously, the point is not to make commercials or music videos — although to earn a living, he has made these as well — but rather to extend their language to say what those genres are not generally permitted to say. On this level, the term pure communication departs from the minimalist and modernist paradigm altogether: it is critical without being critique, without being a negation. It rejects nothing and weighs everything anew.

An acute, masterly example of this is *Electric Earth*. The story of one man left totally and irrevocably alone in an automated world of machines. *Electric Earth* is a music video transmuted into a science-fiction vision of the present.

Aitken relies on the power of visual images to open the symbolic space for the mythic narrative he is inter-ested in telling. It is how his work interrupts the consumption of images and demands our contem-plation of them. This is especially the case in *Eraser* (1998), a video for which the artist adopts a stripped down documentary style that, pre-cisely on account of its photo-graphic quality, is simultaneously empirical and wholly symbolic. It records Aitken's trek across the Caribbean island of Montserrat shortly after it was devastated by the eruption of a volcano.

As we make our way inland, images of lush vegetation and human civilisation give way to houses and buildings covered in thick layers of volcanic ash. Soon, pastures and roads are replaced by dried flows of lava, until, finally, the entire installation wall becomes a screen of grey and white. A nature video turned Ur-myth, *Eraser* is a paean to the destructive power of nature.

Eraser demonstrates that, on one level, Aitken's pure communication is a form of pure cinema compar-able with the movies of the era of silent film and Eisenstein's theory of montage. The American writer Gore Vidal once remarked that 1930s Hollywood was the greatest era of myth in the history of the world. *Eraser*, however, is also an attempt to rescue montage from its own tendency to create generic film styles and the mythic force implied in them. Aitken's visual constructivism reveals that montage has the potential to produce a space for a contem-plative image practice within the mediascape.

SAUL ANTON
excerpt from 'Doug Aitken's Moment',
The Art Magazine, Tate Gallery, No. 19, 1999
quote: interview with Giovanna Amadasi, 1999

eraser 1998
production still
courtesy the artist & 303 Gallery, New York

Matthew Barney

Paradise Lust: Matthew Barney's cinematic piece CREMASTER 2 *scraps the distinctions between Mother Nature and that copycat of hers, art.*

The human body is the last riddle of all. In spite of the pornographic way western society's media approach the body, the latter remains a source of myths, images and kinky fancies — as illustrated in Matthew Barney's films. They have turned the body into a universe in miniature. In Barney's film *CREMASTER 2* anatomical details take on the appearance of landscapes, interior designs replicate human organs and vice versa. Producing art turns into producing 'carnal pictures' which centre on the artist's own anatomy. To all intents and purposes he is the Creator's understudy. His fecundity generates a beauty which is a causal reflection of his author's superiority.

CREMASTER 2 begins with a love-making scene which exalts the merging of two human bodies into a mythical spectacle. The act of copulation symbolizes artistic creativity. The female body's vagina resembles a piece of sculpture coated with a vaseline-like substance; as it is withdrawn *post coitum*, the penis ejaculates bees instead of semen. An eye-catching backdrop, namely a swarm of buzzing bees and a giant hive, highlights and accentuates the copulating couple's gyrations. Virility as a metaphor for boundless fertility, a physical hint at the confidence exuded by a 32-year-old artist already considered to be amongst the pick of his generation.

CREMASTER 2 is the fourth sequel of a five-part video and film series which has been produced with ever-increasing input since 1994,

becoming the driving force of Barney's endeavour. *CREMASTER 2* has feature-film length and has long since outstripped the criteria of a mere art video. To really do it justice, it should perhaps be classed as a multi-discursive film opera. Barney himself plays the part of the murderer Gary Gilmore, Norman Mailer takes on the role of escapologist Harry Houdini. The plot is a stream of consciousness whose myriad images are the stepping stones of free association. This is a sparkling world transformed into a canon of flawless shapes which mirror and replicate physical perfection. Civilization becomes a corporeal figment of its own environment and, in the same process, the body mutates into an object which is alien to the human condition. "In the course of all those transformations," Mailer explains,

"Houdini turns into the very same cage which encases him". It is precisely this split second of transformation, when a human being is simultaneously liberated and encumbered by the surrounding mechanisms, that Barney freezes in his images of metamorphosis. In doing so, his stream of intimate and unconventional images encapsulates the nitty-gritty blueprint of civilization which expresses human delusions of omnipotence as well as the root of all our traumas and fears. Murderer and escapologist are, for all the world to see, of the same ambivalent ilk. The one comes a dreadful cropper and is executed, the other turns the fears of captivity into a game and ends up a living legend …

The thrust of Barney's creative thought processes forces us to delve deeper into our fantasies. Barney, the artist-cum-traveller who set out from the innermost human recesses, now records every single echo of the human body.

ULF POSCHARDT
excerpt from 'Squall in the genepool', *Süddeutsche Zeitung,* 1 October 1999

Vanessa Beecroft

During a panel discussion at The New Museum in New York in December 1998, Beecroft described herself as a "post-feminist". Does that mean her work forecloses on or reverses the "progress" that marks feminist-related performance art? For Beecroft and her generation, "women giving their bodies back to themselves" isn't a big issue, if it's an issue at all. In contrast to performance art of the sixties and seventies, with its utopian tinged ambitions to reconstruct the purely feminine and, in the offing, to change the world, Beecroft isn't out to convince us of anything, much less promote a cause. Beecroft asserts her autonomy and authority by producing images that are considered taboo, or too provocative, or off-limits. In contrast to her feminist predecessors, Beecroft silences the voice, depersonalises the female body, and pumps up its image as a purely visual spectacle, charging it with unmistakable provocation. Beecroft is very correct about the production of her pictures but she doesn't care a toss for political correctness. Everybody who witnesses a performance gets to think whatever they want. The unresolved issue of display and the provocation of desire that plagued early women's performance art is in 'post-feminist' performance the point of it all. What the thing looks like — women's bodies in particular — is the centripetal point for Beecroft's work. The visuality of the event — not its textuality — is what's important.

Beecroft plays with various "looks" ... but the point, over and over again, is that the "look" is exaggerated, brought to our attention, fetishized. Beecroft draws attention to the look, to the act of looking, and to the art of crafting the look, within the artificial confines of something that looks vaguely, oddly, like a dispassionately rendered harem scene.

It's important to notice that Beecroft's pictures keep changing. The picture is never static, never one thing by itself, but always combinations of images, impressions, associations, slippages and stoppages. If one looks long and thoughtfully enough, there's probably all the world to see. The picture Beecroft sets in motion is one of disintegration, a façade that is comprised by the "human-ness" of the girls who grow tired over the duration of the performance, which spans several hours. Inevitably, the "picture" begins to twitch and fidget, to sag, droop and collapse. The perfect, the perfectly problematic, picture quite literally falls apart. Some will read this collapse as a critique on glamour or conventional feminine stereotypes, but such interpretations, to the degree that they "fit", must never overshadow the gradual deterioration of the picture plane as intended to be primarily a poetic and visual event.

Counterpoint to this visual decline of the picture and its gradual but unmistakable inclination to a horizontal axis are the paradoxical shifts that underscore Beecroft's performances. Her performance events are described as "non-events" because it looks like nothing ever happens. In one sense that's true. The girls stand around doing nothing. There's no narrative, plot, beginning, middle or end. But in another sense the picture is gradually and continually changing. The pictures are controversial and titillating. People get mesmerized by them; people get incensed by them; people get off on them. It's a busy performance arena.

Beecroft makes pictures that can't be looked at like "regular" (that is, non-living) pictures. She produces events that qualify as "non-events" but that are terribly eventful. She uses real girls but takes them out of real life. She creates performances in which no one performs yet in which everyone has a role to play. She makes installations that are performances in slow time; that are, at once, like painting, billboards, beauty pageants, sex fantasies and pure technology wrapped into a strange production number of "take notice" images — naked-bottomed girls in high heels; blond dominatrixes with military accessories; a phalanx of lean, pale-skinned models occupying the Guggenheim in New York. While the work is super-charged with erotic texture, Beecroft's style is subliminal and cool. Its edginess is the bait that brings the audience to the work. But it's the human-ness of the girls that brings the picture, ultimately, to its knees.

JAN AVGIKOS
excerpt from *Parkett* 56, 1999, pp. 106-109

vb40.067.vb.pol
VB40 Museum of Contemporary Art,
Sydney, Australia 1999
© 2000 Vanessa Beecroft
courtesy the artist
photography: Vanessa Beecroft

Gordon Bennett

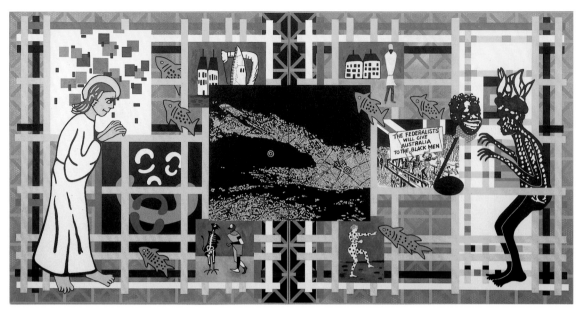

Over the last decade, Gordon Bennett has produced a powerful body of critical art that has ranged widely, in engaging with the iconography of Australian history, with the quest for purity in western modernism, with the language of racial stereotyping, and with the presentation of the body in art. He has consistently been concerned with the pain and violence of colonialism, and much of the power of his work arises from the way these themes have been drawn together. His highly energized compositions have, for instance, recontextualized Pollock's drip style in such a way that the lines of paint suggest the welts on a whipped body, and their turbulent tracery not the angst of an artistic genius but the tortuous cycle of racial violence arising from the foundational myths of dispossession in Australia.

He has described his effort as a kind of history painting, and this is certainly apt, especially if we understand history not as the way it really was, as the way it has been imaged and imagined, particularly in myths of national origin. Gordon Bennett has engaged, not so much with the actualities of early encounters between Aboriginal people and settlers, as with the popular iconography of these moments, which have been extensively represented in bad nineteenth century history paintings, in primary school social studies texts of the 1950s and 1960s, and in many other literary and visual genres. The cruder evocations typically purged the colonial history of its invasive and violent character, and produced a monumental narrative, that endowed explorers, early settlers, and pioneers with a kind of nobility. Bennett's work recasts and often defaces these images, overwriting them with the dots that have become a hallmark of Aboriginal art, framing them with western perspectival geometry, and imposing a conjunction of images that richly evoke the confusion of identities that arises from colonial narcissism and stereotyping. Although Australian colonial history is directly referred to in many of these works, and though it has been continually present, as a reference point, Bennett links the Australian conflict to a global history of slavery and racism, and relates that dynamics to deeper antinomies between self and other, transparency and obscurity, purity and impurity ...

For Bennett, the expression of ideas and feelings always has a historical context, often one burdened by conflict and contradiction. The project of purity cannot escape a politics of purity, and is implicated in colonial transactions energized by a language of violence, which Bennett has often deployed in his work, forcing the viewer to confront terms of abuse such as 'coon', 'darkie' and 'abo'. If this assimilation of high art to colonial savagery would seem shocking to many art historians, who would insist that the works quoted possess some degree of autonomy, Bennett's oeuvre turns a gesture of defacement into a sustained and elaborated argument. What he presents is not merely a negative response to colonial imagery, but the positive fabrication of a new if always historicized and conflicted subjectivity.

NICHOLAS THOMAS
excerpt from 'Home décor and dance: the abstraction of Aboriginality', *In Place (Out of Time): Contemporary Art in Australia,* exhibition catalogue, ed Rebecca Coates & Howard Morphy, Museum of Modern Art, Oxford, 1997
quote: Gordon Bennett, 'The Manifest Toe', *The Art of Gordon Bennett*, ed Ian McLean, Craftsman House, G & B Arts International, Australia, 1996, p. 8

Home Décor (Preston + De Stijl = Citizen) Then And Now 1997
acrylic on linen
182.5 x 365 cm
private collection, Brisbane
courtesy Bellas Gallery, Brisbane
& Sutton Gallery, Melbourne
photography: Richard Stringer

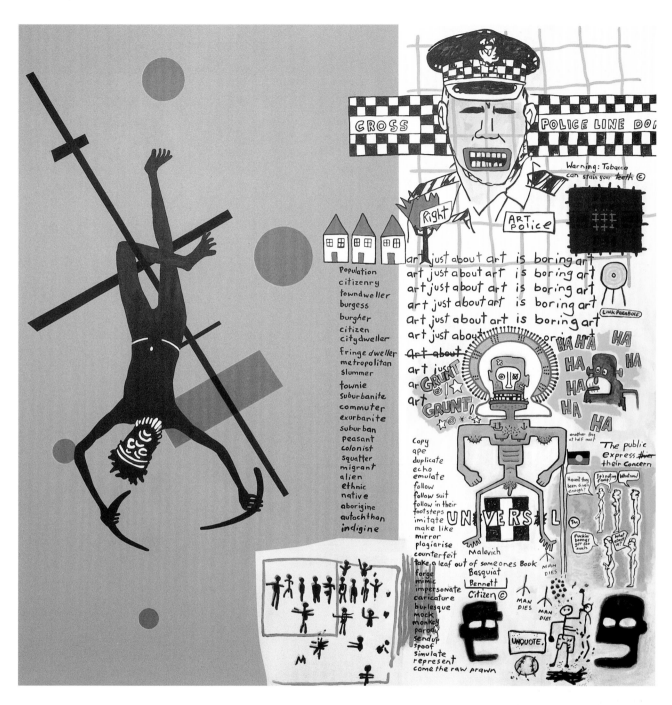

Notes to Basquiat (in the Future
Art will not be Boring) 1999
collection: the artist
courtesy Sherman Galleries, Sydney
photography: John O'Brien

Louise Bourgeois

THESE SCULPTURES ARE INHABITED

We are witnesses to a phenomenon. At 89 Louise Bourgeois is proving that artistic radicality is not by definition the province of youth. By pursuing her longstanding formal innovations and psychological scenarios to obsessional extremes she is changing the way we look at sculpture — and the way we experience it. The satisfactions of her work are those of surprise as well as continuity, partially proving and partially disproving Nietzsche's adage that "it is not the strength, but the duration of great sentiments that makes great men". For in this great woman, emotion is both sustained *and* intense.

C.O.Y.O.T.E. (1941-48) established the paradigm for what Bourgeois is making today. One of several wooden assemblages created in the late 1940s and early 1950s in which spindly legs extend downwards from a dorsal ridge — by this simple but unprecedented means the artist inverted the traditional idea of a sculptural group on a base and put the unifying plane above rather than below the figurative forms — the piece is, so to speak, Bourgeois's *Burgers of Calais*. Renamed and repainted in the 1970s but structurally unaltered from the original, it is a cluster of spare but clearly anthropomorphic elements linked to one another and fated to stand or fall together. However, Bourgeois's inventiveness in this case was not confined to the

formal reversal described above. Scaled to her own height, she physically placed herself on an equal footing with these skeletal representations and photographed herself clinging to them as if she were trying squeeze into the line-up. Thus, this modular, precociously minimal sculpture anticipated what we now call installation art by directly annexing the space around it, absorbing the spectator into its reality. When one looks at a work of this kind, one does not stand back in the normal way, and if one tries to it almost seems as though the object itself, sensing that physical and psychological distance, starts to approach.

Fifty years later Bourgeois is doing the same thing — but very differently.

Two bodies of work have preoccupied her over the last decade — and when speaking of a 'body' in this respect, the term is employed literally and metaphorically. The first is the 'Cells'. This word also has compound connotations, since it refers to biological units of growth, rooms for contemplation and prison chambers. Typical of Bourgeois's way of turning things upside-down or inside-out, *Cell VIII* (1998) with its mysterious arrangement of drapes and carved marble enclosed by steel grid and wire mesh is designed as much to exclude as to confine, to keep the passers-by away as to visually lure them. Such

double readings are the poetic essence of Bourgeois's art; they reflect profound ambivalences in her own nature — fear of intimacy coupled with fear of isolation, talismanic evocations of the past framed by harsh material realism — and sculpturally project back onto the viewer. The second ensemble of works from the 1990s is made from clothes Bourgeois had put in storage and only recently rediscovered. Each of these garments — a child's smock, an adult's dress — is a self-portrait. Arranged together on hangers they describe the ages of woman in a kind of one-person family tree in which the person Bourgeois became at various stages of her life confronts the person she was. But here too logic — in this case temporal — is subtly turned around, for in effect this chain of being implicitly defines the young Louise as the mother rather than the daughter of the older Louise. That existential fact is the core around which the clothes accumulate like rings of a tree, and from which her distinct, staggered identities branch out. Moreover, with each fabric husk suspended from the privotal armature but not touching the ground, the overall construct is a linear though utterly transformed descendent *C.O.Y.O.T.E.*

And we circle or walk up to and among these fragile surrogates as we would ghostly presences hanging from a battered maypole or delapidated jungle-gym. As always the artist's alternately, or simultaneously, embracing and deflecting configurations implicate us in their drama. As always, we feel an uncanny kinship with her forms. As always, Bourgeois's sculpture is inhabited — and we are invited to inhabit with her.

ROBERT STORR
February 2000

Cell VIII 1998 (two views)
mixed media installation
274.3 x 335.2 x 254 cm
courtesy the artist
photography: Peter Bellamy

Untitled 1996 (opposite)
cloth, bone, rubber & steel
283.2 x 297.1 x 254 cm
courtesy the artist
photography: Allan Finkelman

Cai Guo-Qiang

Roads are not yet paved in the beginning, words are not yet definite from the beginning. — Zhuangzi

Cai handles fire. To be more precise, he manoeuvres the explosion that is a metamorphosis of energy. His methodology is grounded in the archetypal experience of moments in which violence transforms into beauty. His birthplace, China's Fujian Province, is famous for the manufacture of firecrackers; in his childhood, the region, dubbed the Fujian Front, was the front base against Taiwan. The roar of reconnaissance planes flying over his head and flashes emitted from explosions made an impression of both violence and beauty on him.

Cai accepts the contradiction that destruction and violence can be perceived as beautiful. His thinking is founded on Daoism (Taoism), the cornerstone of Chinese thought: each and every existence in this world from humans to other living beings to lifeless beings consists of qi (ch'i, invisible energy) and, according to Zhuangzi (Chuang Tzu), the true phase of being is chaos. Qi, the origin of life, is omnipresent and perpetual, indivisible, beginningless and endless in space-time, constantly in motion and ever changing. Qi recurs, like the four seasons, yet is without purpose or program, and thus natural and without artifice. Moreover, any two beings imbued with qi mutually respond. However distant they may be, they engender something new by responding to each other. Their correspondence is an interaction with no causal relationship.

This is quite contrary to Western thought, which articulates the world, linguistically demarcates and defines things, and equates essences of things with their names. In other words, it is the opposite of pronouncing "this or that is, in essence, absolutely this or that". Nothing in this world is, in essence, absolutely defined. Since we postulate the notion of "beautiful", that of "ugly" arises in contrast; the same is true of "good" vs "evil". All exist in relative distinction, in relative opposition. All belong to a single mechanism in perpetual motion and change, with no observer existing outside the working of this mechanism. For example, the form of a human being is a coalescence of qi that disperses after a destined time, returning to the original vessel, which was temporarily rendered empty — this is how death is visited upon them. Seeing the world from the viewpoint of qi, life and death are indivisible ...

There are three kinds of qi; heavenly qi, earthly qi, and human qi. In the process of affording them a visual form, Cai employs fire, gunpowder, wind, the body's pressure points, Chinese herbal medicine, and the art of feng shui. His operation is not dissimilar to Daoist diagnostics and prescription, yet the artist metaphysically prescribes the spirit, intellect, and sensitivity ...

It is logical that Cai emerged in the 1990s. As the theories of chaos and complex systems flourish in mathematics and science, as geopolitics become more intricate after the end of the Cold War, as multiculturalism gathers momentum, he knowingly names his own place "chaos" and invokes its name to the face of audiences everywhere, as if he had anticipated all these historical developments.

YUKO HASEGAWA
excerpt from 'Circulating Qi (Energy) of Mind and Intellect', *I Am The Y2K Bug*, exhibition catalogue, trans. Reiko Tornii, Kunsthalle Wien, Vienna, 1999
quote: ibid

Drawing for Dragon Sight Sees Vienna
1999 (opposite)
i) during the explosion
ii) after the explosion
Kunsthalle Wien, Vienna
courtesy the artist
photography: Hertha Humaus

Dragon Sight Sees Vienna, Project For Extraterrestrials No. 32 1999 (left)
Kunsthalle Wien, Vienna
photography: Fritz Simak

Sophie Calle

In his 1992 novel, *Leviathan*, Auster included a note in which he thanked Calle for allowing in him to mingle fact with fiction in his portrayal of the character, Maria, an artist whose work the narrator describes as "too nutty … too idiosyncratic, too personal to be thought of as belonging to any particular medium or discipline".

This, if you're not familiar with Calle's work, is a pretty spot-on summary. Auster credits his character with some of Calle's more enigmatic art projects from the 1980s: following strangers on the streets of her native city [Paris], photographing them from a distance; pursuing one of these strangers to Venice and back again; examining the sleeping habits of strangers she invited to sleep in her bed; calling up every name in an address book she finds to piece together the story of a life; taking a job as a hotel chambermaid to gain access to guests' rooms, the contents of which she secretly photographs.

For such a keen chronicler of strange metropolitan life as Auster, these games on city streets — themselves blending fact and fiction — proved irresistible. But little can he have guessed how his own narrative would unfold. Some artists would have been flattered by the reference to their work, kept a copy of the novel in the house to show friends — that sort of thing. Not Calle. She decided to do a little fact and fiction mingling of her own …

First, she set about getting to know Maria better (that's Maria, the fictional character based on herself, you understand). Maria made art of strange, obsessive rituals as Calle does, but she had some fine oddities of her own — restricting herself to foods of one colour on a given day, for example, and living under the spell of one letter of the alphabet. Calle makes quick, funny work of copying this, as if to let the fictional artist know she's an absolute beginner in the idiosyncratic stakes.

Sticking to a rigidly chromatic diet for a week last December, Calle photographed the unappealing offerings before tucking in with matching plastic cutlery. It's hard to say which day looks worse, the white (fish, rice, fromage blanc and milk) or the pink (ham and taramasalata, washed down with strawberry ice cream and rose wine). But she has the greatest fun with the letter game, dressing up and living life to the letter B, C and W. For B, Calle is transformed into a Bardot-like babe surrounded by cute, furry animals (all beginning with the letter B, of course); for C, she's in a cemetery; and for W she goes for a weekend in Wallonia surrounded by W-inspired objects.

Now on quite intimate terms with Maria, Calle took the fact and fiction game one stage further: "I asked Paul to write the story of a character I would obey," Calle explains in wonderfully deadpan style, as if this is all completely normal. "Instead of writing about Maria imitating me, I wanted him to say her name was Sophie, that she was 45, lived in Paris and did this and that, which I would obey. I gave him one year of my life."

Unsurprisingly perhaps, Auster didn't take up the chance to take fiction out of the equation … Would [she] really have gone through with whatever Auster had scripted? …"Yes. It was my proposal. I was ready. But instead he sent me instructions for the amelioration of life in New York which I obeyed for one week."

These instructions included smiling at strangers, letting them talk to her for as long as they liked, distributing food and cigarettes and cultivating her own spot on the city streets, tending it for an hour each day. Calle chose a phone booth, making it comfy with a chair, small change, reading material, food and drinks, and decorating it with flowers, photographs and paint …

"Everything about it was hard," admits Calle, "because it was not my natural behaviour. I did it as a job, I did it because I said I would obey. The work's more about how I deal with it — it's more about me than usual and it involved me doing things I don't normally do, like talking to crazy people."

This new work, in loose collaboration with Auster, is indeed different in atmosphere from Calle's previous projects. It's lighter in tone, more playful, and obviously ironic. But like all her work, it involves some risk on the part of the artist and the artwork itself is not one precious object in a gallery, but a long (sometimes painfully so) drawn out process. When [asked] why she works in this way … "My work started for personal rather than artistic reasons. After travelling for seven years, I returned to Paris and began following people in the streets because I didn't know what to do with my life, I was lost."

From this aimless wandering came her first art projects, then Calle hired a private detective to follow and photograph her. After the address book project, she was publicly attacked (by the book's owner and critics alike) for intrusiveness, so her work turned to autobiographical, culminating in the new work inspired by Auster's novel.

Through it all, there's a thread of voyeurism and impropriety, fact and fiction, sadism and masochism. It's as if Calle, like some latter-day *flâneur* on the streets of Paris, is still chasing the thrill that eludes us in the ennui of our daily lives but which might just lurk around the next dark corner. She's still fascinated by the danger and unpredictability of urban life.

ELISABETH MAHONEY
excerpt from 'My life as a fictional character', *The Independent,* London, 13 November 1998

De L'Obeissance Lettre B 1998
photograph
courtesy the artist
photography: JB Modino

In his novel *Leviathan*, Paul Auster describes Maria: "At other times, she would make divisions based on the letters of the alphabet. Whole days would be spent under the spell of b, c, or w."

To be like Maria, I spent the day of Tuesday, 10 March 1998, under the sign of B by taking on the appearance of a Big-time Blonde Bimbo (regarding the model for this photograph, see *Paris Match* of 2 November 1989 and the portrait of BB, who in recent years has taken her preference for the cause of animals over that of humans to the point of caricature).

B for Beauty and the Bestiary, for Bat, Bantam, Boar, Bull, for Bug, Badger, Bray, Bellow, Bleat, Bark, for Beastly Birdbrain, for BB.

Destiny Deacon

Photography is white people's invention. Lots of things seem really technical, for example, the camera and the dark room … I've started taking the sort of pictures I do because I can't paint … and then I discovered it was a good way of expressing some feelings that lurk inside.
— Destiny Deacon

Destiny Deacon has remained a Kafkaesque artist, her mutilated dolls still portraying 'subcultural' gender and hybridity critiques. She remains the committed satirist, alerting us to the messages of contempt and derision for indigenous men, women and children in Australia's colonial and postcolonial iconography.

To really understand Destiny and her work, it is almost essential to have been in a share household, probably a squat, with a group of Aboriginal single mothers and/or black separatists — whether inspired by Sappho or Malcolm X or both — but more relevant, perhaps, to have been poor, very

poor, to have a big intellectual take on the world, and to have been marginalised from the discourses of power. Or at least this is the impression Destiny gives and likes to give to the wider audience, one which can hardly read acrylic Western Desert art and is not likely to tune into Deacon's deconstructionist reading of urban Australian Aboriginal survivors of the colonial wars now exiled in the Housing Commission 'burbs …

Oh, the dilemmas of a black woman! She plays hard ball with gender and hybridity stereotypes or tropes and translates them through, for instance, kitsch busts, dolls, performance pieces and installations …

Her installation, *Welcome to Never Never*, 1995, is just one example of her reading of Australian history. It consists of a museum glass display cabinet containing a collection of 'white Australian Aboriginal artefacts'. The trash and

kitsch stand in for … the degrading history of white representations of Aboriginal people, particularly women and children, or, in the language of the settlers, 'lubras' and 'piccaninnies'.

Destiny's target includes constructions of Australian national identity through this demotic pictorial degradation of the Aboriginal subject. In the Australian craft movements and in the kitsch of popular culture, appropriation of Aboriginal imagery as a marker of Australian identity has remained a consistent theme. In the 1950s, as ethnographers collected bark paintings for museums, Australian popular culture was marked by an enthusiastic appropriation of Aboriginal motifs …

Destiny owns an enviable collection of ashtrays and other paraphernalia produced by the amateur plate painters of this period, who depicted 'lubras'

Blak lik mi 2 1991 (opposite)
from *Blak lik mi* series
polaroid
42 x 54.4 cm
private collection

Venus Half Caste, series I 1991
polaroid
42 x 59.4 cm
collection: the artist

and 'piccaninnies' in the browns, blacks and whites of the 'Aboriginalist' style. She evokes this emblematic infantilisation of Aboriginal people in her *Teatowel — Dancing dolly* 1993-95, a laser transfer on linen, which presents two dancing black dolls in Aboriginal flag vestments ... Deacon loves to resurrect the imagery of our oppression, position her favourite dolls or people in her stage sets, and eke out the discomfort ...

She positions herself sharply as a public intellectual, pouring out images and performances from the heart of the hybrid native woman, teetering on the edge of any classification, lacerating the easy, hip images thrown up by New Ageists, Aboriginal people themselves and the colonial cultural machine. Her work serves as a barometer of post-colonial anxiety, as a window of understanding for new generations of Australians turning away from the psychosis of the colonial

relationship but seeking to establish a considered and meaningful grammar of images in an environment full of colonial memories.

MARCIA LANGTON
excerpt from 'the valley of the dolls', *Art and Australia,* Vol. 35, no. 1, 1997, pp. 100-107
quote: Destiny Deacon, 'You Can Be the President, I'd Rather be the Pope', Djon Mundine, *Tyerabarrbowaryaou II: I Shall Never Become A White Man,* exhibition catalogue, 5th Havana Biennial, 1994, pp.17-18

Stan Douglas

[Much of my work deals with] certain aspects of modernity, its dissemination in the world and its transformation into a global condition. However, my two most recent video installations are definitely the most specific with regard to this project. I used to describe my work as a reflection on moments of utopian failure. Perhaps I became more aware in the course of time that works such as *Pursuit, Fear, Catastrophe: Ruskin B.C.*, *Der Sandmann* and *Hors-champs* were also about identifying potential lines of development where societies had the option of going one way or another, at paradigmatic crossroads, so to speak. The two most recent works, *Nu•tka•* and *Win, Place or Show*, refer to exemplary, however specific, places on the North Western coast of the American continent — in the vicinity of Vancouver, where I live. In a way, they frame the beginning and end of modernity there: the first appearance of colonizers in *Nu•tka•*

and the way they failed to take possession of the place in their first attempt. *Win, Place or Show* shows a kind of science-fiction version of a modernist housing project and the totalitarian concept of space behind it. During the post-war years, a number of the utopian ideas which modern architects had developed for individual dwellings and public housing were taken up — and transformed by private developers. The housing estate I am referring to is comparable to many examples we know of utilitarian public housing complexes in the United States or Eastern Europe. These last projects are strangely close to the places associated with my biography but they refer to the general conditions of present-day life in a more complex way than the earlier works ...

Only two complexes of the original master plan for the housing development from the fifties were actually built. These two projects

literally frame the neighbourhood of Strathcona. In these buildings, I recognized a historical symbolism to which I had been blind, a representation of the modernist utopias of *cité radieuse* in the tradition of Le Corbusier which was, in bad faith, to become a reality all over the world in the post-war years ...

The suture, the separation that can be seen in my dual projections, is also metaphorical in nature. The concept forms a real thread through my work even though I have always tried not to turn it into a stylistic device. I am interested in utilizing this difference to create a dialogic situation in a very simple way, a kind of polyphony ...

[In *Win, Place or Show*] I am expressly referring to a TV show that was shown in Vancouver for one year, in 1968. The costumes and characters are derived from it. As regards the dialogue: the

German version gives you the type of stage language that was used to dub American serials for German TV in the sixties. The work is also about television and its local languages and translocal distribution. The original text of the plot is highly formal and most actors in the serial I am referring to were stage actors. *Win, Place or Show* is about such conventions.

There is a reference to a highly Fordist structural momentum, namely the spatialization of time: the build-up of the storyline in the narrative. It is also cut up and reassembled by the computer. In one sense, in relation to space, you always get to see the same story. But it is always also a different one — in much the same way that the various situations and circumstances of life in this totalitarian space are the variations of a single story. The second soundtrack, the radio on which you can hear the broadcasts of a radio station in real time, like the view from the apartment which you can see time and again, also functions as a representative of the "world outside" which enters this private world … to enforce its standards within its almost entirely contained structure. All this also represents the conditions in which these people lived in the post-war years, and

the institutions of extreme control which form a marked contrast to the bourgeois ideals of the civic society, of the urban and public spaces as embodied in the utopias of the nineteenth-century garden city movement, of which the master plan of the development is a caricature. When you listen to these two people, who have no access to the rationalized forms of self-representation within such a society, talking about co-incidence, games of chance and conspirative theories, it is almost an occult situation …

I believe that *Win, Place or Show* … dramatically speaking, convey[s] to people the feeling of claustrophobia. However, behind it there are a number of further layers. Everything the work says, it says by means of representation. Pictures, words, sounds — my work relies on means you must mistrust because so many traces of power and oppression are stored away in them and their history, the history of their exploitation. This is the fundamental irony about my — and any — artistic work.

STAN DOUGLAS
excerpt from interview with Georg Schöllhammer, in Elisabeth Frank-Grossebner & Georg Schöllhammer, 'Win, Place or Show', *Springerin*, September-November 1998, pp. 32-37

Win, Place or Show 1998 (top)
2 channel video projection,
4 channel soundtrack
204,023 variations with an average duration of 6 minutes each
Installation view at the Vancouver Art Gallery, 1999
photography: Trevor Mills

Untitled (Set for Win, Place or Show) 1998 (detail)
cibachrome photograph
triptych each 76 x 102 cm
courtesy David Zwirner Gallery, New York

Marlene Dumas

When viewers are disturbed by her images, notes Dumas, they often look to her life for explanation. She remembers a woman at a lecture she gave who asked whether she was abused when she was a girl. "She was quite disappointed that I had a happy childhood. Some people try and find out what your problem is," says Dumas. "That's why I am so interested in people's opinions. Viewers inspire me with their prejudices."
— Jonathan Turner

I ON PORTRAITURE AND POLITICS

One cannot help remembering here that Apartheid itself was quite literally the representation or "portrayal" of groups. But Dumas' work goes beyond such a political statement alone. She explores the intricate relationship between the political situation of Apartheid and the representational consequences of looking for essences in mimetic portrayal.

This project becomes inescapably apparent when viewed with hindsight. For Dumas' later portraits suggest by their difference that these earlier works are part of an overall endeavour to explore and challenge systematically the characteristics of the traditional portrait as a politically invested genre. In the later works she continues to pursue the genre's conventions, but takes a slightly different approach.

Black Drawings (1991-92) was the first work by Dumas which no longer presents a single portrait or group portrait, but a group of single portraits. It consists of 112 ink drawings ...

Dumas constructs a conception of subjectivity that is based on variety and diversity but not on unique individuality. The portrayed figures are not endowed with subjectivity in terms of original presence, but they acquire it in relation to one another. They are subjects, because they are all different from one another. "That is why they all deserve their own panel within their collective portrayal."

ERNST VAN ALPHEN
excerpt from 'Facing Defacement "models" and Marlene Dumas' intervention in Western Art', *Models 1995*, exhibition catalogue, Oktagon, 1995, pp. 68-69

II ON PHOTOGRAPHY AND PORNOGRAPHY

Painting and photography keep rubbing up against each other, getting all hot and bothered. A cold-eyed artist like Gerhard Richter just likes to watch, but a more physically and emotionally demonstrative one like Marlene Dumas keeps wanting to join in. Richter's paintings, which treat a portrait, a landscape, or an abstraction as equivalent, introject the camera's horrific indifference to any subject. Dumas's obsessive return to the human face and figure make her a sort of anti-Richter. She understands that to the model, the camera's indifference is no more absolute than a psychoanalyst's silence is to the patient: Both are flagrant invitations to the melodrama of transference. And we are all models, sooner or later. Or as Dumas describes our yearning relationship with the mechanical

Pretty White Guy 1999
oil on canvas
100 x 56 cm
private collection, Israel
photography: Stephen White

eye in the title of a 1997 painting, a group portrait of eight haughty demoiselles stripped down to their frilly white underwear, *We Are All in Love with the Cyclops*.

I don't usually talk dirty in my writing, but around Dumas's recent paintings it's hard to avoid. I keep saying yes. Although her imagery has come to focus on pornography only recently, this survey of the last eight years of her work shows that the difference is merely one of degree. For her, relations between person and camera have always been carnal. Still, in making her paintings more seductive, she has also made them harsher. They put me in mind of an observation made by the philosopher Paul Feyerabend after witnessing Muhammad Ali in the ring: "He is so graceful and when he knocks an opponent to the ground it looks as if he had just stroked his cheek with affection."

BARRY SCHWABSKY
excerpt from 'Marlene Dumas', *Artforum*, January 2000, p. 108

III ON PAINTING AND ALL THE OTHER PROBLEMS

Parted lips, exploring fingers, dirty glances. Bend and spread. Only a woman artist could get away with this kind of thing, without the ramifications of some extremely hard-core art theoretical justification to back it all up.

Baring your bum is a gesture of defiance, a baboon's way of making a face, or a mandrill's brightly coloured way of saying he's in the mood. It is a basic simian sign, at once aggressive and comic. In human cultures it has become something else, and we're inclined to call it lewd. Unless, of course, it is art, in which case we qualify the unavoidable with more elevated thoughts and theoretical complications. These discussions, which turn about the male gaze and the objectification of women, have been so often repeated that they have become anodyne.

There has also been a lot of talk about artists "taking responsibility" for the meaning and implications of the images they create, as if the images were the artists' children, and as if there were some duty not

Lovesick 1994
oil on canvas
60 x 50 cm
private collection, London
courtesy Paul Andriesse, Amsterdam
photography: Peter Cox

just to create, but to give moral guidance. "At the moment", Dumas wrote in the mid-eighties, "my art is situated between the pornographic tendency to reveal everything and the erotic inclination to hide what it's all about."

The moment is still with us, and Dumas still manipulates her images with an extreme ambivalence. Her images are volatile, unstable and difficult to deal with. It is hard to maintain one's critical distance. What they might mean is something else.

Dumas occupies an interesting position. She is an intuitive painter who is also seen as something of a conceptualist …

The women in her paintings, for all their pouts and bedroom glances (some of which are very fierce), are painted with a kind of intimacy, which paradoxically reclaims their independence and their dignity. They're not just sex objects, a collection of orifices and protrusions, and they're not real people either. Paintings don't have psychologies, of course, but they can make the viewer feel self-conscious and awkward just the same.

When she uses oil paint, her paintings often have a kind of tawdriness derived from her use of mixed greys, rubbed-down skin tones, drawing revised on the surface for all to see. We can never forget that these things are painted … A number of the paintings also depict men. They're as vulnerable and as self-

possessed as her women. A very beautiful pale painting has a *Pretty White Guy* reclining, toying with himself with his Egon Schiele hands. He's so pearly and pallid he's fading entirely away into a kind of masturbatory reverie. He has little more substance than a jellyfish. Another guy looks down at his own lurid violet erection. It isn't certain whether he's admiring it, or whether he's utterly astonished. It is as if he's met an alien. Another man dribbles on himself. It is comical, infantile, and somehow full of pathos …

It could only be painted, and that is where description fails; with what can one counter such images? They are uncensored and uncensorious. They are born on the sheet of paper. They relate to the world and to human feelings — the childish, the repressed, the pleasurable and the taboo, but they are ultimately themselves. They are every way up and in every position. They play with themselves and they play with our reactions. They pose for us, and we pose and adopt critical positions for them …

Her work is its own commentary, and deals with its own difficulties. Any other problems are our own.

ADRIAN SEARLE
excerpt from 'I am a dirty woman. That's why I paint', *The Guardian*, March 30 1999, p. 10
quote: Jonathan Turner, 'Sometimes Clever, Sometimes Smutty', *ARTnews*, January 1997, pp. 98-101

Rosalie Gascoigne

James Mollison was a friend when, in the early 1970s, Rosalie Gascoigne entered the art world. She remembers his responses to her work. "Your work is lyrical", he said after watching for a few years. And so it is. Poetic, at times song-like, and invariably expressing the artist's own thoughts and feelings. Rosalie's university courses, forty years before in Auckland, New Zealand, in the classics and the Romantic poets, remain her professional training in a very real sense.

Poets are Nature's best celebrants, when they write from an independent position, paralleling it.

White, yes, pale with the pallor of old timbers
Thistle-stalks, shells, the extreme pallor of starlight –

Rosemary Dobson wrote the magnificent poem which begins with these lines in July [1985], after spending a day with Rosalie in the countryside near Canberra. Rosalie was harvesting the pale, dry thistle-stalks which appear in the work called *Flight*. Denise Levertov, an American poet, wrote a poem after visiting the artist's home in 1981 and seeing

… slabs of old wood, weathered, residual,
formed by the absence of what was cut
for forgotten purpose, out of their past:
they meet now, austere, graceful,
transfigured by being placed,
being seen.

Rosalie was not trained in an art school: "It is no use pretending I am — I can come in late and careless because it is so unlikely and silly that I should". Art and one or two artists had been around for years but for her the watershed was in the late 1960s when, within her family and in a small circle of Canberra friends, there had developed a lively interest in art, especially new art … Leaving the arranging of flowers, her disciplined outlet till then, and never enough, she went for the bigger game.

There was in any case no long-standing tradition for her kind of work — the art of assemblage. It posed a problem of identification for the artist and then for her audience. She wrote in December 1971, "I am thinking … that we call my things 'bush sculpture' — 'bush' partly because of their content and partly in the context of 'bush lawyer', 'bush carpenter'."

The first solo exhibition was in 1974 when Rosalie was aged 57. She came into the art world, like Athena, fully-armed. Her largest work to that date *Last Stand* 1972, a three metre tall stand of white skeletons, had been preceded by a still bolder version — eighteen metres of bones threaded on fencing wire prancing and looping through the garden. She described this work as "harsh weeds". Whatever went into making Rosalie an artist had already done its job by the time she went gathering bones in 1971 but, entering the art community, she responded to new influences. The art community and its gossip, its expectations, and ups and downs, became another of her field trips. Looking at her work, people talked about Joseph Cornell, Man Ray, Marcel Duchamp, "collage" and "assemblage" … In January 1974 James Mollison showed her Duchamp's "cage of marble sugar lumps" and "bicycle wheel on stool" and Man Ray's "mysterious object, wrapped sewing-machine or whatever", in storage with the rest of the Australian National Gallery collection …

One of Rosalie's strengths is clarity. She responds directly to people, to art, to nature, and bounces back as directly. She's not introverted or contemplative. She's responsive. It has been of great benefit to her art, enabling her to see her own work clearly, what it is and how it comes across, and to judge influences as benign, when they are 'true'…

Rosalie had one test of whether her work was art. If her works had presence. If they came across and continued to come across, for other people as well as herself, and in other environments than the one in which they were made, then they were art, good art. Encountering her work at Gallery A, Sydney, in 1975 Daniel Thomas found it "quite unlike anybody else's in Australia". The assemblages he saw, such as "a neat horizontal stack of dried stalks in a piece of convex metal", were organised "with a marvellously sure and fully sculptural taste in setting up contrasts of texture, colour, direction and weight". He too, used the word 'poetic' (*Sydney Morning Herald* 8 May 1975) …

Classical is one of her words, so is 'presence'. Her art hasn't altered all that much, not in the way it would have if she had been discovering *everything* in that time. "Art confirmed me", says Rosalie … So where did she begin if not in the so-called informal sculpture of the 1970s? My guess is that the decisive moment was in 1963 or 1964 on the steps of Mark Foy's, Sydney, drinking coffee and reading a big new book about Ikebana. "I read on, feeling that I knew for myself everything it was saying".

The first lesson in Ikebana, awareness of nature, she had. "I was already bringing back the hill-tops and rivers in the form of dried native flowers, river stones and grasses. I was all wild surmise … Ikebana gave an absolute. It gave form. To do things exactly steadied you down. From practising Ikebana I got the vision of how to use the things I liked".

It sounds like Plato, this vision or precious intimation of a perfect form or absolute, which is the unrealisable aspiration of art. Michelangelo was a neoplatonist. Rosalie is too, though not literally: she doesn't know the term. The vital step for her between a wild surmise and knowing how to realise a work of art was the Ikebana *exercises*. Like practising scales in music … Rosalie abandoned the classes when, their purpose served, she wanted more freedom, but not before Ikebana, like Plato's abstract form, had provided her with an internalised sense of perfect order. She now has her original, passionate acquisitiveness plus the rare sculptural sense which the art community noticed.

"This is a piece for walking around and contemplating. It is about being in the country with its shifting light and shades of grey, its casualness and its prodigality. The viewer's response to the landscape may differ from mine but I hope this piece will convey some sense of the countryside that produced it: and that an extra turn or two around the work will induce in the viewer the liberating feeling of being in open country." (Rosalie Gascoigne on *Piece to Walk Around* 1981)

To see Rosalie Gascoigne's work is properly to feel something bigger. Nature. She respects her materials. She dismantles boxes to get the planks or to cut out images. She removes nails. She saws. She scrubs. But she won't alter the thing that first drew her.

The titles are allusive, signifying something the work might suggest, *Honey Flow* for example. Whereas the title *Flight* refers to what the work is about — birds raking the sky in flight, *Highway code* fits both the material and its cryptic lettering. It is made of yellow road signs the artist found in a tip. They had been purposely scrambled by being cut up and painted with splashes of white. From this deconstruction Rosalie made one of her best wall panels. Moreover, since the yellow is retro-reflective, the panel takes on another, spectral, presence after dark.

MARY EAGLE
excerpt from *Rosalie Gascoigne, 1985*
exhibition catalogue, Fine Arts Gallery,
The University of Tasmania, 1985

Metropolis 1999
retro-reflective road signs
232 x 319.7 x 1.6 cm
gift of the artist 1999
collection: Art Gallery of New South Wales,
Sydney
photography: Christopher Snee for AGNSW

Andreas Gursky

I generally let things develop slowly …

My bookshelves are ordered in an extremely paradoxical way, which roughly reflects the way I live my daily life. As a person who primarily experiences his environment visually, I am always observing my immediate surroundings. Consequently, I am constantly putting things in order, sorting them out, until they become a whole. Perhaps that sounds very general; however I don't sort my books purely according to their content. When I don't feel up to the demands of daily life, which happens often enough, all my tidy principles fly out of the window and there's complete chaos … I also make a categoric division between photography and 'pure art' … Perhaps this has something to do with the fact that I'm fascinated by a few specific characteristics of photography, such as the "photogenic" or what people think of as the "authenticity" of the medium. It could also be because I have had a lifelong relationship with photography, due to the fact that, as a child, my room was part of my parents' advertising studio. Which reminds me of a statement by Gary Winograd: "I take photographs to see how things look when they've been photographed."

The photogenic is a term recently used in connection with the Catherine effect from an article describing how a woman who wasn't particularly good looking was given the aura of a Russian grand duchess thanks to the way she was photographed. It means exactly the opposite of authenticity. As you can see, I have a weakness for paradox. For me, the photogenic and the authentic are two characteristics of the medium that would appear to be mutually exclusive. The photogenic allows a picture to develop a life of its own on a two-dimensional surface, which doesn't exactly reflect the real object. One talks about photogenic people who are often less attractive in real life than they are in pictures …

Several unconscious decisions would appear to be important in photography. Decisions that are subconsciously taken correctly at the first attempt may be the wrong ones in a second picture, which,

one likes to believe, is taken under greater control. Despite the fact that I have twenty years' experience in photography, I still find developing negatives like alchemy …

I deliberately use controversial arguments to show that there are countless ways of taking photographs nowadays, and that since the photogenic medium has been digitalised, a fixed definition of the term 'photography' has become impossible. Amateur photographers take their pictures in seconds, yet the amateurish use of the camera can unintentionally lead to the most brilliant pictures …

This spontaneous, unthought out use of the camera is the extreme end of the spectrum and proves that my theory about the element of surprise is correct. Another, completely different way of working is electronic picture processing, as exemplified by Jeff Wall or Thomas Demand's recording of real, "stage-managed" spaces. This manner of working requires an arbitrary, gradual and utterly controlled procedure, and with these artists I can no longer make the distinction … between photography and painting. As far as my working technique is concerned, there are recurring themes, such as how photographing something is developed into a formalistic picture, but the raw materials for my pictures come from the most diverse sources. I follow no strict method to transform a visual experience or an artistic concept into a picture. I appreciate the seemingly coincidental circumstances which I can't include in my concept and react spontaneously to them, without knowing whether a picture taken like this is going to make sense. In such cases I put the negative aside for months or even years before selecting the photograph. Since 1992 I have consciously made use of the possibilities offered by electronic picture processing, so as to emphasise formal elements that will enhance the picture, or, for example, to apply a picture concept that in real terms of perspective would be impossible to realise. When I work like this, I keep the picture in my mind's eye and approach the final result step

by step without allowing myself to be influenced by spontaneous flashes of inspiration.

One of my most recent pictures, *o.T.V.* is a work of fantasy … of more than 200 different sports shoes on shelves. There are several layers of reality in this picture. The real shoe display was pictorially ineffective and harmlessly presented. That's why I felt it would be all the more interesting to highlight the symbolic dimension of this phenomenon — the fetishism of our material world. Having thought about it for several weeks I decided to go back to New York to photograph these shoes in a specially constructed, artificial room before I lined them up in rows and laboriously created an all-over using digital processing techniques …

My pictures really are becoming increasingly formal and abstract. A visual structure appears to dominate the real events shown in my pictures. On a formal level, countless interrelated micro and macrostructures are woven together, determined by an overall organisational principle … Of course, there are adequate reasons to justify such a formal, schematic representation of reality.

If you talk about my interest in nature, I have to explain my extended notion of nature. I am perhaps more interested in the nature of things in general — again and again, the term "aggregate state" comes to mind when I describe the existential state of things …

The shift in emphasis could also be seen as a logical progression from the seemingly naïve landscapes of the Eighties to today's drier and more abstract pictures. I believe that there's also a certain form of abstraction in my early landscape: for example, I often show human figures from behind and thus the landscape is observed "through" a second lens. I don't name the activities of the human figures specifically and hence do not question what they do in general. The camera's enormous distance from these figures means that they become de-individualised. So I am never interested in the individual, but in the human species and environment …

Klitschko 1999
c-print
207 x 261 cm
courtesy the artist
& Monika Sprüth Galerie, Cologne

Compositional decisions are always important when structuring a picture, but I don't think these are particularly interesting, as they should be a matter of course. The immediately visual experience should in any case be the catalyst for a pictorial decision. Questions of social relevance or contextual strategy should, in my opinion, only be considered in a second phase. In the first instance, what concerns me is the autonomy of the picture and confidence in the power of the image.

I don't intentionally raise issues intrinsic to art in order to formulate them anew in modern terms. In my opinion, a context-related procedure such as this leads to dull results, because the calculated approach denies the irrational laws of creating a picture the necessary freedom. Nonetheless, parallels with historical styles are apparent in many of my pictures, from

Albrecht Altdorfer's *Alexander-shlacht* which can be discerned in my images of stock exchanges, to De Chirico's *Pittura Metafisica* reflected in *Ayamante* or my recent photos such as *Rhein*, which is reminiscent of Barnett Newman, and *Prada II* which can be compared with Dan Flavin's work. The history of art seems to possess a generally valid formal vocabulary which we use again and again. It would perhaps be interesting for art historians to find out why an artist who is not versed in the subject such as myself still has access to this formal vocabulary. My preference for clear structures is the result of my desire — perhaps illusory — to keep track and maintain my grip on the world.

ANDREAS GURSKY
excerpt from a correspondence between the artist and Veit Görner, published in *Andreas Gursky, Fotografien 1994–1998*, Kunstmuseum Wolfsburg, 1998

Fiona Hall

We share a great deal with plants, and use them frequently as erotic metaphors. The basis of our shared existence is something that, scientifically, we are now more fully able and obliged to acknowledge ...

There are more genetic similarities between us and the plant world than there are differences. These are mind blowing concepts that should make us take notice, because if we can't coexist with and maintain the plant world then human life is doomed.
— Fiona Hall

The initial *Paradisus Terrestris* (1997) series was informed in part by Fiona Hall's research into the botanical depictions, including those in exquisite florelegiums such as one by Basilius Besler entitled *Hortus Eystettensis*, and Thornton's *The Temple of Flora*. She also became fascinated by the history of ideas around plants and the ways in which certain vegetables and spices, such as tomatoes or chillies, were sought after — considered to be a bizarre phenomena — when they were introduced to Europe from the Americas. An important aspect of her work was her interest in systems of classification, first devised by scholars such as Carl Linnaeus in the 1700s — based upon looking at the male and female components of each plant. 'At the time of his findings', Hall notes, 'people still believed that the Garden of Eden existed some-where on Earth. So they were shocked when he talked about plants in overtly sexual terms be-cause their view had always been that plants were benign, innocent; they didn't have a sex life.'

Hall, who had long been interested in the potency of words, researched the botanical and common names of the plants she chose; enlivened by the metaphorical associations of 'Venus Fly Trap' or 'Screw Pine'; a sense of entrapment or closure interacting with openly seductive elements. She felt that it was crucial to be as accurate as possible both in the processes of naming and in the depictions themselves — her early training in life drawing clearly providing valuable grounding. In the later *Paradisus Terrestris Entitled* (1989-90) series, depicting specifically Australian plants, Fiona Hall includes a triple naming system: the botanical name, the common name, and an Aboriginal name and the language group to which it belongs. This was partly due to her realisation that naming is highly revelatory of the ways in which we regard the world. It was also a deliberate act of acknowledging the indigenous peoples' connections with the land and plant life.

"It is amazing to me that a section of the Australian population still can't comprehend that this land and the plants that grow in it, and the people whose land that originally was, have together a very long history of coexistence that must be acknowledged and respected. The recent work, *Paradisus Terrestris Entitled*, attempts to make a political comment about this. The multiple parallel systems of plant names seem to me to eloquently indicate widely different outlooks and levels of awareness."

DEBORAH HART
excerpt from 'Fiona Hall's Garden: fertile interactions', *Art and Australia*, Vol. 36, no. 2, 1998, pp. 202-211
quote: ibid, p. 202

Drift Net 1998
pvc pipe, glass beads, mother-of-pearl buttons, wire, engraved bottle, compass, vitrine
vitrine dimensions 129 x 160 x 76cm
courtesy the artist & Roslyn Oxley9 Gallery, Sydney

Paradisus Terrestria Entitled 1999
(opposite)
dumban (Bundajalung)
staghorn
Platycerium superbum
aluminium and tin
25.5 x 15.0 x 2.2 cm
courtesy Roslyn Oxley9 Gallery, Sydney

Bill Hammond

Bill Hammond gets us where we live. So persuasive are the spaces this artist furnishes that when you withdraw from the interior of one of his works, the room you are standing in seems heightened, reordered, strange to itself ... Continuously, furiously, his paintings restage the common-place, unhouse the ordinary, and return us, changed, to the places we dwell in.

Hammond's interiors first clamped themselves on to the imaginations of gallery-goers in the 1980s, a decade in which ... the domestic interior had begun to trump landscape as a subject for local painters ... His convulsive, pressurised spaces harbour two violently opposed dreams about what it means to be housed. One is a nightmare of constriction and enclosure, a claustrophobia that the ego strains to be free of. But there is also, secreted in that nightmare, a dream of protection and retreat: the interior as a refuge for the assailed self ...

In Hammond's paintings of the 1980s the Great New Zealand Landscape has shrunk and come inside; it's part of the furniture of the neurotic imagination. Tables carry alps on their backs in *I've Just Got to Get a Message to You*; and in *Heading for the Last Roundup*, curtains fall like vast guillotine blades toward the plains ... we might plausibly guess that the paintings are about the giddying psychic gap between the space of the studio, in here, and the sinister vastness of the spaces beyond. Ever since early works such as *Making a Break for the Good of the Soul* and *Passover* established an ominous tension between windows and the people they frame, strange views from small rooms have been Hammond's favoured terrain.

The paintings are often treated as if they were only the sum of their "quirky" motifs. Yet the deep strangeness of Hammond's early scenes springs from the way their interiors are put together, from the perverse ways they're *staged*. Long interested in expressionist set design ... Hammond is a master of the architectural panic attack. The engines of that panic are his devious, reversed perspectives,

which drag you from agoraphobia to claustrophobia in one uncanny surge ... To say that Hammond has revolutionised figure/ground relations is true, but insufficient. He wants to make you feel — with the urgency of fingernails dragged down a blackboard — wrenching contradictions between space and actor, body and thing, skull and skin, title and meaning ...

The gleeful grotesquerie of such images secures Hammond's place in a tradition of shape-changing and spatial unease that runs from Bosch's phantasmagoria to Goya's dark hybrids, from de Chirico's anxious arcades to the scrunched and snoutish figures of Jim Nutt. More than that, it reveals Hammond's abiding debt to the pop-surrealism of comics and cartoons and horror movies: a faith that the frame is a place where matter misbehaves and the only constant is metamorphosis. In

Hammondland people become things and things behave like people. Bodies balloon and shrivel, stretch like silly putty, burst forth from furniture with an almost audible graunch of bone and gristle, melt into their clothing, peel free of their skins, and tattoo walls. Elsewhere, drapes stiffen into fences, electrical flex deliquesces, televisions chunder grue. Plugged into guitars, microphones, joysticks, fitness machines, Hammond's people are not men alone in the landscape, rather hapless amplifications of their environments ...

Since 1992, when Hammond began to conduct journeys back to the haunted house of New Zealand history, his nightmares of domestic life have given way to a more distant dream. Among the new paintings' strangest details are the 1950s fabrics — patterned with ferns, with cigarettes — in which

his trademark bird-people are sheathed. These are the same fabrics, often, that partition spaces and clothe people in his mid-1980s images; fabrics inspired, Hammond has said, by his grandmother's and auntie's dresses in an old family photo. Hammond's birds enjoy a silent idyll in the emerald light, twisting through a space that now suggests tapestry as much as it does wallpaper. *Of* their place, tattooed with the patterns of a nation, they stand for the grace and moral dignity of a lost past — a past that mingles the pre-colonial period with his own childhood.

Hammond puts his case with great tact, great subtlety, here. His recent paintings, you see, seem to *anticipate* the earlier, neurotic interiors; the birds look resigned to their fates because they can see what's coming. Joined together, the early interiors and recent landscapes compose a social panorama of rare reach and complexity, stretched between the dead calm of the past and the neurotic energies of the present. Imagine all of Hammond's roomscapes and wallpapers joined end to end in this way, so that they seal one interior in a perpetual frieze. It would be hard to feel at home in the midst of that room, but even harder not to feel alive.

JUSTIN PATON
excerpt from 'Bill Hammond's Apocalyptic Wallpaper', *Bill Hammond: 23 Big Pictures*, exhibition catalogue, Dunedin Public Art Gallery, 1999, pp. 8-12

Hokey Pokey 1998
acrylic on canvas on stretchers
200 x 500 cm
private collection, Auckland
photography: Julia Brooke-White

Gwyn Hanssen Pigott

I have learned a few things about the arrangements. I have to be in neutral when I place the pots together, and alert to tensions and havens of spacing. Then I might find sweet relationships, shy couplings, protecting strengths, in those pared down, waiting forms. Traps are legion, and I easily slip into them: the snares of design, of glibness, of easy predictability or cleverness, as in all areas of the making. There is a lot of self-trust involved here. Not always so easy. Some groupings stand the test of time: some, alas, seem awkward or pretentious now to my changed eyes.

Before coming to Netherdale in far North Queensland, eight years ago, I had started to look more closely at how pots, perfectly contained within themselves, sit with each other, changing each other. I was interested to find what could hold the pots together in a bonding that was neither design nor intention, but could only be discovered after the firing, when everything came into play: lushness, coolness, weight, line. Lately, I would add, 'character'.

I had seen Giorgio Morandi's paintings, etchings and drawings first in Paris at the huge 1972 retrospective, and then again at Bologna at the centenary exhibition in 1990. I love his searching, obsessive, describing of the common objects that were his subject and measure. A bottle: a dense, palpable block of creamy white. A bottle: a wavering half-line holding space. His work is substantial, tenuous, disturbing, resolved. His work is *not* about character. It is about 'essence': the metaphysical expressed through the solidly physical and knowable.

Of some artists' work you can say, yes, if I understood that, I would understand all there is to know about expressed beauty. For me, Morandi's work is like that, and Piero della Francesca's. But so are many bowls.

I could try, perhaps, to scrutinize my pots in the way I imagine Morandi looked at his beloved still life subjects: those old tin cans, assorted bottles, paper roses, coffee bowls, metal boxes, shells, pots and pans, some battered and painted over, that have outlasted him, in Bologna. But it won't do. I don't *intend* to re-present my pots and position them in fields of colour so dense and greyed that they lock and surround or make them poignant or monumental by the solidity of the strong, thick, paint itself. My pots have to stand as they are, as real as my hand; and it seems I have so little time to know them before they are gone.

Morandi's work can inspire and direct my eye, and hint at eccentric joinings, and haunting colour. But it is a big leap from standing, grateful as anything, in front of his canvases, to looking at the very tangible, usable, everyday pots that salt my life: pots which need, too, that kind and urgent attention.

This gap has been, at times, a sadness for me. I *know* the pots I live with and sometimes make can be potent. Potent as language, potent as solace, potent as messages. Writers, poets, artists have described again and again the force of these everyday objects; but who knows how many potters, knowing, finally, the rightness of their work, have despaired of having their work actually perceived.

But you go on, with the colour blends and glaze tests, the accumulating buckets of stained glaze, arranging the wood for the firing that may or may not give you that pulling back of iron in the mixed stain to make that particular purple/ bronze, or that slight bloom that *severe* shape needs to make it tender: wondering if the porcelain you are using, fired for longer, might just soften enough to make the line of that bowl more languid. Paring, honing, adding. Head in hands after the firing, as like as not; but sometimes utterly thankful.

It's an old story, the maker's story …

Not long ago I made two lines of small, very anonymous table pots, one of 19 pieces, the other of 23. The pots have a certain squareness, flat to the ground. The rims are fine, but have no flare. There is some colour, some leaning towards movement, but the mattness suggests quiet. Well, it does for me. I *could* look at them as rock outcrops. I could, but didn't. I saw a displacement: images of resettlement, border crossing, refuge seeking. I called them *Exodus*.

Pots, useful, everyday, ordinary pots, have for most of my life been my daily pleasure mines. Crowding the kitchen shelves, focussing the mind during a coffee conversation, letting the eye rest on considered form, on tenuous line, on languidness, on simplicity, on offered optimism; inviting the hand to cup, the finger to outline a rim, the lip to brush. They have become … my companions; and each meal or smoko I make a choice, inviting the pot like a friend, and seeing, perhaps, something about it I had forgotten or overlooked in the rush of things.

Beauty, and our response to it, remains a mystery. But it seems to me that, in the alchemy of making, the pot becomes subtly humanised. It is as though a kind of knowing — a history of understanding and a sort of longing are translated, through care and consideration, and an intimate connecting with the stuff under our fingers … into a form with an independent life. With its own power to move.

So we speak of pots as though they are animate. We call them gentle or generous or strong or vulnerable. A group of bottles becomes a family. A straggling line of jugs and cups and tumblers becomes an assorted tribe journeying somewhere. A silent line of porcelain beakers waits in a window for the light to hit their rims and their ordinary beauty to become radiant.

GWYN HANSSEN PIGOTT
excerpt from notes and statements supplied by the artist

Exodus II 1996 (top)
porcelain (23 pieces)
private collection, Melbourne
courtesy Christine Abrahams Gallery, Melbourne
photography: Brian Hand

Black Mountain Still Life 1995
11 pieces wheelthrown, glazed
& woodfired at Netherdale, Qld
collection: Bret Walker Collection, Sydney
courtesy Rex Irwin Art Dealer, Sydney

Bill Henson

Henson gives shape to dreams and nightmares, squalor and opulence, darkness and piercing shafts of light: a world charged with erotic tension, and guarded by the spectre of death. It is sweeping, and intricate, slow to surrender its detail. The grandeur of its landscapes and buildings, the immensity of its skies, are subject to the subtlest distinctions of colour and form. Things shift and dissolve into contrary conditions, like stone that erodes into air we breathe or neon that flares like the sunset.

This idea of metamorphosis is central to all Henson's work. We see things at the instant before the evidence of their existence disappears, or becomes the evidence of something else. We understand that this moment, and this moment only, is now ours. An eye becomes a glittering jewel, a building is erased by grains of light. Flesh is marbled or crumbles into darkness. Bodies seem lit from within, the way light can pass through water. Sometimes these pictures almost successfully resist our ability to see them. 'What is that face,' wrote Peter Schjeldahl of one of Henson's pictures, 'breaking our hearts, but a momentary configuration of molecules taking form and changing form and losing form as night falls'...

The faces in Henson's crowd works or in the series of pictures he made of naked junkies, the faces of people in suburban malls or gravely watching the opera in Paris, have this much in common: they are oblivious to us, but attentive to something we cannot see or know. The mystery is not only that the photograph can dramatize this nameless rapture: these people, whom we cannot know, whom we never knew, somehow *are* us as we stand before the work, attending dumbly to their silence. The semblance, magnified and beautiful, of our own concentrated gaze lies before us on the wall.

Henson's recent work can't quite be read like this. We can't surrender to these images but must negotiate our way, seeking a point of entry. This work is undeniably beautiful too, but its beauty has been fractured and displaced. We see a world abandoned to itself and its own

weird logic, a ruined arcadia shattered into its natural elements: air, junk, flesh, foliage. In this terrible place the only gestures that remain for its inhabitants are instinctive: bodies are ferried down buckled terraces of metal, haplessly caressed or abandoned in the mud like the fallen in some obscure battle. These are images of surrender but to what forces we do not know: we are merely witnesses to the wreckage, to the way someone stands, head bowed, waiting; to a hand splayed against a naked back; to a man and woman whose bodies gleam in their embrace with a pale translucent light. This is the meaning of Henson's collage: everything happens at once according to some irrevocable destiny. We may not know what this destiny is, but the resonance of Henson's images tells us it exists.

During the eighties Henson often pursued his ideas across hundreds of images. But now the sequence has become the suite, a handful of pictures, each one an obsessive variation on the others. These images are like palimpsests, each written across another, each abandoned in a different condition. Their layered surfaces suggest that behind the paper on which the images are printed lies more paper, more images in an infinite progression. We are looking at the fragments from one catastrophic image. But perhaps it is true that in every picture Henson has ever taken he has been searching for this essential image — and now he is getting nearer to finding it. Perhaps every idea he has lived with, everything he knows and wants to say, is fated to be contained in a single photograph he is yet to make.

But for now we must settle for the multiplier effect he manages with such power. This is the kind of world Baudelaire imagined, composed of intoxicating scent and colour, of perfume, sweet as the smell of a child's skin, mingled with rust and blood. It is a world in which anything might happen but hardly anything will, of steel, scrub and swamp beneath gigantic biblical skies and funereal trees. There is a kind of desperate splendour about these works; the eye moves gingerly across their surfaces. It is arrested by specific

detail, but drawn again into movement by hairlines, seams, and fissures. It finds pockets of darkness where it can rest, and severed white shapes, blinding areas of cut light. Something is happening in these sectors, but it is not for us to see.

This new work notates a kind of chaos, the beginning of time or the end: are we staring at things at the point of their collapse or at the moment before everything coheres? We know only that more is happening than we can understand, perhaps more than we can bear. So much of Henson's work has gestured at the condition of the dream. But now, with his jagged alignments, his irresistible internal logic, his soaring deathly landscapes, his blurred, receding figures and gashes of white light, he has come nearer to rendering the sensation of dreaming itself than ever before. Dreams are precise, unarguable, immune to what we think of them: we sleep; things happen; we wake; these things never happened at all; and now they are part of us.

MICHAEL HEYWARD
excerpt from 'The Photography of Bill Henson', *Bill Henson,* exhibition catalogue, Australian Pavilion at the 46th Venice Biennale, 1995, pp. 24-26

Untitled 1998/1999/2000 (top)
type c colour photograph
127 x 180 cm
courtesy Roslyn Oxley9 Gallery, Sydney

Untitled 1998/1999/2000
type c colour photograph
127 x 180 cm
courtesy Roslyn Oxley9 Gallery, Sydney

Gary Hill

… the art event takes place within …
process. One has to be open to that event
and be able to … wander in it and feel it
open up. I'm getting further and further into
finding this moment in processes that involve
me with people. — Gary Hill

VIEWER/1996

Slightly larger than life-size color
images of seventeen day laborers,
facing out from a neutral black
background, are projected on a
wall, about 45 feet long, by five
video projectors attached to the
ceiling. Five laserdiscs … are synchronized so that the figures appear
to be standing side-by-side in a
somewhat continuous line … The
men stand almost motionless, their
movement limited to involuntary
stirring — an incidental shuffling
from foot to foot, slight movements
of the hands, and almost imper-
ceptible changes in facial expression. There is no interaction among
them, each man standing quite
alone and gazing out from the plane
of projection towards the viewer.

ON VIEW

When we enter an art space we
implicitly choose the role of viewer,
even when some sort of participation or interactivity is called for.
The history of art is arguably some
"volution" of that role — evolution/
devolution/revolution/convolution —
depending on one's model of
cultural progression over time. In a

sense every act of art "on view"
challenges us to define the role of
viewer, as well as the role of
"viewed." Our presence is request-
ed, so to speak, by the nature of
the event. Yet presence, like
viewing, is an unsettled notion in
more or less continuous need of
reassessment. This is a strange
fact, given that viewing and being
present are "activities" that we can
hardly *not* be doing. Aren't they, like
life itself, in some sense self-
evident? Seemingly. And *Viewer*,
Gary Hill's projective installation,
serves as an arena of such self-
evidence — and the self-question-
ing hidden in the heart of *view* …

THE QUESTION

It's an odd, even awkward fact that
when we gaze into the eyes of
individuals among the seventeen
standing men of *Viewer*, we quickly
find ourselves in the state of
inquiring. Perhaps this state is the
inevitable result of a pervasive
mood of uncertainty — in their
eyes, in how they stand. There's an
impulse to question them — who
are you, where do you come from,
what are you doing here, what do
you want from me, how did you get
into this situation …? *On view* here
means *on the spot*. Yet *who* is on
the spot is part of the question. The
mood of uncertainty is contagious
and soon becomes a mode of
presence in the space.

Everyone's a suspect, all are under
suspicion. The kind of distinction
one draws in lining people up this
way reflects how we set ourselves
and others apart, and participates in
a history of apartness. No one feels
particularly safe in this situation,
neither the one on view, being
stared at and suspected, nor the
one viewing, inquiringly cutting into
the space of the other standing
there. Unsafety is on their faces, a
look learned and adapted to handle
the state, the modus operandi of
everyday on-the-spot identity. And
we, as viewers, just keep looking
on, fixing the face of the one
standing in front of us, facing us.
We quickly develop our own mode
of standing apart. It's a matter of
the survival of the identified,
because by a sort of law of
reciprocity in uncertainty, the
inquiry moves in two directions at
once. An identity adrift in the space
of the viewed soon cuts across the
safety of the art space and feeds
back into the state of the viewer.
Art may be in question, or, at the
very least, in the question. (Might it
even have been beside the point?)

What we are in the midst of here is
viewing. When we came into the
room what we happened upon was
the view. A room with a view,
inside. The view is people looking
out from where they are, *in* to
where we are, here, in the middle

of the space. It seems, perplexingly, that the view itself is viewing — viewing us. Or, by a turn of phrase (a shift in view), viewing itself. In an environment that is saturated with viewing, at a certain point it's as though the space itself views — a topological displacement of agency, a spinning out of grammar in the active relationship of entities in the space. It quickly gets confusing, and it is hard to believe one might be thinking: *the view is viewing itself*. The thought is a kind of trap. To dwell there risks getting lost in the rainforest-like heart of the question: the thicket of identity in the two-way act of viewing. Even when one-half of the equation has the status of *the illusory*.

Who, then, is the viewer? And what constitutes the view *concretely*?

PROJECTIVITY

The view is, at any given moment and in quite different senses, a projection. There's always someone behind it giving it specific life. And the medium itself is projection, which means that some*thing* is being thrown out into "viewing space." In this kind of space there is a reflexive relationship between the thrower and what is thrown, with continuing feedback governing the interchange. And of course the context in which we make these distinctions is projective art, which

is a conscious — meaning responsive and responsible — working within the generative field created by the possibility of projection. The nature of this possibility is as complex as it is attractive, and this becomes obvious when we venture into what projectivity actually gives rise to …

FOCUS

View, viewing space, the viewer's state of presence — key notions that we do not *define* so much as *invoke* in the interest of sustaining an inquiry — are all linked to the matter of focus. In *Viewer* the projection of the seventeen figures is very sharply focused (from an optimal distance, which is not close up to the wall). And as one engages this concrete focus, there is a personal charge relative to each of the men as one views them discretely; this is a *human* focus, a kind of individuation of attention. Then there is the *interactive* focus, by which we mean the phenomenon of focusing on the image of this *other* person in such a way that we ourselves seem to *get focused* … And in so many ways what shows up in this hypersensualized space is how these quite simple and ordinary people, whose living and breathing images are projected on the wall, are in fact quite powerful presences — unavoidably engaging and almost eerily present

presences. Yet they are merely projections.

Projections of whom or what? The artist? To situate the artist relative to the projection we must determine who, which may mean *where*, he is in this art. He is of course not anonymous, but he is in this work somehow an artist *of* the anonymous. His camera has recorded the full-bodied presences of seventeen individuals hired off the street, day laborers (working here, as it were, by the minute), whose identities we have no way of knowing. If we met them, however, we'd almost certainly "know" them, that is, recognize their faces — and maybe more. We do carry these projected faces away with us, so powerful is their presence. And we might be tempted to say: so powerful is the projection, or the art — the view.

GEORGE QUASHA AND CHARLES STEIN
excerpt from *Viewer: Gary Hill's Projective Installations — Number 3,* Station Hill Arts / Barrytown Ltd in association with Barbara Gladstone Gallery, New York, 1997
quote: ibid, p.8

Viewer 1996
five-channel video installation:
five laserdisc players, five projectors,
one five-channel sychronizer
courtesy Donald Young Gallery, Chicago

Ilya & Emilia Kabakov

Ilya Kabakov's installations are full of ghosts. Sometimes they are known simply as "the man who ..." followed by a description of what the particular man in question did. For example, there is *The Man Who Flew Into Space From His Apartment*, *The Man Who Collects the Opinions of Others*, *The Man Who Never Threw Anything Away*, *The Short Man*, and *The Composer*, these being five out of the original *Ten Characters* whose manias were described in Kabakov's most complex project prior to his leaving the Soviet Union in 1988.

A mysterious and unanticipated *Gesamtkunstwork*, from an artist virtually unknown to the general art public, *Ten Characters* announced the advent of a "new" talent who, as it happened, was already in his fifties and had been the center of a small circle of conceptual artists in Moscow since the 1970s. Since then Ilya Kabakov has been busy in virtually every corner of the globe building replicas of his own half-remembered, half-imaginary world. Some look like ordinary rooms recently abandoned by their inhabitants — apartments filled to overflowing with relics of interrupted lives, hospital wards, schools or other institutional settings where private need or whimsy fights to a stalemate with public planning and the average good. Others have a fantastic aura, as if one had entered into an alternate universe — an Insect Kingdom, a Gulliverian State symbolised by Lilliputian monuments or a Noah's Ark of memories — which, nevertheless, is made to seem wholly familiar by virtue of the odd bits of detritus laying around, all of them indicating that the mini-Utopias one has discovered behind the looking glass are still "under construction," or, in the process of fitful deconstruction.

The sheer proliferation of these environments is astonishing. Altogether the archipelago of altered or invented places Kabakov has created in the last decade constitute one of the most sustained demonstrations of the maturity of the art form that we have. Once an avant-garde novelty, installation has, since the 1970s, become one of the dominant modes of art-making. Exponent of "total installation," a genre that instead of adapting itself to a given site, utterly transforms its location so as to transport the spectator to physical and mental spaces far removed from their daily experience yet provocatively parallel to them, Kabakov has created an unprecedented hybrid of sculpture and theatre, in which the gallery-goer is the only substantial being in a realm otherwise populated by phantoms.

ROBERT STORR
excerpt from 'Blinded by the Light', *Ilya Kabakov: Life and Creativity of Charles Rosenthal (1898-1933)*, exhibition catalogue, Art Tower, Mito, 1999

The installation *Monument To A Lost Civilizahon* radiates from two centrally placed architectural models — one showing the internal layout for a proposed underground 'museum' and the other, its roof — a city park which covers over and therefore disguises the site. The garden however, unlike other green, tree-lined squares, is surrounded by a deep trench and is accessible only via footbridges on each side. Viewed together, the two models mirror each other: both are formally arranged — the corridors and rooms below reflected in the layout of gardens, lawns and paths above.

Surrounding these two marquettes are eight vitrine-like tables describing the project, each outlining the seven divisions or categories to be found within the *Monument*: aspects of government under Soviet ideology; its bureaucracies; communal living; medical/scientific research; cultural institutions; the education system and the art school; personal memories and childhood. Around the walls of the gallery are 38 framed panels, each with a small architectural model of a specific room attached to its surface. These panels contain drawings, notes and 'found documents' relating to the content of each 'exhibit'. Under the guise of an anthropological or archaeological museum, the Kabakovs', in fact, are re-presenting installation projects completed over the last decade.

The journey begins at a small door with a sign 'To the Summer Garden' — and for the viewer, an expedition unfolds not unlike Alice's beyond the looking glass. The motivation for the project is life in the USSR — from its auspicious beginning, the Russian Revolution, to the inventiveness of the Constructivists, the Soviet avant-garde, to repression under Stalin. And then the aftermath — Cold War diplomacy, fascination in the west with espionage and daring escapes from life behind the Iron Curtain. Grounded as it is in the social conditions of the Soviet Union, the installation reveals through its exhibits the constraints of an enforced ideology — but more, it suggests totalitarianism is an ever-present political reality, something that could happen in any society ... a reminder that individual freedom is worth fighting for.

The assemblage of 'archival' and 'archaeological evidence' is laid out under one roof: each chamber like a separate building or constituent institution of a small city. Classified under the appropriate institutional category, each fragment is a chapter within a narrative structure that reads as a blueprint for the future. As a record, the installation reveals a society in crisis — a society that suffered under and then threw off the legacy of Communism, only to face the traps of modern capitalism. It illustrates how over-zealous bureaucracies can denigrate the lives of citizens.

Unlike ancient burial mounds, this hidden museum has few spectacular treasures. This 'Palace of the Future' instead has the appearance of a hastily-built, red brick domestic bunker, its surrounding 'moat' nothing more than a concrete ditch. Its interior —poorly lit and barely maintained — is a somewhat dusty and pathetic encapsulation highlighting the transience of material things. The intention is not didactic: rather the artists celebrate the poignancy and humour associated with storytelling. Soviet utopianism is experienced through the eyes of daily experience. If the *Monument* represents a world where human endeavour has been curtailed by oppression, paranoia and alienation, then it could well be a memorial to the 20th century.

EWEN MCDONALD
March 2000

Monument to a Lost Civilization,
courtesy FRONTIERE per Cantieri
Culturali alla Zisa, Palermo
photography: © SHOBHA

Seydou Keïta

Seydou Keïta was born around 1921 in Bamako. He was a cabinet maker who taught himself photography. In 1935 following a trip to Senegal his uncle gave him his first camera, a Kodak Brownie Flash. An apprentice photographer, he specialised in portraits in black and white using natural light with a *chamber 13 x 18*. This format enabled him to produce high quality prints of very high optical quality without the use of an enlarger.

In 1948 Keïta opened a workshop in Bamako. He became popular very quickly — the most sought after portrait artist by the people of Bamako, then Mali and neighbouring countries such as Guinea. Between 1949 and 1977, when he ceased all professional activities, he would have photographed every one in Bamako — they all wanted their portrait taken by the great Keïta.

Keïta has said over and over again that his only aim was to satisfy his clients by producing the clearest and most advantageous portrait. The portraits reflect this obligation to meet his clients' wishes. They pose on their own, as a couple, or a family, standing or framed as a bust. Sometimes they include an object symbolising their trade such as a sewing machine, a feather and ink well, or symbolising their family — a radio, bicycle, or scooter. The photographer used backdrops with decorative motifs, which he changed every two to three years. Today these are used as a reference to date his work.

On 2 February 1962, Seydou Keïta became the official photographer of the Mali government — a position that he held until 1977. Shots of that era, which are kept by the government, cannot be viewed. Keïta "covered" the main events that took place during the new independent state of Mali presided over by Modibo Keïta, and then ruled by the National Liberation Military Committee: meetings with heads of state, official visits, various commissions ordered by the administration … historical shots relating to the first fifteen years of independence.

Seydou Keïta's photography provides an exceptional testimony of Mali society in a particular time.

But there is also a timeless dimension. Keïta seems intuitively to have invented or reinvented the art of portraiture by seeking perfect precision: "I knew that my pictures were beautiful … beauty is art". A gracefulness, a certain elegance is emitted through these pictures — of a woman or a man, alone, as a couple or in a group, as a bust, lying down or standing. Keïta's mastery of light, of subject, of centring brings things back to basics. He managed to keep in equilibrium his personality as a photographer and that of his subjects, not models but clients who were awaiting a result.

ANDRÉ MAGNIN
modified excerpt from *Seydou Keïta,* Scalo, Zurich, 1997

Untitled
photograph
50 x 60 cm
courtesy André Magnin, Paris &
Ray Hughes Gallery, Sydney

Untitled (opposite)
photograph
50 x 60 cm
courtesy Ray Hughes Gallery,
Sydney

42 x 59 Seydou Keita 2000 Paris

Bodys Isek Kingelez

For the last ten years a dialogue between cultures has been in operation. Artworks from Asia, Australia, South America and Africa have broken down cultural barriers … we are witnessing the manifestation of cultural pluralism.

The African art we knew was mainly a mystical and metaphysical art — our focus was on traditional sculpture and the role it played in social cohesion. In the last twenty years, however, individual artists have come to the fore, representing the struggle for creative freedom and through this the search for unique personality.

Some of these artists were 'discovered' at the exhibition *Magiciens de la terre*, Paris. Bodys Isek Kingelez, from the Belgian Congo, is without doubt one such 'discovery'. At the end of the 1970s he was restoring antique African sculptures at the Kinshasa National Museum. Under Mobutu, Kinshasa was a large, chaotic, anarchic and corrupt metropolis … and this had an impact on Kingelez' work. Power and the search for truth are themes in his work, which aims to displace the occult. He focuses on aesthetic, political and poetic commitments challenging mankind. He still lives and works in the centre of Kinshasa, in an enclave surrounded by a high wall that is practically inviolable,. Perhaps this is why his eyes are turned towards the sky.

For Kingelez, "art is a rare product … of deep thought about the dynamics of the imagination. Art is, above all, knowledge, a vehicle for the individual's revival, as well as for a better future of the collective".

At the beginning of the 1980s Kingelez started building architectural pieces. Each of his "supra maquettes" made out of cardboard, plastic and paper carries a serial number, a title, a date and annotations as if part of a real manifesto. On his return from Paris, in 1989, he began a series about four cities — Kimbembele Ihunga, The Phantom City, Kin Third Millennium and the City of the Future.

Recently the artist wrote: "I just want to make my art available to the community which is in the midst of rebirth, with a view to create a new world, because the pleasures of this earth are dependent on the people who live on it. I therefore set up this city to create lasting peace, justice and worldwide freedom. This city will function as a small State with its own politics — where police, soldiers, body guards, jails will never be needed … as the sky on earth, a gem noticed by the whole world."

ANDRÉ MAGNIN
March 2000

Projet pour le Kinshasa du troisième millénnaire 1997
mixed media with wood, paper and card (two views, opposite)
100 x 332 cm
collection: Fondation Cartier pour l'art contemporain, Paris
photography: André Morin

Miami City 1980s (detail)
pens, pencils, biro on paper, plastic card and plywood
58 x 50 x 50 cm
courtesy Ray Hughes Gallery, Sydney
photography: Penelope Clay

Martin Kippenberger

I am rather like a travelling salesman. I deal in ideas. I do much more for people than just paint them pictures. — Martin Kippenberger

Martin Kippenberger likes to make others work for him … The artist's social intelligence, which has evolved into real instinct, found its expression in the fact that he considered certain stereotypes extremely ridiculous, yet at the same time regarded their simple negation as a similarly reprehensible undertaking. Hence everything had to be transformed into actionistic travesty in order to demand from latent knowledge something like an identification with the subject matter by means of diving into filthy conditions …

Kippenberger's strategy: i.e. turning his art and his life as an artist into literature, implies a tendency for leniency. For instance his self-portraits: what could they be considered but literary forms? They often even refer to illustrious examples and then continue spinning their own story. Picasso's self-idolization in a photograph showing him in bathing trunks accompanied by an elegant Afghan hound provoked Kippenberger's respectful mockery and inspired a couple of self-portraits in which he poses with paunch and in grandpa's double-knit underwear — long before the value of cotton underwear was increased by attaching a designer label. In most of these self-portraits Kippenberger is standing in front of a mirror and trying to evade the flying Moorean holed sculptures, i.e. balloons, i.e. kinder surprise eggs. In linguistics the triggering of a picture by means of a — randomly chosen — fragment of another is called metonymy. In Kippenberger's work this minimalistic mechanism is of course an exception. Normally the extreme opposite dominates, i.e. the repeatedly over-encoded, crammed and cluttered figure: "Santa Claus disguised as a frog on a fried egg (island) with streetlight disguised as a palm" …

This close relationship of any artistic activity with the happenings and circumstances of real life was the focus of Kippenberger's attention. In this concentration he was absolutely alert, and this is what makes his attitude unmistakably anti-metaphysical. He mercilessly exposed artists' petty bourgeois weaknesses — intellectual laziness, yearning for a professor's chair, living in a small castle, the spouse's suits by Chanel, the cultivation of good taste, the misery of manual perfection. Yet despite his taking offence at the art business which surrounded him, this did not mean to distance himself angrily but rather to stew in his own juices. Kippenberger was merciless in tracking down the wish for distancing oneself from ordinary life. In the analysis of this feeling alien, he was uncompromising — because it had to do with the crucial question about the reality of art. This is also the context in which he applied his notion of kitsch, which certainly has to be discussed if one wants to appreciate the intellectual heritage of this artist who died in 1997 at the age of 44. Kippenberger's notion of kitsch has hardly anything to do with what we see on canvas, but rather with the question why is it there and how is it dealt with. He is always interested in the kitsch in one's attitude and the kitsch in one's mind, i.e. in one's refusal to analyse how the art business works, what one's own position is and what one can contribute in terms of realizations and practices to prevent it from becoming dreadful. According to Kippenberger one has to "look at the rules" and not just hang a painting on the wall and declare it art.

RUDOLF SCHMITZ
excerpt from 'The Unfinished Happy End', *The Happy End of Franz Kafka's Amerika*, exhibition catalogue, Deichtorhallen, Hamburg, 1999
quote: Martin Kippenberger, *Martin Kippenberger: Ten Years After,* Taschen, Germany, 1991

Jetzt gehe ich in den Birkenwald, denn meine Pillen wirken bald (I am going into the birch forest as my pills will be taking effect soon)
1990
20 birch tree trunks
111 wooden pills
room size: 770 x 460 x 240 cm
installation view: Anders Tornberg, Lund
courtesy Galerie Gisela Capitain, Cologne

Yayoi Kusama

Yayoi Kusama was born to a well-known family deep in the mountains of Nagano prefecture. From her childhood, she was plagued with a nervous disorder that made her hear voices and see visions. She accepted these things as mysterious signals from nature, from the universe. She came to feel that these signals enveloped the world, as if with a curtain, or a net, and started expressing this in her work via polka dots. "One day," she writes, "looking at a red-flower patterned tablecloth on the table, I turned my eyes to the ceiling and saw the same red-flower pattern everywhere — even on the ceiling, the window glass, and the pillars." After images seemed to cover everything, and it seemed as if she herself would fade away into that dot-filled world. She feared that she might scatter and diffuse into her own private world, yet, she also had a feeling of returning back to the infinite universe.

Drawing was one way for Kusama to take a stand in this world, by giving reality to what she saw. And so she began to paint polka dots. While dots or spots are simple geometric figures, they are also organic shapes that suggest the cells, molecules, particles, and seeds that are the fundamental building blocks of life. In other words, they continually give the impression of dissolving and accumulating, proliferating and separating, appearing and dissappearing.

In 1957, Kusama moved to America whose wide-open spaces provided an outlet for the destinationless vortexes she created in her small canvases ... She said that the self became a single dot that had lost its existence in the universe, that was diffused. It goes without saying that this feeling was reflected in her work. And out of this situation she was able to find techniques that allowed her escape. The act of burying the world behind very small objects (dots) is a kind of suppression, a covering-up of reality with shapes with which one is familiar. It might be considered a form of escapism, but it can also be considered a constructivist, intelligent method of changing or transforming the world.

One method utilized by Kusama was collage. In her youth, she took paper or cloth or pages from books she had finished reading and cut them into shreds with scissors or a razor blade. She also took windowpanes, mirrors, and plates and pulverized them to powder with a hammer. In this she dissected, then re-constructed the world. Further, as though probing the alien forms of her own neurospace she became fascinated with the web pattern found in the veins of leaves or on butterfly wings. In works of great detail and simple colors, she portrayed the micro-world of tree trunks or leaf veins in a close-up view, making studies to assist in her re-construction.

In the 1960s, she began making minimalist collages, using the fragments obtained through her dissections to once again completely cover the world. She even covered all the white space on her work with hundreds of portraits cut out of magazines, with dollar bills, and with airmail stickers ... For Kusama dots and spots were positive images, nets were negative, and out of these interstitial spaces her art was born. The repetition of dots was a minimalist way of rejecting gestures, of rejecting self, and a direct response to the male-dominated world of Abstract Expressionism which, at that time, prided itself on its grand gestures. Through her art of simple repetition Kusama anticipated Minimal Art, but her repeated dots were not nonfunctional; rather her thick applications of paint gave a tactile power to her works: "I made these polka dots like suns to indicate a masculine energy, that is, the source of life. Further, since they also symbolize the feminine principle of birth and development, I made them in the shape of the [full] moon." The positive and negative co-exist and oppose each other, obliterate each other, and dissolve into the chaos of nothingness ...

In 1963, the nets within Kusama's vision went beyond her canvases and started to cover chairs, desks, and even floors. In space, her work developed as environmental art. The spots that had been one-dimensional began to sprout from the floor and grow ... Phallus shapes arose from her attempt to banish her deep-rooted fear of the male sexual organ yet, since they had an appearance symbolic of implements used in religious rituals and festivals, they appeared ... without any sense of the grotesque.

While Kusama had a particular obsession with sex, she had another with food, and she started to produce environmental works using macaroni. Western-style clothes, shoes, chairs, desks and dressers, things which had been covered in dots and spots, were liberated from their polka dots only to be buried in sprouting phalluses or macaroni. Sex and food are both essential — for life. As the title of one of her exhibitions, *Driving Image* (1986), suggests, the premise of Kusama's works is an acceptance that in the end we have no choice but to continue living our lives.

Using environmental processes as a starting point, Kusama's imagination became more focussed on immediate issues. In a series of guerrilla-like happenings, she took part in painting dots on naked bodies, raising her voice in protest against the government, and organizing orgy performances ... Among these "happenings" was her performance at the Venice Biennale entitled *Garden of Narcissus*, for which she created 1,500 mirror balls. The silvered balls, placed on the lawn in front of the pavilion, reflected all those who came to view them — narcissistically — along with the background scenery. The work was a reflection of Kusama's vision of the self returning to a single dot. When Kusama started selling the balls during the Biennale this was immediately forbidden by the authorities, and she was withdrawn from the exhibition.

When Kusama returned to Japan in 1974-1975, putting an end to her days of scandal she announced that the theme for her work would now be the theme of "Death." Joseph Cornell, an artist she loved and respected, died around this time, followed by her father. Wanting to help their souls find eternal rest, Kusama started to produce collages with a nostalgic, classical quality... an art closely connected with loss of life.

YUKO HASEGAWA
excerpt from 'Yayoi Kusama: Traveling Life', *A Guide to Contemporary Art: a pleasure to meet "Now"*, Heibon-sha Ltd, Japan, 1998

*Infinity Mirror Room – Phalli's Field
(or Floor Show)* 1965
(no longer extant:
Reconstructed 1998)
sewn stuffed fabric, plywood, mirrors
room measures 250 x 500 x 500 cm
courtesy the artist

John Mawurndjul

Johnny Mawurndjul is a leader among Kuninjku (the eastern dialect of Kunwinjku) language speaking artists in the western Arnhem Land region of the Northern Territory. As a young artist he was taught to paint by a number of major figures in the history of western Arnhem Land bark painting and Mawurndjul is now active in interpreting the religious traditions of the region in a dynamic way.

The primary medium for Mawurndjul's work is painting with naturally occurring ochres on the flattened bark of the stringybark tree (*eucalyptys tetradonta*) although he has also been known to paint hollow log coffins for the market. His clan lands are called Nakurulk and lie adjacent to the Mann River, a tributary of the Liverpool River that stretches south from Aboriginal township of Maningrida situated on the coast. Mawurndjul has lived for a number of years in Maningrida but now prefers to live closer to his freshwater clan lands at Mumeka.

With the passing of the Aboriginal Land Rights (Northern Territory) Act 1976 all of Arnhem Land was returned to Aboriginal owners. In this part of Arnhem Land there has been a strong move away from government settlements such as Maningrida. With the return to traditional lands, a strong ceremonial life has been rekindled and the production of art has become a key way of circulating knowledge about religious topics within the community.

Mawurndjul's art is grounded in a strongly traditional religious life: his subjects are the major creator beings of the western Arnhem Land region. He shares his interest in these subjects with many other senior artists in the region. The creation journeys of these beings form the main subjects celebrated in major ceremonies and the journeys are renewed in the present as Kuninjku hunt and travel across their clan lands, visit particular sacred sites imbued with the power of the Ancestral beings, and marvel at the majesty of Ancestral creation.

In Mawurndjul's lands there are rock shelters covered with the art of previous generations. Kuninjku lands are on the north-eastern extremity of the vast body of sandstone escarpment that comprises the Arnhem Land plateau. The escarpment is dotted throughout with shelters which were once important home bases for families during the wet season. The floodplains around the base of the cliffs are incredibly rich in fish and birdlife while the dry hill country provides shelter for larger game such as kangaroo and emus. In Mawurndjul's lands there are images of all these species as well as extinct species. The earliest art in the region has been dated to the time of Lascaux and there is a recognisable sequence of different styles through to the present ...

Mawurndjul has developed a reputation for the strong patterning of his large barks which feature swathes of very fine multicoloured cross-hatching. Kuninjku call these cross-hatched designs *rarrk*, and they feature as an important component of body paintings worn in Mardayin ceremonies. The use of such designs in paintings for the market is in part an attempt by Kuninjku to reveal more important religious subjects to a non-Aboriginal audience, while *mimih* [trickster spirits with special powers] are considered more important images and Kuninjku expect that they should command more respect. Kuninjku artists are eagerly seeking ever new ways of communicating the power of their Ancestral beliefs to a largely untutored audience.

Mawurndjul frequently paints the subject of the Rainbow Serpent Ngalyod devouring young girls known as Yawk Yawk. In earlier works from the mid 1980s, Mawurndjul clearly distinguishes the snake-like form of Ngalyod from the figures of the girls. As in many Kuninjku bark paintings, the figures of these early works can be clearly distinguished against the plain red ochre of the background. Occasionally the girls may be shown in a dismembered state or as bones after Ngalyod has killed them. Ngalyod may be shown twisting and turning back on itself, the dynamism of the image reflecting the huge energy and power that Ngalyod is perceived to have. This figure is one of the original creators in the western Arnhem Land region and every year Kuninjku perform ceremonies to ensure that Ngalyod maintains the cycle of wet season rains that replenish the earth. The cyclonic power of Ngalyod is also said to be involved in the protection of sacred sites in the clan lands where Ngalyod killed these women and where features of the landscape are considered the transformed bodies of the beings involved. If people were to damage these places Ngalyod would send a cyclone to kill them.

Mawurndjul's images of this theme painted in the 1990s show much more complex arrangements of figures than his earlier works. In contemporary paintings the twists and turns of Ngalyod are elaborated to fill almost the entire painting surface.

Some of these later works re-semble the geometric designs of body paintings in a much more direct way. The whole rectangular frame of the bark painting is filled with patterns of cross-hatching and representations of Ancestral landscape in a format much like the format of designs painted on the torso of ceremonial participants. Figures, if they appear at all, are barely discernible against the rhythmic waves of cross-hatching that evoke Ancestral power and creation in a more abstract sense. Here Mawurndjul plays on the intersection between geometric and figurative art, in his paintings of the Ancestral actions that resulted in the creation of these lands. Mawurndjul has become a master at manipulating the surface texture and interlocking compositions of these works to cryptically reveal the stories that lie in the lands that are so dear to him.

LUKE TAYLOR
excerpt from 'John Mawurndjul: Weaver in Ochre', *In Place, Out of Time: Contemporary Art in Australia,* ed Rebecca Coates & Howard Morphy, Museum of Modern Art, Oxford, 1997, pp. 12-15

Mardayin Ceremony 1999
natural pigments on eucalyptus tetradonta
153 x 88 cm
collection: The Laverty Collection, Sydney
photography: Annandale Galleries, Sydney

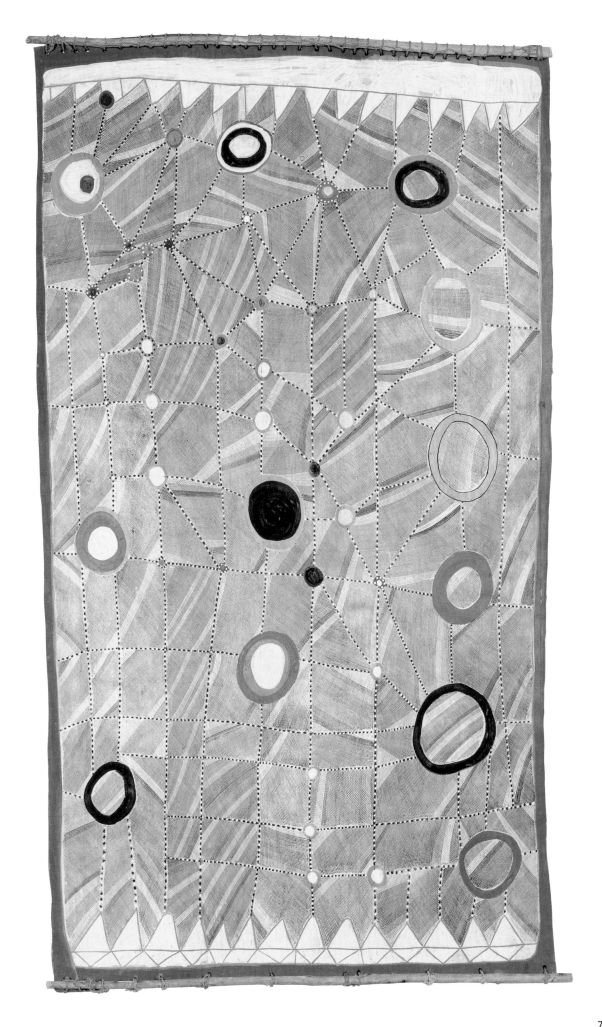

John Mawurndjul / Maningrida Sculpture

England Banggala

Jimmy Bungurru

James Iyuna

Willie Jolpa

Mick Kubarkku

Crusoe Kuningbal

Crusoe Kurddal

Jack Laranggai

Jimmy Wood Maraluka

Jacky Maranbarra

Les Midikurriya

Ivan Namirrkki

Michael Ngalabiya

Alec Wurramala

Owen Yalandja

Lena Yarinkura

left to right

Owen Yalandja
Yawk Yawk 1999
natural pigments on Kurrajong
227.5 x 9.8 x 8.4 cm
collection: Art Gallery of New South Wales,
Sydney
Mollie Gowing Acquisition Fund for
Contemporary Aboriginal Art 2000
photography: Jenni Carter for AGNSW

Owen Yalandja
Yawk Yawk 1999
natural pigments on Kurrajong
261.5 x 12.2 x 8.5 cm
collection: Art Gallery of New South Wales,
Sydney
Mollie Gowing Acquisition Fund for
Contemporary Aboriginal Art 2000
photography: Jenni Carter for AGNSW

Mick Kubarkku
Mimih Spirit from Yikarrakkal 1995
natural pigments on bombax ceiba
269 x 12 cm
courtesy Gallery Gabrielle Pizzi, Melbourne

Mick Kubarkku
Mimih Spirit from Yikarrakkal 1995
natural pigments on bombax ceiba
270 x 11 cm
courtesy Gallery Gabrielle Pizzi, Melbourne

Alec Wurrmula
*Galabarrbarra Male/Female Spirit from
Jinamarda* 1995
natural pigments on bombax ceiba
283 x 15 cm
courtesy Gallery Gabrielle Pizzi, Melbourne

THE MIMI SPIRIT AS SCULPTURE

The *Mimi* figure is an ancient theme in the Aboriginal art of western Arnhem Land. As it has been established that certain rock paintings of *mimi* are several thousand years old, the representation of these spirit figures may be the most enduring artistic tradition known. The most recent manifestation of the *mimi* in art – as painted wooden sculpture – is considered here in relation to its mythological context, historical development and stylistic variations.

Aborigines say that *mimi* are spirits in human form who, along with Aboriginal people, occupy the rugged sandstone country of the Arnhem Land escarpment. They hunt only in calm weather as their elongated bodies are extremely fragile. Their physical delicacy is combined with magical strength; they float above the ground rather than walk and are reputed to raise or lower cave roofs to paint images of themselves. *Mimi* are shy and have acute powers of sight and hearing so they escape detection by slipping through cracks in the rock walls. Within these rocks is a separate *mimi* world which, with its animals and trees, sea and sky, is identical to the human world outside.

While the characteristics of *mimi* are well known to Aboriginal people only a few old men are reputed to have seen them … Mandarrk, a famous bark and rock painter, is said to have had a special friendly relationship with *mimi*. His sons tell how Mandarrk left camp for extended periods when he felt sick to live with *mimi* until he was better.

Although *mimi* are frail and shy their magical powers make them potentially dangerous so Aborigines are very wary of them. Only *marrkidjbu* or magic-men have powers strong enough to part rock to enter the world of the *mimi* and resist the temptations they offer to make them stay away forever.

Carved wooden *mimi* figures are a dramatic recent variant on the images of rock and bark painting. The first of these sculptures appeared in museum collections during the 1960s. Their distinctive appearance is characterised by an extremely slender sculptured form with rudimentary limbs and panels in relief across the shoulder and hips. The whole of the front of these *mimi* is painted with a readily identifiable dotted pattern.

While details of the sculptured form and painted decoration of *mimi* figures vary slightly, they are distinctive for their obvious frontality and geometric dotted patterning. The rough cylindrical form of the tree trunk is retained in the elongated body and stylised head and neck. *Mimi* sculptures always have tiny stick-like arms and slender legs without feet. Although the front of each figure is fully rounded and painted over its length with horizontal or vertical rows of dots on an ochred ground, the back of the figure is flattened and often roughly painted with white pigment.

The Kuninjku evidently feel a certain ambivalence toward *mimi* spirits. By day these frail creatures are harmless, even helpful as they occasionally show lost hunters the way home. By night their character is transformed and both *mimi* and *namorrodo* become more aggressive, waiting to steal people's flesh, lure them away from their family to trap them in *mimi* caves. The Kuninjku exploit the dramatic qualities of this relationship, weaving the harmless and malevolent elements into their ceremonies and stressing each aspect by turn. This aura of ambivalent power and mystery is also clearly apparent in the carved and painted *mimi* figures. Are the simple faces smiling blandly or staring with open-eyed menace? Do the attenuated bodies convey elegant movement or a more threatening alertness?

JENNIFER HOFF & LUKE TAYLOR
excerpt from 'The Mimi Spirit as Sculpture'
Art and Australia, Vol. 23 No. 1, Spring
1985, p. 73

nb: Mimi & Mimih are accepted variations

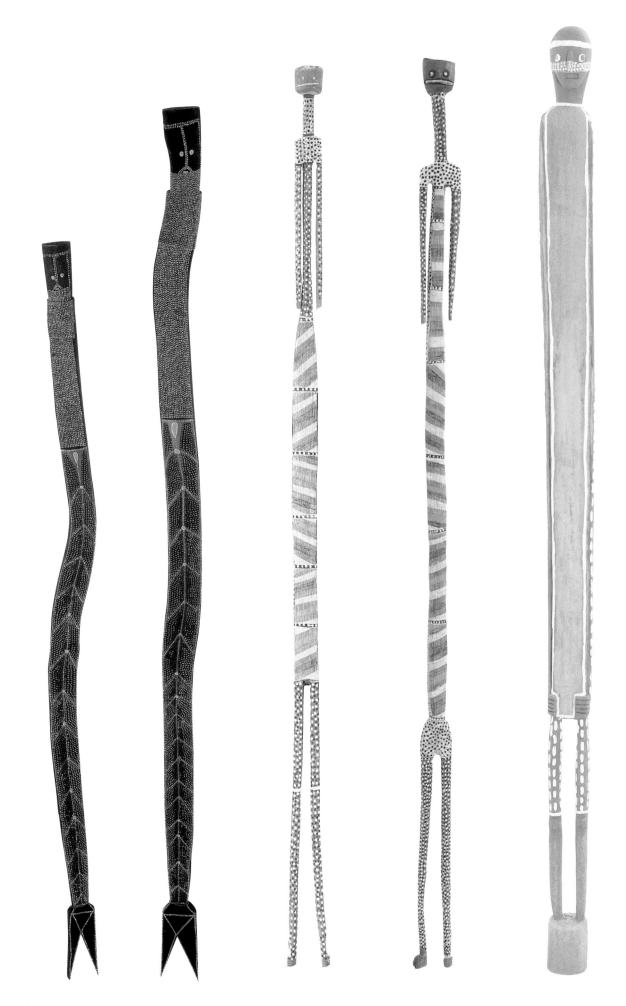

Paul McCarthy

As they excavate pop culture's repressed fantasies, Paul McCarthy's demented mock-instructional videos, Audio Animatronics-type sculptures, Hollywood-style sets, and mutant figures look like distorted family entertainments more than the objects of art history. At once eerie and comic, his bestiary teems with robotic goat-fuckers, giant furry skunks with human genitals, psychoactive human/vegetable hybrids, and mannequin legs afflicted with multiple personality disorders. Looking like mutants from a theme-park slum, they allegorize the traumas of consumer culture in terms of sexuality, identity, and body-boundary confusion …

The unstable humour of this work, as well as its dumb pathos, characterizes many contemporary esthetic exercises in desublimation, but while McCarthy wreaks havoc with childhood's idealized images, he's less concerned with transgressing taboos than with examining the perverse nature of authoritarian hierarchies. Instead of being about "killing the father", as in the avant-garde wish to shock authority, his work obsessively returns to the scene of paternal violence. The trauma of cultural conditioning in the consumerist family is McCarthy's great motif; his performance and videos from the 1970s and 1980s are rife with allusions to children's TV shows, with McCarthy often taking on the persona of a buffoonish male authority enacting a deranged educational program …

Violated bodies are scattered like casualties throughout McCarthy's oeuvre; dwarfish, armless mascots and eviscerated robots lie stretched out as if victims at a crime scene. Poignantly freakish, these creatures appear as emblems of pain and loss, anxiety and horror. To the theme-park esthetic they add the perfume of sexual violence, calling to mind the Surrealist legacy of hybrid figures: Max Ernst's human/bird composites, Hans Bellmer's recombinable *poupée*. As Hal Foster has pointed out, these monstrous hybrids spoke to a cultural anxiety over the mechanizing and commodifying of body and psyche alike. McCarthy's work marks a different crisis — the confusion between media images and embodied experience. His cartoony anatomies are typically ruptured, penetrated by an invasive Toontown logic …

Much of McCarthy's recent work probes these disciplinary uses of delirium. He is exploring a change in the manifestation of patriarchal authority: the Fatherland's return as Disneyland, no longer transcendent order but stage-managed hallucination and airbrushed utopia. Even as his work evinces hallmarks of the uncanny, it raises questions about this area largely untouched elsewhere. What is the role of the uncanny in a culture of the simulated uncanny, the manufactured uncanny, the uncanny of consumer desire? In a theme-park world, how does one identify the return of the "real" repressed?

At the same time, McCarthy's hybrid figures acknowledge the allure of the absurd and violent transformation. The root of the word 'hybrid' comes from the Greek *hubris*, which means violence, excess, outrageousness, and so carries with it the idea of a dangerous sensory excitement. The dark eroticism of transformative esthetics is evident in many of the Surrealists' sexually charged hybrids, and it may well be that every monster can be considered an erotic figure, inasmuch as its composite body reflects a principle of joining and connecting. The face it shows the world is the face of an orgy, a commingling and union of diverse parts.

McCarthy has been telling us all along that our cultural Father is a pervert, that the Law is besmirched with lewd and irrational pleasures. His cartoon hybrids rearticulate this theme, but the chaotic rhythms of their mutation point to another kind of violence besides the violence of repression: that of seduction, fuelled by the power of metamorphosis. If the lowly tomato can be irradiated and genetically engineered, conflating the natural and the artificial in a way that renders both these terms meaningless, we too can be made traitors to our own interests and identities. McCarthy's art shows us how we both devour and are eaten up by these strange fruits of our theme-park culture.

RALPH RUGOFF
excerpt from 'Deviations on a Theme', *Artforum*, October 1994, pp. 80-83

Painter 1995
stills from performance/installation
collection: Rubell Family Collection, Miami
photography: Karen & Damon McCarthy

Boris Mikhailov

Culture This is the selection of a set of limitations.

A paradigm This is the dominating system of central ideas, principles, patterns accepted by a professional society or scientists and which, over time, is no longer doubted as to its truth.

PG 5 NOTES FROM BORIS MIKHAILOV'S
UNFINISHED DISSERTATION

A discussion between Ilya Kabakov and the critic Victor Tupitsyn cites the term "panicking" in discussing Mikhailov's photographic work depicting the homeless of his home city of Kharkiv. It seems only appropriate that this term refer to the condition endemic to the subjects of Mikhailov's work who seem indifferent to the ecological and economic conditions in their environment …

These images differ from what may be referred to as the obscene representation … of the subjects in his *Outcast Series*, whereby the subject almost challenges the viewer in heralding their predicament, a position sitting uncomfortably for the viewer who is accustomed to a pathetic reading of such conditions …

Mikhailov's work is represented by nearly three decades of photographic work reflecting the subtle shifts in the Soviet social fabric over this time, his own role as photographer forever shifting to seek out the optimal manner to instigate and reveal. This body of work includes: *The Red Series*, as a response to the massive propaganda campaigns of the 1970s; *Sots Art* from the late 1970s at the time the Soviet machinery witnessed the beginnings of its deterioration; *Luriki*, coded images drawn from official portrait studios manipulated by montage and reconstruction; *Berdyansk* and the *Salt Lake* series, narrative series of photographs which illustrated the toxic conditions of the Soviet vacationer's leisure environment. *Uncompleted Dissertation* serves at the artist's personal archive organized and compiled throughout the Glasnost period, made up of loose papers upon which the artist arranged snapshots and jotted down autobiographical notes relating to photography at the time. Within the dissertation, Mikhailov aptly cites the term "phenomenology" in recognizing the very way to describe the predicament of the artist both then and now "as an abstraction from any claims on existence".

MARTA KUZMA
excerpt from 'The Ubiquitous Contract With Culture: or the Abstract Notion of Ukrainian Contemporary Art', exhibition catalogue, *The Future is Now*, Museum of Contemporary Art, Zagreb, Croatia, 1999

The Snowy People from Case History series 1998
photographs
125 x 185 cm each
collection: the artist

Tracey Moffatt

I am not concerned with verisimilitude ...
I am not concerned with capturing reality,
I'm concerned with creating it myself.
— Tracey Moffatt

Tracey Moffatt was catapulted to critical attention on the cusp of the 1990s on the basis of two quite distinct works made almost simultaneously: a nine-part phototableau, titled *Something More*, and a 35 mm short film, *Night Cries: A Rural Tragedy* (both made in 1989). Increasingly overlaying, intersecting, even interrogating each other, these two media remain the cornerstone of her practice as a visual artist, notwithstanding occasional forays into video and music television.

Something More is comprised of both color and black-and-white photographs ... organized along a three-tiered grid. The intermittent placement of the trio of monochromatic works serendipitously interrupts the smooth flow of the "storyboarded" narrative. The resulting discontinuity, a kind of Brechtian device that stimulates a reflexivity in the viewer, impairs the seductive unfolding of what is a familiar, even clichéd, fable of shattered aspirations and failed dreams. A young woman, born in the margins with few options, embraces stereotypical delusions of the romance, riches, and glamour of urban life. Redolent of sagas like Tennessee Williams' *Baby Doll* and Erskine Caldwell's *Tobacco Road*, with the Deep South finding its counterpart here in the Outback, *Something More* is at once local and generic. The telltale red earth and brilliant searing light, hallmarks of the Australian desert, are presented unmistakably as broadly painted flats. They provide a backdrop for the opening photograph, which depicts a scene played out as if on a stage, with all the principals present.

Certain features in Moffatt's rendition of this well-rehearsed tale are critical for her future work. The conflict — a rivalry between women — not only reverses conventional roles but invites a reading in racial terms. The bottle-blonde, who has become the antagonist, also inhabits the land to which her mixed-race counterpart (played by Moffatt) has only a dispropriated relation. The site of the drama is rural, far from the big city (Brisbane) yet dialectically connected to it. Sex and violence are closely intertwined, with, tellingly, the female aggressor assuming macho signifiers while the males are reduced to minor parts, as indifferent or ineffectual bystanders. Retelling this hackneyed fable through a local dialect, Moffatt deftly uses paraphrase and pastiche, not to imbue it with a compelling sense of singularity and specificity, novelty and poignancy, but by insisting wryly on its ubiquity and normality — locating the archetype within the stereotype, the mythic within the mass cultural.

In many respects, *Night Cries* could be deemed the reverse of *Something More*, even though again artifice and stylization inform Moffatt's visual language, and again a fundamental and paradigmatic relationship constitutes her point of departure, the mother-daughter bond. Manifestly contrived, its mise-en-scene owes as much to theater and painting as to film, while the story-line is structured into a continuous narrative in the present with two flashbacks to the daughter's childhood ...

In the final scene in which the bereft Aboriginal daughter assumes a fetal position on a railway siding next to her dead, white foster mother, the setting is significantly a place of transition, a site of departure, suggesting that she is reenacting her recurrent nightmare of abandonment in infancy and, simultaneously confronting the possibility of rebirth, of a new life.

Moffatt's work has been interpreted as a pointed critique of traditional ethnographic film, which typically addressed Aboriginal issues through the idioms and conventions particular to naturalistic documentary film and photography. Recognizing both the constructed nature of the fundaments of anthropological practice and the impossibility of portraying through the camera a reality that is inherently fictional, ethnography has recently focused on redefining the traditional relationship between the anthropologist and the object of study, and on exploring recording techniques that address the limitations and presuppositions integral to representation itself. Paralleling some of these more innovative current practices, Moffatt's synthetic approach also owes much to its roots in fine-art practices of the eighties. Like many of her peers ... she eschewed straight photography in favor of staged and fictive representations. While also informed loosely by cultural theory, her art is far from didactic or doctrinaire, and can never be reduced to a feminist or ethnic polemic. Welding tropes from painting, film, theater, and photography into a patently hybrid entity, her nuanced heteroglot style speaks to the complexity of a postcolonial society in which mixed-race relationships ... cannot be approached as already known, as preordained. By not reproducing reality, that is, by not *taking* pictures but by *making* pictures, Moffatt suggests metaphorically that such relationships in their specificity are not given but must be constructed — created, literally, from the shards of older stereotypes.

LYNNE COOKE
excerpt from 'A Photo-Filmic Odyssey',
Tracey Moffatt Free-Falling, Dia Center for the Arts, New York, pp. 23-39
quote: ibid, p. 23

Scarred For Life II, Suicide Threat, 1982 1999
offset print
80 x 60 cm
collection: Amanda Love, Sydney
courtesy Roslyn Oxley9 Gallery, Sydney

Suicide Threat, 1982

She was forty-five, single and pregnant for the first time. When her
mother found out, she said *"If I wasn't Catholic I'd commit suicide."*

Tracey Moffatt

Mariko Mori

All living beings are connected at every moment in inner space. Every life form with its own life cycle is part of the outer universe and there is only one planet earth. In the next millennium, the power and the energy of the human spirit should unify the world in peace and harmony without any cultural or national borders. — Mariko Mori

Stanley Kubrick's assertion that with *2001: A Space Odyssey* he wanted to create an overwhelming "visual experience, one that ... directly penetrates the subconscious with an emotional and philosophical content"[1] just as aptly describes Mariko Mori's art since the mid-1990s. Her fantastic photographs and video installations aim to likewise convey transformative and transcendental experiences on a similarly grand and enthralling visual scale. Just as the "Star-Child" scene from *2001* provides a coda to a string of events that encapsulates centuries of human progress, so too does Mori's work reach across the ages, combining Japanese tradition, Eastern and Western art historical forms and motifs, and more contemporary phenomena like fashion, science fiction, popular culture, and high technology. Her panoramic, technicolor images repeatedly assert themes of transformation, transcendence, and visual and other pleasures. Like Kubrick's vision in *2001*, Mori's highly stylized and reservedly hopeful view of the future presents the interface between man, technology, and an ethereal "Other" (for Kubrick, extraterrestrials, for Mori, the spiritual dimension of Buddhist enlightenment) as a possible way for humankind to progress into a new era of peace and understanding ...

In her most recent work, Mori ... favors more cosmic and spiritually inspired female forms. In the interrelated 1996 photograph and video *Last Departure* and *Miko no Inori* ("The Shaman-Girl's Prayer"), she poses on Osaka's Kansai International Airport as a futuristic, Kaleidoscope-eyed vision who, in the video, gently and meaningfully caresses a crystal ball to a haunting Japanese song. Mori effects an ethereal, techno/traditional shaman — a human figure who serves as a medium between earth-bound humans and the spiritual unknown — who is at once both a cyborg and

a bodhisattva figure from Buddhist Mandala imagery. In *Last Departure* this figure appears in triplicate, with two versions appearing as ghostly doppelgängers flanking the central figure. Her shape changes again in the *Nirvana* series of photographs and video from 1996-97. Mori floats above infinite stretches of land and seascape as goddess figures who now move deeply and explicitly into the spiritual realm of Buddhist art. Her transformative impulse, once used to confront quotidian concerns, has now evolved into a

divining rod for matters of mystical importance.

DOMINIC MOLON
excerpt from 'Countdown to Ecstasy', *Mariko Mori*, exhibition catalogue, Museum of Contemporary Art, Chicago and Serpentine Gallery, London, 1998, pp. 1-16
quote: ibid, p. 11

[1] Stanley Kubrick, 'Stanley Kubrick: Playboy Interview' (1968) reprinted in *The Making of Kubrick's 2001,* ed Jerome Agel (New York: Signet Books, 1970), p. 328

Entropy of Love 1996
glass with photo interlayer
305 x 610 x 216 cm
collection: William & Maria Bell
courtesy Deitch Projects, New York

Juan Muñoz

For the past fifteen years, Juan Muñoz's work has been structured around a dialectic of attention and indifference. In pictures and places both peopled and empty, he holds in balance seemingly contradictory positions: an attempt to be public and a desire to remain private; a promise of access and a denial of entry; the representation of actions which cannot be seen. In a sequence of beautifully choreographed interior landscapes, Muñoz builds a quiet drama of inclusion and exclusion, of presence and absence.

How do the work and the viewer communicate with each other, or fail to? What is the condition of the work which is being seen, and the person who is seeing it; how does the onlooker approach the work, and how does the work address the onlooker? Muñoz has a love for the mechanics of attraction and deception, of concealment and disclosure. Like a magnetic field in which the positive and negative are pulling at the same time, Muñoz's work both invites involvement and remains indifferent to it.

Michael Fried has called this indifference the 'supreme fiction', that the person looking at the work of art is not there at all. Fried's discourse is based on a study of the art of the middle of the 18th Century in France and its reception; but it is no less pertinent to current questions about attention and autonomy. To perfect the fiction, the work should not simply disregard the spectator, it needs to deny his or her existence. It is the work's absolute obliviousness to anything outside of itself which paradoxically enables the spectator's absorption into the world of the work. To put it another way, the muted monologue of the work creates the condition for the silent dialogue which is its reception.

Fried speculates as to the well-being and sense of self-sufficiency which this supreme fiction engendered in Diderot's time. But Muñoz's work does not pretend to create a similar experience. In expanding the two-dimensional world of the picture into a three-dimensional world of figures, objects and space, he creates a

dislocated landscape. But it is a landscape which it is possible to be within. You are not only looking at a dwarf, or a ventriloquist's dummy, or a row of silenced drums, or figures sitting in corners, you are in the room amongst them. The threshold separating the viewer and the viewed has been transgressed. But physical proximity does not bring a greater closeness; it creates a greater distance. Being amidst the work creates a powerful sense of apartness.

Like a sentence of few words and long pauses, Muñoz activates, even dramatises, the spaces in-between, the gaps which can't be closed, the places where nothing will happen. The figures do not perform as figurative sculpture used to (indeed, their refusal to perform is one of their most poignant characteristics). Rather than declaring power by seeking to control the space around them, they withdraw into themselves. Immersed in their own worlds, the sculptures, the tableaux, the configurations and conversations quietly absorb the attention of those who approach them. Powerless and mute, they embody no universal values, no common truths, they propose no programs for the future or the past. Friezes or freeze frames of arrested moments or movements, perhaps they are allegories of communication and its failures, of the impasse of language. The work may be there, before us, but it is also elsewhere. There is often a feeling that something or someone has departed. Empty balconies, bannisters which connect to nowhere, uninhabited rooms, silent corridors. And most particularly of all, the absence of sound …

JAMES LINGWOOD
excerpt from *Juan Muñoz: Monologues and Dialogues,* exhibition catalogue, Museo Nacional Centro de Arte Reina Sofía, Madrid, 1997, pp. 16-17

Conversation Piece (Dublin) 1994
22 figures in resin, sand and cloth
each 170 x 40 x 40 cm
courtesy the artist
& Irish Museum of Modern Art, Dublin

Bruce Nauman

Bruce Nauman's philosophical framework is of our era, not that of Pascal's wager that state of grace might exist but can never be achieved through reason or Montaigne's critical appreciation of man's imperfections that give rise to the "noble savage" who eats his fellows but does so with exemplary dignity. Nor does Nauman's often harsh vision really correspond to that of Pascal's approximate contemporary, Thomas Hobbes, the English materialist who viewed man "in a state of nature" as an animal at war with other animals for whom life was "nasty, brutish, and short." Nauman is, instead, of a generation whose intellectual points of reference encompass B.F. Skinner and Ludwig Wittgenstein, that is to say behavioral psychology and linguistic theory — with topology thrown in. Still one may clearly distinguish in Nauman's repertoire of themes and images a pattern of terms and counter terms that evoke the classical polarities just cited.

At the one philosophical extreme lies the apparently unqualified idealism of the simple phrase "The true artist is an amazing luminous fountain." This patently romantic declaration — which first appeared on a transparent plastic window shade in Nauman's studio in 1966 and later, in a 1968 exhibition, as jigsaw-cut letters around a doorway — is matched in moral fervor by the words of a 1967 neon which read, "The true artist helps the world by revealing mythic truths." When I say that the former — like the latter — bespeaks an "apparently unqualified" idealism, the element of uncertainty Nauman introduces is of a piece with his literal assertion. We are not dealing here with Duchamp-style systematic irony, much less Salon cynicism of a more contemporary variety, but rather with the sympathetic resonance of hopeful affirmation and gnawing doubt.

Using neon to publicly advance metaphysical propositions rather than to flash commercial messages, Nauman tested the aesthetic conviction of his audience, along with his own, in a medium usually employed by copyrighting hacks. "Will you 'buy' this idea of the 'true' artists' vocation?" the sign frankly entreats the bedazzled viewer. "Do

I buy that idea?" its author implicitly asks himself as its glare hits him. Nauman's 1968 doorway text provokes the same ambivalence. When passing under it, is one tacitly subscribing to the belief that the artist is an inspired being and the gallery a quasi-sacred precinct? The work's final version, where the letters that had composed it were dumped on the floor and scrambled, seemingly placed the sentence's potential for meaning forever out of reach, yet somehow, knowing the significance these verbal shards once had, they continue to emit a conceptual aura …

At the other philosophical extreme of Nauman's work is the hallucinatory pessimism of formally similar pieces such as the 1972 neon EAT/DEATH. Once again turning to the signmaker's craft — this time exploiting electronically cycled text overlays — this on-again, off-again message-board frames the first, apparently positive word in the cold light of the second, negative one, reducing the quest for nourishment to an ultimately futile struggle against death. Effectively transforming the conventional expression "Eat to Live" into "Eat to Die," Nauman renders man's fate — and his desperate orality — with pitiless concision. In *From hand to mouth* (1967) Nauman likewise takes a bit of common parlance and literally transfigures it in such a way that the idea it originally expressed of eking out an existence by feeding off what is nearest at hand turns into a disturbingly complex emblem not only of subsistence living, but also of the link between gesture and utterance, between word and deed.

Drawings such as *Punch and Judy II birth & life & sex & death* (1985) elaborate on this struggle to survive without offering any more reason for hope. A fullscale study for another synchronized neon in which male and female silhouettes face-off and sequentially kill one another, kill themselves or sexually "eat" their doppelgangers, it depicts the puppetry of human compulsion as "nasty and brutish," but never-ending rather than mercifully "short," as it was in Hobbes's dictum … In related studies, similarly archetypal figures replay the battle of the sexes in comparably

grotesque variations of this murderous orgy, while in other drawings and neons, same sex antagonists engage in clownish phallic duels and slapping contests, and in still others confrontational heads and hands pick the noses and poke the eyes of their opposite number, marking a progression from slapstick sexual aggression to regressive intimacy and violation and finally, when a solitary head swallows the mucous oozing from its own nose, to primitive self-consumption. Thus portrayed, "human nature" is wholly conditioned by crude appetites and their inevitable frustrations. The men and women who populate these infernal images would seem to be beyond the help of the "true artist," and given the intensity with which Nauman describes their routine degradations — an intensity fired by identification with them — one suspects that the "true artist" is, in fact, among the damned.

Nauman's art is rife with examples of such violent comedy, as well as references to violence unrelieved by humor of any kind. Some works point indirectly to the political dimension of human conflict. Various drawings of the 1980s show chairs suspended in space — upright, sideways and upsidedown — sometimes alone, sometimes in awkward conjunction with fundamental geometric shapes: crosses, squares, circles and triangles. Based on the principle of Foucault's pendulum which hangs from a great height under the dome of the Pantheon in Paris and oscillates gently in response to the earth's rotation, Nauman's image refers to the manner in which upheavals on one part of the globe register in faraway places. More specifically, the chair refers to the solitary confinement of the Argentine newspaperman Jacobo Timmerman, whose memoir of imprisonment Nauman read at the time he made these sculptures, of which three from 1981 carry the titles *South America circle*, *South America square*, and *South American triangle*. A sketch of the same period in which the chair appears with a block lettered inscription makes the point with a sobering clarity that implicates both North and South. Half of them inverted, the four stacked lines of text are: "AMERICAN/DELICATE/BALANCE/VIOLENCE." When Nauman takes the measure of man the results are fragmentary, inconclusive and contradictory ...

Nauman's frank use of his own body as sculptural material extends to the grotesque "modelling" of his own features in the five *Study for hologram* screenprints of 1970 — a childishly regressive experiment in "making faces" that ends up rivaling the physiognomic caprices of the 18th-century Viennese sculptor Franz Xavier Messerschmidt — and to the Beckett-like musical mimicry of the videotape *Violin tuned D E A D* (1969) in which the artist reiterates his morbid tonal phrase — the notes spell DEAD — by striking the strings of his instrument as if he were a hopelessly untalented student condemned to eternal, solitary practice.

In this regard, one is once again reminded of the arc that joins "hand to mouth," for in the universe of aesthetic possibilities Nauman has opened up for himself, mind and matter, speech and action, conceptual means and more or less traditional studio processes are all inseparably connected to the overall project of articulating the basic contradictions and anxieties around which his work revolves. Each medium recommends itself as an expressive mode or analytic — one might even say diagnostic tool — within a given set of artistic circumstances. Nauman's preeminence rests not only on his mastery of many ways of making — a mastery revealed as much by his refusal to succumb to the temptations of superficial refinements as by his actual abilily to delineate forms, fashion objects, orchestrate sounds, lights and moving pictures of great albeit austere beauty — but also on his ability to relate such stylistically disparate approaches to an economically as well as logically coherent core of concerns.

ROBERT STORR
excerpt from 'The True Artist', *XXIV Bienal de São Paulo,* exhibition catalogue, Paulo Herkenhoff and Adriano Pedrosa, Fundação Bienal de São Paulo, 1998, pp. 492-497

Window or wall sign 1967
fluorescent tubes
149.9 x 134.7 cm
collection: National Gallery of Australia, Canberra

Shirin Neshat

Rapture (1999) is an installation of two synchronized black-and-white video sequences projected on opposite facing walls. A soundtrack written and performed by the noted Iranian musician Sussan Deyhim accompanies the work. Blending Middle Eastern and North African folk traditions with contemporary world music influences, Deyhim's composition combines lyrics with abstract, primal utterances, natural ambient sounds, electronic noise, and percussion. Installed in an adjacent gallery, five black-and-white photographs complement the video-and-sound installation.

In her previous photographic work, the use of handwritten Farsi (Persian) text on the surface of photographs had become something of a trademark device for Neshat. Although the artist has chosen not to overlay text on the images in this new series, the spirit of recent Iranian poetry and fiction continues to inform Neshat's work …

Rapture was filmed, under Neshat's direction, on location in Morocco in 1998. Working with hours of footage and a team of editors, the artist constructed two parallel narratives (each thirteen minutes) that play in continuous loops. In the sequence projected on one side of the room, men populate an architectural environment; in the other sequence, women move within a natural environment. The piece begins with images of a stone fortress and a hostile desert, respectively. The fortress dissolves into a shot of over one hundred men — uniformly dressed in plain white shirts and black pants — walking quickly through the cobblestone streets of an old city and entering the gates of the fortress. Simultaneously, the desert scene dissolves into a shot of an apparently equal number of women, wearing flowing, full-length black veils, or *chadors*, emerging from different points in the barren landscape. In some sense, the work can be seen in relation to ancient sources. Narratives of desert migration and liberation — such as Moses leading the Jews out of Egypt across the Sinai to the Red Sea and into Canaan — exist in both the Judeo-Christian and Muslim traditions.

In *Rapture*, Neshat self-consciously exploits entrenched cliches about gender and space: namely, woman's relationship to nature (like the soul, irrational and wild) and man's relationship to culture (like the mind, rational and ordered). "To me the built architecture represents the authority and the principles of a traditional society," the artist has stated. In contrast, the women are assumed "to represent human nature and all of its frailty." Neshat's desire to articulate the ways in which space and spatial boundaries are politicized in Islam was fundamental to the conception of this project. Influenced by the writings of Moroccan sociologist and feminist critic Fatima Mernissi, Neshat is seeking to make legible Islam's need to use space as a device for sexual control. "Islam has always relied on the wall," the artist has observed. "In many ways the fortress defines Islam's relationship to the West." Both men and women, Neshat argues, are contained and controlled by a fortress mentality — women behind the veil, men behind the wall …

Extending the autobiographical narrative of Neshat's larger project, *Rapture* exists as a poignant meditation on the rootless, unsettled psychology of exile. As an Iranian expatriate living in the United States, Neshat maintains a critical distance that has allowed her to locate both the poetics and the power of the veil. At the same time that she celebrates the strength and beauty of Islamic women, however, she remains keenly aware of the horrors of repression. Ultimately, *Rapture* gives visual form to the diasporan experience itself.

JAMES RONDEAU
excerpt from *Shirin Neshat,* exhibition brochure, Art Institute of Chicago, 1999

Rapture 1999
video stills
courtesy Barbara Gladstone
Gallery, New York

Chris Ofili

DATA: SBM AGE: 27 NIGERIAN FROM MANCHESTER

The ex-altar boy arrived. He came bearing gifts: gold, frankincense and elephant shit. To place at the feet and at the breast of his Holy Virgin Mary.

CANVASSES: *Someone described them as being like an African front room. Yes. A wealthy Nigerian front room in the decadent late seventies. Flocked wallpaper. Fitted shagpile carpets. Plastic covered velour furniture. Smoked glass coffee tables and gilt framed photos of ancestors that stared down at you sombrely.*

And the room full of your parents' friends, glamourously dressed in every colour and fabric you've ever seen: textured brocades, ornate lace, jacquard, decorative damask, dazzling gold jewels and fuschia pink lipstick. Drinking gin and laughing at jokes you didn't understand.

Like the smell of palm oil, Dax and Omo. Like old, torn copies of Ebony, Essence, Black Hair and Beauty and Hustler.

THE JOURNEY: was long. The search intense. The descent to London arduous. Strolling briskly through the Green Channel of Her Majesty's Customs, Heathrow airport, he feigns confidence and a sense of belonging, whilst carrying a suitcase stuffed with illegal elephant doo-doo.

Like space dust in your mouth and Super Trooper lights. Like game show sets and Saturday night TV.

He has presented himself at the table of High Art, but will he partake of the pork? Will he engage in the debate?

"Excuse me sir but where are you coming from?

What was the weather like there?

Where are you going to? How will you get there?"

"Er .... dunno"

Like fireworks in the night sky. Like the intrigues of orifices.

Customs official No. 667, so busy busy busy scrutinising this Briton's passport for forged truths and illegal entries, forgets to check the case. From the corner of his eye, the ex-altar boy watches. It seems to glow, radioactive, and the faintest waft of fetid shit seeps through the zip.

AKURE WALL
excerpt from *About Vision — New painting in the 1990's,* exhibition catalogue, Museum of Modern Art, Oxford, UK, 1997

Double portrait
watercolour
courtesy Victoria Miro Gallery, London

The Adoration of Captain Shit and the Legend of the Black Stars 1998 (opposite)
acrylic, oil, resin, paper collage, glitter, map pins and elephant dung on canvas
200 x 270 cm
courtesy Victoria & Warren Miro, London

Yoko Ono

EX IT. DEATH AND ABANDONMENT. THAT WHICH NO LONGER IS AND CANNOT BE NAMED.

Yoko Ono designed a unique installation for the magnificent medieval building l'Almodi of Valencia. It occupies practically the whole of the 700m (sq) of the splendid building and is, without doubt, one of the most moving and impressive works created by the artist …

From the first moment when Yoko Ono saw l'Almodi — an ancient wheat silo — in the photos of a catalogue in which the space was reproduced, she felt a special attraction for its beauty in form and volume, for the decoration with religious murals and commemorative inscriptions, for the atmosphere …

In the installation Yoko Ono develops a direct reflection on the human condition, existential fragility and the uncertain outcome of our hopes after the drama that is death. *Ex It* is a reflection on life and death, a vindication of human beings from their anonymity. As I have pointed out earlier, the title of the work could refer to 'exit' (of life) and to 'no longer be' or in a more linguistic interpretation to 'that which can no longer be named or has no name'. As we will see, there is enough evidence to support all interpretations.

One hundred simple, unadorned wooden coffins — 60 for men, 30 for women and 10 for children — fill the central nave of l'Almodi. Following Yoko Ono's instructions they were to be robust, simple affairs, like those we imagine filling battlefields or after a natural catastrophe. A citrus tree, so representative of this country, grows from each of them, from the opening where you can normally see the face of the dead. Such an extraordinary number of coffins together is both moving and disturbing, despite the silence and sadness of death which emanates from this orchard of citrus trees.

From this landscape of anonymous coffins — which have no name or which cannot be named — springs life, hope and desire for the future. This is nature renewing itself, feeding from the same apparently inert and sterile human material. The tree and its fruit are a message for the future, the evidence of life after catastrophe, feeding from the spiritual and material of the earth in which trees and people have their roots, asserting our belonging to a group, to a way of being and understanding the world (as identity, as culture).

In creating this forest of orange trees (a symbol of Mediterranean culture) within, and on, these simple anonymous coffins, Yoko Ono has made a moving homage to those anonymous people who give sense to our precarious existential drama with their life and death. The future, in the form of a tree, a beautiful orchard of orange trees, springs once again from where it once seemed there was only sorrow and absence.

L'Almodi is wrapped in a mysterious atmosphere created especially by Yoko Ono for this occasion using confused and overlapping sounds of birds and human voices. They sound like dialogues, distant echoes that reverberate in our memory. Where do they come from? Where are we going? Does paradise exist, or hell? Yoko Ono: "The gates of hell are only a play of light".

PABLO J. RICO
excerpt from 'En Trance — Ex It', catalogue essay, Generalitat Valenciana, Spain, 1997

Yoko Ono with 'Ex It', 1998
100 coffins, 100 trees
Ex It, El Almudin, Valencia
floorspace 8. 00 x 28. 60 m
courtesy Lenono Photo Archive
& Generalitat Valenciana
photography: Miguel Angel Valero

Mike Parr

SOME NOTES

There isn't a specific relationship between the wax bride (*Untitled Self Portrait*, 1998) and the photograph from the series, *The Umbrella of Glass (Fading)*, 1981-93. I am more interested in a kind of fugal relationship where each piece remains cocooned and autonomous but related thematically, harmonically. 'Separate but echoing parts' describes what I have in mind perfectly. Fugue-like form, counter-point, contradiction even, is the basis for the Self Portrait Project because the forms taken by actual works, while resolved and in my mind acute, are only ever provisional. Sensing this instability is an essential part of the experience of the work …

I've often discussed my work in terms of "photodeath". Duchamp's subtitle "Delay in Glass" also seems very interesting to me. It is the sense of the lens and the speci-men; of process trapped by representation. The cast wax figure is set in a peculiarly unstable pose. The right arm is raised and tense. There is the sense of 'stoppage' or arrest in time, while the associations provoked by the object swirl around it. Life casting seems to me to produce something like a 3-dimensional photograph. There is a strong sense now, as we leave the 20th Century, that

photography is somehow or other anachronistic. That the photographic image is passing away, that it is a memento mori in relation to itself. The first bride performance was done in 1993. Incidentally, its title *Black Mirror/Pale Fire* includes a Nabokovian reference …

To enter the empty gallery rooms the audience stepped over the sleeping bride. I was very interested in the notion of *threshold*. The idea of the bride being carried across the threshold of the conjugal home. Brides and photography seem to go together as though the camera imposes the first stages of a paralysis that is consummated by entrance into the institution of marriage. But this 'cultural criticism' is only an aspect of the bride performances. Between the bride laid out on the floor and the blacked-out Australian National Dictionary on its wooden table, there was a strong sense of homology, as if symbolic order and the conventions of representation collude, producing an inevitable status.

Brides and death also seem to go together. *Brides of Christ* implies an interminable chastity; sacrifice without end. I recall an alchemical/Gnostic text that talks about Christ 'getting into the marriage bed of the Cross and

there-in hearing the sighs of all living creatures'. Here the grid of representation, sacrifice, the tongues of Babel, androgyny and transfiguration are suggested and made explicit in a way that is extraordinary, clear. I am interested in the cultural connection between *paralysis and authority* …

The Self Portrait Project is driven, in a deeply ironical and I think inventive way, by the same traumas of reproduction and point of view. There is no narrative in my work, only the constant process of its displacement and futility. A *process* of symbolic order that fails. Osten-sibly my congenitally unformed left arm provides some sort of explan-ation for my work as a whole, but of course it doesn't, because I realised long ago that it's absence is a kind of hyphen; a gap; as well as a kind of connection or mirroring.

The character of the exhibition room is fundamental to the piece. The isolation of the wax bride, the veiled presence of the photograph and the peculiarity of self sur-veillance are enlarged by an odd feeling of distraction.

MIKE PARR
excerpt from letter to Andrew Sayers, Director, National Portrait Gallery, Canberra, 8 February 1999

Performance photograph from Day One of *Deep Sleep [The Analytical Disabling of Mind and Matter]* (left)
3 day performance from evening June 17 to evening June 20, 1999 inclusive, Old Parliament House, Canberra
courtesy Anna Schwartz Gallery, Melbourne
photography: Paul Green

opposite
Slash your arm. Smear blood on your face
performance, Sydney 1973
Push a fish up your nose
performance, Sydney 1975
courtesy Sherman Galleries, Sydney

nb: the artist acknowledges Viridian Press as a collaborator in the production of prints

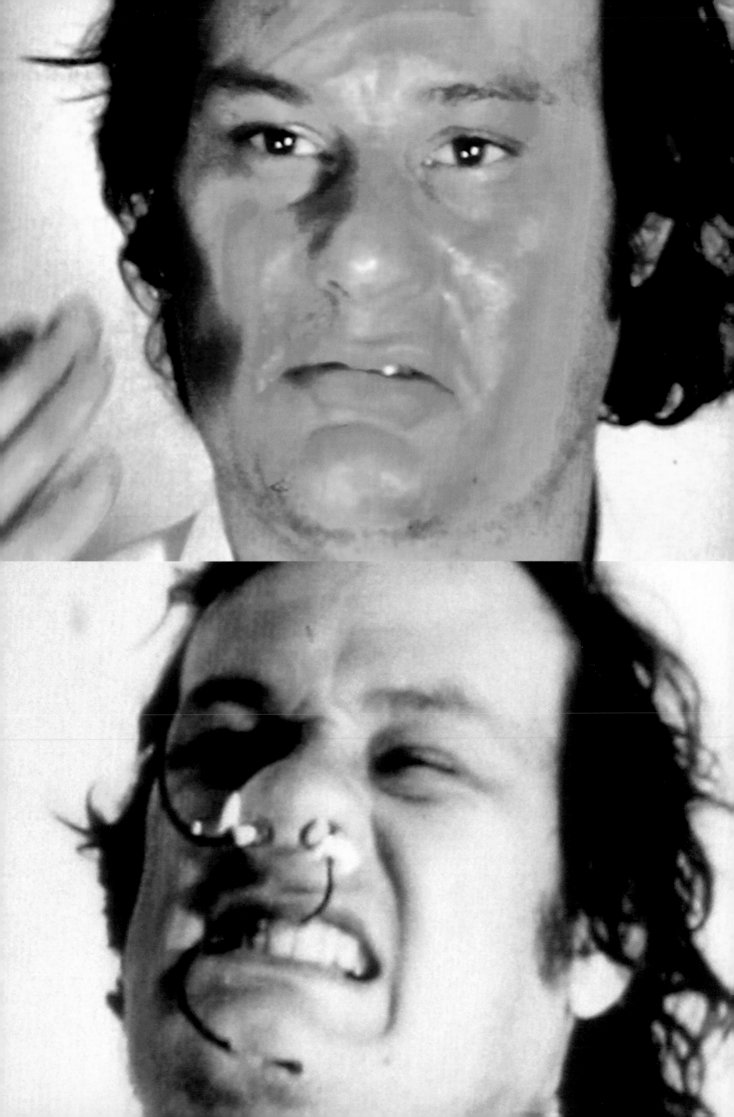

Lisa Reihana

I use my artwork as a point of self-discovery and a key into my Maori culture. I create my own interpretation of traditional concepts and art forms in a way that I feel comfortable with, whilst still pushing the boundaries …
— Lisa Reihana

Lisa Reihana describes herself as a video fibre artist. She interweaves digital images, creating associations, patterns and narratives. Her video walls are at the same time a Rubik's cube and a quilt made up of moving images or textures, and her slick digital images contain the illusion of tactile surfaces or the juxtaposition of real textiles with electronic constructions. Reihana is versatile, her concepts determine the medium, which can be as varied as velvet patchwork, animation, short dramas or experimental films, feather installations, photographs and copy collages.

All Reihana's work references her Maori heritage in some manner. She is not prescriptive or imposing, preferring to work on a multitude of levels to produce subtle, cultural pieces, such as the velvet quilt in *Korurangi* and particularly the laser-copied panels in *inei/konei*. Reihana creates associations with seemingly disparate concepts, so that contemporary music beats can co-exist harmoniously with the swinging and noise of long *poi* (a lightweight ball on string used in customary dance).

Based in Auckland, New Zealand/ Aotearoa, she deliberately seeks cultural spaces like the *marae* (site with meeting house), and, as her extended family are far in the North, Reihana is interested in constructing an imaginary sacred, personal space which she calls 'a virtual marae'. Most of her work can be understood as a development of this idea.

Reihana works predominantly with electronic media because it is symptomatic of the times, with its emphasis on speed and maximising information, and because 'there is only so much that an object can convey. My works present a great deal of material. People are then free to choose what they want from it'. It is this aspect of information saturation that has a universal appeal. Much of the content references Maori practices or features Maori people, yet is presented in an accessible form to a mixed audience. This could be due to the music, which links traditional sounds with contemporary beats, and Reinhana's visual referencing of other time periods such as the late 1970s. By playing with these readily recognisable patterns, music and styles she accesses Euro-American viewers' collective memories.

In *Native Portraits n.19897*, 1998, commissioned by the Museum of New Zealand Te Papa Tongarewa … Reihana examines colonial photographs and aspects of the past in order to reclaim them for the 1990s. Reihana and collaborator Hinemoana Baker chose examples from the museum's photographic collection portraying indigenous generic styles ranging from the 'Maori Belles' to the 'Dying Race' and 'Native Warrior' types. They then reconstructed the narrative moments before the historical photographs were taken, making them into filmic moments. Although contemporary in their execution, the narratives and video portraits are played on television monitors within the museum glass cabinets, reminding the viewer of the negative complexity of recent museum practice. The positioning of video portraits alongside the drama shows Maori as very much alive.

Native Portraits responds to the curatorial brief of works about time, tourism and technology. Reihana constructed a *waharoa*, which is the entrance to the marae, out of television monitors. This fictional, symbolic gateway combines images of customary dancing with Maori men in colonial and contemporary army uniforms. Interjections of road workers with 'stop' and 'go' signs create a visual bank of commonly seen depictions of Maori.

Reihana deliberately avoids using the Maori language, which she does not speak fluently: "I always use my own original material, I re-create everything so that I'm sure not to trample on any community's sensitivities".

MAUD PAGE
excerpt from 'Interdigitating Reihanamations: Lisa Reihana's Video Weavings', *Art Asia Pacific*, Vol. 21, 1999, pp. 41-43
quote: Megan Tamati-Quennell, 'Lisa Reihana, *Native Portraits n.19897*', *Photofile*, p. 48

*'native portraits n.19897'
(waharoa component)* 1997
installation & video
collection: Museum of New Zealand
Te Papa Tongarewa, Wellington
CT.9987/32A
photography: Michael Hall

Lisa Reihana / The Pacific Sisters

Henry Ah-Foo Taripo

Ani O'Neill

James Pinker

Rosanna Raymond

Suzanne Tamaki

Niwhai Tupaea

21st Sentry Cyber Sister is the intriguing alter ego of the Pacific Sisters multi-media collective. As envisioned by her creators Ani O'Neill, Rosanna Raymond, Suzanne Tamaki, and Niwhai Tupaea, she projects a vibrant personality indicative of Pacific Islands' identity. She stands at the nexus of identity, time, and imagination in contemporary Pacific culture.

In the elusive space between imagination and identity, body and adornment, Cyber Sister takes shape. Strong ankles encircled by tupe anklets; powerful thighs wrapped with elastic and shell bands; precise wrists adorned with red, white, and black plastic bracelets. The wisdom of her eyes is shaded with a feather mask; a multi-coloured choker protects the pulse at her neck; and a beef bone

necklace marks the bounty of her heart. An intricately designed tupe, pu'a and cowrie waistcoat/armour shields her torso and shoulders.[1] Korari and feather 'spears' tucked away in a black PVC backpack attest to her fierce nature and impeccable fashion sense.

Commissioned by Te Papa for its 1998 opening, she was unveiled in an elaborate ceremony on the museum's marae Te Hoko ki Hawaiki that challenged protocol in a vital way. Evoking the spirit of Maui's sister, the women asserted their right to speak in the sacred and transformatory realm. In a significant departure from protocol that only allows men to speak, each designer stood up, proudly naming the meaning of their adornment. Uncertainty marked this moment; the women spoke as creators, as sisters, as women who define reality in spite of the obstacles.

During the moving ceremony, each item was removed from model Ema Lyons for presentation to museum representatives until she stood, alert as a sentry in a black and red slashed body stocking. The gift was accepted. In the act of peeling away layers, the Pacific Sisters revealed the essence of female identity in liminal space; through vulnerability, there is power.

For Pacific Island women of all generations, their work is especially meaningful. Of Te Papa's com- mission O'Neill says, "Having a Sister in the House is important. It's important in all ways to have a Pacific Sister [costume] in the Pacific Fashion collection. She guards the Pacific collection, Pacific pride and Pacific women."[2] Due to her guardianship status, Cyber Sister grants membership in an encompassing Sister-hood. She is a composite costume assembled by individual artists that embodies the link between women across cultures.

As a composite of traditional and contemporary adornment, she reflects the fluid nature of identity in urban Aotearoa/New Zealand. Polly Ullrich writes, "This theme of the body 'as fusion of our earthly world and its cybernized, conceptualized shadow' stands as a major paradigm for art at the turn

of this century".[3] Beyond the margin of body and adornment, the true nature of Cyber Sister emerges; her shadow identity is that of the 'cyborg'.

Donna Haraway suggests the "cyborg is a kind of disassembled and reassembled, postmodern collective and personal self".[4] The spatial body maps social reality; adornment traces the continuum of past, present, and future construct- ions of identity in Pacific cultures.

Contemporary Pacific identity can project and reflect itself at will in liminal space. The artistic and personal identity of each Pacific Sister is negotiable in the realm of imagination. As the alter ego of the Pacific Sisters, Cyber Sister guards their collective hope through time. For any viewer, she soothes anxieties about the present and sharpens visions for the future. Cyber Sister is the alert sentry at the border of transgressions and possibilities.

BERNIDA ANNE WEBB
excerpt from *Adorned Identity in Aotearoa/New Zealand*, unpublished thesis, University of Denver

[1] Fashioned of any combination of natural or manufactured materials, the waistcoat resembles a vest and is the official uniform of the Pacific Sisters.
[2] Interview with Ani O'Neill by the author, 20 October 1999
[3] Polly Ullrich, 'Beyond Touch: The Body as Perceptual Tool,' *Fiberarts 26*, Summer 1999, p. 44
[4] Donna Haraway, 'A Cyborg Manifesto' in *Simians, Cyborgs, and Women*, New York: Routledge, 1991, p. 163.

21st Sentry Cyber Sister cloaked in pandanus mat, leading the Pacific Sisters (Ema Lyons, Rosanna Raymond, Te Itirawa Nepia & Suzanne Tamaki) Museum of New Zealand Te Papa Tongarewa, Wellington, 1998

opposite
i) adorning Ema Lyons
ii) fully adorned Cyber Sister & Pacific Sisters await formal acknowledgement of their presentation
iii) Ani O'Neill presents her work. Niwhai Tupaea removes it watched by Lisa Reihana

Gerhard Richter

In 1983 Richter wrote: "I have always been resigned to the fact that we can do nothing, that Utopianism is meaningless, not to say criminal. This is the underlying 'structure' of the Photo Pictures, the Colour Charts, the Grey Pictures. All the time, at the back of my mind lurked the belief that Utopia, Meaning, Futurity, Hope might materialize in my hands, unawares, as it were; because Nature, which is ourselves, is infinitely better, cleverer, richer than we with our short, limited, narrow reason can ever conceive ..."

There is something expansive and liberating in Richter's latest abstract paintings, more than in the preceding phases of this work, something we can designate "nature" in a positive sense, an extra dimension we are unable to grasp in plain and simple terms. In his manifesto from *dokumenta 7* in 1982 Richter declares:

When we describe a process, or make out an invoice, or photograph a tree, we create models; without them we would know nothing of reality and would be animals. Abstract pictures are fictive models, because they make visible a reality that we can neither see nor describe, but whose existence we can postulate. We denote this reality in negative terms: the Unknown, the incomprehensible, the infinite. And for thousands of years we have been depicting it through surrogate images such as heaven and hell, gods and devils.

The manifesto continues:

In abstract painting we have found a better way of gaining access to the unvisualisable, the incom-

prehensible; because abstract painting deploys the utmost visual immediacy — all resources of art, in fact — in order to depict 'nothing'. Accustomed to pictures in which we recognise something real, we rightly refuse to regard mere colour (however multifarious) as the thing visualised. Instead we accept that we are seeing the unvisualisable: that which has never been seen before and is not visible. This is not some abstruse game but a matter of sheer necessity: the unknown simultaneously alarms us and fills us with hope, and so we accept the pictures as a possible way to make the inexplicable more explicable, or at all events more accessible. Of course, pictures of objects also have this transcendental side to them. Every object, being part of an ultimately incomprehensible world, also embodies that world; when represented in a picture, the object conveys this mystery all the more powerfully, the less of a 'function' the picture has.

Rather than "dematerialise" as did abstraction in the early 20th century, Richter sets himself the task of bringing into focus that which we still do not know. In that sense the Abstract Pictures are the answer to the desire mechanism that was launched in the Photo Landscapes, according to Jill Lloyd [*Gerhard Richter, The London Paintings,* Anthony d'Offay Gallery, London, 1998]. They do not give an answer, but they provoke a creative response and hence continue to stretch the limits of what is possible for painting in our times.

In spite of all the apparent "style confusion", there is continuity in Richter's work, a continuity which with Richter rather signifies an attitude towards life than a style, an attitude characterised by a questioning, experimenting approach to the potential in his medium, something that must not be mistaken for eclecticism. He insists himself on the irrevelance of style — either abstract or figurative — in a formalistic sense, that it is something significant in itself. And as he has said in the catalogue for the Venice Biennale in 1972, he has no aesthetic problem, and means that the way to paint is irrelevant. The paintings do not differ from each other, he

says, and he changes his method wherever he sees fit.

Perhaps the following Richter quotation can round off his creative process up until the present:

I don't have a specific picture in my mind's eye. I want to end up with a picture that I haven't planned. This method of arbitrary choice, chance, inspiration and destruction may produce a specific type of picture, but it never produces a pre-determined picture. Each picture has to evolve out of a painterly or visual logic: it has to emerge as if inevitably. And by not planning the outcome, I hope to achieve the same coherence and objectivity that a random slice of Nature (or a Readymade) always possesses. Of course, this is also a method of bringing in unconscious processes, as far as possible. I just want to get something more interesting out of it than those things that I can think out for myself.

He makes great demands — both on himself as an artist and on art in general: "Painting is a moral action. Now that there are no priests or philosophers left, artists are the most important people in the world ... Art does have a moral function; it is a kind of substitute for religion; and it can transform, shape, invest-igate, delight, show, provoke ..."

JUTTA NESTEGARD
excerpt from 'Gerhard Richter: Trying to Jump Over His Own Shadow', *Gerhard Richter: The Art of the Impossible — Paintings 1964-1998,* exhibition catalogue, Astrup Fearnley Museum of Modern Art, Oslo, Norway, 1999, pp. 53-55
quotes: *Gerhard Richter, The Daily Practice of Painting,* Hans-Ulrich Obrist, Insel Verlag, Frankfurt-Main and Leipzig, 1993, pp. 103, 100, 100, 216, 69

Abstract Painting (812) 1994
oil on canvas
250 x 200 cm
Art Gallery of New South Wales Foundation Purchase 1999
collection: Art Gallery of New South Wales, Sydney
photography: Christopher Snee for AGNSW

Schädel (548/1) 1983 (left)
oil on canvas
55 x 50 cm
courtesy the artist

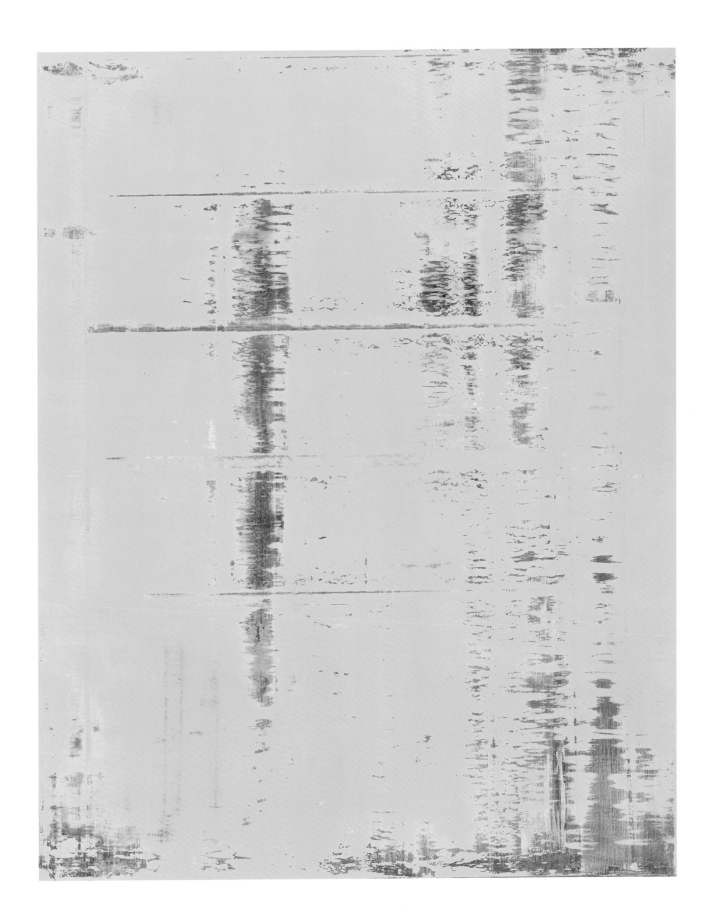

Ginger Riley

The iconography of Ginger Riley's art remains constant, the same, being focused on a sequence of events which took place in his mother's country for which he is *jungkayi*, or custodian. He knows this country and can sing and name it in ritual contexts, but not for outsiders. In accord with Mara law, the role of *jungkayi* passed to him from his mother and will pass from Riley to an appropriate person. He also knows the country and important stories belonging to his father but does not paint these because he is not entitled to by law. As he himself often puts it in explaining his art: 'My mother country is in my mind.' This country includes the riverine lands adjacent to the Limmen Bight River, from near the river to its tidal reach near the Four Archers, some fifty-five kilometres inland.

Artistically, Riley does not stray beyond this particular country or from the ancestral beings whose actions left their mark on the land and who then became the land of which he is part. Ginger adheres strongly to what he is entitled to paint and divulge through Mara law, and does not trespass upon anyone else's territory or cross the line between public and secret knowledge. As he puts it: 'That ceremony, (you) should know not to talk about it, leave the ceremony alone, otherwise it will kill you.' The constancy of iconography is not, however, a limitation to Riley but a source of inspiration and empowerment. He returns again and again to his mother country … The artist's whole body of work can be read as a series of variations upon a single theme of great substance and moment.

Central to Riley's art and spiritual vision of this land are the Four Archers, which he describes as 'the centre of the earth, where all things start and finish'. From the air, the Four Archers, perfectly formed pyramidal hills, rise dramatically out of the surrounding plain. In accord with its profound significance in the scheme of things, the rock formation commands attention for its visual splendour and power.

Sometimes this important rock formation is shown in close-up, cut off from the surrounding country,

like a detail of a map, or seen from different viewpoints in the one composition, so that it appears both in foreground close-up and in the distance. In other paintings, the stony hills, topped with vegetation, may be viewed from a wider angle in relation to the Limmen Bight River and other landmarks …

The Four Archers stand out in the artist's mind and figure again and again in his work as markers of his country. The rock formation was created by Garimala, 'a taipan which can strike you dead in a minute', according to Ginger. Although referred to as if it were a single being, Garimala is commonly understood to be two, and often appears in Riley's work as two snakes rising to face each other over the Four Archers.

Distinct from Garimala is Bandian, the King Brown snake, Ginger's father's mother's Dreaming. Bandian travelled through and formed places with Ginger's mother's country, including Nyamiyukanji, a site associated with Riley's own Dreaming, Jatukal (Plains Kangaroo). Nyamiyukanji is not explicitly painted or discussed. According to Ginger, Plains Kangaroo travelled towards the mouth of the Limmen Bight River in search of a woman. Failing to find one, he was advised by Bandian, who was resting in a nearby waterhole, to look for a young girl instead. Ginger says that Jatukal, 'the first being', needed a mate and the sexual act took place at Nyamiyukanji.

Riley is *jungkayi* for Bandian, but King Brown snake and Plains Kangaroo are much less visible in his paintings than Garimala and Ngak Ngak (Sea Eagle) which are dominant icons …

Perhaps the most striking image in Riley's work is Ngak Ngak, the white-breasted sea eagle, shown singly or repeated, but almost invariably depicted in profile and facing to the left. He plays the role of a sentinel or guardian, protecting the country. Ngak Ngak created an island near the mouth of the Limmen Bight River when he flew over it. This island, associated with Bulukbun's punishment of initiated boys, is Beatrice Island or

Yumunkuni, an important place for Ginger's mother's Dreaming, Yulmunji (Shark).

Ngak Ngak is generally painted white but may be yellow, brown, grey, charcoal or green … For Riley, depicting Ngak Ngak is an act of homage, a means of honouring this protective spirit. Sometimes Ngak Ngak is shown without an eye, indicating that he may be asleep or is looking at nothing in particular. Ngak Ngak's attributes include his hunting prowess and keen eyesight.

Human figures occasionally occur in Riley's art but are of secondary importance to the ancestral beings Garimala and Ngak Ngak, and the land itself. Ancestral people, the *Gor-yi-mar*, are shown in groups engaged in everyday activities, small in scale. Often described by the artist as unimportant, they rarely occupy centre stage. Sometimes, Riley represents their bark shelters to refer to life before white contact …

The presence of human beings is more commonly invoked indirectly through the decoration that often frames Riley's compositions. The distinctive wedge shapes which frame the outer, and sometimes inner, sections of his works are derived from his shoulder and chest body-paint designs. The patterned edge serves to anchor the work within the law and point to another layer of meaning, that of song, dance and ceremony, visible but not spoken.

JUDITH RYAN
excerpt from 'My Mother Country is in my mind: the iconography of Ginger Riley's art', *Ginger Riley*, exhibition catalogue, National Gallery of Victoria, 1997, pp. 29-32

The Four Arches 1994
synthetic polymer paint on canvas
186.2 x 233 cm
courtesy the artist & Alcaston Gallery, Melbourne

Pipilotti Rist

Taped almost entirely underwater, Rist's video SIP MY OCEAN offers a "fish-eye" view of swaying seaweed gardens and coral kingdoms. Wafting sybaritically over the ocean beds, the camera records trajectories of household objects as they sink to the depths of the sea; kitsch coffee mugs with heart-shaped patterns, a bright yellow teapot, a plastic toy truck, and an old LP settle into the sand. Schools of tropical fish whizz in and out of this ever-shifting marine vista, while a bikini-clad woman cavorts in the waves ...

Rist's video works are often double-edged in their delivery, being at once coquettish and rebellious. Her aesthetic reference is not so much the real-time task-oriented video of the 1970s as the slickly packaged porno-pop of MTV. In particular, her 1986 single-channel piece I'M NOT THE GIRL WHO MISSES MUCH — a spectacle of frenzied rock-and-roll dancing glimpsed through deliberate technical disruptions — playfully satirizes the commodified eroticism of television's music videos, while exposing their sexist underpinnings. For her projection pieces, which tend to be environmental in scale and immersive in feeling, Rist manipulates the technology of video to emulate cinematic effects. These hybridisations of film and video emit a profusion of captivating audio and visual stimuli that invite corporeal, if not libidinal, identification. Far from being "politically correct", these installations problematize feminism's interrogation of visual pleasure as it is manifest in the cinema.

If Rist claims a feminist agenda for her work, which I believe to be the case, her theoretical sources lie in the lyrical writings of Helene Cixous and Luce Irigaray, who each espouse pure female embodiment as the vehicle for psychological and sexual emancipation from the inequities inherent in the heterosexual gender difference. Cixous' poetic call for women to inscribe their own history with "milk" instead of ink, and Irigaray's directive for women to employ a science based on the "mechanics of fluids" as a methodology for self-analysis, resonate in the leitmotif of aqueous imagery running throughout many of Rist's videos. Visions

of water — and the metaphors of mutability and transformation they invoke — abound in the work: from the swimming pool shots in (ENTLASTUNGEN) PIPILOTTIS FEHLER (Absolutions: Pipilotti's Mistakes, 1988), to the floating, interpenetrating bodies in PICKELPORNO (Pimple Porno, 1992), to the scenes of the deep blue sea in SIP MY OCEAN.

Rist's saturated, ever-mutating imagery imparts a polymorphous pleasure in the physical. The pervasive sensuality of SIP MY OCEAN, with its multiple screens and hallucinogenic mirroring effects, suggests the elusive state of jouissance — unadulterated, boundless, pre-Oedipal pleasure. Associated with the female, this metaphoric realm imagines a body with no boundaries, a body with multiple and autonomous erotic zones, a body in full possession of its own desire. However, Rist's erratic vocals — which range from sweetly lyrical to maniacal screaming — disrupt these utopian dreams of total gratification. For desire always demands an "other", one who may or may not yield to the seduction, one who may or may not return the favour. As the soundtrack to this deliriously enchanted underworld, Rist's version of Chris Isaak's tune expresses the dangers (and pleasures) of desire; it also suggests a person trying to maintain control against the rising tides of passion. SIP MY OCEAN is Rist's invitation to participate in this game of desire and fulfillment; yet it is also a dare to survive its perilous undertow.

NANCY SPECTOR
Curator of Contemporary Art, Guggenheim Museum, New York.
excerpt from 'The Mechanics of Fluids', Parkett 48, 1996, pp. 83-85

GROSSMUT BEGATTE MICH (SIP MY OCEAN)
1994-1996
6 video stills
courtesy Galerie Hauser & Wirth, Zürich
& Luhring Augustine, New York

Dieter Roth

the aim of this book is to set down and write up everything that appeared in my work between 1947 and 1971 as piles or groups of **flat objects**   and now stands out   flat though it was   excepting old things which could no longer be found   and new things that were produced on this or that side of the so-called deadline (which it was decided should be drawn roughly down the middle of the year 1971)
(some of them though were produced with the united efforts of richard hamilton or stefan wewerka)

flat (objects) refers to those items that have been printed   squeezed   pressed   squashed   or sieved in a squashy manner to a height of under two centimetres

books are called here   or in this context   all that is gummed or sewn and piled up   either in groups or as company for its kind   or stands around or stands about   or stands there wedged in or lies around   (not wedged in)

prints are called in this context (of flat objects) all that appears   or has appeared   alone or lonesome and lies around singularly or hangs about solitarily   as well as wedged in

so-called **printing** (which should actually be called pressing) is done when something flat   and simultaneously hard   lies there and someone   or -thing or -body has dabbed or daubed ink over it   and then someone   or -thing or -body presses a sheet of paper on it so that he she or it gets a bit of the ink stuck to the paper as soon as the paper (after pressing) is removed   or torn away (manually or mechanically)   from the no-longer-quite-so-bedaubed-as-prior-to-printing hard flatness   so that there is then ink on the sheet   which may then be termed an impression (not con-cession   although sometimes a con-tour or con-figuration can be seen on it)[1]

now whenever the hardness that was just mentioned here can be referred to as a relief or as relief-like   where the ink perches on the mountain peaks and ranges   (so that the ink gets torn away from them with the paper) one can talk of **relief printing** (although little relief is generally involved because little pressure is exerted) in which the so-called mechanical aspect plays   or drives   a very large roller

now   if the hardness   which has already come to be mentioned twice   can be called a relief   or the like on which the ink nestles between the peaks   namely in the depths and vales   (so that when someone or -thing or -body tears the paper away   the ink is torn up out of them together with the paper   or when any two of them or even all three tears it up and away) then one can call this **intaglio printing**   but however it is done swiftly or otherwise   the chief characteristic (straight or bent) here is that once again the mechanical aspect dominates

and when   by comparison   the hard flatness   which has already been employed here verbally for some time (hopefully a not yet worn out hard flatness)   lacks any particular relief and is purely (hopefully not poorly) and simply smooth   and lies there   as it were   flat to the power of two   and the ink on top can rest neither on peaks nor in vales   but is forced simply to stay somewhere there on the plane   (so that one can and has to simply knock off a copy   by slapping the paper on top   which once again leads to a poor copy but now in the verbal sense   inasmuch as it is followed by the proof copy)   then one can speak of **planographic** or **flat printing**   in which chemistry assumes   and also plays   the role of both the thick and the thin   and that with success   and for a good hundred years already   which is to say (in passing) the flat print[2] has shut agatha's mouse-trap good and proper   has squeezed it shut and snapped it flat   as it were

but in cases when the ink is pressed onto the paper (and not the paper onto the ink)   ie when the ink is squidged through a partially open sieve (which is partially sealed)   through the parts that are open   (to land squidgily sieved on the paper)   one may talk of or write about or type about what is termed **silk-screening**

pressings   on the other hand   are something that is done with pressure   when something none too flat or soft is pressed down and flattened on something hard and flat   thus making it wide and seem to want to descend from three dimensions to two   and although it does not want to   it must   it is forced and pressed to do so and is simply left there   and without the need of any proof-pulling   because the flat-pressed and de-pressed object on (and with) its bed underneath is (are) already what was wanted   (what one wanted to have)   and which would   as it were   itself have wanted to be called a pressing   if it could want   so once again one has what one wants   and calls it a **pressing**   (and happily so   for it is not a print)

but under no circumstances may it be called a **squashing**   because **squashings** are produced by pressure at right angles   applied **parallel** to the base   (which may be termed the bed)   whereas pressings are only produced by **downward vertical** pressure on the same   (although there is no contradiction or -distinction or -vention between the two   one can nevertheless say **'nevertheless'**)
printing forme is   however   (in contradistinction or -vention or -diction to all that has been blabbered about or blabbered around here   or should have been jabbered about there)   the name or term to be given to the strictly pictorial   or the image (to put it succinctly)   that gives rise to the form of the printed calls it forth and shouts out and kicks up a row   (so as to lend a quick acoustic dimension to the pictorial side of the images)   to wit the forme   being the image that is printed in one solitary printing process which is also called a **sheet pass** and should also be called as such here   to wit sheet pass   because   is it not necessary   (assuming one wants colour in the picture)   to see   and recognize   the form of the colour   and apply it to the frequently mentioned hardness and lay the paper on top   so that the colour can appear in its specific form on the paper and form the picture   and is it not necessary to do (and not die) this several times if the picture is in several colours?
wherever the maker of the printing forme (i.e. the printing forme maker)   who created the shape of the single

(and basically solitary)   or at any rate forever separated colours that appear on the paper   or on the card
or on the tin   or on the wallpaper   has been left unnamed at the end   (but not finally)   it was in
fact me (except where it was the photographer   who may also have done it   when no one else is named
additionally as the photographer)

colour separation is what is referred to when someone goes off   or drives off   or rushes off   (or perhaps
even somebody   or something   for the world of civilised people   who are not in fact civilised at all
has a great deal more tucked away in its bosom   or on its programme   or under its cap)   and produces the
forms of the various colours   or the printing formes in the form of colour printing formes   after or beside
or before a model (which lies there before   beside   or on the other side beside him   and which is the
object of the desire that he harbours to get it like that onto paper   or wallpaper   just the way it looks
there before   beside or on the other side beside him)

and i would like the same to be said here about their **maker**   (who may just as equally be a **makeress** or
makerling)   that i wanted to have said earlier regarding the printing forme and its maker   (by first writing
it   and then having it printed)   by which the pressure here appears as the head of steam behind the will to
imagine

unique print is   on the other hand   an expression   and moreover an expression that is designed here to
take the place of the more attractive   (yet more ugly)   expression   unique thing   (there is no skill in
pleasing everybody because anyone can do that   meaning that art must be what no one can do)   so the
expression unique thing is not to be used here   but **unique print** is certainly not meant to say that that thing
there   (called unique print)   stands   or lies   or indeed moves   all alone and lonesome in this awful
world   not all alone and forsaken   but rather as a thing that only differs slightly (if not greatly) from
the things with which it appears as a group   (or as a series or such like)   which is called   all said and
done   (or not done)   an edition   so in cases where it is slightly (or greatly) different from the things
the stuff   or even junk   with which it appears in its group   (it has   after all   been produced   or
tossed off   using the same printing formes)

the term **publisher** is given to such persons   or person   or he or she or it   who have met or has met or
meet or meets   the requirements for living as a publisher (a publisher's life)   namely ordering and funding
and supervising and distributing the items in question   which may be termed marketeererly art objects
assuming they are such   which they often are   not least   because the time passes so fast and loose   and
the faster one makes it pass   (the more effectively one kills it)   the more space there is   (there where
time was)   and   the more business that can be done (or not done) on those places   especially with the flat
objects
in keeping with my thoughtful and understanding (or rather thoughtless and overkind) nature   (a nature that is
often described as timid)   i have also given in to those who have failed to meet the aforementioned
requirements   and entered them beside the words **published by**   (meaning that people appear here as
publishers who have only ordered   say   or only paid   or only met as few as possible of the requirements
that a publisher requires   or people who in other ways have instilled fear and dread in me

yet I remained firm when it came to the **dimensions** of the flat objects   for here height always comes before
width (apart that is from those exceptions where   or in which   only one pair of dimensions has been given
(or put there)   in these cases i sometimes mean the size of the paper   but sometimes the size of the picture
on the paper   (and not the paper behind the picture))

the **titles**   which the things   (meaning once again the flat objects)   go by   or go under   will be found
by the upright observer   if they have the right inclination   in correct   reliable form in the german
section of the index   the english section merely provides translations   titles by which the flat objects in
question are not known on the market   and which are only to be found in this catalogue   although when an
english title is given in the german section of the index   then that is the right one (and not the left one
even though it is on the left side of the page)   and thus not the wrong one   rather it is precisely the one
which accompanied the item onto the market

artists copies designates   (or designate)   that which   or those prints that   are printed over and above
the number set for the edition (and thus printed over and beyond the whole of that)   quite recently   people
have started to talk of artists proofs   in fact they are only referred to so revoltingly as artists proofs
because this is being done quite fraudulently   for artists proofs are the proofs that the artist (who is often
quite genuinely an artist   and sometimes not)   has printed single-handedly and single-mindedly for himself
during the course   and flow   of the preliminary work prior to printing the edition   so that he could see
what was there and what was not there   as such   then   they can best be termed artists copies

once again   time goes by   whereby the time passes and makes space for new times   which is to say modern
times   which people regard as really their element (or in which people see themselves as being really in their
element)   good health!

dieter rot   16.12.71

¹ The original wordplay, "Abzug - Abriß - Umriß" means roughly impression - outline - contour. (Translator)
² The German "Flachdruck" can also mean "flat pressure." (Translator)

Sanggawa

The art collective Sanggawa, meaning "one work", is composed of Elmer Borlongan, Federico Sievert, Mark Justiniani, Karen Flores, and Joy Mallari — all of whom have impressive credentials as individual artists. Formerly of ABAY (Artista ng Bayan/Artists of the People) and Grupong Salingpusa, these artists find in the act of collaboration an alternative ethos in art making. The joint creation of murals entails a painful but fulfilling process of discussion and debate among the various temperaments of the group.

Sanggawa breathes new vigor into the Philippine mural tradition, which was blazed by Philippine National Artist Carlos Francisco and reconfigured by Imelda Marcos' New Society projects in the 1970s; the former First Lady commissioned artists to put up murals (actually enlarged easel works copied by hired artists) around her kingdom, supposedly to give Manila, her City of Man, a cultural face. The murals of Sanggawa, however, resist the grandeur of great history and the propaganda of regimes, and instead tackle topical issues which speak to very particular audiences ...

The *Second Coming* is part of a series of editorial artworks documenting in a satirical mode the key events and dramatis personae which defined the news in Manila in 1994 and early 1995. Filipinos who were in the know at the time would surely recognize the Ms Universe Pageant, Mike Verlarde's emergence as the religious leader of the burgeoning charismatic renewal group called El Shaddai and Cardinal Sin battling the methods of contraception. Sanggawa portrays these events under a carnival tent and with the trappings of a circus. The group identifies religion and entertainment as twin pivots around which the events of the time turned. But Sanggawa is not slave to factual documentation; its members take liberties in organizing schemes of relations within which figures and details interact. Ferdinand Marcos' son crowns the fairest of them all, a Virgin Mary statue sneers at the woman in a swimsuit but clutches a scepter that matches hers. The Cardinal and the President compete for a shaman-showman's favors.

Amid this gaiety are envelopes, filled with either money or prayers, flying in the air as a woman with a basket waits on the ground for their fall. As in so many of its works, Sanggawa puts forth recurrent motifs like ominously charged landscapes, a sense of imminent catastrophe, and money drifting in the air. The whole approach to mural making is political but playful, alluding to the sensibility of *komiks* (local cartoons) and editorial cartoons.

The *Second Coming* re-creates the frenzy that surrounded the Pope's second visit to the Philippines. On the canvas, a messianic festival of alms, prayers, and penance told as a fairy tale-like morality play unfolds, with a White God in attendance and a Christ figure summoning the multitude to destroy the temple which blind faith built. The Pope blesses his flock from a podium stamped with the symbol of the State. On the side, the Supreme Pontiff's exaggeratedly gargantuan high chair remains empty beside a Vatican guard who dutifully attends. And as in all of Sanggawa's murals, the sky is heavy with impending change, to herald either holocaust or utopia. The whole scene is framed by the architecture of the Church which encompasses the structures of the State, fusing the two institutions.

PATRICK FLORES
excerpt from *At Home & Abroad: 20 Contemporary Filipino Artists,* exhibition catalogue, Asian Art Museum of San Francisco, 1998, p. 120

Palo-sebo 1995
oil on canvas
197 x 305 cm
purchased 1995 with a special allocation from the Queensland Government celebrating the Queensland Art Gallery's Centenary 1895-1995
collection: Queensland Art Gallery, Brisbane

Mick Namarari Tjapaltjarri

While the precise detail will never be known of the negotiations among the men at Papunya back in 1971, one thing is becoming ever clearer and more certain. The contribution made by Mick Namarari Tjapaltjarri to launching and establishing the Papunya painting movement, and the direction he gave to the Pintupi men in so doing, has been one of the absolutely essential ingredients to achieving whatever success the extraordinary Papunya Tula painting school may have secured.

A quiet, unassuming and inward man as is the Pintupi way, Tjapaltjarri's intensity and intuitive brilliance were key forces in developing the characteristic Pintupi painting orientation at Papunya. More thoroughly steeped in the ways of the bush and the desert, and more earnestly observing the rigorous disciplines of the ancient tradition through which they were formed, the Pintupi men were least ready and able to disclose the secret-sacred images that were the decisive constituents of profound ceremonies. It was Tjapaltjarri's great achievement to form a compositional attitude through which the secret-sacred designs received interpretation, rather than explicit re-statement.

In his artistic and spiritual struggle to release the meaning embodied in the ancient and profound diagrams, Mick was able to focus on the more substantial and higher issues of Pintupi consciousness, while preserving the appropriate respect and awe for the secret-sacred objects and images. Such an artistic policy allowed Tjapaltjarri to make paintings of great intensity, importance and merit: indeed his work *Naughty Boys' Dreaming* of 1971, (showing a story that Tjapaltjarri indicated belongs to all people and all tribes), stands as the central interpretative piece of the Papunya movement, the starting point for us from which all other paintings may be brought into intelligible perspective.

In proceeding in this manner, Tjapaltjarri was responding, it seems, to the 'policy' recommendation of Old Walter Tjampitjinpa, the most senior Pintupi man, under whose wing Geoff Bardon had been taken in the earliest days of the painting movement. In fulfilling his responsibilities, Tjapaltjarri forged the basic principles of the Pintupi art style, wherein powerful abstract images bearing allegorical meaning were formed and where deeper and unified spiritual meanings imparted the overall coherence to the free visual elements by which the paintings were constituted. Leading Pintupi artists, such as Turkey Tolsen Tjupurrula and Ronnie Tjampitjinpa, are greatly influenced by his ways.

As his 'interpretative-abstract' style preserves the secrecy and integrity of the sacred forms, Tjapaltjarri has painted works which address the issues and spiritual substance known only to men of High Degree. In so doing, many of Tjapaltjarri's works look distinctly different to many Papunya, and even Pintupi, paintings. His works must be regarded as particularly precious, because it is through them that the most sublime consciousness of the Pintupi man receives direct as well as philosophical revelation through artistic statement. By means of his art Mick Namarari Tjapaltjarri has bequeathed to his people the deeper wisdom that forms the inner essence of the traditional culture of the ancient Australian land.

RUDOLF TALMACS
courtesy Utopia Art, Sydney

Tjuningpa (Desert Mouse) Dreaming at Tjiterulpa 1994
synthetic polymer on Belgian Linen
181 x 121 cm
private collection, Adelaide
courtesy Gallerie Australis, Adelaide

Luc Tuymans

These days, painting is in itself a risky business. Everything, absolutely everything, has already been said and done and shown over the past five hundred years. Particularly throughout the 20th century. The genre of painting has proved to be particularly rich in invention, destruction, new beginnings and more than one reconsidering to traditional forms. Every artist who chooses the medium of painting as his (or her) means of expression knows that …

The best paintings confront us, the observers, with images which we have been waiting for, images which we dream of, which we love and can hate, which attract and repel us, which are provocative, which are inaccessible, dull and intolerable and which, because they are one or all of these things, will never let us go. During the past ten years, Luc Tuymans has succeeded in presenting himself to the art world with such pictures.

Tuymans has tackled two key artistic problems of the late 20th century. First, he questions the necessity and expressiveness of a painted picture, which after all must always hold its ground against competition from other media images. Second, he intensifies this problem within artists themselves by adding the dimension of the collective recollection of the Holocaust. Tuymans believes that this is not a specifically German problem but a European one, and it concerns him directly, as an artist who thinks in pictures and images. His credo of 'The image is the negation of the image' refers, therefore, to both aspects. The medialized images of the crimes are part of the common stock of images, but what do they actually express? Can they still usefully serve as memories? Tuymans often uses historical documents and pictures from the Nazi era as motifs for his paintings. The artist uses the pessimism and distrust of images to create a new means of remembering.

Naturally, we are not talking here about a survivor's memories, but instead about memories from one born post-war to others born post-war. This makes his paintings the antithesis of impartial. They come to us burdened down with knowledge, scruples and scepticism.

Whence does Tuymans draw the driving force for this demanding and risky undertaking? I believe it comes from his fascination with those impossible, taboo, terrible and unfathomable aspects of human nature, together with his desire to not make things easy for himself and others. This is shown not least by an extraordinary mental tension between his constant talk of failure — we are dealing with a very eloquent painter here — and the pictorial transformation of this failure into pictures of laconic beauty.

ANNELIE LÜTGENS
excerpt from *The Purge,* exhibition catalogue, Bonnefantenmusuem/ Kunstmuseum, Wolfsburg, 1999

Schwarzheide 1986
oil on canvas
60 x 70 cm
private collection, Ghent
courtesy Zeno X Gallery, Antwerp
photography: Felix Tirry

Blessing 1996 (opposite)
oil on canvas
143 x 187 cm
collection: Bonnefanten Museum, Maastricht
courtesy Zeno X Gallery, Antwerp
photography: Felix Tirry

Ken Unsworth

Ken Unsworth's work often incorporates kitsch pranks and contrived melancholy in its use of metaphor to evoke psychological and emotional experience. Humour in Unsworth's work operates as it does in society, as a means of keeping at bay the fear of mortal confrontation and personal tragedy. Sexual puns and material frivolity give voice to our ambivalent relationship with death and with the contested land that we inhabit, which, combined with a distinct lack of social ritual, manifests in feelings of social isolation and helplessness. We cope by shifting between identities, playing out our dreams, fears and desires in the uncomfortable grey terrain which lies between diversion and despair.
— Felicity Fenner

My first encounter with Ken Unsworth's work was in a formerly grandiloquent, yet vaguely harrowing, building in Lodz, Poland.

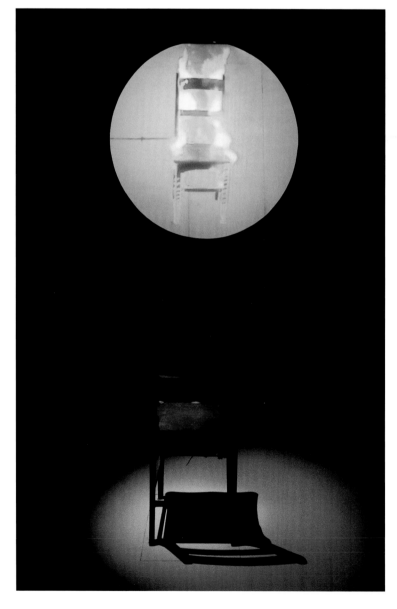

Two sizeable mounds of hay on the floor suggested similar piles in vast rows that you find all over Poland, but just as likely those in Australia, which also reach way, way back to Australia's complicated agrarian past. Tucked into and around the circular base of one were several intricate dollhouses, which seemed simultaneously protected and about to be either crushed or overwhelmed, and which also indicated that these haystacks might be chock-full of secrets. Nearby, more hay was atop a piano, this time just barely revealing charred sheet music by the Polish composer Gracyna Bacewicz, while a handmade female figure, presumably the spirit of Bacewicz, blasted upwards, taking with her the top of the piano. A lot came together around this spare yet complex work: playfulness and whimsy, but also fragility, mortality, startling visual drama, music and elusive signals of transcendence. Unsworth is an acutely poetic artist, and by poetic I mean the way multiple associations keep deepening and expanding the longer you spend time with his works. His is an especially generous work and it rewards patient attention on the part of the viewer. What struck me immediately about this piece — and indeed what still strikes me about Unsworth's work — is its mix of visceral grittiness and crackling, effervescent magic. There is something earthy about his aesthetic, wilfully rough, and alertly democratic, especially in the way he incorporates familiar things (stones, hay, framed mirrors, furniture) or other found objects that don't have a rarefied air. Still, what emerges are logic-bending situations which can be whimsical or near-beatific, but also dark and conflicted — often at the same time. Figures fly, heavy stones levitate or morph into hybrid flying creatures with motorised wings, tools and devices also appear suspended in the air, and fragrant mounds of hay can take on the look of mysterious devotional or meditative objects, but you're in the presence of an art which, while rooted in the visceral, is cathartic, risky, transformative, and enormously inventive …

Ken Unsworth's work is animated by a largeness of scope or vision — call it what you will — which ultimately has less to do with aesthetics than it does with its profoundly human core

GREGORY VOLK

excerpt from 'Immediate humanity: several thoughts on the work of Ken Unsworth', *Ken Unsworth*, exhibition catalogue, Art Gallery of New South Wales, 1998, p. 15
quote: Felicity Fenner, 'Vernacular Vagaries', ibid, p. 21

The Skidderump, 2000 (opposite)
working drawing
collection: the artist

Litost 1984-1998
video, motorised chair, sound
photography: Christopher Snee

Adriana Varejão

Hers is a painting of thickness — in fact, of many different degrees of thickness. To understand the body of the painting is also to understand the possible pain of painting and not abdicate from its sensuality and its specters. The thickness here comprehends not only the materiality but also the symbolic density of the pictorial discourse. Adrian Varejão's work is the practice of an intricate cartography that covers the span from China to Brazil's history town of Ouro Preto, between the image of a portolano and the signs of painting, from body to history. It is a collection of apparently scattered signifiers that acquire a connection within a logic of scenes constructed by the artist in a theatricalization of history …

Varejão's work is also an icono-logical operation through which images extracted from the history of art — where they were sculptures, monuments, chinaware, engravings, maps and ex-votos printed in books — shift to the condition of painting, their filter and denominator. The method, insistently, is to render the migrations of images. The artist does not paint an angel, but rather the tile on which the angel is impressed.

She paints "a flor da pele" [literally, the flower of the skin, that is, the skin's finest and outermost layer in a tattoo]. Angels and flowers transform themselves into flesh and dwell among us through Varejão's painting. Therein we find a prime dimension of this painting, which consists of the symbolic thickness of the images …

Oleg Grabar, in his work "The Mediation of Ornament," argues that the ornament can establish the immediate meeting of the spectator and an object of any culture whatsoever. To Varejão, ornaments and images, as results of the exchanges and circulation of symbols and technology, are propitiatory offerings of the meeting of cultures …

Varejão's painting is located in a region between tactile, visual and plastic sensuality and reason. The oval Mapa de Lopo Homem (Map of Lopo Homen) refers to the map of the year 1519, in which the geographical continuity between Asia and America is drawn. Homem's cartographical fancy reconciled the ancient Ptolemaic conceptions in face of the discovery of America. It provided reassurance of Adam's Biblical role as the father of humanity. Varejão explores the continuity as cultural contagion from the perspective of the trauma of the knowledge and dogma regarding the order of the world. The slits in the canvas, stitched together with surgical material, procure the scar. A window on the world in the Renaissance, the picture places itself in the situation of a body in the world … Varejão knows that to articulate the visual past historically means to take possession of a reminiscence, of a visual evidence so that it produces flashes of light in a moment of danger. In this respect, her art acts as an agential process of history …

In Adriana Varejão's work, any citational manifestation is not a mere embarkation in the History of Art, but a production of understanding of the thickness of history and its process of condensation and exchange. After all, it is Walter Benjamin who declares, "The past brings with it a mysterious index, which impels it to redemption. The past, like an irreversible image that emits flashes of light, only lets itself become fixed, at the moment in which it is recognised" …

Now tiling that is vulgar and geometrical, abstract, appears in Varejão's work. The neighbourhood café-bar and the butcher shop substitute Portugal's landed estates (of the art movement) of the 1700s and the Brazilian convents with their panels of painted tiles. In her most recent work, the imagerial base on which Varejão casts her pictorial dramas is becoming thinner in consistency, as in programmed loss of thickness. The tiles no longer bear designs inscribed on their body. They are modern. Monochromatic. Severe and blind, aseptic. The white ones, like a canvas, suffer in the purity from the fissures of experience.

PAULO HERKENHOFF
excerpt from *Adriana Varejão Painting / Suturing*, exhibition catalogue, Galeria Camargo Vilaça, São Paulo, 1996

Carne à Moda de Franz Post
1995
oil on canvas & porcelain
60 x 80 (canvas), 25 cm
diameter (porcelain pieces)
collection: Brondesbury
Holdings Ltd, Caracas
courtesy Galeria Camargo
Vilaça, São Paulo
photography: Vicente de Mello

Tongue with Winding Pattern
1998 (opposite)
wood, aluminium,
polyurethane & oil paint
220 x 170 x 57 cm
collection: Frances & José
Marinho, Rio de Janeiro
courtesy Galeria Camargo
Vilaça, São Paulo
photography: Vicente de Mello

Jeff Wall

I attempted to create an image of a way subjected people might try to build a space for themselves. I imagined the picture as a speculative project. All my pictures about talking are in fact about the ways people work on creating something in common, about how they work to find a way to live together. — Jeff Wall

The corpus of photographic tableaux produced by Jeff Wall since *The Destroyed Room* in 1978 can be situated (defined by the historian) as a post-conceptual attempt at the reconstruction of a pictorial tradition in the age of the media. The English expression 'a pictorial tradition' is appropriate here, in that it designates a repertory of pictures extending far beyond painting, able to include, in particular, a history of photography, more or less institutionalised and marked out by works ascribed to 'auteurs'. But the artist did not wait for historians to situate his project. He precisely articulated his own intentions and strategy by defining the tradition to which he refers — and which he seems to perpetuate — as that of 'painted drama', transformed by a technology associated with the media, the 'spectacle', etc. In 1986 he declared: "The fascination of this technology for me is that it seems that it alone permits me to make pictures in the traditional way. Because that's basically what I do, although I hope it is done with an

effect opposite to that of technically traditional pictures. The opportunity is both to recuperate the past — the great art of the museums — and at the same time to participate with a critical effect in the most up-to-date spectacularity. This gives my work its particular relation to painting. I like to think that my pictures are a specific opposite to painting" ...

It seems to me that a significant aspect of Wall's work is his acceptance of the notion that critical lucidity (a conceptual and dialectical approach) can participate in a rhetoric of ambiguity, in accordance with the 'mannerisms' that emerged from pop art in the sixties. Parodic imitation — which is not necessarily equivalent to satire — has been the most common form of this rhetoric since the late seventies, particularly in painting. But parody allows only for the appropriation of fragments of the pictorial tradition, while Jeff Wall aims at a systematic reconstruction. *Parody* enabled the so-called 'neo-expressionist' (or neo-figurative) painters to feign a critical lucidity, the better to reaffirm their status as authors; whereas Wall conceives his photographic *tableaux* in a dialectical relation to the tradition of figurative painting. At issue for him is the possibility of redefining modern art by situating it in the historical (and logical) gap

between the fine arts and the media, between the artistic tradition — that is, the transmission of cultural norms through technical knowledge — and the technology of the spectacular image. Modern art is no longer to be cast exclusively as a break with the past, not even as a utopian breakthrough; rather it appears as the history of an unresolved conflict which can and should be replayed, restaged, until it is brought to a form enabling us to imagine its overcoming ...

Wall's images possess a pronounced theatrical character: but it is a pictorial theatricality, enclosed within the flat, strictly delimited space of two-dimensional re-presentation. The support structure of the light box, replacing stretcher and frame, further complicates things by reducing the physiological complexity of the painter's coloured light, with its qualities of emanation, envelopment, etc., to the literal effect of a technical procedure. Finally, it is tempting to consider this treatment of the photographic *tableau* as the exemplary pictorial form of the unresolved conflict of modern art ...

The perception of the photographic *tableau* is an experience of confrontation that prohibits both the empathy of an imaginary participation in the pictorial work and the

Rear, 304 East 25th Ave, Vancouver, 9 May 1997, 1.14 & 1.17 pm 1997
black and white gelatin photograph on fibre base paper
246.4 x 363.2 x 7 cm
courtesy Marian Goodman Gallery, New York

Diagonal Composition 1993 (left)
transparency in light box
40 x 46 cm
collection: the artist

appropriation made possible by a manipulable photographic print (or a printed reproduction). Standing before each work, the viewer is invited, indeed obliged, to mentally reconstitute a specific compositional procedure which derives in varying degrees from something seen, and forgoes any standard technique in favour of a subtle and oblique play on the believability of the photographic image …

In the course of an interview accompanying the 1990 exhibition in Vancouver, Jeff Wall insisted on exactly this element of black humor in his pictures, which he related to the definition of 'reduced' or 'suppressed' laughter given by Mikhail Bakhtin in *Rabelais and his World*: "Black humor, diabolic humor, and the grotesque are very close to each other. Bakhtin talked about the 'suppressed laughter' in modern culture. Things can be laughed about, but not openly. The fact that the laughter is not open gives it a sinister, neurotic, bitter, and ironic quality. It is a kind of mannerist laughter that is similar to Jewish humor, Schadenfreude, and gallows humor. I feel that there is a kind of 'suppressed laughter' running through my work, even though I am not sure when things are funny. *Humour noir* is not the same as the comic, although it includes the comic; it can be present when nobody seems to be laughing."

JEAN-FRANCOIS CHEVRIER
excerpt from 'Play, Drama, Enigma', *Jeff Wall*, trans. by Brian Holmes, exhibition catalogue, The Museum of Contemporary Art, Chicago, 1995, pp. 11-16
quote: ibid, p. 13

Gillian Wearing

Much of Wearing's work is split between ... seemingly contradictory poles — the piece occupies our attention as an objective document of the symbolic in search of the real, while at the same time never vacating the position it holds as an expressive statement of the artist's own subjective experience.

This paradoxical split is potentially a feature of works of a documentary nature. In *10-16*, [for instance] the rigorously nonfictive language of video magnifies these split tendencies following the medium's propensity to de-centre the subject and dissolve the author and spectator alike in the wake of its total flow. It is along these cleavages that Gillian Wearing's art interacts with various documentary traditions and means of representing the self alongside the Other. This same conjuncture serves as the source for many of the rhythmic tensions that one can grasp in her work: those between an interior feeling self and the external display of a mask, between private identifications and their public expression, and ultimately, that area between thought and expression over which is spread a lifetime. It is the slippage back and forth between these states that fascinates Wearing. To chart these fault lines

and trace such movement leads in her work to an intense involvement with identity and its embodiment in language.

As the named author of *10-16*, Gillian Wearing maintains a position both inside and outside the frame of this piece. As in much of her lens-based art that includes collaborators and co-authors from the streets of London, Wearing frames herself as she frames the Other. This builds a reflexivity into the work which helps her negotiate the contradictory status of otherness as both given and constructed, real and fantasmatic. In turn, this reflexive aspect of Wearing's art allows her to retain a fragile, yet tangible, sense of critical distance as she weaves threads from her own biography into the fabric of her subjects' biographies. The Other remains other and is neither subsumed by the whole nor lost in a cloud of over-identification, which leaves ample space in her work for the Othering inherent to representation. This is not to say that her representations are not problematic; they are, deeply.

But rather than brushing aside the problems that arise in representing the Other, Wearing reaches out to the frustrations and the traumas

that we each experience in attempting to represent that which we feel to be real, and part of ourselves. These adversities — that amount to a crisis of representation which we all can relate to personally — then become the matter out of which she makes her art.

In a way, the authors of *10-16* are both resoundingly present and conspicuously absent. This video-text emerges eloquently out of the anonymous and sometimes painfully awkward murmurs of language and identity that unfurl in childhood. As such, *10-16* strikes at the centre of Wearing's person and practice. Perhaps more than any other, this piece shows her art to be not so much about human language and humane communication as material examples of just that. From the start, Wearing aimed to construct a narrative that would recount the rites of passage that take place from ten to sixteen years of age. Seven film segments mark the expansive development and maturation of language and identity that is compressed into those seven short years ... The rites of passage that are elaborated in *10-16* follow the insertion of the subject into the symbolic order and codes of language and identity. The story that Wearing tells here is one

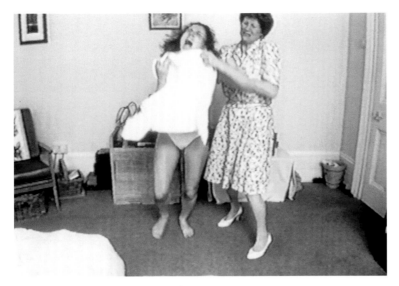

humans and is only mediated by the analogue features of language. The words in her work always take precedence over and above any prized production values. Presentation is in fact only a recent concern — for Wearing, the collusive relationship she forms with her collaborators is still essentially the primary end product of her art …

Gillian Wearing does not suffer the indignity of speaking for others. She listens with an empathy beyond that of language while bringing voices into frame that speak to us all. That one can identify on a humane level with these unconstrained voices means that, in the end, the question that really matters is not: *Who* is speaking? The question is rather: *who* is willing to enter the space Gillian Wearing leaves for us in these very human discourses, and, in so doing, become a subject that speaks, but more importantly, one who also listens.

JOHN SLYCE
excerpt from 'Focus: 10-16, or Life Under the Conditions of Art', *Gillian Wearing*, Phaidon, London, 1999, pp. 74-85

of the birth of a speaking subject. It is, consequently, as much about discovery as it is about loss …

It is through language that we can find the kind of material evidence of social relations that lies embedded in communicative relations. For Wearing this is a crucial factor, since in the cultural context in which her consciousness was formed, language and identity are inseparable — your destiny is defined by the shape, cadence and pronunciation of your words, even more than by your anatomy.

Wearing's employment of video allows us to witness the full range of possibilities and potentialities of the medium in a way that illuminates its more restricted uses. She comes to video through the television screen. Wearing is more a product of British documentaries — broadcast into her home and

family life as a young teen in the mid-1970s — than the offspring of early video artists working in the same period … In her work, her video functions as a theatre of the self. Her pieces are full of electronic intimacy, and yet Wearing consistently pushes this inherently self-referential and narcissistic device, to take stock of and respond to the structural conceits and codes upon which the amassed media of electronic broadcasts rely.

Culture today is wholly a matter of media. Technology and the machine not only govern the mechanization of culture, but increasingly these regimes regulate the flow of private feelings between individuals. Even when saturated by their electronic glow, Wearing's video pieces caution us that meaningful communication, hazardous and imperfect as it may be, takes place in the space between two or more

Take Your Top Off 1993 (opposite)
c-type colour print
75 x 100 cm
courtesy Maureen Paley / Interim Art, London

Sacha and Mum 1996
2 video projection stills
courtesy Maureen Paley / Interim Art, London

Franz West

West's work engenders moments of psycho-physical well-being … It embraces the realization, in the form of direct experience, that the best way to exercise the mind is to allow oneself moments of relaxation …

For instance, all this involves lying half-draped over sofas made out of scrap iron cushioned with soft carpets and placed outdoors during the Documenta before last; sprawling on the roof of the Dia Center in New York; or lounging indoors during the last Lyon Biennale, for the purpose of watching other artists' films or simply to pass the time. Or sitting around on benches and seats in Vienna's National Gallery, observing oneself becoming absorbed in historical paintings. Or strolling through the gardens of the Villa Arson in Nice, or along Münster's public promenade, tempted momentarily to transgress social taboos and use a work of West's in the manner for which it seems to have been intended — that is, as a urinal. How can you not like such an artist?

Is this why curators are so fond of West? Because he forces them to constantly re-examine the criteria on which they base their craft, even the most basic one of assigning artistic value? Do they like him because he rewards minds strained by critical thinking with work that is agreeable or uplifting? Because he brings people together through leisure?

At issue here is not just the relationship between the art work and the consumer … Rather, it is the work's radicalization through the consumer's own actions. By unleashing a chain of interpersonal communication, that is, the work's principal aim becomes affectivity rather than aesthetic value. Over twenty years ago, West initiated a body of research around these topics whose influence is still evident today, in the experiments of many younger artists … Video art, for example, is the dominant mode of the moment. Having attained a spectacular opulence, however, it rehabilitates the concept of art as exorbitant, specialized knowledge; the concept of the artist as demigod; and the notion of spectator as passive consumer

contemplating wonders … West first started questioning this artistic vision in the mid-seventies with his series of *Paßtücke* — literally, "fitting parts", or as he now wishes the word translated, *Adaptives*. At the beginning of that decade, he drew and then painted monochromes. Not long afterwards, he began to deploy the spectator's body, specifically as a qualitative element of the work. In 1973-74, he fastened a pair of red plastic shoes to a length of wood painted yellow, inviting people to put them on; another work required people to undress, put on a shower cap and stand in front of a panel painted green. The same invitation applied to a tie and a pair of socks.

Following these early efforts, West created sculptural pieces out of papier-mâché, plaster and then polyester, ranging from white to colored, from two-dimensional to portable (equipped with handles) to completely free-standing forms, and modeled on everyday objects, only later to become more abstract. As opposed to contemporaries such as Rebecca Horn, whose early body "extensions" … were prostheses for modifying and expanding habitual corporeal experience, West's creations introduced from the first a social element. His work, that is to say, is meaningless until handled, put on, or "lived" — not via the artist's own body or those of his assistants, as in a performance, but via the public body, an anonymous collectivity …

Social collaboration, or interactivity, was West's principal contribution to that multifarious period of exploration during the sixties and seventies, gathered under the rubric of "process art," a generic term which nonetheless calls into question the work of art as an autonomous, marketable end in itself. This contribution was also a strategic way out for the artist, enabling him to differentiate himself from the Viennese *Aktionismus* group which — in spite of his interest in it — he observed with the critical eye of an artist of the following generation …

West redefines artistic labor in the anti-heroic terms of everyday existence. West took this bold step after a long apprenticeship (almost ten years without producing or exhib-

iting anything) in the avant-garde tradition, whose problematic he shares, though, for the most part, it is based upon an organic, all-encompassing vision of global systems and ideologies West abjures.

Undoubtedly … West was one of the first to question the avant-garde's aristocratic isolation from the world, the cultural necessity of which can no longer be ignored today. During the eighties this interrogation was to be found in his utilitarian works, such as the chairs, sofas and, later on, other bits of furniture for which the artist received international recognition. Experientially related to the *Adaptives*, these were first made in similar materials, such as plaster or polyester; since 1987, they have been fabricated in metal, either painted or not. Nothing about the furniture's construction even remotely resembles formal design, its primitive appearance seeming to disavow even the merest trace of style or decoration. Yet these pieces, scavenged from already existing, usually abandoned material, are given new life by West.

West opens up his art to this historical immediacy, offering the public a moment of leisure which, thanks to the sensual stimuli he offers, also becomes a moment of awareness. The social relationships West sets up are thus operational, requiring first presence, then cognizance, evaluation, and eventually the understanding of art as a collective activity, embedded in a social field — this as compared to art as an embrace of the mundane and its myriad instruments. Such a comparison totally vindicates, and in fact revolutionizes, the premises of seventies process art. It offers, as well, a possible solution to the oft-agonized problem of integrating what we are pleased to call "art" and "life".

GIORGIO VERZOTTI
excerpt from *Art/Text* 61, 1998, pp. 61-65

Three times the same 1998
paper mache, gauze, plastic, paint, wood
A: 83 x 26 x 33 cm; B: 57 x 39 x 43 cm;
C: 62 x 42 x 33 cm
courtesy the artist & David Zwirner Gallery,
New York

Xu Bing

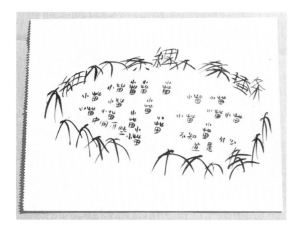

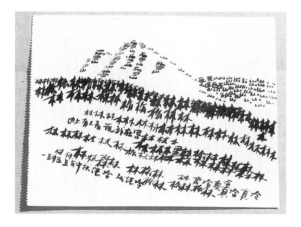

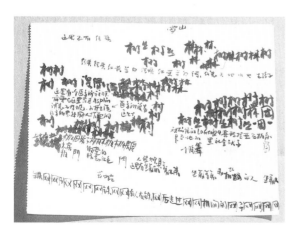

Xu Bing's *Picture Window* has been five years in the making. He first conceived the idea for a window project when he was invited to do a new work for the Joan Miró Foundation in Mallorca, Spain. The Foundation's windows looking out onto the beautiful island landscape provided an ideal vista for Xu to continue his exploration of language and signification. He had planned to adhere printed Spanish words — such as montaña, mar and casa — to the inside surface of the windows according to their relative position in the landscape as viewed from the window. Thus as the viewer moved past the windows the relationship between words and objects would shift, underscoring the arbitrary nature of the relationship between sign and referent. This project seemed particularly well-suited to the Miró Foundation in light of Joan Miró's use of words or fragments of words in his own landscape paintings of the mid-1920s, such as *The Hunter (Catalan Landscape)* (1923-24). That Xu did not realize his window project at the Miró Foundation was due, in large part, to technical difficulties.

In the past few years, Xu has been occupied primarily with developing his system of "New English Calligraphy", in which letters from the English alphabet are combined in a systematic fashion to form words that have the appearance of Chinese characters. This project has taken a number of different forms, including *Introduction to New English Calligraphy* (1996), a classroom where visitors can learn Xu's new calligraphic system by watching an instructional video and practising in exercise books; *Your Surname, Please* (1998), a computer program that translates the visitor's name into the hybrid characters; and *Art for the People* (1999), a banner for The Museum of Modern Art in New York bearing a dictum by Mao Tse Tung printed in "New English Calligraphy".

Xu renewed his relationship to the landscape in 1999 when he was invited to take part in the *Himalaya Project*, as one of six artists who were invited to hike in the Himalayan mountains in preparation for their June 2000 exhibition at Kiasma, Museum of Contemporary Art, in

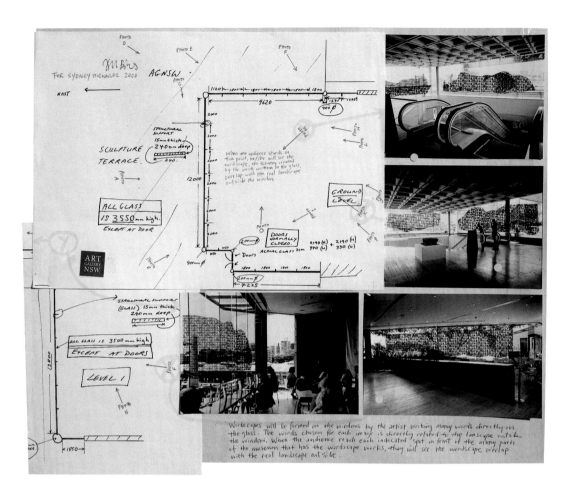

working drawings (left) and proposal (above) for the window project, Art Gallery of New South Wales, *Biennale of Sydney 2000*, courtesy the artist

Helsinki. The terrain and communal atmosphere of the expedition reminded him of the compulsory relocation to the countryside to work alongside peasants that he had experienced as a student. Though Xu Bing was only able to participate in the Himalayan hike for a week, he did a series of small drawings in the area around Namche, rendering images of the mountainous land-scape, winding rivers and roads, and simple wooden edifices in ink using the ancient and modern Chinese characters corresponding to the objects depicted. In Xu's drawings, modern Chinese characters are intermingled with their ancestral forms, which first appeared in the Shang dynasty (1600-1050 BC) and were systematized under Qin rule (221-206 BC). For example, in one drawing a rock partially submerged in a stream is made up of dozens of densely arranged modern characters denoting rock. Encircling the base of the rock is the modern character for moss. The old, squiggly pictographic character for water is scattered around the rock. Xu signifies the

solidity of the rock and the fluidity of the water by modulating the proximity, density, and form of the characters.

After a five year hiatus, Xu has returned to his window project which is finally being realized for the 12th Biennale of Sydney. In many ways the projects Xu undertook in the intervening years have helped him to hone his conception of *Picture Window*. Rather than using the phonetic Roman characters he originally envisioned for the Miró Foundation, Xu has settled on a mixture of the ancient and modern logographic Chinese characters to draw the landscape just beyond the windows of the Art Gallery of New South Wales, demonstrating how language mediates our perception of the world. With the aid of several assistants, he will apply the words designating the elements of the landscape in ink on the window, based on the perspective of a viewer standing at a point approximately eight meters from the window. The words and objects

in the landscape will only be aligned from this one particular position. Although the relationship between words and objects will constantly shift as the viewer moves about the gallery, this is not simply a case of an arbitrary sign system. Xu's landscape refuses to completely dissipate because of the relatively stable relationship of sign and referent engendered by the logographic basis of the Chinese writing system. His *Picture Window* is, moreover, rooted in the long tradition of Chinese landscape painting, in its dual interest in painting and calligraphy, and in its concern with the viewer's experi-ence of the landscape. As with his "New English Calligraphy", Xu has seamlessly merged two distinct traditions — Chinese landscape painting with Western perspectival conventions — subtly disrupting our expectations and point of view once again.

LYDIA YEE
Curator, The Bronx Museum of the Arts
March 2000

Yun Suknam

Although Yun Suknam devoted herself to becoming a professional artist without the baptism of an institutional art education, she is representative of the female artists who have catalysed and formalised discussions on female art in South Korean society. She tells the harsh history of women through the image of the 'mother' which is both a general image of womanhood and a personal matter for the artist.

Yun Suknam's work is an elegy for all mothers who were made to accept obedience as a virtue by Confucian society, and who had to endure the labour of life. It is also a hymn to the mothers who despite the hardship survived with great strength and did not lose dignity. It was not until after the mid-1980's that discussion on feminist art gained a wider forum in South Korea. This parallelled the 1980's social commentary *minjung* art movement in dealing with fundamental human rights issues. However, deep-rooted patriarchal attitudes exist within the progressive art circle as well as within

society generally. Consequently, feminist art has been considered an inferior and peripheral art. Yun Suknam overcomes the double oppression of being a woman and an artist by successfully fusing the themes of her work with an epistemological approach to her work process that is based on her memories and her life.

The artist paints on and engraves the aged and battered pieces of wood found in her surroundings. Her choice of this very manual method of production legitimates the sculptural language which has been neglected because it has been seen as unprofessional.

In previous works the artist has looked back at the past from the eyes of a mother … Her recent installations explore women's issues as a subject which has interested the artist since early 1995, used as a tool to suggest women who are both psychologically and physically insecure. The cushioning, curves and luxurious colours refer to the identity of middle class middle-aged women.

Her brilliantly coloured work expresses women's hopes and their desire to escape from a society that demoralises rather than accepts them.

SOYEON AHN
Curator, Samsung Museum of Modern Art, Seoul
excerpt from *The Second Asia-Pacific Triennial of Contemporary Art,* exhibition catalogue, Queensland Art Gallery, 1996, p.77

The Kitchen 1999
mixed media: clothes, chair, acrylic colour on wood, acrylic beads, glass
300 x 220 x 300 cm approx.
courtesy the artist
photography: Choi Si Young

Pink Room III 1999 (opposite)
mixed media: sofa, clothes, acrylic beads (detail)
dimensions variable
courtesy the artist
photography: Choi Si Young

Artists' biographies

Doug Aitken

Lives and works in Los Angeles. Born in 1968, Aitken has been exhibiting since 1991.

SELECTED SOLO EXHIBITIONS SINCE 1990
1999 *Concentrations 33: Doug Aitken, Diamond Sea*, Dallas Museum of Art, Dallas; Victoria Miro Gallery, London; Doug Lawing Gallery, Houston; Pitti Discovery Series, Pitti Immagine, Florence **1998** 303 Gallery, New York; Jiri Svestka Galleru, Prague; Taka Ishii Gallery, Tokyo; Gallery Side Two, Tokyo **1997** 303 Gallery, New York **1996** Taka Ishii Gallery, Tokyo **1994** 303 Gallery, New York **1993** AC Project Room, New York

SELECTED GROUP EXHIBITIONS SINCE 1990
1999 *Regarding Beauty in Performance and Media Arts*, Smithsonian Institution, Hirshorn Museum and Sculpture Garden; *Biennale di Venezia*, Venice; *Natural Order*, Edmonton Art Gallery, Alberta; *Clues, An Open Scenario Exhibition*, Monte Video, Amsterdam; *Montreal International Festival of New Cinema and New Media*, Montreal; *International Film Festival Rotterdam*, Rotterdam **1998** *New Selections from the Permanent Collection*, Walker Art Centre, Minneappolis; *Portrait – Human Figure*, Galerie Peter Kilchman, Zurich; *La Voie Lactee*, New York; *LA Times*, Palazzo Re Rebaudengo, Guarane; *New Visions: Video 1998*, Long Beach Museum of Art, Long Beach; *Unfinished History*, Walker Art Centre, Minneapolis; *I Love New York – Crossover of Contemporary Art*, Museum Ludwig, Cologne; *Speed*, Photographer's Gallery, London; *Poor Man's Pudding, Rich Man's Crumbs*, AC Project Room, New York; *International Film Festival Rotterdam*, Rotterdam; International Film Festival, Geneva **1997** *The 1997 Whitney Biennal*, The Whitney Museum of American Art, New York; *We Gotta Get Out of the Place*, Cubitt Gallery, London; *One Minute Scenario*, Le Printemps de Cahors, Saint-Cloud; *Doug Aitken and Peter Gehrke*, Galleri Index, Stockholm; *Camera Ascura*, San Casciano dei Bagni; *Doug Aitken, Alex Bag, Naotaka Hiro*, Taka Ishii Gallery, Tokyo; *(re)Mediation: The Digital in Contemporary American Printmaking*, 22 International Ljubljana Biennal of Graphic Art, Cankarjevdom-Cultural and Congress Centre, the Modern Gallery and the Tivoli Gallery, Ljubljana; *Montreal International Festival of New Cinema and New Media*, Montreal; *film+arc.graz*, 3th International Biennale, Graz, Austria **1996** *Campo 6: The Spiral Village*, Galleria Civica D'Arte Moderne e Contemporanea, Turin; Bonnefanten Museum, Maastricht; *29' – 0/ East*, Kunstraum Vienna, Vienna; *29' – 0 /East*, Kunsthalle, New York; *Art in Anchorage*, The Brooklyn Bridge Anchorage, New York; *Doug Aitkin, Mariko Mori, Ricardo Zulueto*, Elga Wimmer Gallery, New York **1995** *La Belle et la Bete*, Museé d'art de la Ville Paris, Paris; *The Image and The Object*, Museo Laboratorio di Arte Contempranea, Roma; Universta Degli Studi di Roma, Rome **1994** *Beyond Belief*, Lisson Gallery, London; *Audience 0.01*, Flash Art Museum, Trevi; Vera Vitagioia, Naples; *New York, New York*, Ma'nes Space, Prague; *Out West and Back East*, Santa Monica Museum of Art, Santa Monica; *Not Here Neither There*, Los Angeles Contemporary Exhibitions, Los Angeles **1993** *Okay Behaviour*, 303 Gallery, New York; *Underlay*, 15 Renwick St, New York; *Doug Aitkin and Robin Lowe*, AC Project Room, New York **1992** *Multiplicity*, Christopher Middendorf Gallery, Washington; *The Art Mall, A Social Space*, The New Museum of Contemporary Art, New York; *Invitational 92*, Stux Gallery, New York **1991** *Artworks/Artworkers*, AC Project Room, New York

PUBLICATIONS
Has featured in numerous international journals and magazines SELECTED READING **1999** *Concentrations 33: Doug Aitken, Diamond Sea*, exhibition catalogue, Dallas Museum of Art, Dallas, TX USA; *EXTRAetORDINAIRE*, exhibition catalogue, Le Printemps de Cahors, St Cloud, France; *Video Cult/ures*, exhibition catalogue, Zentrum fur Kunst und Medientechnologie, Karlsuhe, Germany **1998** *Unfinished History*, exhibition catalogue, Walker Art Center, MN USA; *I Love New York – Crossover of Contemporary Art*, exhibition catalogue, Museum Ludwig, Cologne, Germany; *Metallic Sleep*, artist's book, Taka Ishii Gallery, Tokyo; *Dreams*, artist's book, Sandretto Re Rebaudengo Foundation for Art, Italy

Matthew Barney

Lives and works in New York. Born in San Francisco in 1967, Barney has been exhibiting since 1988.

SELECTED SOLO EXHIBITIONS SINCE 1990
1999 *CREMASTER 2: The Drones' Exposition*, Walker Art Center, Minneapolis **1998** *March with the anal sadistic warrior*, Kunst Kanaal, Amsterdam; *CREMASTER 5*, Fundació La Caixa, Barcelona, Spain; *CREMASTER 5*, Regen Projects, Los Angeles; *CREMASTER 1*, Öffentliche Kunst-sammlung Basel, Kunstmuseum **1997** *CREMASTER 5*, Portikus, Frankfurt; *CREMASTER 5*, Barbara Gladstone Gallery, New York; *CREMASTER 1*, Kunsthalle Wien, Vienna **1996** *Transexualis and Repressia*, *CREMASTER 1* and *CREMASTER 4*, San Francisco Museum of Modern Art, San Francisco **1995** Barbara Gladstone Gallery, New York; The Tate Gallery, London; Fondation Cartier, Paris; Museum Boymans-van Beuningen, Rotterdam, Holland; *PACE CAR for the HUBRIS PILL*, Musée d'art Contemporain, Bordeaux & Kunsthalle Bern (1996) (cat) **1994** *Portraits from CREMASTER 4*, Regen Projects, Los Angeles **1991** Barbara Gladstone Gallery, New York; San Francisco Museum of Modern Art; Regen Projects Los Angeles

SELECTED GROUP EXHIBITIONS SINCE 1990
2000 *Picturing the Modern Amazon*, New Museum, New York **1999** Carnagie International, Carnagie Museum of Art, Pittsburgh; *Regarding Beauty*, Hirshhorn Museum and Sculpture Garden, Washington; *The Promise of Photography: selected works from the DGBank collection*, PS 1, New York **1998** *Wounds Between Democracy and Redemption in Contemporary Art*, Moderna Museet, Stockholm; *Scratches on the surface of things*, Museum Boymans van Beuningen; *Die Rache der Veronika*, Fotosammlung Lambert, Deichtorhallen Hamburg; *Emotion: Young British and American art from the Goetz collection*, Deichtorhallen, Hamburg (cat); *+Zone*, Palazzo Re Rebaudengo, Guarene d'Alba; *Global Vision, New Art from the 90s, with new acquisitions from the Dakis Joannou Collection*, Deste Foundation, Athens; *Extensions: Aspects of the figure*, The Joseloff Gallery, Hartford Art School **1997** *De-Genderism*, Setagaya Art Museum, Tokyo, Japan (cat); *Rrose is a Rrose* is a Rrose, Gender Performance in Photography, Solomon R; Guggenheim Museum (cat), and Andy Warhol Museum, Pittsburgh; *sous le manteau*, Gallery Thaddaeus Ropac, Paris (cat); *Loco-Motion*, Cinema Accademia Dorsoduro, Venice; Biennale de Lyon, Lyon, France **1996** *Hugo Boss Prize Exhibition*, Guggenheim Museum SoHo Branch, New York; *Jusassic Technologies Revenant*, 10th Biennale of Sydney, Sydney (*CREMASTER 1* screening); *Matthew Barney, Tony Oursler and Jeff Wall*, Sammlung Goetz, Munich (cat); *Foreign Body*, Museum fur Gegenwartskunst, Basel; *Hybrids*, De Appel, Amsterdam (cat); *Defining the Nineties: Consensus-making in New York, Miami and Los Angeles*, Museum of Contemporary Art, Miami; *Picasso: a Contempoary Dialog*, Galerie Thaddeaus Ropac, Salzberg; *Passions Privees*, Museé d'Art Moderne, Paris; *Faustrecht der Freiheit*, Neues Museum Weserberg, Bremen; *Art at Home, Ideal Standard Life*, The Spiral Garden, Tokyo (cat) **1995** *Drawing on Chance*, Selections from the Collection, The Museum of Modern Art, New York; *DASAMERICAS II*, Museu de Arte de São Paulo, Brasil; *Ripple Across the Water 95*, WATARI-UM Museum of Tokyo; Biennial Exhibition, Whitney Museum of American Art, New York; *ARS '95*, Museum of Contemporary Art, Helsinki (cat); *The Masculine Masquerade*, MIT List Visual Center, Cambridge; *Altered States: American Art in The 90s*, Forum For Contemporary Art, St. Louis (cat) **1994** *Hors Limites*, Centre Georges Pompidou, Paris (cat); *Of the Human Condition: Hope and Despair at the End of the Century*, Spiral Gallery, Tokyo; *Acting Out – The Body in Video: Then and Now*, Royal College of Art, London; *Sammlung Volkmann*, Berlin; *The Ossuary*, Luhring Augustine, New York; *Drawing on Sculpture*, Cohen Gallery, New York **1993** *Exhibition to Benefit the Mapplethorpe Laboratory for AIDS Research*, Barbara Gladstone Gallery, New York; *Aperto '93*, 45th Venice Biennale, Venice; Biennial Exhibition, Whitney Museum of American Art, New York; *Action/Performance and the Photograph*, Turner-Krull Galleries, Los Angeles; *Works on Paper*, Paula Cooper Gallery, New York **1992** *documenta IX*, Kassel (cat); *Périls et Colères*, CAPC Musée Bourdeaux, Bordeaux; *Post Human*, FAE Musée

d'Art Contemporain, Pully/Lausanne & Castello di Rivoli & Dete Foundation, Athens & Deichtorhallen, Hamburg (cat); *Matthew Barney, Sam Reveles, and Nancy Rubins*, Stein Gladstone Gallery, New York; *Spielhölle*, U-Bahn Station, Frankfurt am Main **1991** Barbara Gladstone Gallery, New York; Regen Projects, Los Angeles; Paula Cooper Gallery, New York **1990** *Viral Infection: The Body and its Discontents*, Hallwalls Contemporary Arts Center, Buffalo; *Drawings*, Althea Viafora Gallery, New York

FILM SCREENINGS
2000 Goteborg Film Festival, Sweden (CREMASTER 2); Metro, London (CREMASTER 2); Kunsthalle Wien, Filmcasino (CREMASTER 2); Ecole des Beaux Arts, Tours, France (CREMASTER 5); Grand Illusion Cinema, Seattle (CREMASTER 2) **1999** Sammlung Goetz, Munich (CREMASTER 5 & 4); Hirschhorn Museum & Sculpture Garden, (CREMASTER 2); Carrnegie International, PA, (CREMASTER 2); MCA Chicago (CREMASTER 2); Film Forum, NY (CREMASTER 2); Detroit Institute of Art (CREMASTER 5 & 1); Pitti Immagine Discovery, Florence (CREMASTER 2); Temple Bar Production, Dublin (CREMASTER 1 & 4); Galssel School of Art, Houston (CREMASTER 4 & 5); Astrup Fearnley Museet, Oslo (CREMASTER 5 & 1); Walker Art Center, Minneapolis (CREMASTER 2); IVAM, Valencia (CREMASTER 4 & 5); Artspace, New Zealand (CREMASTER 5); Temple Bar Production, Dublin (CREMASTER 5); Austin Museum of Art, Texas (CREMASTER 5); Nanjo and Associates, Tokyo (CREMASTER 1); International Film Festival, Cleveland (CREMASTER 4 & 5) **1998** Slamdance Film Festival, Park City Utah (CREMASTER 5); Kunsthalle Vienna (CREMASTER 1 & 4); Rotterdam International Film Festival (CREMASTER 5, *March of the anal sadistic warrior*); Facts and Fiction: Film and Video Festival (CREMASTER 5), Cinema De Amicis, Milano; NAT Film Festival (CREMASTER 5, *March with the anal sadistic warrior*) Copenhagen; Nuart Theater (CREMASTER 5 & 4) Los Angeles; METRO Cinema (CREMASTER 5 & 1) London **1997** Nexus Contemporary Art Center, Atlanta (CREMASTER 1 & 4); C3, Center for Culture and Communication, Budapest (CREMASTER 5); Film Forum, New York, (CREMASTER 5) **1996** Film Forum, New York (CREMASTER 1 & 4); Flicks, Boise, Idaho, (CREMASTER 1 & 4); San Francisco Museum of Modern Art (CREMASTER 1 & 4); Museum of Modern Art, New York (CREMASTER 1); School of the Museum of Fine Arts, Boston (CREMASTER 4) **1995** New York Film Festival (CREMASTER 1); The Metro, London (CREMASTER 4); Joseph Papp Public Theater, New York (CREMASTER 4)

PUBLICATIONS
Has featured in numerous international journals and magazines.

Vanessa Beecroft
Lives and works in New York. Born in Genoa, Italy in 1969, Beecroft has been exhibiting since 1993.

SELECTED SOLO EXHIBITIONS & PERFORMANCES
1999 Galleria Massimo Minini, Brescia; Museum of Contemporary Art, Chicago; Galerie Analix, Geneva; Museum of Contemporary Art, San Diego; Museum of Contemporary Art, Sydney; Galerie Deux, Tokyo; Wacoal Art Center, Tokyo **1998** Galleria d'Arte Moderna, Bologna; Galerie fur Zeitgenossische Kunst, Leipzig; Solomon R. Guggenheim Museum, New York; Fondation Cartier pour l'Art Contemporain, Paris; Galerie Ghislaine Hussenot, Paris; Galerie Axel Morner, Stockholm; Moderna Museet, Stockholm **1997** Galerie Jean Bernier, Athens; Institute of Contemporary Art, Boston; Galerie Analix, Geneva; Institute of Contemporary Art, London; FRAC, Le Nouveau Museé, Lyon; Kunstmuseum, Milwaukee; Stadtisches Museum Abteiberg, Monchengladbach; Galleria Lia Rumma, Naples; Site Santa Fe, II Biennial, Santa Fe; Galleria Il Capricorno, Venice; XLVII Esposizione Internazionale d'Arte, Venice Biennale, Venice **1996** The Dakis Joannou Collection, Athens; CAPC, Musée d'Art Contemporain, Bordeaux; The Renaissance Society at the University of Chicago, Chicago; Ludwig Museum, Cologne; Stedelijk Van Abbemuseum, Eindhoven Fri Art, Centre d'Art Contemporain, Kunsthalle, Fribourg; Galerie Analix, Geneva; Galleria Massimo De Carlo, Milan; Deitch Projects, New York; Galerie Ghislaine Hussenot, Paris; Institute of Contemporary Art, Philadelphia; Galerie Tre, Stockholm **1995** *Inizio di Partita*, Comune di Castelvetro di Modena, Italy; Galerie Analix, Geneva; Palazzina Liberty, Milan; Fondation Cartier pour l'Art Contemporain, Paris; Fuori Uso 95, Pescara **1994** Galerie Schipper & Krome, Cologne; PS 1 Museum, Long Island City; Galleria Massimo De Carlo, Milan; Andrea Rosen Gallery, New York; Trevi Flash Art Museum, Trevi; Castello di Rivoli, Museo d'Arte Contemporanea, Rivoli **1993** Galleria Inga-Pinn, Milan

SELECTED GROUP EXHIBITIONS
1999 *Heaven*, Kunsthalle Düsseldorf, Düsseldorf; *Passagen*, Linkopings Konsthall, Center for Contemporary Art, Linkoping; *The 3rd Art Life 21 – Spiral TV*, Wacoal Art Center, Tokyo; *Photography Salon*, Elizabeth Cherry Contemporary Art, Tucson; *Examining Pictures*, Whitechapel Art Gallery, London; *Unheimlich*, Fotomuseum Winterthur, Switzerland **1998** *Room mates*, Stichting Museum Van Loon, Amsterdam; *Millenovecento*, Galerie Analix, B. Polla & C. Cagnel, Belluno, Italy; *Encyclopedia 1999*, Turner + Runyon, Dallas; *Kritische Elegantie*, Museum Dhondt-Dhaenens Deurle, Deurle, Belgium; *Photographie als*

Handlung, 4 Internationale Photo-Triennale, Galerie der Stadt Esslingen, Esslingen, Germany; *Mille Neuf Cent*, Galerie Analix, Geneva; *Helmut Newton, Vanessa Beecroft, Alix Lambert*, L'Elac, L'espace Lausannois d'Art Contemporain, Lausanne; *Then and Now*, Lisson Gallery, London; *Male Female*, Palazzo Abatellis, Palermo; *Exterminating Angel*, Galerie Ghislaine Hussenot, Paris; *FIAC pas FIAC – Le Théâtre de L'amour*, Galerie Analix, B. Polla + C. Cargnel, Paris; *Veronica's Revenge, from Man Ray to Matthew Barney*, Prague City Gallery, Lambert Art Collection, Prague; *Wounds, Between Democracy and Redemption in Contemporary Art*, Moderna Museet, Stockholm **1997** *Odisseo (Ulysses)*, Stadio Della Vittoria, Bari, Italy; *Arte Italiana, Ultimi Quarant'anni Materiali Anomali*, Galleria d'Arte Moderna, Bologna; *Enterprise, Venture and Process in Contemporary Art*, Institute of Contemporary Art, Boston; *1 Minute Scenario*, Les Printemps de Cahors, Cahors; *Display*, Charlottenborg Exhibition Hall, Copenhagen; *Fatto in Italia*, Centre d'Art Contemporain, Geneva; *Veronica's Revenge, from Man Ray to Matthew Barney*, Centre d'Art Contemporain, Lambert Art Collection, Geneva; *Fracturing the Gaze*, Lawing Gallery, Houston; *Fatto in Italia*, Institute of Contemporary Art, London; *Some Kind of Heaven*, South London Gallery, London; *Identité*, FRAC, Le Nouveau Museé, Lyon; *Vanessa Beecroft, Diana Thater, Tracey Moffatt*, Stadtisches Museum Abteiberg, Monchengladbach; *Heaven*, PS 1 Museum, New York; *Young and Restless*, Museum of Modern Art, New York; *The Name of the Place*, Casey Kaplan Gallery, New York; *Ein Stuck vom Himmel*, Kunsthalle Nurnberg, Nurnberg; *Partito Preso Internazionale*, Galleria Nazionale d'Arte Moderna, Rome; *Persona x*, Salzburger Kunstverein, Salzburg; *Truce, Echoes of Art in an Age of Endless Conclusions*, Site Santa Fe, II Biennial, Santa Fe; *Vanessa Beecroft, Jennifer Bornstein, Martin Kersels & Gillian Wearing*, S.L. Simpson Gallery, Toronto; *BV97, Future, Present, Past*, XLVII Esposizione Internazionale d'Arte, Venice Biennial, Venice; *World Speak Dumb*, Karyn Lovegrove Gallery, Victoria **1996** *Carte Italiane*, Parco Eleftherias, Athens; *Everything that's Interesting is New*, The Dakis Joannou Collection, Deste Foundation, The Factory, Athens; *Push-ups*, The Factory, Athens; *Persona* (The Renaissance Society at the University of Chicago), Kunsthalle Basel, Basel; *To Die by One's Own Hand*, Link, Bologna; *Traffic*, CAPC Musée d'Art Contemporain, Bordeaux; *Museumsfest*, Wallraf-Richartz-Museum and Museum Ludwig, Cologne; *Beige*, Saga Basement, Copenhagen; *ID: An International Survey on the Notion of Identity in Contemporary Art*, Stedelijk Van Abbemuseum, Eindhoven; *Autoreverse 2*, Le

Magasin, Grenoble; *The Scream*, Arken Museum of Modern Art, Ishöj, Denmark; *Doppel Haut*, Kunsthalle zu Kiel, Kiel; *Campo 96*, Konst Museet, Malmo; *Shopping*, Deitch Projects, New York; *Global Tekno 2*, Hotel de Retz, Paris; *You Talking to me? Conversation Piece II*, Institute of Contemporary Art, Philadelphia; *Aufnahmen der Normalität*, Galerie der Stadt Schwaz, Vienna; *Moving*, Projokt Raum, Zurich **1995** *This is Today (Trailer)*, Mediapark, Cologne; *Inizio di Partita*, Comune di Castelvetro di Modena, Modena, Italy; *Vidéos et Films d'Artistes*, Ateliers d'Artistes de la Ville de Marseille, Marseille; *Anni 90, Arte a Milano*, Palazzo delle Stelline, Milan; *Inizio di Partita*, Comunedi Castelvetro di Modena, Modena, Italy; *Show must go on, Les Soirees Nomades*, Fondation Cartier Pour l'Art Contemporain, Paris; *Fuori Uso 95*, Ex Aurum, Pescara, Italy; *Aperto Italia 95*, Trevi Flash Art Museum, Trevi; *Campo 95*, Corderie dell'Arsenale, Venice **1994** *Incertaine Identité*, Galerie Analix, Geneva; *Winter of Love*, P.S.1 Museum, Long Island City; *Prima Linea, The New Italian Art*, Trevi Flash Art Museum, Trevi; *Soggetto-Soggetto, Una Nuova Relazione NellArte di Oggi*, Castello di Rivoli, Museo d'Arte Contemporanea, Rivoli **1993** *Film*, Galleria Inga-Pinn, Milan; *Nuova Ingegneria per l'Osservazione*, Villa Montalvo, Serre di Rapolano

PUBLICATIONS
Has featured in numerous international journals and magazines SELECTED READING **1999** *Art at the Turn of the Millennium*, edited by U. Grosenick & B. Riemschneider, Taschen, Cologne, Germany; *Contemporanee*, E. De Cecco, G. Romano, Costa & Nolan, Milan, Italy; *Regarding Beauty: A View of the Late Twentieth Century*, exhibition catalogue, N. Benezra, O. M. Viso and A. C. Danto, Smithsonian Hirshhorn Museum, Washington, USA **1998** *Cream*, edited by G. Williams, Phaidon, New York, NY USA; *Roommates*, exhibition catalogue, Stichting Museum Van Loon, Amsterdam, Netherlands

Gordon Bennett
Lives and works in Brisbane. Born in Monto, Qld in 1955, Bennett has been exhibiting since 1987.

SELECTED SOLO EXHIBITIONS SINCE 1990
1999-2000 *History and Memory in the Art of Gordon Bennett*, Brisbane City Gallery, Brisbane; Ikon Gallery, Birmingham; Arnolfini, Bristol; Henie Onstad Kunstsenter, Oslo, **1999** *Gordon Bennett*, Sutton Gallery, Melbourne; *Notes to Basquiat: One Tense Moment*, Bellas Gallery, Brisbane; *Notes to Basquiat: One Tense Moment (episode two)*, Sherman Galleries, Sydney **1998** *Home Decor (Calculus)*, Sutton Gallery, Melbourne; *Gordon Bennett*, Bellas Gallery, Brisbane; *Notes to*

Basquiat, Grammercy International Art Fair, New York **1997** *Home Decor (Algebra)*, Bellas Gallery, Brisbane; *John Citizen: Flatland*, Bellas Gallery, Brisbane; *Preston + De Stijl = Citizen (Cold Comfort),* Sutton Gallery, Melbourne; *John Citizen: Sacred Cows*, Sutton Gallery, Melbourne **1996** *Mirror Mirror: The Narcissism of Coloniality*, Canberra School of Art Gallery, Canberra; *John Citizen: Sacred Cows*, Bellas Gallery, Brisbane; *Home Decor (after Margaret Preston)*, Bellas Gallery, Brisbane **1995** *John Citizen: Works on paper*, Sutton Gallery, Melbourne; *BLACK: Fear of Shadows*, Bellas Gallery, Brisbane **1994** *Mirror Mirror (The Inland Sea)*, Sutton Gallery, Melbourne; *Surface Veil*, Bellas Gallery, Brisbane; *Dismember/Remember*, Bellas Gallery, Brisbane; *How to Cross the Void – works on paper*, Sutton Gallery, Melbourne; *Present Wall*, Installation, Institute Building, Adelaide **1993** *A Black History*, Sutton Gallery, Melbourne; *Painting History*, Contemporary Art Centre of South Australia, Adelaide; Drill Hall Gallery, Australian National University, Canberra; *Mirrorama*, Ian Potter Gallery, University of Melbourne, Melbourne; *How to Cross the Void*, Bellas Gallery, Brisbane **1992** *The Colour Black and Other Histories*, Bellas Gallery, Brisbane; *Relative/Absolute*, Bellas Gallery, Brisbane **1991** *Gordon Bennett*, Bellas Gallery, Brisbane; *Dialogues with Self*, Art Gallery of Western Australia, Perth; **1990** *Psycho(d)rama*, Institute of Modern Art, Brisbane; *Gordon Bennett*, Bellas Gallery, Brisbane

SELECTED GROUP EXHIBITIONS SINCE 1990
1999 *Australian Perspecta 99: Living Here and Now – Art and Politics*, Museum of Contemporary Art, Sydney; *The Third Asia-Pacific Triennial of Contemporary Art*, Queensland Art Gallery, Brisbane; *New Worlds, Contemporary Art from Australia, Canada & South Africa*, Canada House Gallery, London; Edmonton Art Gallery, Edmonton; Australian Centre for Contemporary Art, Melbourne; Johannesburg Art Gallery, Johannesburg; *Conceptualist Art: Points of Origin 1950s - 1980s,* Queens Museum of Art, New York; Walker Art Centre, Minneapolis; *Art – Worlds in Dialogue,* Ludwig Museum, Cologne, Germany **1998** *Remanence*, Old Magistrates' Court, Melbourne Festival, Melbourne; *Telling Tales*, Ivan Dougherty Gallery, Sydney; Neue Galerie, Graz, Austria; *The Australian Drawing Biennale*, Drill Hall Gallery, Australian National University, Canberra (touring exhibition) **1997** *Video Positive '97: Escaping Gravity*, Open Eye Gallery, Liverpool; *In Place (Out of Time): Contemporary Art in Australia*, Museum of Modern Art, Oxford **1996** *Systems End: Contemporary Art in Australia*, OXY Gallery, Osaka; Hakone Open-Air Museum, Hakone, Japan; Dong-Ah Gallery, Seoul; Kaohsiung

Museum of Fine Arts, Kaohsiung, Taiwan; *Perception and Perspective*, Next Wave Festival, National Gallery of Victoria, Melbourne; *Inclusion/Exclusion: Art in the Age of Post Colonialism and Global Migration*, Kunstlerhaus Burgring, Graz, Austria; *Colonial Post Colonial*, Museum of Modern Art at Heide, Melbourne; *Fourth Adelaide Biennial of Australian Art*, Art Gallery of South Australia, Adelaide **1995** *Interfaces: Art and Technology*, Regional Touring Exhibition hosted by Griffith University, Brisbane; *TransCulture*, Palazzo Giustinian Lolin, Venice Biennale, Venice; *Naoshima Contemporary Art Museum*, Naoshima Island, Japan **1994/95** *Antipodean Currents*, Guggenheim Museum, SoHo, New York; John F. Kennedy Center for Performing Arts, Washington; *Virtual Reality*, National Gallery of Australia, Canberra **1994** *Localities of Desire: Contemporary Art in an International World*, Museum of Contemporary Art, Sydney; *Fifth Havana Biennial*, Cuba; *Identities: Art from Australia,* Taipei Fine Arts Museum, Taipei; Wollongong City Gallery, Wollongong; Gold Coast City Gallery, Gold Coast; *Adelaide Installations: Incorporating the Adelaide Biennial of Australian Art*, Adelaide **1993** *Inner-Land: Australian Contemporary Art*, Soko Gallery, Tokyo; *Confess and Conceal: 11 Insights from Contemporary South East Asia and Australia*, Art Gallery of Western Australia, Perth, touring South East Asia; *Fifth Australian Sculpture Triennial*, Melbourne; *Aratjara: Art of the First Australians*, Kunstsammlung Nordrhein-Westfalen, Dusseldorf; Hayward Gallery, London; Louisiana Museum of Contemporary Art, Louisiana; Humlebaek, Denmark; *9th Biennale of Sydney: The Boundary Rider*, Bond Store 3/4, Sydney; Art Gallery of New South Wales, Sydney **1992** *Strangers in Paradise: Contemporary Australian Art to Korea*, National Museum of Contemporary Art, Seoul; *Australian Artists In Paris*, Parvi: Pour l'Art Visuel, Paris; *Tyerabarr-bowaryaou: I Shall Never Become A White Man*, Museum of Contemporary Art, Sydney; *Southern Crossings: Contemporary Australian Photography*, Camerawork Gallery, London, touring Britain to 1994 **1990** *Paraculture*, Artists Space, New York; *Adelaide Biennial*, Art Gallery of South Australia, Adelaide

PUBLICATIONS
Has featured in numerous international journals and magazines
SELECTED READING **1998** *White Aborigines. Identity Politics in Australian Art*, Ian McLean, Cambridge University Press, Cambridge, UK **1996** 'The Manifest Toe', *The Art of Gordon Bennett*, Gordon Bennett, Craftsman House / G+B Arts International, Australia **1995** 'Gordon Bennett', *Transculture: La Biennale di Venezia 1995*, Dana Friis-Hansen & Fumio Nanjo, Palazzo Giustionian Lolin, Venice, Italy **1993**

'Painting History', *Gordon Bennett*, Bob Lingard, exhibition catalogue, Contemporary Art Centre of South Australia, Adelaide, Australia; 'Aesthetics and Iconograohy: An Artist's Approach', *Aratjara: Art of the First Australians*, Gordon Bennett, Kunstsammlung Nordien-Westfalen, Dusseldorf, Germany, pp. 85-91

Louise Bourgeois
Lives and works in New York. Born in Paris in 1911, Bourgeois has been exhibiting since 1938.

SELECTED SOLO EXHIBITIONS SINCE 1990
2000 *Louise Bourgeois*, Galerie Hauser & Wirth, Zurich; *Louise Bourgeois: Inaugural Installation of the Tate Gallery of Modern Art at Tubine Hall*, Tate Modern, London; *Louise Bourgeois*, National Museum of Contemporary Art, Kyungki-do, Korea **1999** *Louise Bourgeois*, Galerie Karsten Greve, Köln; *Louise Bourgeois*, Dartmouth College, Jaffe-Friede & Strauss Galleries, Hanover; *Louise Bourgeois*, Kunsthalle Bielefeld, Bielefeld, Germany; *Louise Bourgeois: Topiary*, Piece Unique, Paris; *Wexner Prize Wall*, Wexner Center for the Visual Arts, Columbus; *Louise Bourgeois*, Grafiska Sallskapet, Stockholm; *Louise Bourgeois: Graphic Works*, Remba Gallery, West Hollywood; *Group Show of Drawings and Prints*, William Shearburn Gallery, St Louise; *Louise Bourgeois: Metamorfosis and other works on paper*, Galerie Lelong, New York; *Louise Bourgeois Prints: 1989-1998*, Maier Museum of Art, Randolph-Macon Women's College, Lynchburg & Cleveland & Minneapolis; *Louise Bourgeois: Architecture and Memory*, Museo Nacional Centro de Arte Reina Sofia, Madrid **1998** *Carte Blanche à Annee Djian: The Drawings of Louise Bourgeois*, Espace Saint-Francois, Lausanne; *Sacred and Fatal: The Art of Louise Bourgeois*, North Carolina Museum of Art, Raleigh; *Louise Bourgeois: Topiary,* Whitney Museum of American Art, New York; *Present Tense: Louise Bourgeois*, The Art Gallery of Ontario, Toronto; *Louise Bourgeois: New Work*, Galerie Lars Bohman, Stockholm; *Louise Bourgeois: Art is a Guarantee of Sanity*, Wood St Galleries, Pittsburgh; *Louise Bourgeois: Geometry of Pleasure,* Barbara Krakow Gallery, Boston **1997-1998** *Louise Bourgeois: Homesickness*, Yokohama Museum, Tokyo; *Louise Bourgeois*, The Arts Club of Chicago **1997** Commissioned by the French Government, *Toi Et Moi* is installed in the new Bibliothèque Nationale de Paris; *Louise Bourgeois,* Locks Gallery, Philadelphia; *Louise Bourgeois: Ode à Ma Mere*, The Contemporary Arts Center, Cincinnati; *Louise Bourgeois: Recent Drawings*, Galerie Karsten Greve, Paris; *Louise Bourgeois,* Galerie Karsten Greve, Cologne; *Louise Bourgeois: Blue Days and Pink Days,* Prada Foundation, Milan; *Louise Bourgeois: Drawings*, Rhona

Hoffman Gallery, Chicago **1996-1997** *Louise Bourgeois: Red Room Installation / Drawings*, Galerie Hauser & Wirth, Zurich; *Louise Bourgeois*, Xavier Hufkens Gallery, Brussels **1996** *Louise Bourgeois: Drawings*, University Art Museum, University of California, Berkeley & The Drawing Center, New York & The List Visual Art Center, Massachusetts Institute of Technology, Boston; *Louise Bourgeois: Works on Paper*, Galerie Karsten Greve; *Louise Bourgeois: Spiders,* Baumgartner Galleries, Inc, Washington; *Louise Bourgeois: Sculptures and Objects,* Rupertinum, Salzburg, Austria; *Louise Bourgeois: The Forties and Fifties*, Gallery Joseloff, Harry Jack Gray Center, University of Hartford, Westford; *Louise Bourgeois*, Galerie Soledad Lorenzo, Madrid; **1995-1996** *Louise Bourgeois,* MARCO, Monterrey, Mexico & Centro Andaluz de Arte Contemporaneo, Seville & Museo Rufino Tamayo, Mexico City; *Louise Bourgeois,* National Gallery of Victoria, Melbourne & Museum of Contemporary Art, Sydney **1995** *Louise Bourgeois: Drawings,* L'Ecole Nationale de Beaux Arts de Bourges, France & Galerie Karsten Greve, Paris & Musée National d'art Moderne, Centre Georges Pompidou, Paris; *Louise Bourgeois: Dessins pour Duras,* Theatre du Vieux Colombier, Paris; *Louise Bourgeois,* Mitsubishi-Jisho Artium, Fukuoka City & Walker Hill Art Center, Seoul **1994-1996** *Louise Bourgeois: Print Retrospective,* Museum of Modern Art, New York & Bibliotheque Nationale, Paris & Musée du Dessin et de l'Estampe Originale, Gravelines & The Museum of Modern Art, Oxford & Bonnefanten Museum, Maastricht **1994** *Louise Bourgeois*, Galerie Espace, Amsterdam; *Louise Bourgeois: Drawings and Early Sculptures,* Galerie Karsten Greve, Cologne; *Louise Bourgeois: The Personages,* The Saint Louis Art Museum, St Louis; *Louise Bourgeois,* Nelson-Atkins Museum of Art, Kansas City; *The Louise Bourgeois Papers: A Promised Gift to the Archives of American Art,* Archives of American Art, New York **1993-1996** American Pavilion, Venice Biennale, Venice & The Brooklyn Museum of Art, New York & The Corcoran Gallery of Art, Washington & Galerie Rudolfinum, Prague, Musée d'Art Moderne de la Ville de Paris, Deichtorhallen & Hamburg, Musée d'Art Contemporain de Montreal, Canada **1993-1994** *Louise Bourgeois,* Galerie Ramis Barquet, Monterrey **1992-1993** *Louise Bourgeois,* Ydessa Hendeles Art Foundation, Toronto; National Gallery of Art, Washington **1992** *Louise Bourgeois: C.O.Y.O.T.E,* Parrish Art Museum, Southampton, NY; *Louise Bourgeois: Drawings*, Reykjavik, Iceland; *Louise Bourgeois: Prints 1947-1991*, Barbara Krakow Gallery, Boston; *The Fabric Workshop's 15th Anniversary Annual Benefit Honoring Louise Bourgeois and Anne d'Harnoncourt,* The Fabric

Workshop, Philadelphia **1991** Ydessa Hendeles Art Foundation, Toronto; *Louise Bourgeois: L'Oeuvre Gravée,* Galerie Lelong, Zurich; *Louise Bourgeois: Recent Sculpture,* Robert Miller Gallery, New York **1990** *Louise Bourgeois: Drawings and Sculpture,* Barbara Gross Galerie, Munich; *Louise Bourgeois: 1984-1989,* Riverside Studios, London; *Louise Bourgeois: Bronzes of the 1940s and 1950s,* Galerie Karsten Greve, Cologne; *Bourgeois Four Decades,* Ginny Williams Gallery, Denver

SELECTED GROUP EXHIBITIONS SINCE 1990
2000 *The End: An Independent Vision of Contemporary Culture 1982-2000,* Exit Art, New York; Société des Expositions Du Palais Des Beaux-Arts, Brussels; *Hypemental – Rampant Reality 1950-2000,* Kunsthaus Zurich **1999** *Signs of Life,* The 1999 Melbourne International Biennial; *Art Focus,* The Israel Museum, Jerusalem; *Rosso Vivo,* The Commune di Milano, Milan; *Regarding Beauty: A View of the Late Twentieth Century,* Hirshhorn Museum and Sculpture Garden, Washington & Haus der Kunst, Munich; 48th Venice Biennale, Venice; *Zeitwenden,* Municipal Museum, Bonn; *The Hand,* The Power Plant, Toronto; *Toward a Society for All Ages: World Artists at the Millennium,* United Nations, New York; *The Body in Question: Tracing, Displacing, and Remaking the Human Figure in Contemporary Art,* J.B. Speed Art Museum, Louisville; *Mother and Care: The Image of the Mother in Contemporary Art,* Trinitatiskirche, Köln; *Impact: Revealing Sources for Contemporary Art,* Contemporary Museum, Baltimore; *54x54x54,* Museum of Contemporary Art, London; *The American Century: Art and Culture, 1950-2000,* Whitney Museum of American Art, New York; *Surrealists in Exile and the Beginning of the New York School,* Reina Sofia, Madrid & Musée d'Art Moderne et Contemporain, Strasbourg; *Encounters – New Art from Old,* The National Gallery, London; *Presumed Innocent,* Musée d'art Contemporain de Bordeaux; *The Wounded Film Goddess/Star: Hysteria, Body and Technology in the Art of the 20th Century,* Städtische Galerie im Lenbachhaus, Munich; *Louise Bourgeois,* National Museum of Contemporary Art, Kyungki-do, Korea **1998** *Mirror Images: Women, Surrealism and Self-Representation,* MIT List Visual Arts Center, Cambridge & Miami Art Museum & San Francisco Museum of Modern Art; *Wounds: Between Democracy and Redemption in Contemporary Art,* Moderna Museet, Stockholm; Reykjavik Arts Festival, Iceland; Rene Magritte and Contemporary Art Museum voor moderne Kunst, Oostende; *Premises: Invested Spaces In Visual Arts and Architecture from France 1958-1998,* Solomon R. Guggenheim Museum, Soho, New York & Guggenheim Museum Bilbao;

Cannibalism, XXIV Bienal de São Paulo; *Maschile/Femminile,* Palazzo Abatellis, Palermo & Museo di Castel Nuovo, Napoli & Summer Show Xavier Hufkens Gallery, Brussels; *Les Champs de La Sculpture,* Taipei Fine Arts Museum, Taiwan; *Corps a vif – Art et anatomie,* Ville de Geneve, Musée d'art et d'histoire; *Twentieth Century Sculpture: Inspired by Rodin,* The First Ladies Garden, The White House, Washington; *50 Years of Art: An Exhibit Honoring the Golden Anniversary of The Joe and Emily Lowe Art Gallery at Hudson Guild,* Hudson Guild, New York **1997-1998** *Changing Spaces,* Galerie Rudolfinum, Prague & Miami Art Museum & Arts Festival of Atlanta & Detroit Institute of Arts & ICA, Philadelphia; *Trash,* Museo di Arte Moderna e Contemporanea, Trento; *Frauenmacht und Mannerherrschaft im Kulturvergleich,* Josef-Haubrich-Kunsthalle, Köln **1997** *Chimeriques Polymeres,* Musée d'Art Moderne et d'Art Contemporain, Nice; *L'Empreinte,* Centre Georges Pompidou, Paris; *Inside the Visible: Alternative Views of 20th Century Art Through Women's Eyes,* Art Gallery of Western Australia, Perth; *Form and Function,* Messe Frankfurt, Frankfurt; 1997 Biennial Exhibition, Whitney Museum of American Art, New York; *Epicenter Ljubijana* Moderna Galerija Ljubljana; *Biennale d'art Contemporain de Lyon,* Maison De Lyon; *Masters in Sculpture,* Kukje Gallery, Seoul; *A Decade of Collecting: Recent Acquisitions in Modern Drawing,* The Museum of Modern Art, New York; *Angel, Angel,* Kunsthalle Wien, Vienna & Biennale de Kwangju, Seoul; Fifth International Istanbul Biennial **1996-1997** *Art / Fashion,* Biennale di Firenze, Forte Belvedere, Florence; *Partners in Printmaking: Works from Solo Impression,* The National Museum of Women in the Arts, Washington **1996** São Paulo Bienal, São Paulo, Brazil; *Inside the Visible,* The Institute of Contemporary Art, Boston & National Museum of Women in the Arts, Washington & Whitechapel Gallery, London; *The Material Imagination,* Solomon R. Guggenheim Museum Soho, New York; *Portrait of the Artist,* Anthony d'Offay Gallery, London; *From Figure to Object: A Century of Sculptors' Drawings,* Galerie Karsten Schubert, London **1995-1996** *Surrogates,* Ydessa Hendeles Art Foundation, Toronto **1995** *Revolution in Contemporary Art: The Art of the Sixties,* Museum of Contemporary Art, Tokyo; *Rites of Passage,* The Tate Gallery, London; *ARS 95 Helsinki,* Nyktaiteen Museo, Helsinki; *Drawing the Line,* Southampton City Art Gallery & Manchester City Art Gallery & Ferens Art Gallery, Hull & Whitechapel Art Gallery; *XLVI Esposizione Internazionale d'arte,* Venice Biennale; *A Heart as a Friend,* Triennale di Milano; *In Three Dimensions: Women Sculptors of the 90s,* The Newhouse Center for Contemporary Art, Snug Harbor

Cultural Center, Staten Island; *XI Mostra da Gravura de Curitiba/ Mostra America,* Fundacao Cultural de Curitiba, Brazil; *23 Artistas Para Medicos del Mundo,* Museo Nacional Centro de Arte Reina Sofia, Barcelona; *Feminin-Masculin: Le Sexe de l'Art,* Centre Georges Pompidou, Paris **1994-1995** *From Beyond the Pale,* The Irish Museum of Modern Art, Dublin **1994** *Between Transcendence and Brutality: American Sculptural Drawings from the 1940s and 1950s,* Aspen Art Museum & Arkansas Art Center, Little Rock & The Parrish Art Museum, Southhampton; *le temps d'un dessin,* Ecole des Beaux Arts, Lorient; *Drawings,* Frith Street Gallery, London; *Against All Odds: The Healing Powers of Art,* The Ueno Royal Museum, Tokyo & The Hakone Open-Air Museum, Kanagawa-ken; *Statues Into Sculpture: Twentieth Century Selection from Mid-Western American Art Museums,* The First Ladies Garden, The White House, Washington; *This is the Show and the Show is Many Things,* Museum van Hedendaagse Kunst, Gent **1993-1994** *The Body of Drawing,* Graves Art Gallery, Sheffield & The Mead Gallery, Coventry, Aberdeen Art Gallery, Scotland, Victoria Art Gallery, Bath, Oriel Mostyn Gallery, Llandudno; *Andere Länder – andere Sitten: Zeichnungen aus dem Kunstmuseum Bern,* Palais Kinsky, Nationalgalerie Prague **1993** *Drawing the Line Against AIDS,* Peggy Guggenheim Collection, Venice; *Sculptor's Drawings,* Linda Farris Gallery, Seattle; *Et tous ils changent le monde,* Iléme Biennale d'art Contemporain, Lyon; *Zeitreise. Bilder. Maschinen. Strategien. Rätsel,* Museum fur Gestaltung, Zurich; *Zeichnungen Setzen Zeichen. 44 Künstler der Documenta IX: Arbeiten auf Papier,* Galerie Raymond Bollag 1, Zürich; *De la main à la tête, l'objet théorique,* Centre d'Art Contemporain du Doamine de Kerguéhennec, Bignan, Locminé; *Real Sex,* Salzburger Kunstverein, Salzburg **1992** *documenta IX,* Kassel; *The Coming of Age of American Sculpture,* Lehigh University Art Gallery, Bethlehem & Brunnier Gallery, Iowa State University & Paine Art Center, Oshkosh & Mitchell Art Gallery; *American Masters: Six Artists from the Permanent Collection of the Whitney Museum of American Art,* Whitney Museum at Equitable Center, New York & Whitney Museum of American Art at Champion, Stamford; *In Your Face: Politics of the Body and Personal Knowledge,* A / C Project Room, New York; *From Brancusi to Bourgeois: Aspects of the Guggenheim Collection,* Guggenheim Museum Soho, New York; *Masterpieces From the Guggenheim Collection,* Solomon R. Guggenheim Museum, New York **1991-1992** *Devil on the Stairs: Looking Back on the Eighties,* Institute of Contemporary Art, Philadelphia & The Forum and Washington University Gallery of Art,

St Louis & Newport Harbor Art Museum, Newport Beach & The Hudson River Museum, Yonkers; *Dislocations,* Museum of Modern Art, New York **1991** Illème Biennale de Sculpture, Monte Carlo; *Carnegie International,* The Carnegie Museum of Art, Pittsburgh; *Art of the Forties,* The Museum of Modern Art, New York; *Die Hand Des Künstlers,* Museum Ludwig, Köln **1990** *Inaugural Exhibition Part II – Art in Europe and America: The 1960s and 1970s,* Wexner Center for the Visual Arts, The Ohio State University, Columbus; *The Matter at Hand: Contemporary Drawings,* University of Wisconsin Milwaukee Art Museum; *Coming of Age: American Sculpture,* Emily Lowe Gallery, Hofstra University, Hempstead; *Scultura in America,* Il Biennale Internazionale de Scultera Contemporanea di Matera; *David Smith, Louise Bourgeois, Michael Heizer, Robert Rauschenberg, Donald Sultan, Mark di Suvero,* London Hill Gallery, Birmingham

PUBLICATIONS
Has featured in numerous international journals and magazines.

Cai Guo-Giang
Lives and works in New York. Born in Quanzhou City in 1957, Cai has been exhibiting since 1985.

SELECTED SOLO EXHIBITIONS SINCE 1990
1999 *I Am The Y2K Bug,* Kunsthalle Wien, Vienna (cat) **1998** *No Construction, No Destruction: Bombing the Taiwan Museum of Art,* Taiwan Museum of Art, Taichung, Taiwan (cat); *Daydreaming,* Cheung Piin Gallery, Taipei (cat) **1997** *Cultural Melting Bath: Projects for the 20th Century,* Queens Museum of Art, New York (cat) *Flying Dragon in the Heavens,* Louisiana Museum of Modern Art, Humblebaek, Denmark (cat) **1996** *The Century with Mushroom Clouds – Projects for the 20th Century,* Nevada, Nuclear Test Site, Salt Lake, New York **1994** *Chaos,* Setagaya Art Museum, Tokyo (cat); *Concerning Flame,* Tokyo Gallery, Tokyo (cat); *The Horizon from the Pan-Pacific,* Iwaki, Fukushima, Japan; *From the Pan-Pacific,* Iwaki City Art Museum, Fukushima, Japan (cat); *Calendar of Life,* Gallery APA, Nagoya (cat) **1993** *Project to Extend the Great Wall of China by 10,000 Meters,* Jiayuguan City, China; *Long Mai (The Dragon Meridian),* P3 art and environment, Tokyo **1992** *Wailing Wall – From the Engine of Four Hundred Cars,* IBM Kawasaki City Galley, Kawasaki (cat) **1991** *Primeval Fireball – The Project for Projects,* P3 art and environment, Tokyo (cat) **1990** *Works 1988/89,* Osaka Contemporary Art Center, Osaka

SELECTED GROUP EXHIBITIONS SINCE 1990
1999 *Zeitwenden,* Kunstmuseum Bonn, Bonn; *Art-Worlds in Dialogue,* Museum Ludwig, Cologne; *Beyond The Future,* The Third Asia-Pacific

Triennial of Contemporary Art, Brisbane; *Looking for a Place*, The Third International Biennial, SITE, Santa Fe; *Aperto over All*, 48th Venice Biennial, Venice; *Panorama 2000*, Centraal Museum Utrecht, Netherlands; *Opening SMAK* Museum of Contemporary Art, Gent, Belgium **1998** *Remanence*, Melbourne Festival, Melbourne; *Issey Miyake Making Things*, Fondation Cartier pour l'art contemporain, Paris & ACE Gallery, New York; *Crossings*, National Gallery of Canada, Ottawa; *Inside Out: New Chinese Art*, PS 1, New York & San Francisco Museum of Modern Art & Asian Art Museum of San Francisco & MARCO, Monterey, Mexico & Tacoma Art Museum & Henry Art Gallery, Seattle; *Global Vision: New Art from the 90's part II*, Deste Foundation, Athens; Taipei Biennial *Site of Desire*, Taipei Fine Arts Museum, Taipei; *Where Heaven and Earth Meet*, Art Museum of the Center for Curatorial Studies, Bard College, New York; *La Ville, le Jardin, la memoire: 1998, 2000, 1999*, Academie de France a Rome, Rome; *Wounds: Between Democracy and Redemption in Contemporary Art*, Moderna Museet, Stockholm **1997** *Cities on the Move*, Secession, Vienna & Museum of Contemporary Art Bordeaux, Bordeaux & PS 1, New York & Louisiana Museum of Modern Art, Humblebaek, Denmark & Hayward Gallery, London & Kiasma Museum of Contemporary Art, Helsinki; *On Life, Beauty, Translation, and Other Difficulties*, 5th International Istanbul Biennial, Turkey; *Future, Past, Present*, 47th Venice Biennial, Venice; *Performance Anxiety*, Museum of Contemporary Art, Chicago & Museum of Contemporary Art, San Diego & SITE, Santa Fe,; *Promenade in Asia II*, Shiseido Gallery, Tokyo **1996** *The Hugo Boss Prize 1996*, Guggenheim Museum Soho, New York; *The Red Gate*, Museum van Hedendaagse Kunst, Gent, Belgium; *Origins and Myths of Fire – New Art from Japan, China and Korea*, The Museum of Modern Art, Saitama; *Universalis*, 23rd International Biennial of São Paulo, São Paulo; 2nd Asia-Pacific Contemporary Art Triennial, Queensland Art Gallery, Brisbane; *Between Heavens and Earth – Aspects of Contemporary Japanese Art II*, Nagoya City Art Museum, Japan & Tamayo Museum, Mexico City; *In the Ruins of Twentieth Century*, The Institute for Contemporary Art, PS 1, New York **1995** *Contemplation*, The Ho-Am Museum, Seoul; *Ripple Across the Water*, Watarium Museum of Contemporary Art, Tokyo; *Transculture*, 46th Venice Biennial, Venice; *Art in Japan Today 1985-1995*, Museum of Contemporary Art, Tokyo; The 1st Johannesburg Biennial, Johannesburg; The 51st Scripps Ceramics Annual, Ruth Handler Williamson Gallery, Scripps College, USA **1994** *Heart of Darkness*, Rijksmuseum Kruller-Muller, Otterlo, Holland; *Creativity in*

Asian Art Now, Hiroshima City Museum, Hiroshima; *Well Spring*, Bath Festival Exhibition, Bath; *Open System*, Contemporary Art Gallery, Art Tower Mito, Ibaragi; *Making New Kyoto '94*, Kyoto,; *Promenade in Asia*, Shiseido Gallery, Tokyo **1993** *Silent Energy*, Museum of Modern Art, Oxford; *Outdoor Workshop '93*, The Shigaraki Ceramic Park, Japan **1992** *Encountering the Others*, The Kassel International Art Exhibition, Hann. Monden, Germany; *Das Kunstwerk in Zeitaleer Seiner Telekommunizerbarkeit*, Vienna; *Looking for Tree of Life*, The Museum of Modern Art, Saitama, Japan **1991** Exceptional Passages, Fukuoka **1990** The 7th Japan Ushimado International Art Festival, Okayama, Japan (cat.); *Chine Demain pour hier*, Pourrieres, France (book); *Museum City Tenjin '90*, Fukuoka

PUBLICATIONS
Has featured in numerous international journals and magazines
SELECTED READING **1999** *No Destruction, No Construction – Bombing*, Taiwan Museum of Art, Taichung, Taiwan. **1998** *Cai Guo-Qiang: Day Dreaming*, Chern Piin Gallery, Taipei; *Cai Guo-Qiang Making Oil Paint Drawings in Rome*, Academie de France a Rome-Villa Medicis;. *The Origins of Postmodernity*, Perry Anderson, Verso, London **1997** *Cai Guo-Qiang: Flying Dragon in the Heavens*, Denmark Louisiana Museum of Modern Art; *Cai Guo-Qiang: Cultural Melting Bath: Projects for the 20th Century*, Queens Museum of Art **1994** *Project for Extraterrestrial No. 10, Project to Add 10,000 Meters to the Great Wall of China*, text by Cai Guo-Qiang, Peyotoru Kobo, Tokyo **1992** *Project for Extraterrestrials No. 9, Fetus Movement II*, text by Cai Guo-Qiang, Nomart, Osaka **1989** *Gunpowder paintings of Cai Guo-Qiang*, text by Cai Guo-Qiang, Guilin:Liang Publishing House

Sophie Calle

Lives and works in Paris. Born in 1953, Calle has been exhibiting since 1980.

SELECTED SOLO EXHIBITIONS SINCE 1990
1999 *Double Game*, Camden Arts Centre, London; *Les Tombes*, Galeria Clara Rainhorn, Brussels **1998** *The Birthday Ceremony*, The Tate Gallery, London; *Double Game*, Site Gallery, London **1997** *Relatos*, Centre Cultural de la Fundación "la Caixa", Barcelona; *Comme si de rien n'était*, Fondation Ledig-Rowohlt, Château de Lavigny, Vaud, France; *Suite Vénitienne*, White Cube, London; Donald Young Gallery, Seattle; *Sophie Calle: Last Seen*, in conjunction with *Crossings '97: France/Hawaii*, Honolulu Academy of Arts, Honolulu **1996** *True Stories*, Tel Aviv Museum of Art, Israel; High Museum of Art, Atlanta; *Sophie Calle: Des historires vraies,* Gallery Koyanagi, Tokyo; *Journees d'Art contemporain de*

Porto, Sinagoga de Oporto; *The Detachment*, Galerie Arndt & Partner, Berlin **1995** *Last Seen,* Portalen, Koge Bugt Kulturhus, Greve, Denmark; *Proofs*, University Art Museum, University of California, Santa Barbara & Cleveland Center for Contemporary Art, Cleveland & David Winton Bell Gallery, Brown University, Providence **1994** *Romances*, Contemporary Arts Museum, Houston; *The Husband: Nine Autobiographical Stories*, Fraenkal Gallery, San Francisco; *L'absence*, Musée cantonal des Beaux-Arts, Lausanne; *Absence*, Galerie Chantal Crousel, Paris; FRAC, Provence-Alpes Côte d'Azur, Marseille; Galerie Sollertis, Toulouse; *Sophie Calle: Proofs*, Contemporary Arts Center, Cincinnati; Bockley Gallery, Minneapolis; Sala Amarica, Vitoria-Gasteiz, Spain **1993** *Last Seen*, Leo Castelli, New York; *Sophie Calle: Proofs*, Hood Museum of Art, Dartmouth College, Hannover; Sala Mendoza, Caracas, Venezuela; Museo d'Arte, Maracay, Venezuela **1992** Donald Young Gallery, Seattle; *The Graves*, Mills College Art Gallery, Oakland; *A suivre*, Lunds Konsthalle, Sweden; *Sophie Calle – Les Tombes*, Galerie Sollertis, Toulouse; Galerie Crousel-Robelin, Paris; Centre Cultural Français, Palermo **1991** *Sophie Calle: á suivre*, ARC Museé d'art Moderne de la Ville de Paris; Luhring Augustine/Pat Hearn, New York; Kulturhuset, Stockholm **1990** Institute of Contemporary Art, Boston; Matrix Gallery, University of California at Berkeley, Berkeley; Galeria La Maquina Espanola, Madrid; Galerie Crousel-Robelin Bama, Paris

SELECTED GROUP EXHIBITIONS SINCE 1990
1999 The Jewish Museum, New York; Carlton College Art Gallery, Northfield **1997** *Veronica's Revenge: Photographs form the Lambert Art Collection*, Centre d'Art Contemporain, Genéve; *Trade routes: History and Geography*, Johannesburg Biennale, Johannesburg; Montenegro Biennale, Montenegro; *Sophie Calle: The Husband (Autobiographical Stories) and Other Works*, Society for Contemporary Photography, Kansas City **1996** *NowHere*, Louisiana Museum of Modern Art, Humblebaek, Denmark; *By Night*, Fondation Cartier, Paris; *Imagined Communities*, Oldham Art Gallery, Oldham & John Hansard Gallery, University of Southhampton & Firstsite at the Minorities, Colchester & Walsall Museum and Art Gallery & Royal Festival Hall, London & Gallery of Modern Art, Glasgow; *Pasions Privées*, Musée d'Art moderne de la Ville de Paris, Paris; *More than Real*, Palazzo Reale: Caserta, Galleria Raucci/Santa Maria, Naples; *Carte blanche á fouad bellamine*, Villa Roudani, Casablanca; *Dites-le avec des fleurs*, Galerie chantal Crousel, Paris; *Reels, Fictions, Virtuel*, XXVIIemes: Recontres Internationales de las Photographie, Arles; *1989-*

1995: deuxième époque, FRAC Limousin, France; *For the Museum of Contemporary Art: Sarajevo 2000, the 1996 Collection*, Moderna Galerija, Liubliana, Slovenia; *Art Focus*, Jerusalem; *Féminin-Masculin Cinéma*, Centre Georges Pompidou **1995** *Incidents*, Casa da Parra, Santiago de Compostela; *Art Museum*, Center for Creative Photography, University of Arizona, Tucson; *Els límits del museu*, Fundació Antoni Tàpies, Barcelona; *Photography and Beyond: New Expressions in France*, The Boca Raton Museum of Art, Boca Raton Florida & Museum of Contemporary Photography, Chicago & Museum of Photographic Arts, San Diego & Bard College Museum, New York & The Israel Museum, Jerusalem; Printemps de Cahors, France; *Fetishism*, Brighton Museum & Art Gallery, Brighton & Sainsbury Center for Visual Arts, University of East Anglia, Norwich; *Fantômes et autres revenants*, Château de Biron, Monpazier; *The Vision of Art in a Paradoxical World*, Bienal Internacional de Istanbul, Turkey **1994** *Art & the Social conscience*, Project Row Houses, Houston; *The Psycho-Pathology of Everyday Life*, Ruth Bloom Gallery, Santa Monica; *Arte in Francia, 1970/1993*, Galleria Comunale d'Arte Moderna, Bologna; *Evidence of Death*, The Light Factory, Photographic Arts Center, Charlotte; *Some Went Mad...Some Ran Away*, Serpentine Gallery, London & Museum of Contemporary Art, Chicago & Portalen, Copenhagen; *Endstation Sehnsucht*, Kunsthaus, Zurich; *Gift*, The InterArt Center, New York; *ou les oiseaux selon Schopenhauer*, Musée des Beaux-Arts, Agen, France **1993** Luhring Augustine, New York; *Biennial Exhibition*, Whitney Museum of American Art, New York; *Memories, Facts & Lies*, BlumHelman Gallery, New York; *Blind color*, Leo Castelli, New York; *Doubletake*, Kunsthalle, Vienna; *Documentario 2*, Spazio Opos, Milan; *Nachtschattengewächse*, Museum Fridericianum, Kassel; Luhring Augustine, New York; *Histoire de voir*, Château de Villeneuve, Venice; *Strange Hotel*, Aarhus Kunstmuseum, Aarhus, Denmark **1992** Donald Young Gallery, Seattle; *Doubletake: Collective Memory and Contemporary Art*, Hayward Gallery, London; *Avstand*, Museét fôr Nutids Konst, Helsinki; *Le portrait dans l'art contemporain*, Musée d'Art Moderne et d'Art Contemporain, Nice; *Theoretically Yours*, Chiesa di S Lorenzo, Aosta, Italy; *Bedroom Eyes: Room with a View*, California State University, Fullerton; *France, troisième génération*, World Fair, Sevilla **1991** *L'esprit nouveau: une exposition de l'art contemporain en France*, Museé d'Art Contemporain de Lyon, Lyon; Carnegie International, Pittsburgh **1990** *Autour de Rene Payant*, Museé d'Art Contemporain, Montreal; *The Readymade Boomerang*, 8th Biennale of Sydney,

Sydney; *Seven Obsessions*, Whitechapel Art Gallery, London; *Keys for a Building*, Galerie Crousel-Robelin/Bama, Paris; *Beyond the Photographic Frame*, Mito Arts Foundation, Mito-shi, Japan; *Images in Transition: Photographic Representation Towards the 90s*, The National Museum of Modern Art, Kyoto & The National Museum of Modern Art, Tokyo; Donald Young Gallery, Chicago; *Exposed*, Vivian Horan Fine Art, New York; *Strip-tease de l'intime*, Galerie Urbi & Orbi, Paris

VIDEO SCREENINGS
Double Blind (screened in collaboration with Greg Shephard) **1996** Tel Aviv Museum of Art, Tel Aviv **1994** ICA, London; Festival of Belfort; Festival of Taormina, Taormina, Italy **1993** Kunsthalle, Vienna; Whitney Biennale, New York; Telluride Film Festival, Telluride, Colorado; New York Film Festival, New York

PUBLICATIONS
Has featured in numerous international journals and magazines.

Destiny Deacon
Lives and works in Melbourne. Born in Maryborough, Vic in 1957, Deacon has been exhibiting since 1990.

SELECTED SOLO EXHIBITIONS SINCE 1990
1998 *Postcards From Mummy*, Australian Centre for Photography, Sydney; *It Won't Rub Off, Baby*, Gallery Gabrielle Pizzi, Melbourne **1997** *Inya Dreams*, Festival of Dreaming, Olympic Arts Festival, The Performance Space, Sydney; *No Fixed Dress*, Melbourne International Fashion Festival, Melbourne; *Destiny Deacon*, Gallery Gabrielle Pizzi, Melbourne **1996** *Beauty's Back on Duty*, Hogarth Galleries, Sydney; *Welcome to Never Never*, Gallery Gabrielle Pizzi, Melbourne; *Destiny Deacon*, Rebecca Hossack Gallery, London **1995** *Welcome to Never Never*, Gallery Gabrielle Pizzi, Melbourne; Rebecca Hassock Gallery, London **1994** *My Boomerang Won't Come Back*, Contemporary Art Centre of South Australia, Adelaide

SELECTED GROUP EXHIBITIONS SINCE 1990
2000 *Beyond the Pale*, 2000 Adelaide Biennial, Art Gallery of South Australia, Adelaide **1999** *The Thin Line*, Midsumma Gay and Lesbian Arts Festival, Platform Space, Melbourne; *Signs of Life: The 1st International Melbourne Biennial*, Melbourne; *Processes: ARX5*, Singapore Art Museum, Singapore; *Close Quarters – Art from Australia and New Zealand*, Australian Centre for Contemporary Art, Melbourne **1997** *City Provoked* (Public Art Project), Melbourne International Festival, Royal Melbourne Institute of Technology, Melbourne **1996** *The 2nd Asia-Pacific Triennale*, Queensland Art Gallery, Brisbane; *Abstracts, New Aboriginalities: Destiny Deacon and Brenda L. Croft*, Watershed Media

---

Centre, Bristol; *Inheritance*, Australian Centre for Photography, Sydney **1995** *In the Picture: Creative Australians from the National Library's Portrait Collection*, National Portrait Gallery, Canberra,; *Africus: The 1st Johannesburg Biennale*, Johannesburg; *National Women's Art Exhibition*, Hogarth Galleries, Sydney; *Octette: The Critic's Choice*, Eva Breuer Gallery, Sydney **1994** *Blakness: Blak City Culture!* Australian Centre for Contemporary Art, Melbourne; *Descriptions*, Next Wave Festival, 200 Gertrude Street, Melbourne; *Tyerbarrbowaryaou II*, The 5th Havana Biennale, Havana, Cuba & the Museum of Contemporary Art, Sydney; *True Colours: Aboriginal and Torres Strait Islander Artists Raise the Flag*, Bluecoat Gallery, Liverpool; *An Eccentric Orbit – Electronic Media Art from Australia*, Museum of Modern Art, New York; *Urban Focus: Aboriginal and Torres Strait Islander Art from the Urban Areas of Australia*, National Gallery of Australia, Canberra **1993** *Australian Perspecta* Art Gallery of New South Wales, Sydney; *Can't See for Looking – Koori Women Artists Educating*, National Gallery of Victoria, Melbourne; *Caste Offs: Destiny Deacon and Brenda L. Croft*, Australian Centre for Photography, Sydney; *Yanada, New Moon*, Ivan Dougherty Gallery, Sydney **1992** *Kitch'en Koori*, Fringe Studio, Melbourne **1991** *Kudjeris*, Boomalli Aboriginal Artists Cooperative, Sydney; *Aboriginal Women's Exhibition*, Art Gallery of New South Wales, Sydney & National Gallery of Victoria, Melbourne & Tandanya, Adelaide **1990** *Pitcha Mi Koori*, Friends of the Earth Gallery, Melbourne

PUBLICATIONS
Has featured in numerous international journals and magazines. SELECTED READING **1997** *No Fixed Dress*, exhibition catalogue, D. Deacon and V. Fraser, Gallery Gabrielle Pizzi, Melbourne, Australia; *Inya Dreams by Destiny Deacon*, exhibition catalogue, J. Harding, Performance Space, Sydney, Australia **1996** 'Destiny Deacon', *The 2nd Asia-Pacific Triennial*, exhibition catalogue, C. Williamson, Queensland Art Gallery, Brisbane, Australia **1993** 'Destiny Deacon', *Perspecta 1993*, exhibition catalogue, Hetti Perkins, Art Gallery of New South Wales, Sydney, Australia

---

Stan Douglas
Lives and works in Vancouver. Born in 1960, Douglas has been exhibiting since 1981.

SELECTED SOLO EXHIBITIONS SINCE 1990
1999 *Stan Douglas*, Vancouver Art Gallery, Vancouver & Edmonton Art Gallery, Edmonton & The Power Plant, Toronto & De Pont Museum, Tilburg & MOCA, Los Angeles (cat); *Double Vision, Stan Douglas and Douglas Gordon*, DIA Center for the Arts,

---

New York; *Stan Douglas: Pursuit, Fear, Catastrophe: Ruskin, B.C.*, Fondation Cartier pour l'art contemporain, Paris; *Detroit*, Art Gallery of Windsor, Windsor **1998** *Stan Douglas*, Salzburger Kunstverein, Salzburg; *Detroit Photos*, David Zwirner, New York **1997** *Der Sandmann*, Freedman Gallery, Albright Center for the Arts, Reading; *Evening*, Museum of Contemporary Art, Chicago; *Photography*, Centre genevois de gravure contemporaine, Geneva; *Overture y Monodramas*, Museo Alejandro Otero, Caracas **1996** *Stan Douglas*, Musée d'Art contemporain Montréal, Montréal (cat); *Stan Douglas*, Museum Haus Lange & Museum Haus Esters, Krefeld (cat); *Nootka Sound Photographs*, Zeno X Gallery, Antwerp; *Stan Douglas: Two Early Works*, David Zwirner, New York **1995** *Overture and Marnie*, David Zwirner, New York; *Stan Douglas, Monodramas*, Neueraachenerkunstverein, Aachen; *Stan Douglas*, Marstall, DAAD, Berlin; *Evening and Hors-champs*, The Renaissance Society at the University of Chicago, Chicago (cat); *Stan Douglas: Pursuit, Fear, Catastrophe: Ruskin BC*, Walter Phillips Gallery, Banff **1994** *Currents 24: Pursuit, Fear, Catastrophe: Ruskin BC*, Milwaukee Art Museum, Milwaukee; *Hors-champs*, Contemporary Art Museum, Houston; *Stan Douglas* (with Diana Thater), Witte De With, Centre for Contemporary Art, Rotterdam; *Stan Douglas*, Institute of Contemporary Art, London & Viewpoint Photography Gallery, Salford, England; *Hors-champs/Matrix 123*, Wadsworth Atheneum, Hartford, Connecticut; *Stan Douglas*, Macdonald Stewart Art Centre, Guelph & York University, Toronto (cat); *Stan Douglas*, Centre Georges Pompidou, Paris & Museo Nacional Centro de Arte Reina Sofia, Madrid & Kunsthalle Zurich & Witte de With, Rotterdam & Marstall, DAAD, Berlin (cat) **1993** *Monodramas*, Galerie Christian Nagel, Cologne; *Hors-champs*, Transmission Gallery, Glasgow & World Wide Video Centre, Den Haag & David Zwirner, New York **1992** *Monodramas*, Art Metropole, Toronto; *Monodramas and Loops*, UBC Fine Arts Gallery, Vancouver (cat) **1991** *Monodramas*, Galerie Nationale du Jeu de Paume, Paris

SELECTED GROUP EXHIBITIONS SINCE 1990
2000 *Let Me Entertain You*, Walker Art Center, Minneapolis; *Insistent Memories*, Harn Museum, University of Florida, Gainsville **1999** *Rewind to the Future*, Bonner Kunstverein, Bonn; *The Modernist Document*, Leonard + Bina Ellen Art Gallery, Concordia University, Montreal; *Artist Once-Removed*, Kunstlerhaus Stuttgart; *Liverpool Biennial of Contemporary Art*, Liverpool; *Moving Images: Film-Reflection in Art*, Stedelijk Museum voor Actuele Kunst, Gent; *Gallery Artists Summer Show*, David Zwirner, New York;

Sharawadgi, Felsenvilla, Vienna; *So Faraway, So Close*, Encore Gallery, Brussels; *Notorious: Alfred Hitchcock*, Museum of Modern Art, Oxford: *Views from the Edge of the World*, Marlborough Gallery, New York; *Ecstatic Memory*, Art Gallery of Ontario, Toronto; *Stories of the Moment*, Stadtische Galerie im Lenbachhaus, Munich; *Searchlight: Consciousness at the Millenium*, California College of Arts and Crafts, Oakland; *Seeing Time: Selections from the Pamela and Richard Kramlich Collection of Media Art*, San Fransisco Museum of Modern Art, San Fransisco; *Umwelt/Umweld*, Palais des Beaux-Arts, Brussels; *Crossings*, Rudolfinum, Prague **1998** *Auf Der Spur*, Kunsthalle Zurich, Zurich; *Play Mode*, The Art Gallery, University of California, Irvine & Jean Paul Slusser Gallery, University of Michigan, Ann Arbor; *Stretch*, Tensta Konsthalle, Stockholm; *1998 Images Festival of Independent Film and Video*, Toronto; *Crossings*, Kunsthalle Wien, Vienna & Rudolfinum, Prague; *Ghost Story*, Kunstlerhaus Wien, Vienna; *Reservate Der Sehnsucht*, Hartware Projekte, Dortmund; Herzliya Museum of Art, Herzliya, Israel; *Berlin Biennale*, Berlin; *Altered States Festival*, Utrecht; *Five Years, 1993-1998*, David Zwirner, New York **1997** *Trade Routes: History and Geography*, 1997 Johannesburg Biennale, Institute of Contemporary Art, Johannesburg; *Longing and Memory*, Los Angeles County Museum of Art, Los Angeles; *documenta x*, Kassel; *Skulptur: Projekte in Münster*, Münster; *4e Biennale de Lyon*, Lyon; *The 5th International Biennale in Nagoya-Artec '97*, Nagoya; *Twenty Years … almost*, Robert Miller Gallery, New York; *Between Lantern and Laser: Video Projections*, Henry Art Gallery, Seattle; *Public Service and Other Announcements*, Philadelphia Museum of Art, Philadelphia; *Sharon Lockhardt/Stan Douglas/Hiroshi Sugimoto*, Museum Boymans Van Beuningen, Rotterdam; *MUUten anniversary exhibition*, Museum of Photography, Helsinki; *'97 Kwangju Biennale*, Kwangju; Inaugural Exhibition, Museo Guggenheim Bilbao, Bilbao; *Timeframes*, Freedman Gallery, Albright Center for the Arts, Reading **1996** *100 Photographs*, American Fine Arts, New York; *1996 Hugo Boss Prize*, Solomon R. Guggenheim Museum, New York; *The Red Gate*, Museum van Hedendaagse Kunst, Gent; *Art in the age of Post-colonialism and Global Migration*, Steirischer herbst 96, Graz; *Hall of Mirrors: Art and Film Since 1945*, Museum of Contemporary Art, Los Angeles & The Wexner Center for the Arts, Columbus & Palazzo delle Esposizioni, Rome & Museum of Contemporary Art, Chicago; *Ideal Standard Life*, Spiral Garden, Tokyo & Gallery Seomi, Seoul; *NowHere*, Louisiana Museum of Modern Art, Humblebaek; *Jurassic Technologies Revenant*, 10th Biennale of Sydney, Sydney; *Real*

Fictions: Four Canadian Artists, Museum of Contemporary Art, Sydney; *Antartica Artes com a Folha*, Museum of Image and Sound, São Paulo; *Defining the Nineties: Consensus-making in New York, Miami, and Los Angeles*, Museum of Contemporary Art, Miami; *Instants photographiques: & Oeuvres choisies de la Collection*, Couvent des Cordeliers, Paris; *Everything that's interesting is New*, The Deste Foundation, Athens & The Guggenheim Musem of Art, New York & Museum of Modern Art, Copenhagen; *Nach Weimar*, Kunstsammlungen zu Weimar, Weimar; *Un-frieden: Sabotage von wirklichkeiten*, Kunstverein und Kunshaus in Hamburg, Hamburg; *The Culture of Nature*, Kamloops Art Gallery, Kamloops; *Shifting Shapes: Reading the Shadows*, Bard College, Annandale-on-Hudson; *Rough Bush*, Or Gallery, Vancouver **1995** *3e Biennale d'art Contemporain de Lyon*, Palais de Congres, Lyon; *1995 Carnegie International*, The Carnegie Museum of Art, Pittsburgh; *Video Spaces*, Museum of Modern Art, New York; *A Notion of Conflict: A Selection of Contemporary Canadian Art*, Stedelijk Museum, Amsterdam; *Public Information: Desire, Disaster, Document*, Museum of Modern Art, San Francisco; *L'Effet cinema*, Musée d'Art Contemporain de Montréal, Montréal; *Trust*, Tramway, Glasgow; *Displaced Histories*, Canadian Museum of Contemporary Photography, Ottawa, Ontario; *Spirits on the Crossing*, Setagaya Museum of Art, Tokyo & Hokkaido Museum of Modern Art, Sapporo & National Modern Art Museum, Kyoto; *Das Ende der Avant Garde, Kunst als Dienstleistung*, Sammlung Schürmann, Kunsthalle der Hypo-Kulturstiftung, Munich; *1995 Whitney Biennial*, The Whitney Museum of American Art, New York; *Temporary Translation(s): Kunst der Gegenwart und Fotografie*, Sammlung Schürmann Deichtorhallen, Hamburg; *En passant*, Institut für Gegenwartskunst, Vienna **1994** *In the Field. Landscape in Recent Photography*, Margo Leavin Gallery, Los Angeles; *First Light: Celebrating African Canadian Cinema*, Canadian Artist's Network: Black Artists in Action, Toronto; *Summer Group Show*, David Zwirner, New York; *Notational Photographs*, Metro Pictures and Petzel/Borgmann Gallery, New York; *Theoreticalevents*, Naples; *Beeld/Beeld (Image/Image)*, Museum van Hedendaagse Kunst, Gent; *Een keuze uit de collectie*, Museum van Hedendaagse Kunst, Gent; *Stain*, Galerie Nicolai Wallner, Copenhagen; *The Media*, Magic Media Company, Hürth, Germany **1993** *Self Winding*, Sphere Max, Tokyo & Nanba City Hall, Osaka; *Out Of Place*, Vancouver Art Gallery, Vancouver; *Tele-Aesthetics*, Procter Art Center, Bard College, Annandale-on-Hudson; *Canada – une nouvelle génération*, Musée de Beaux Arts & FRAC Franche-Comté, Dole & Musée

de L'Abbaye Sainte-Croix, Les Sables-d'Olonne; *Working Drawings*, Artspeak Gallery, Vancouver; *Private/Public: Privé/Public*, Winnipeg Art Gallery, Winnipeg; *Behind the Signs*, Artspeak Gallery, Vancouver; *Gent te Gast, de keuze van Jan Hoet uit de collectie van het Museum van Hedendaagse Kunt in Gent*, De Beyerd, Breda **1992** *documenta IX*, Kassel; *The Creation ... of the African-Canadian Odyssey*, The Power Plant, Toronto **1991** *Schwarze Kunst: Konzept zur Politik und Identität*, Neue Gesellschaft für bildende Kunst, Berlin; *Northern Lights: An Exhibition of Canadian Video Art*, Canadian Embassy, Tokyo & Nagoya City Art Museum, Nagoya & Hokkaido Museum of Modern Art, Sapporo; *The Projected Image*, San Francisco Museum of Modern Art, San Francisco **1990** *Privé/Public: Art et Discours Social*, Galerie d'art Essai & Galerie du Cloitre, Rennes & Winnepeg Art Gallery, Winnepeg; *Passage de l'image (Video Program)*, Centre Georges Pompidou, Paris & Fundació Caixa de Pensions, Barcelona; *Aperto '90*, Biennale di Venezia, Venice; *Issues in Contemporary Video*, Mendel Art Gallery, Saskatoon; *The Readymade Boomerang: Certain Relations in 20th Century Art*, The 8th Biennale of Sydney, Art Gallery of New South Wales, Sydney; *Reenactment, Between Self and Other*, The Power Plant, Toronto

PUBLICATIONS
Has featured in numerous international journals and magazines
SELECTED READING **1999** *Moving Images*, exhibition catalogue, Galerie fur Zeitgenossische Kunst Leipzig, Leipzig, Germany; *Stan Douglas*, exhibition catalogue, D. Augaitis, G. Wagner, and W. Wood, Vancouver Art Gallery, Vancouver, Canada. **1998** *Berlin/Berlin*, edited by K Biesenbach, H Ulrich-Obrist and N Spector, Cantz Verlag, Berlin, Germany; *Play Mode*, exhibition catalogue, A. Walsh, The Art Gallery, University of California at Irvine, CA USA; *Stan Douglas*, S. Douglas, Diana Thater, S. Watson, C. J. Clover, Phaidon Press Limited, London, England

Marlene Dumas
Lives and works in Amsterdam. Born in Capetown in 1953, Dumas has been exhibiting since 1979.

SELECTED SOLO EXHIBITIONS SINCE 1990
1999 *MD – Light*, Frith Street Gallery, London; *MD*, Muhka, Antwerp; Camden Arts Centre, London & Henie Onstad Artcenter, Hovikodden **1998** *Miss World*, Galerie Paul Andriesse, Amsterdam; *Fantasma*, Fundacao Calouste Gulbenkian, Centro d'Arte Moderna, Lisbon; *Damenwahl*, Kasseler Kunstverein, Kassal **1997** *Wolkenkeiker*, Produzentengalerie, Hamburg **1996** *Marlene Dumas*, Tate Gallery, London; *Pin-Up*, Museum het Toreke, Tienen; *Youth and Other Demons*, Gallery Koyanagi, Tokyo

1995-1996 *Models*, Salzburger Kunstverein, Portikus-Frankfurt am Maine, NGBK, Berlin **1995** *The Particularity of Being Human: Francis Bacon, Marlene Dumas*, Malmo Konsthall, Castello di Rivoli, Turino **1994** *Not From Here*, Jack Tilton Gallery, New York; *Chlorosis*, Douglas Hyde Gallery, Dublin; *Manneransichten*, Kunst Station Sankt Peter, Cologne **1993** *Give the People What They Want*, Zeno X Gallery, Antwerpen **1992** *Miss Interpreted*, Stedelijk Van Abbemuseum, Eindhoven & ICA, Philidelphia; *Marlene Dumas*, Kunstverein, Bonn & ICA, London & Moore College of Art Philadelphia & Arts Club, Chicago & Art Gallery, Toronto **1990** *The Question of Human Pink*, Kunsthalle Bern

SELECTED GROUP EXHIBITIONS SINCE 1990
1999 *Trouble Spot Painting*, Muhka, Antwerp; *Examining Pictures*, Whitechapel Art Gallery London & Contemporary Art Museum, Chicago; *Regarding Beauty*, Hirschorn Museum and Sculpture Garden, Washington DC **1998** *Szenenwechsel XIII*, Museum fur Moderner Kunst, Frankfurt; *Wounds: Between Democracy and Redemption in Contemporary Art*, Moderna Museet, Stockholm; *Eight People from Europe*, The Museum of Modern Art, Gunma **1997** *Floating Images of Women in Art History*, Tochigi Prefectural Museum of Fine Arts, Tochigi **1996** *Distemper*, Hirshorn Museum, Smithsonian, Washington DC **1995** *Africus, Johannesburg Biennial*, Johannesburg; *XLVI Biennale di Venezia*, Dutch Pavillion, Venice; *Identita e Alterita*, Palazzo Grassi, Venice; *Carnegie International*, Carnegie Museum of Art, Pittsburgh **1994** *Art Pays BAs XXe Siecle: De Concept a L'Image*, Museé d'Art Moderne de la Ville de Paris, Paris; *Cocido Y Crudo*, Museo Nacional Centro de Arte Reina Sofia, Madrid **1992** *documenta IX*, Kassel; *De Opening*, De Pont Stichting, Tilburg; *The 21st Cenury*, Kunsthalle, Berlin; *Der Zerbrochene Spiegel*, Kunsthalle Wien, Deichtorhallen, Hamburg

PUBLICATIONS
Has featured in numerous international journals and magazines.

Rosalie Gascoigne
Born in Auckland in 1917. Rosalie Gascoigne died in Canberra in 1999. Gascoigne began exhibiting in 1972.

SELECTED SOLO EXHIBITIONS SINCE 1990
2000 City Gallery, Te Whare Toi, Wellington **1999** Roslyn Oxley9 Gallery, Sydney **1998** Roslyn Oxley9 Gallery, Sydney; Greenaway Art Gallery, Adelaide; *Material as Landscape*, National Gallery of Australia, Canberra **1997** *Material as Landscape*, Art Gallery of New South Wales, Sydney **1996** National Gallery of Australia, Canberra; Greenaway Art Gallery, Adelaide **1995** Roslyn Oxley9 Gallery, Sydney; Pinacotheca

Gallery, Melbourne **1994** Roslyn Oxley9 Gallery, Sydney **1993** Pinacotheca Gallery, Melbourne **1992** Roslyn Oxley9 Gallery, Sydney **1991** Pinacotheca Gallery, Melbourne

SELECTED GROUP EXHIBITIONS SINCE 1990
1999 *Toi Toi Toi*, Museum Fridericianum, Kassel & Auckland Art Gallery Toi o Tamaki, Auckland; *Clemenger Art Award*, Museum of Modern Art, Heide, Melbourne **1998** *Expanse: Aboriginalities, spatialities and the politics of ecstasy*, University of South Australia Art Museum, Adelaide; *Every Other Day*, Roslyn Oxley9 Gallery, Sydney **1997** *In Place (Out of Time)*, Museum of Modern Art Oxford; *Other Stories: Five Australian Artists*, Bangladesh Biennale, Dhaka & Kathmandu, Nepal & Colombo, Sri Lanka & Hanoi, Vietnam **1996** *Islands*, National Gallery of Australia; *Spirit + Place: Art in Australia 1861-1996*, Museum of Contemporary Art, Sydney **1995** *Island to Island Australia to Cheju*, Cheju Pre-Biennale, Korea; *In the Company of Women: 100 Years of Australian Women's Art from the Cruthers Collection*, Perth Institute of Contemporary Art; *Group Show*, Roslyn Oxley9 Gallery; *Perceived Differently*, Canberra National Sculpture Forum 95, Drill Hall Gallery, Australian National University, Canberra **1994** *Aussemblage*, Auckland City Art Gallery & City Gallery, Wellington; *Reinventing the Grid*, Robert Lindsay Gallery, Melbourne; *Circle, Line, Square – Aspects of Geometry*, Campbelltown Regional Gallery; *Romantisystem*, Canberra Contemporary Art Space, Canberra; *100% Tracy*, 24 Hour Art, NT Centre for Contemporary Art, Darwin **1993** *Clemenger Triennial Exhibition of Contemporary Australian Art*, National Gallery of Victoria, Melbourne; *Identities: Art from Australia to Taiwan*, Taipei Fine Arts Museum, Taiwan & Wollongong City Gallery **1992** *Conversions: Festival of Installation Works*, Canberra Contemporary Art Space, Canberra **1991** *Diverse Visions*, Queensland Art Gallery, Brisbane; *Cross Currents: Contemporary New Zealand and Australian Art from the Chartwell Collection*, Waikato Museum of Art, Hamilton **1990** *Rosalie Gascoigne – Colin McCahon: Sense of Place*, Ivan Dougherty Gallery, Sydney & Ian Potter Gallery, Melbourne; *L'Ete Australian a Montpellier*, Musée Fabre, Montpellier, France; *Strange Harmony of Contrasts*, Roslyn Oxley9 Gallery, Sydney & *Adelaide Biennial of Australian Art*, Art Gallery of South Australia, Adelaide & *The Readymade Boomerang*, 8th Biennale of Sydney, Art Gallery of New South Wales, Sydney

PUBLICATIONS
Has featured in numerous international journals and magazines
SELECTED READING **1997** *In Place: Out of Time*, exhibition catalogue, Museum of Modern Art, Oxford, UK; *Material as Landscape*, exhibition

catalogue, Art Gallery of New South Wales, Sydney, Australia; *Art in Australia: From Colonisation to Postmodernism*, Christopher Allen, Thames and Hudson, UK **1995** *Art Now*, Donald Williams, McGraw Hill Publications; *Islands: Contemporary Installations*, exhibition catalogue, Kate Davidson, Michael Desmond, National Gallery of Australia, Canberra, Australia

Andreas Gursky
Lives and works in Düsseldorf. Born in Leipzig in 1955, Gursky has been exhibiting since 1985.

SELECTED SOLO EXHIBITIONS SINCE 1990
1999 Serpentine Gallery, London; Scottish National Gallery of Modern Art, Edinburgh; Museo d'Arte Contemporanea, Castello di Rivoli; Centro Cultural de Belém, Lissabon; Matthew Marks Gallery, New York; Regen Projects, Los Angeles **1998** The Henry Art Gallery at the University of Washington, Seattle; Columbus Museum of Art, Columbus; Kunstmuseum Wolfsburg; Fotomuseum Winterthur; Contemporary Arts Museum, Houston; Milwaukee Art Museum, Milwaukee; Kunsthalle Düsseldorf **1997** Galerie Javier Lopez, Madrid; Galerie Mai 36, Zürich; Galerie Rüdiger Schöttle, München; Matthew Marks Gallery, New York **1996** Galerie Jean Bernier, Athen; Galerie Ghislaine Hussenot, Paris; Victoria Miro Gallery, London; Monika Sprüth Galerie, Köln **1995** 303 Gallery, New York; Lumen Travo, Amsterdam; Rooseum Centre for Contemporary Art, Malmö; Tate Gallery, Liverpool; Galerie Mai 36, Zürich; Portikus, Frankfurt **1994** Deichtorhallen, Hamburg; De Appol Foundation, Amsterdam; Le Case d'Arte, Mailand **1993** Monika Sprüth Galerie, Köln **1992** Kunsthalle Zürich; Victoria Miro Gallery, London; Galleria Lia Rumma, Neapel **1991** Galerie Rüdiger Schöttle, München; Galerie Johnen + Schöttle, Köln; 303 Gallery, New York; Galerie Rüdiger Schöttle, Paris; Künstlerhaus, Stuttgart

SELECTED GROUP EXHIBITIONS SINCE 1990
1999 *Photography: An Expanded View*, Solomon R. Guggenheim Museum, New York; *Contemplating Pollock*, Victoria Miro Gallery, London; *Räume: Lucinda Devlin, Andreas Gursky, Candida Hofer*, Kunsthaus Brenenz; *Tomorrow for Ever: Photographie als Ruine*, Kunsthalle Krerns; *Robert Grosvenor, Andreas Gursky, John Wesley*, Carnegie Museum of Art, Pittsburgh; *The Big Plcture: Large-Format Photography*, Middlebury College Museurn of Art, Vermont; *Reconstructing Space: Architecture in Recent German Photography*, The Architectural Association, London; *Große Illusionen: Demand, Gursky, Ruscha*, Kunstmuseum Bonn **1998-1999** *Thinking aloud*, Kettle's Yard, Cambridge & Cornerhouse,

Manchester & Camden Arts Centre, London **1998** *Citibank Private Bank Photography Prize 1998*, The Photographers' Gallery, London; *Situationism*, Galerie OMR, Mexico **1997** *Belladonna*, ICA, London; Yokohama Museum of Art; *Junge Deutsche Künstler 2*, Saatchi Gallery, London; *Positionen künstlerischer Photographie in Deutschland seit 1945*, Berlinische Galerie, Martin-Gropius-Bau, Berlin; *Alpenblick*, Kunsthalle Wien; *Landschaften*, Kunstverein für die Rheinlande und Westfalen, Düsseldorf; *About Painting*, Robert Miller Gallery, New York; *Michael Ashkin, Andreas Gursky, Fischli & Weiss*, Andrea Rosen Gallery, New York **1996** *Prospect '96*, Schirn Kunsthalle, Frankfurt; Galerie Antoni Estrany, Barcelona; *Private View*, Bowes Museum, Barnard Castle; *Stadtansichten*, Otto Nagel Galerie, Berlin; *Jurassic Technologies Revenant*, 10th Biennale of Sydney, Sydney; Galerie Specta, Kopenhagen; *La fatografia nell'arte tedesca contemporanea*, Claudia Gian Ferrari Arte Contemporanea, Milano **1995** Fotografiska Museet, Stockholm; *Dicht am Leben*, Internationale Fototriennale, Esslingen; Galerie Busche, Berlin **1994-1996** *Junge deutsche Kunst der 90er Jahre aus NRW*, Sonje Museum of Contemporary Art, Kyongju & Pao Galleries, Hong Kong Arts Centre, Hong Kong, Taipei Fine Arts Museum Centre, Taipei, Kulturpalast der Werktätigen, Peking, National Museum of Art, Osaka, Sun Tec Exhibition, Singapore, National Gallery, Bangkok, Neues Museum, Klovo; **1994** *Vis-à-vis*, Ruhrlandmuseum, Essen; Centre Culturel A. Malraux, Nancy; *The Epic and the Everyday*, Hayward Gallery, London; *Zum gleichen Thema*, Stadtische Galerie, Nordhorn; *La Ville: Intimité et froideur*, Galerie des Archives, Paris; Centro Atlantico de Arte Moderno, Las Palmas, Gran Canaria **1993** *Doubletake: Collective Memory & Current Art*, Kunsthalle Wien; *Siemens Fotoprojekte 1987-1992*, Neue Pinakathek, München & Sprengel Museum, Hannover; *Die Photographie in der deutschen Gagenwartskunst*, Museum Ludwig, Köln; *Distanz und Nähe*, Nationalgalerie Berlin; *Stipendiaten für zeitgenössische deutsche Fotografie der Alfried Krupp von Bohlen und Halbach Stiftung(1990/91)*, Museum Folkwang, Essen; Galerie Tabea Langenkamp, Düsseldorf **1992** *Doubletake: Collective Memory & Current Art*, Hayward Gallery, London; *Mythos Rhein*, Wilhelm-Hauck-Museum, Ludwigshaten; *Qui, quoi, où? Un regard sur l'art de Allemagne en 1992*, Musée d'Art Moderne de la Ville de Paris **1991** *10 Jahre Kunstfonds*, Kunstverein Bonn; Galerie Ghislaine Hussenot, Paris; Photoprojekt München, Kunst im öffentlichen Raum, München; *Aus der Distanz*, Kunstsammlung Nordrhein-Westfalen, Düsseldorf;

Squardo di Medusa, Cestello di Rivoli; *Bremer Kunstpreis*, Kunsthalle Bremen; *Renta Preis*, Kunsthalle Nürnberg; **1990** *Aperto*, Biennale Vendig; *De Afstand*, Witthe De With, Rotterdam; *Der klare Blick*, Kunstverein München; *The Past and the Present of Photography – When Photographs enter the Museum*, The National Museum of Modern Art, Tokyo

PUBLICATIONS
Has featured in numerous international journals and magazines.

Fiona Hall
Lives and works in Adelaide. Born in Sydney in 1953, Hall has been exhibiting since 1974.

SELECTED SOLO EXHIBITIONS SINCE 1990
1999 *Fieldwork*, Roslyn Oxley9 Gallery, Sydney; *A Transit through Paradise*, Gallery 706, Colombo **1998** *Global Liquidity* (with Nalini Malani), Gallery Chemould, Bombay, India & Roslyn Oxley9 Gallery, Sydney; *Cash Crop*, Institute of Modern Art, Brisbane **1997** Canberra School of Art, Canberra **1996** *Call of Nature, Lana H. Foil*, Roslyn Oxley9 Gallery, Sydney **1995** *The Price is Right*, Roslyn Oxley9 Gallery, Sydney **1994** *Garden of Earthly Delights*, National Gallery of Australia, Canberra & National Gallery of Victoria, Melbourne & Art Gallery of New South Wales, Sydney & Plimsoll Gallery, Hobart & Art Gallery of Western Australia, Perth & Brisbane City Hall, Brisbane **1990** *Fiona Hall, Words*, Contemporary Art Centre of South Australia, Adelaide

SELECTED GROUP EXHIBITIONS SINCE 1990
1999 *New Worlds: Contemporary Art from Australia, Canada and South Africa*, Canada House Gallery, London; *Signature Works*, Australian Centre for Photography, Sydney; *Clemenger Art Award*, Museum of Modern Art, Heide, Melbourne; *Tensions*, Griffith Artworks, Griffith University, Queensland; Tasmanian Museum and Art Gallery, Hobart **1998** *Every Other Day*, Roslyn Oxley9 Gallery, Sydney **1997** *Contempora5*, National Gallery of Victoria (Winner inaugural Contempora5 Art Award); *The Enigmatic Object*, Art Gallery of New South Wales; *Perspecta*, Art Gallery of New South Wales; Roslyn Oxley9 Gallery, Sydney; *Archives and the Everyday*, ANU Canberra School of Art Gallery **1996** *The Power To Move; Aspects of Australian Photography*, Queensland Art Gallery, Brisbane; *96 Containers*, Adelaide Festival of the Arts, Adelaide; *Death*, Lewers Bequest and Penrith Regional Art Gallery; *How Say You*, Australian Centre for Contemporary Art, Melbourne; *Inheritance*, Australian Centre for Photography, Sydney; *Colonial/Post Colonial*, Museum of Modern Art at Heide, Melbourne; *Container 96 – Art Across Oceans*, Copenhagen; *Asia Pacific Triennale*, Queensland

Art Gallery, Brisbane; *Photography is Dead! Long Live Photography!* Museum of Contemporary Art, Sydney; *Art Cologne Internationaler Kunstmarkt*, Köln Messe; *Art Rage 96*, compilation for ABC TV video (collaboration with Destiny Deacon) **1995** *The Object of Existence*, Australian Centre for Contemporary Art, Melbourne **1994** *Biodata*, Adelaide Installations, Adelaide Festival; *Fania*, University of South Australia Art Museum; *Localities of Desire*, Museum of Contemporary Art, Sydney; *Sydney Photographed*, Museum of Contemporary Art, Sydney **1993** *Dante in Australia*, Dante Centre, Ravenna, Italy **1992** *Adelaide Festival Artists' Projects*, Festival Centre, Adelaide; *The Temple of Flora*, Waverley City Gallery, Melbourne **1991** *Photodeath*, Australian National Gallery, Canberra; *The Corporeal Body*, Drill Hall Gallery, Australian National University, Canberra; *Australian Perspecta*, Art Gallery of New South Wales, Sydney; *Stranger than Fiction*, Australian National Gallery, Canberra; *Second Nature*, P3 Art and Environment, Tokyo **1990** *Harbour Hymns, City Songs*, Art Gallery of New South Wales, Sydney; *Adelaide Biennale of Australian Art*, Art Gallery of South Australia, Adelaide; *Art Contemporain Australien*, Noumea, New Caledonia; *Photography: Recent Acquisitions*, Australian National Gallery, Canberra; *Fragmentation and Fabrication: Recent Australian Photography*, Art Gallery of South Australia, Adelaide; *Terminal Garden*, Experimental Art Foundation, Adelaide; *Twenty Contemporary Australian Photographers*, National Gallery of Victoria, Melbourne & Art Gallery of New South Wales, Sydney; *Art from Australia: Eight Contemporary Views*, Bangkok & Jakarta & Singapore & Kuala Lumpur & Manila, VACB & Dept. of Foreign Affairs and Trade

PUBLICATIONS
Has featured in numerous international journals and magazines
SELECTED READING **1998** *Canberra Projects*, exhibition catalogue, National Gallery of Australia, Canberra, Australia; *Cash Crop*, exhibition catalogue, Institute of Modern Art, Brisbane, Australia **1997** 'Fiona Hall: Retro-spect Leura's Theme', *A Small History of Photography*, G. Newton, in Stuart Koop ed, CCP Melbourne, Australia; *Archives & the Everyday*, exhibition catalogue, Canberra Contemporary Art Space, Australia **1995** *Subject to Change*, exhibition catalogue, Experimental Art Foundation, Adelaide, and Piper Press Sydney, Australia

Bill Hammond
Lives and works in Lyttleton, New Zealand. Born in Christchurch in 1947, Hammond has been exhibiting since 1982.

1999 *Melting Moments*, Brooke/Gifford Gallery, Christchurch **1998** *Blood Bin, Sin Bin*, Gregory Flint Gallery, Auckland; Brooke/Gifford Gallery, Christchurch; Peter McLeavey Gallery, Wellington **1997** *Headscape*, Gregory Flint Gallery, Auckland; *Plain and Fancy*, Brooke/Gifford Gallery, Christchurch; Peter McLeavey Gallery, Wellington **1996** Peter McLeavey Gallery, Wellington; Gregory Flint Gallery, Auckland; Brooke/Gifford Gallery, Christchurch **1995** Gregory Flint Gallery, Auckland; Brooke/Gifford Gallery, Christchurch; *Bill Hammond Unplugged*, Peter McLeavey Gallery, Wellington **1994** *Walter Buller Blind*, Gregory Flint Gallery, Auckland; Peter McLeavey Gallery, Wellington **1993** Gregory Flint Gallery, Auckland; Brooke/Gifford Gallery, Christchurch; Peter McLeavey Gallery, Wellington **1992** *Japan*, Gregory Flint Gallery, Auckland **1991** Gregory Flint Gallery, Auckland; Peter McLeavey Gallery, Wellington; Brooke/Gifford Gallery Christchurch **1990** Peter McLeavey Gallery, Wellington

SELECTED GROUP EXHIBITIONS SINCE 1990
1999 *Home and Away: Contemporary Australian and New Zealand Art From the Chartwell Collection*, Auckland Art Gallery; *The Asia Pacific Triennial*, Queensland Art Gallery, Brisbane **1998-1999** *Dream Collectors*, Museum of New Zealand Te Papa Tongarewa, Wellington & Auckland Art Gallery, Dunedin Public Art Gallery **1998** *Skywriters and Earthmovers*, McDougall Contemporary Art Annex, Christchurch **1995-1996** *Hangover*, Waikato Museum of Art and History, Hamilton & Govett-Brewster Art Gallery, New Plymouth & Robert McDougall Art Gallery, Christchurch & Dunedin Public Art Gallery **1995** *A Very Peculiar Practice*, City Art Gallery, Wellington **1994** *Good Works*, Robert McDougall Art Gallery, Christchurch; *Frizzell, Hammond, Stevenson: Three Painters*, Gregory Flint Gallery, Auckland **1993** *Comfort Zone*, Govett-Brewster Art Gallery, New Plymouth **1992** *Distance Looks Our Way: Ten Artist From New Zealand*, Sarjeant Gallery Wanganui & Pubellon de las Arles, Expo, Seville & Stelling Gallery, Leiden & Centro Cultural de Conde Duque, Madrid & Centro Cultural de Caja Espana, Zamora & Centre Civic Casa Elizaide, Barcelona & Auckland City Art Gallery & City Art Gallery Wellington; *Headlands Thinking Through New Zealand Art*, Museum of Contemporary Art, Sydney & Museum of New Zealand, Wellington; *Vanitas*, McDougall Contemporary Art Annex, Robert McDougall Art Gallery, Christchurch; *Prospect Canterbury '92*, Robert McDougall Art Gallery, Christchurch **1991** *Jamming*, Brooke/Gifford Gallery, Christchurch; *Chilcott/Hammond*, Gregory Flint Gallery, Auckland; *Telling Pictures* Dunedin Public Art Gallery

PUBLICATIONS
Has featured in numerous international journals and magazines
SELECTED READING **1999** *Home and Away: Contemporary Australian and New Zealand Art from the Chartwell Collection*, edited by W. McAloon, Auckland Art Gallery in association with David Bateman, Auckland, New Zealand **1998** *Dream Collectors: One Hundred Years of Art in New Zealand*, A. Johnston and I. Wedde, Te Papa Press, Wellington and Auckland Art Gallery, Auckland, New Zealand; *Skywriters and Earthmovers*, E. Caldwell and F. Milburn, Robert McDougall Art Gallery and Annex, Christchurch, New Zealand **1997** *Contemporary New Zealand Art 1*, E. Caughey and J. Gow, David Bateman, Auckland, New Zealand **1995** *Hangover*, ed R. Leonard, P. Pitts and L. Strongman, Dunedin Public Art Gallery, Govett-Brewster Art Gallery, New Plymouth & Waikato Museum of Art and History, Hamilton, New Zealand

Gwyn Hanssen Pigott

Lives and works in Brisbane. Born in Ballarat in 1935, Hanssen Pigott has been exhibiting since 1961.

SELECTED SOLO EXHIBITIONS SINCE 1990
2000 Galerie Besson, London **1999** Garth Clark Gallery, New York **1998** Christine Abrahams Gallery, Melbourne; Rex Irwin Art Dealer, Sydney **1997** *Gwyn Hanssen Pigott: Bowls and Still Lifes*, Craftwest Gallery, Perth; Galerie B15, Munich **1996** *Gwyn Hanssen Pigott: A Twenty Year Survey*, Queensland Art Gallery, Brisbane; Garth Clark Gallery, New York; *Small Works*, Narek Galleries, Canberra **1995** Christine Abrahams Gallery, Melbourne; Rex Irwin, Sydney **1993** Crafthouse Gallery, CCBC, Vancouver; Garth Clark Gallery, New York **1992** Galerie Besson, London; Ballarat Fine Art Gallery, Victoria **1991-1995** *PRO-ART*, St. Louis; **1990-1991** Narek Gallery, Tharwa; Margaret Francey Gallery, Brisbane

SELECTED GROUP EXHIBITIONS SINCE 1990
2000 *Defining Moments in Contemporary Ceramics*, Los Angeles County Museum of Art, California; *Return of Beauty*, Jam Factory Gallery, Adelaide **1999** *(Un)Limited: Repetition and Change in International Craft*, UK Crafts Council, London; *Artists from the World*, Faenza, Italy; *Contemporary Australian Craft*, Hokkaido Museum of Modern Art, Japan **1998-1999** *The Ceramic Still Life*, Dowse Art Museum & Auckland Art Museum, New Zealand; *10th Anniversary Exhibition*, Campbelltown City Bicentennial Art Gallery, NSW **1998** *A View of Clay*, Contemporary Applied Arts, London; *The Contemporary Teapot*, Keramikmusset Grimmerhus, Middelfart, Denmark **1997** *International Ceramic Art*, Faenza, Italy; *Australische Keramik*, Galerie Handwerk, Munich & Kunstgewerbemeuseum, Dresden;

Then & Now, Meat Market Craft Centre, Melbourne; *The Somatic Object*, Ivan Dougherty Gallery, Sydney; *Sydney Myer Fund Acquisition Award*, Shepparton Art Gallery; *Containment*, Plimsoll Gallery, Hobart & Tasmania & Victoria; *Still-Life Still Lives*, Art Gallery of SA; *Material Perfection: Minimal Art and its Aftermath, A Selection from the Stokes Collection*, Lawrence Wilson Art Gallery, University of WA **1996** *Australian Wood-Fire Survey*, Strathnairn Ceramics Association and *Vessel: Contemporary Australian Ceramics*, Canberra School of Art Gallery, both in conjunction with the 8th National Ceramics Conference, Canberra; *Aurora*, Australian wood, metal, glass, fibre & ceramics RMIT, Melbourne & Seoul Arts Centre, Korea; *Objects of Ideas*, Ten Approaches to Contemporary Craft Practice, touring exhibition by Queensland Regional Galleries **1995** *Aspects of Minimalism*, Garth Clark Gallery, New York; *VicHealth National Craft Award 1995*, NGV, Melbourne **1994-1995** *Sydney Myer Fund Acquisition Award*, Shepparton Art Gallery **1994** *The Art of the Object*, Craft Australia touring exhibition, Uruguay, Brazil & Chile; *Martin Hanson Memorial Art Award*, Gladstone Regional Art Gallery; *Gold Coast National Ceramic Art Award*, Gold Coast City Art Gallery; *Daikyo North Queensland Award*, Cairns Regional Art Gallery **1992-1995** *Fletcher Challenge Ceramics Award* **1993** *Woodfire*, Studio 20 Galley, Blackwood; *Delegates Exhibition*, 7th National Ceramics Conference University of SA; *The Raw and the Cooked*, Barbican Art Gallery, London; *Confrontations*, Ivan Dougherty Gallery, Sydney; *48th International Ceramic Art*, Faenza, Italy **1992** *Australia: New Design Visions*, 2nd Australian International Crafts Triennial, AGWA; *Le Bol*, Galerie Leonelli, Lausanne; *The Ceramic Still Life*, Garth Clark Gallery, New York; *VicHealth National Craft Award*, NGV, Melbourne; *Cinafe Exhibition*, Narek Gallery, Chicago; *Jahresmesse Kunsthandwerk*, Hamburg, Applied Art Museum; *6th National Ceramics Exhibition*, Thailand; *Small Works Wide Vision*, Downlands Art Exhibition, Qld; *Sturt Potters*, NSW Government Exhibition, Tokyo **1991** *Une Passion pour la Ceramique*, La Collection Fina Gomez, Museé des Arts Decoratifs, Paris; Asia Pacific Crafts Exhibition, Kyoto **1990** *La Borne en Feu*, La Borne, France; *Homage to Morandi*, Garry Anderson Gallery, Sydney

PUBLICATIONS
Has featured in numerous international journals and magazines
SELECTED READING **1998** 'Truth in Form', *Studio Potter*, G. Hanssen Pigott, USA January; *Ceramic Form: Design and Decoration*, P. Lane, Collins, London & Rizzoli NY, revised edition; *Material Perfection: Minimal Art & its Aftermath*, catalogue essay, J. Stringer, Lawrence Wilson Art

Gallery, University of Western Australia **1997** *Masters of their Craft*, N Ioannou, Craftsman House; 'Notes from Netherdale', *Ceramics Art and Perception*, G. Hanssen Pigott, No. 27 **1993** *The raw and the cooked: new work in clay in Britain*, exhibition catalogue, Museum of Modern Art, Oxford

Bill Henson

Lives and works in Melbourne. Born in 1955, Henson has been exhibiting since 1974.

SELECTED SOLO EXHIBITIONS SINCE 1990
2000 *Bill Henson*, Roslyn Oxley9 Gallery, Sydney **1999** *Bill Henson*, Karyn Lovegrove Gallery, Los Angeles **1998** *Bill Henson*, Roslyn Oxley9 Gallery, Sydney; *Bill Henson*, ACP Galerie Peter Schuengel, Salzburg **1997** *Bill Henson*, Deutscher Fine Art, Melbourne; Melbourne International Festival of Arts, Melbourne **1996** *Bill Henson*, Banning and Associates, New York; *Bill Henson, Works from the 46th Venice Biennale*, Lawrence Wilson Gallery, Perth & Museum and Art Gallery of the Northern Territory, National Gallery of Victoria, Melbourne, Art Gallery of New South Wales, Sydney, Plimsoll Gallery University of Hobart; *Bill Henson: Photographs from the Monash City Council Collection*; *Bill Henson, Recent Works from 1995/96*, Roslyn Oxley9 Gallery **1995** *Bill Henson, 46th Venice Biennale*, Australian Pavilion; *Bill Henson*, Galerie Froment & Putman, Paris; *Bill Henson, Photographs*, Peter McCleavey Gallery, Wellington **1993** Bill Henson, Tel Aviv Museum of Art; Bill Henson, University of Tasmania, Tasmanian School of Art, Hobart; *Bill Henson, Works from Untitled 1992-93*, Roslyn Oxley9 Gallery; *Bill Henson Work from Two Decades 1970s – 1990s*, Deutscher Fine Art, Melbourne; *Bill Henson Selected Works*, Geelong Regional Art Gallery **1992** *Works From The Paris Opera Project*, Roslyn Oxley9 Gallery, Sydney; *Bill Henson*, Perspektief Gallery, Rotterdam **1991** *Bill Henson Photographies*, Les Ateliers Nadar, Marseille; *Works from the Paris Opera Project*, Realities Gallery, Melbourne; *Bill Henson*, Peter McCleavey Gallery, Wellington **1990** *Bill Henson Installation 1985/86*, Urbi et Orbi, Paris; *Bill Henson Photography*, Denver Art Museum; *Bill Henson Photography*, Marta Cevera Gallery, New York; *Bill Henson*, Nathalie Karg Gallery, New York Bill Henson, Glendash Gallery, Los Angeles; *Bill Henson Photographs*, Bibliotheque Nationale, Paris; *Bill Henson Untitled 1977/87*, Milburn + Arte, Brisbane; *Bill Henson. Images from 'Untitled 1987/88'*, Roslyn Oxley9 Gallery, Sydney; *Bill Henson Photographs 1974-84*, Garry Anderson Gallery, Sydney

SELECTED GROUP EXHIBITIONS SINCE 1990
2000 *Biennale of Sydney*; *Millennium Exhibition*, Los Angeles County Museum of Art Museum; *Presumed*

Innocent, CAPC Museé d'Art contemporain de Bordeaux, France **1999** The Promise of Photography: Selections from the DG Bank Collection, P.S.1 Contemporary Art Center, New York; Moral Hallucinations: Channelling Hitchcock, Museum of Contemporary Art, Sydney; Ghost in the Shell – Photography and the Human Soul 1850-2000, Los Angeles County Museum of Art; 13 – Blind Spot Summer Show, Robert Mann Gallery, New York **1998** Liberamente, Comune di Cescna **1997** Body, Art Gallery of New South Wales, Sydney; Roslyn Oxley9 Gallery, Sydney; Bill Henson, Philip-Lorca DiCorcia, Sarah Jones, Galerie Gebauer, Berlin **1996** System's End: Contemporary Art In Australia, Oxy Gallery, Osaka; From The Street: Photographs From The Collection of Art Gallery of New South Wales, Sydney; Inheritance, Australian Centre for Photography, Sydney; International Basel Art Fair '96, Basel; Photography is Dead! Long Live Photography! Museum of Contemporary Art, Sydney; Australian Art-Colonial to Contemporary 1780-1990, DFA; Face Value, Waverley City Gallery, Sydney; Cologne Art Fair, Cologne **1995** 30th Artists Today Exhibition, Yokohama Citizen's Art Gallery, Yokohama; Through a Glass Darkly, Guinness Contemporary Art Project, Art Gallery of New South Wales; Passions Privee, ARC Museé D'Art Modern D'La Ville De Paris **1994** Bill Henson & Ranier Usselmann, Cambridge Darkroom; Pride-of-Place, Art Gallery of Western Australia; The Full Spectrum: – Colour Photography in Australia 1860s to 1990s, National Gallery of Victoria; Printemps de Cahors France, Cartier Foundation **1993** Clemenger Triennial Exhibition of Australian Contemporary Art, National Gallery of Victoria; Presences, London Photographers Gallery; Museum of Contemporary Art, Korea; Sights of the Imagination: Contemporary Photographers View Melbourne and Its People, National Gallery of Victoria; Art Cologne 1992, Roslyn Oxley9 Gallery; Group Show, Roslyn Oxley9 Gallery **1991** Des De El Fin Del Imperio, Circulo De Bellas Artes, Madrid; The Corporeal Body, Australian National Gallery, Canberra; Corriger Les Lieux, Apres La Photographie De Voyage, Maison de la Culture, Frontenac, Montreal; Photodeath, Australian National Gallery, Canberra; Egypt From the Nineteenth Century Until Now, Montpellier Museum; Sphynx: Bathazar Burckhard, Bill Henson, Thomas Ruff, & Susan Wides, Galerie Pierre Bernard, Nice; Peuples En Image: Weegee, Bill Henson, Roy Arden, Raymonde April and Anne Favrat, Le Lieu Galerie de Photographies, Lorient; Elegia de la Mirada, Raymonde April, Bill Henson, Patrick Tosani, Thomas Ruff, Jeff Wall. Sala de Arte la Recova, Santa Crus de Tenerife **1990** Edge 90, Newcastle upon Tyne & Glasgow, London; Twenty Contemporary Australian Photographers 'From the Hallmark Cards Australian Collection', National Gallery of Victoria & Art Gallery of New South Wales, Queensland Art Gallery, regional galleries; Passages De L'Image, Centre George Pompidou, Paris; Wexner Art Centre, Colombus & San Francisco Museum of Modern Art; Fundacio Caixa de Pensions, Barcelona

PUBLICATIONS
Has featured in numerous international journals and magazines
SELECTED READING **1998** The Promise of Photography: The DG Bank Collection, edited by L. Sabau, Prestel, Munich, Germany **1997** Body, exhibition catalogue, Art Gallery of New South Wales, Sydney, Australia; Art in Australia – From Colonisation to Postmodernism, C. Allen, Thames and Hudson **1995** 'Bill Henson', Through A Glass Darkly, exhibition catalogue, M. Heyward, Art Gallery of New South Wales; Bill Henson, exhibition catalogue, Australian Pavilion, 46th Venice Biennale, Venice **1993** Bill Henson: Paris Opera Project, exhibition catalogue, P. Craven, Tel Aviv Museum of Art

Gary Hill
Lives and works in Seattle. Born in California in 1951, Hill has been exhibiting since 1972.

SELECTED SOLO EXHIBITIONS SINCE 1990
1999 Aarhus Kunstmuseum, Aarhus, Denmark; School of the Museum of Fine Arts, Boston; Gary Hill: Video Works, NTT InterCommunication Center (ICC), Tokyo; A name, a kind of chamber, two weapons and a still life, Barbara Gladstone Gallery, New York; Galleria Lia Rumma, Milan; Whitney Museum of American Art, New York; Barbara Gladstone Gallery, New York **1998** Musée d'Art Contemporain de Montréal, Montreal, Quebec; Gary Hill: Reflex Chamber, Rice University Art Gallery, Houston; Fundação de Serralves, Porto, Portugal; Donald Young Gallery, Seattle; Capp Street Project, San Francisco; St. Norbert Arts and Cultural Center, Manitoba, Canada; Museu d'Art Contemporani, Barcelona; Saint-Gervais, Genève; The Kitchen, New York **1997** Westfälischer Kunstverein, Münster; Tall Ships: Gary Hill, Museum of Art, University of California, San Diego; Midnight Crossing and Remarks on Color, Ujazdowski Castle, Centre for Contemporary Art, Warsaw **1996** Gary Hill: Withershins, Institute of Contemporary Art, Philadelphia; Galerie des Archives, Paris; Kunst- und Ausstellungshalle der Bundesrepublik Deutschland, (Forum) Bonn; Galleria Lia Rumma, Naples; Donald Young Gallery, Seattle; Barbara Gladstone Gallery, New York; White Cube, London **1995** Gary Hill, Moderna Museet, Stockholm & Museet for Samtidskunst, Oslo & Kunstforeningen, Copenhagen & Helsingfors Konsthall, Helsinki & Bildmuseet, Urneå, Sweden &Jönköpings Läns Museum, Jönköping, Sweden & Göteborgs Konstmuseum, Göteborg, Sweden & Busch-Reisinger Museum, Harvard University Art Museums, Cambridge **1994-95** Gary Hill, Hirshhorn Museum and Sculpture Garden, Washington, & Henry Art Gallery; Museum of Contemporary Art, Chicago & Museum of Contemporary Art, Los Angeles & Guggenheim Museum SoHo, New York & Kemper Museum of Contemporary Art and Design, Kansas City **1994** Gary Hill, Musée d'Art Contemporain, Lyon; Imagining the Brain Closer than the Eyes, Museum für Gegenwartskunst, Öffentliche Kunstsammlung, Basel **1993-94** Gary Hill: In Light of the Other, Tate Gallery Liverpool, Liverpool & Museum of Modern Art, Oxford **1993** Gary Hill: Sites Recited, Long Beach Museum of Art, Long Beach; Gary Hill, Donald Young Gallery, Seattle **1992-93** Gary Hill, Musée National d'Art Moderne, Centre Georges Pompidou & IVAM Centre Julio Gonzalez, Valencia & Stedelijk Museum, Amsterdam & Künsthalle, Vienna **1992** Stedelijk Van Abbemuseum, Eindhoven, The Netherlands; Gary Hill, Le Creux de L'Enfer, Centre d'Art Contemporain, Thiers; I Believe It Is an Image, Watari Museum of Contemporary Art, Tokyo **1991** Galerie des Archives, Paris; OCO Espace d'Art Contemporain, Paris; Nykytaiteen Museo: The Museum of Contemporary Art, Helsinki **1990** Galerie des Archives, Paris; Galerie Huset/Ny Carlsberg Glyptotek Museum, Copenhagen; YYZ Artist's Outlet, Toronto; Museum of Modern Art, New York

SELECTED GROUP EXHIBITIONS SINCE 1990
1999-2000 The American Century: Art & Culture, Part II 1950-2000, The Whitney Museum of American Art, New York; Seeing Time: Selections from the Pamela and Richard Kramlich Collection of Media Art, San Francisco Museum of Art, San Francisco **1999** Somewhere Near Vada, Project Arts Centre, Dublin; TV Gallery, Moscow; Passage a l'art: des lieux et des choses, Forum Culturel du Blanc-Mesnil, Le Blanc-Mesnil, France; Umedalen Skulptur 99, organized by Galleri Stefan Andersson, Umeå, Sweden; The Hand, The Power Plant Contemporary Art Gallery, Toronto; Transmute, Museum of Contemporary Art, Chicago; Romancing the Brain, Pittsburgh Center for the Arts, Pittsburgh; Re-Structure, Grinnell College Art Gallery, Grinnell; Surrogate: The Figure in Contemporary Sculpture and Photography, Henry Art Gallery, Seattle; Crossings, Kunsthalle Wien, Austria, & Galerie Rudolfinum, Prague; Blickwechsel, ZKM, Karlsruhe, Germany **1998** Anos 80, Culturgest, Gestão de Espaços Culturais, Lisbon; Tuning up #5, Kunstmuseum Wolfsburg, Wolfsburg; Made in Corpus, Odyssud, Blagnac, France; Personal Effects: The Collective Unconscious, Museum of Contemporary Art, Sydney; 3rd Werkleitz Biennial, Werkleitz, Germany **1997** Angel, Angel, Kunsthalle Wien, Vienna; Citta' Natura, Palazzo delle Esposizioni, Rome; The Twentieth Century: The Age of Modern Art, Martin-Gropius-Bau, Berlin & Royal Academy of Arts, London & Biennale d'Art Contemporain, Lyon; Unimplosive Art, Milan; Water: The Renewable Metaphor, University of Oregon Museum of Art, Eugene; Kwangju Biennale, Kwangju; World Wide Video Festival, Amsterdam; The Objects in Hangar 2, Seattle Arts Commission, Sand Point Naval Base, Seattle; Surveying the First Decade: Video Art and Alternative Media in the United States, San Francisco Museum of Modern Art, San Francisco; Amours, Fondation Cartier pour l'art contemporain, Paris **1996-97** Being and Time: The Emergence of Video Projection, Albright-Knox Art Gallery & Cranbrook Art Museum, Bloomfield Hills & Portland Art Museum, Portland & Contemporary Arts Museum, Houston & Site Santa Fe, Santa Fe **1996** One and Others: Photography and Video by Juan Downey, Angela Grauerholz, Gary Hill, Alfredo Jaar, Annette Messager, Galerie Lelong, New York; NowHere, Louisiana Museum of Modern Art, Humlebaek, Denmark; Worldwide Video Festival, Den Haag, The Netherlands; Le Printemps de Cahors Photographie & Arts Visuels, Fondation Cartier pour l'art contemporain, Paris & Portalen Koge Bugt Kulturhus, Greve, Denmark; The Last Supper, Donald Young Gallery, Seattle; Hamburger Bahnhof - Museum für Gegenwart, Berlin; The Red Gate, Museum Van Hedendaagse Kunst Gent **1995** ARS '95 Helsinki, The Finnish National Gallery, Helsinki; Pour un couteau, Le Creux de l'Enfer, Le Centre d'Art Contemporain, Thiers, France; Altered States: American Art in the 90's, Forum for Contemporary Art, St Louis; Sculptures Sonores: Une Certaine Perspective Communique, Ludwig Museum im Deutschherrenhaus, Koblenz, Germany; Identità e Alterità, Venice Biennale, Venice; Video Spaces: Eight Installations, Museum of Modern Art, New York; Longing and Belonging: From the Faraway Nearby, Site Santa Fe, Santa Fe; Carnegie International, Carnegie Museum of Art, Pittsburgh; Biennale d'Art Contemporain, Lyon **1994** Beeld, Museum van Hedendaagse Kunst, Ghent; Múltiplas Dimensões, Centro Cultural de Belém, Lisbon; São Paulo Bienal, São Paulo; Facts and Figures, Lannan Foundation, Los Angeles; Light Into Art: From Video to Virtual Reality, Contemporary Arts Center, Cincinnati; Cocido y Crudo, Centro de Arte Reina Sofia, Madrid; Intelligent Ambience and Frozen Images, Long Beach Museum of Art, Long Beach

1993 London Film Festival, London; *'Strange' HOTEL*, Aarhus Kuntsmuseum, Aarhus, Denmark; *American Art in the 20th Century, Painting and Sculpture 1913-1993*, Royal Academy, London; Centro Cultural Arte Contemporaneo, Mexico City, Mexico; *1993 Whitney Biennial in Seoul*, National Museum of Contemporary Art, Seoul; *Fifth Fukui International Video Biennal*, Fukui, Japan; *American Art in the 20th Century, Painting and Sculpture 1913-1993*, Martin-Gropius-Bau, Berlin; *The 21st Century*, Künsthalle Basel, Basel; *The Binary Era: New Interactions*, Künsthalle, Vienna; *Biennial Exhibition*, Whitney Museum of American Art, New York; *Doubletake: Collective Memory and Current Art*, Künsthalle, Vienna **1992** *Performing Objects*, Institute of Contemporary Art, Boston; *Metamorphose*, St. Gervais-Genève, Geneva; *Manifest*, Musée national d'art moderne, Centre Georges Pompidou, Paris; *Art at the Armory: Occupied Territory*, Museum of Contemporary Art, Chicago; *The Binary Era: New Interactions*, Musée d'Ixelles, Brussels; *Filmladen Festival*, Kassel, Germany (also Botschaft Festival, Berlin & Hinterhaus, Wiesbaden); *Dance*, California Museum of Photography, Riverside; *documenta IX*, Museum Fridericianum, Kassel; *Passages de l'image*, San Francisco Museum of Modern Art, San Francisco; *Japan 92 Video and Television Festival*, Tokyo; *Doubletake: Collective Memory & Current Art*, Hayward Gallery, London; *Japan: Outside/Inside/Inbetween*, Artists Space, New York; Donald Young Gallery, Seattle **1991** *Biennial Exhibition*, Whitney Museum of American Art, New York; *Currents*, Institute of Contemporary Art, Boston; *The Body (2)*, The Renaissance Society at the University of Chicago, Chicago; *In Public: Seattle, 1991*, Security Pacific Gallery, Seattle; *Metropolis*, Martin-Gropius-Bau, Berlin; *Topographie 2: Untergrund*, Wiener Festwochen, Vienna; *Artec '91 International Biennale*, Nagoya, Japan; *Glass: Material in the Service of Meaning*, Tacoma Art Museum, Tacoma **1990** *Tendances multiples (Videos des Annees 80)*, Musée national d'art moderne, Centre Georges Pompidou, Paris; *Energieen*, Stedelijk Museum, Amsterdam; *Passages de l'image*, Musée national d'art moderne, Centre Georges Pompidou, Paris, France (travelling exhibition); *L'Amour de Berlin: Installation Video*, Centre Culturel, Cavaillon, France; *Bienal de la Imagen en Movimiento '90*, Centro de Arte Reina Sofia, Madrid; *God & Country*, Greg Kucera Gallery, Seattle

SELECTED PERFORMANCES

1998 Performance by Gary Hill, George Quasha and Charles Stein at the Musée d'art contemporain de Montreal **1996-1998** *Splayed Mind Out*, Collaboration with Meg Stuart and the dance company Damaged Goods. Performed in Europe, South

America and the United States **1996** *Touching*, & other works, at the Speakeasy Cafe, Seattle **1993** Performance by Gary Hill, George Quasha and Charles Stein for "Gary Hill: Day Seminar" at the University of Oxford in conjunction with the exhibition entitled *Gary Hill: In Light of the Other*; Performance by Gary Hill, George Quasha, Charles Stein and Joan Jonas at Long Beach Museum of Art, Long Beach

PUBLICATIONS

Has featured in numerous international journals and magazines SELECTED READING **1999** *Gary Hill*, edited by A. Kold, Aarhus Kunstmuseum, Aarhus **1998** *Gary Hill: HanD HearD – Withershins – Midnight Crossing*, exhibition catalogue, H. Liesbrock, G. Quasha and C. Stein, Museu d'Art Contemporani de Barcelona, Barcelona; *Gary Hill*, exhibition catalogue, Musée d'art contemporain de Montréal, Montreal **1994** *Gary Hill*, exhibition catalogue, texts by L. Cooke, B. W. Ferguson, J. G. Hanhardt, and R. Mittenthal, Henry Art Gallery **1993** *Gary Hill: In Light of the Other*, exhibition catalogue, texts by C. Diserens, B. Ferguson, S. Morgan, L. Nittve and R. Mittenthal, The Museum of Modern Art Oxford and Tate Gallery Liverpool **1991** *L'Oeuvre Video de Gary Hill*, C. Devriendt Université de Rennes II, Rennes

---

Ilya & Emilia Kabakov

Ilya (1933) and Emilia Kabakov were born in Dniepropetrousk, Ukraine, USSR. They live and work in New York. Ilya Kabakov has exhibited since 1965, and worked with Emilia since 1989.

SELECTED SOLO EXHIBITIONS SINCE 1990

2000 *Monument To A Lost Civilization*, Telstra Adelaide Festival, University of South Australia Art Museum, Adelaide & Cantiera Culturali alla Zisa, Palermo **1998-1999** *The Children's Hospital, Kabakov in Moscow*, The Irish Museum of Modern Art, Dublin; *Art Angel Project, The Palace of Projects by Ilya and Emilia Kabakov*, The Roundhouse, London & Upper Campfield Market, Manchester, Reina Sofia, Crystal Palace, Madrid **1998** *The Meeting*, Deweer Art Gallery, Otegem; *The Collector*, Thaddaeus Ropac Galerie, Salzburg; *16 Installations*, Muhka Museum, Antwerp; *The Healing with Memories*, Nationalgalerie im Hamburger Bahnhof, Museum fur Gegenwartskunst, Berlin **1997** *The Life of Flies*, Babara Gladstone Gallery, New York; *Monument to the Last Giove*, Public Art Fund, New York; *The Artist's Library*, Satani Gallery, Tokyo; *The Fallen Chandelier*, Hochhaus zur Palme, Zurich; *The Hospital: Five Confessions*, Capp Street Project, San Fransisco; *Drawings and*

Albums, Weisses Schloss Gallery **1996** *Ilya Kabakov: Storyteller*, Portalen I Greve, Koge Bugt, Kulturhus, Copenhagen; Nordjyllands Kunstmuseum, Aalborg; *Der Lesesaal (The Reading Room)*, Deichtorhallen, Hamburg; *Books: A Retrospective with Drawings*, Barbara Gladstone Gallery, New York; *The Healing with Painting*, Kunsthalle, Hamburg; *The World of Ilya Kabakov*, guild Hall Museum, East Hampton **1995** *Metaphysical Man*, Kunsthalle Bremen; *The Man Who Never Threw Anything Away*, Meseet for Samtidkunst; *C'est ici que nous vivons*, Centre George Pompidou, Paris; *No Water*, Osterreichisches Museum fur Angewandte Kunst, Wein; *The School Library*, Stedelijk Museum, Amsterdam; *The Boat of My Life, Unrealised Projects*, Festspeilhaus Hellrau, Dresden **1994** *Operation Room*, Nykytaiteen Museo, Helsinki; *Die Verzweiflung des Künstler oder die Verschwörung der Untalentierten*, Galerie Barbara Weiss, Berlin; *Album of My Mother, The Golden Underground River, Boat of My Life*, Le Magasin, Grenoble; *In the Apartment of Nikolai Victorovich*, Jablonka Galerie, Köln; *Unrealized Projects*, Art Centre, Reykjavik **1993** *Het Grote Archief*, Stedelijk Museum, Amsterdam; *Das leere Museum*, Staaliche Hochschule für Bildende Künst, Frankfurt; XLV Venice Biennale, Venice; *The Boat of My Life*, Salzburger Kunstverein; *NOMA oder der Kreis der Moskauer Konzeptualisten*, Kunsthalle, Hamburg; *Communal Kitchen*, Museé Maillol, Paris **1992** *Das Leben der Fleigen*, Kunstverein, Köln; *Unaufgehängtes Bild (Unhung Pictures)*, Ludwig Museum, Köln; *Illustration as a Way to Survive*, Kanaal Art Foundation, Kortrijk & Ikon Gallery, Birmingham, Centre of Contemporary Arts, Glasgow; *Incident at the Museum of Water Music*, RFFA, New York; Museum of Contemporary Art, Chicago; Hessisches Landesmuseum, Darmstadt, Centro de Asrte Moderna da Fundaçao Gulbenkian, Lisbon **1991** *Meine Heimat: die fliegen (My Motherland: The Flies)*, Wewerka und Weiss Galerie, Berlin; *Die Zielscheiben (The Targets)*, Peter Pakesch Galerie, Wein; *Ilya Kabakov, Sezon Museum of Modern Art, Nagano; *52 Entretiens dans la Cuisine Communautaire*, Ateliers Municipaux d'Artistes, Marseille; La Criée, Rennes **1990** *He lost his mind, Undressed, Ran Away Naked*, RFFA, New York; *The Rope of Life and Other Installations*, Fred Hoffman Gallery, Santa Monica; *Ten Characters*, Hirshon Museum and Sculpture Garden, Washington; *Seiben Austellungen eines Bildes (Seven Exhibitions of a Painting)*, Kasseler Kunstverein, Kassel; *Das Schiff (The Ship)*, Neue Galerie, Sammlung Ludwig, Aachen

SELECTED GROUP EXHIBITIONS SINCE 1990

1998-1999 *The History of Interior: from Vermeer to Kabakov*, Stadel Institute, Frankfurt **1998** *7 Triennale der Klinplastik*, Struttgart **1997** Whitney Biennal, New York; *Monde Future*, XLVII Biennale, Corderie, Venice; *Sculpture of XX Century*, Münster; *Collection of Centre Georges Pompidou*, Museum of Contemporary Art, Tokyo **1996** *G7 Summit*, Museé d'Art Contemporain, Lyon; *Les peches captaux: la Paresse*, Centre George Pompidou, Paris **1995** *Africas*, Biennale Johannesburg; *Eks limits del museu*, Fundacion Antoni Tapies, Barcelona; *Changes of Scene VIII*, Museum fur Modern Kunst, Frankfurt; *The Test of Destiny*, International Biennale, Kwangju; *New Orientation, The Vision of Art in a Paradoxical World*, 4th Biennale, Istanbul **1994** *Toponimias: ocho ideas del espcio*, Fundacion La Caixa, Madrid; *Tyanneir des Schonen*, Osterreichesches Museum fur Angewandte Kunst, Wien; *Virtual Reality*, National Gallery of Australia, Canberra **1993** *Le Magasin*, Centre Nationale d'Art Contemporain, Grenoble; *Rendez(-)Vous*, Museum van Hedendaagse Kunst, Gent; *Et tous ils changent le monde*, Biennale d'Art Contemporain, Lyon; *Russusche Avantgarde in 20 Jahrhundert: von Malevitch bis Kabakov*, Kunsthalle, Köln **1992** *documenta IX*, Kassel; *A Mosca ... A Mosca*, Villa Campolieto, Ercolano; Galeria communale d'arte moderna, Bologna; *Parallel Visions: Modern Artists and Outsider Art*, County Museum of Art, Los Angeles **1991** *Binationale: Sowietsche Kunst um 1990, The Red Wagon*, Kunsthalle, Dusseldorf & Israel Museum, Jerusalem; *Devil on the Stairs: Looking Back on the Eighties*, Institute of Contemporary Art, Philadelphia & Newport Harbour Art Museum, Newport Beach; *Dislocations*, Museum of Art, Pittsburg; *Schereios (Weightless)*, Grosse Orangerie of Charlottensburg Palace, Berlin; *Wanderlieder*, Stedelijk Museum, Amsterdam **1990** *The Readymade Boomerang: Certain Relations in the 20th Century Art*, 8th Biennale of Sydney, Sydney; *Die Endlichkeit der Freiheit Berlin 1990: ein Ausstellungsprojekt in Ost und West*, DAAD-Galerie, Berlin; *In de USSR en erbuiten*, Stedelijk Museum, Amsterdam; *Works on Hanji Paper*, Art Festival, Seoul; *Rhetorical Image*, The New Museum of Contemporary Art, New York

PUBLICATIONS

Have featured in numerous international journals and magazines SELECTED READING **1999** *Monument To A Lost Civilization*, exhibition catalogue, ed Chiara Bertola & Paulo Falcone, Charta, Milan **1998** *The Palace of Projects*, Artangel, London; *Stimmen Hinter Der Tür 1964-1983 (Voices Beyond the Door)*, Galerie für Zeitgenossuche-Kunst, Leipzig; *16 Installaties (16 Installations)*, Mukha, Museum

143

van Hedendaagse-Kunst, Antwerp **1996** *Ilya Kabakov: The man Who Never Threw Anthything Away*, A Wallach, Abrams, New York **1995** *On the Total Installation*, Stuttgart/Cantz

Seydou Keïta

Lives and works in Bamako. Born in 1921, Keïta has been exhibiting since the end of the 1980s.

SELECTED SOLO EXHIBITIONS SINCE 1990
1999 PhotoEspana 99, Madrid **1998-1999** Saint Louis Museum of Art, Saint Louis, Missouri; **1997** Museum of Modern Art, San Fransisco **1996** Fotofest, Houston; National Museum for African Art, Smithsonian Institute, Washinton **1995** Fruit Market Gallery, Edinburgh **1994** Fondation Cartier pour l'Art Contemporain, Paris; Ginza Arts Space, Tokyo

SELECTED GROUP EXHIBITIONS SINCE 1990
1998 Fundacio Joan Miro, Barcelona; *2nd Biennale Photographique de Moscou*, Moscow; *1st Biennale du Mois de la Photo et de l'Image Numerique et de Film au Liban*, Beirut; *Bienale de São Paulo*, São Paulo **1996** *African Photographers*, Guggenheim Museum, New York **1995** Serpentine Gallery, London

PUBLICATIONS
Has featured in numerous international journals and magazines SELECTED READING **1998** *Zeitschrift fur Kultur Austausch 1/98*, Die Global Herausfordrung, Institut fur Auslandsbeziehungen (IFA); 'Talk of the Town' *Art Forum*, M. Diawara, February **1997** *Seydou Keita*, edited by A Magnin, Scalo; 'Bamako – Full Dress Parade: Seydou Keita', *Parkett*, R. Storr, No. 44

Bodys Isek Kingelez

Lives and works in Kinshasa, Zaire. Born in 1948, Kingelez has been exhibiting since 1989.

SELECTED SOLO EXHIBITIONS SINCE 1990
1996 *D'autres Ajouts d'Ete Bodys Isek Kingelez*, Museé d'Art Moderne et Contemporain Geneve **1995** *Bodys Isek Kingelez*, Fondation Cartier pour l'Art Comtemporain, Paris **1992** *Bodys Isek Kingelez*, Haus der Kulturen der Welt, Berlin

SELECTED GROUP EXHIBITIONS SINCE 1990
1999 *The 1999 Carnegie International*, Carnegie Museum of Art, Pittsburgh; *1 Monde Reel*, Fondation Cartier pour l'Art Contemporain, Paris; *Art-Worlds in Dialogue*, Museum Ludwig, Köln; *Zeitwenden*, Kunstmuseum Bonn, Bonn **1998** *Africa Africa*, Tobu Museum of Art, Tokyo; *Unfinished Story*, Walker Art Center, Minneapolis, Museum of Contemporary Art, Chicago **1997** *97 Kwangju Biennale: Unmapping the Earth*, Kwangju; *Projects 59: Architectural Metaphor*, Museum of Modern Art, New York; *Biennale de Johannesburg*, Johannesburg;

Veilleurs du Monde, Cotonou; Fundacio Joan Miro, Barcelona **1996** *Neue Kunst Aus Africa*, Haus Der Kulturen Der Welt, Berlin; *Wall and Space. Reality and Utopia. Bodys Isek Kingelez Architechtural Visions*, Oksnehallen, Copenhagen **1995** *Dialogues de Paix*, Palais des Nations, Geneve; *Big City*, Serpentine Museum, London **1994** *Crudo y Cocido*, Museo Nacional Centro de Arte Reina Sofia, Madrid **1993** *La grande Verite, Les Astres Africans*, Musée des Beaux Arts, Nantes; *Home and the World Architectural Sculpture by two African Artists*, The Museum of African Art, New York **1992** *Out of Africa*, Saatchi Gallery, London **1991-1992** *Africa Hoy (Africa Now)*, Centro de Arte Moderno, Las Plamas de Gran Canaria, Groninger Museum, Groningen; Centro de Arte Contemporaneo, Mexico; **1990** *WAAAAW A Far African Art*, Courtrai, Belgique

PUBLICATIONS
Has featured in numerous international journals and magazines SELECTED READING **1995** *Bodys Isek Kingelez*, exhibition catalogue, Fondation Cartier pour l'Art Contemporain, Paris; *Jeune Afrique*, A. Magnin, No. 1803 August, pp. 64-65; 'La Nouveau Quotidien', *Journal Suisse et Européen*, June **1989** 'Les Extremes architectures de Bodys Kingelez', *Art Press*, C. Girard, No. 136 May, p. 47

Martin Kippenberger

Born in Dortmund in 1953. Martin Kippenberger died in Vienna in 1997. Kippenberger began exhibiting in 1977.

SELECTED SOLO EXHIBITIONS SINCE 1990
2000 Galerie Gisela Capitain, Köln **1999** Deichtorhallen, Hamburg; National Gallery in Prague **1998** Castello Di Rivoli, Turin; MAK Center, Schindler House, Los Angeles; Kunsthalle, Basel; Kunsthaus, Zürich **1997** Galerie Hubert Winter, Wien; Museé d'Art Moderne et Contemporain, Genf; Städtisches Museum Abteiberg, Mönchengladbach; Galerie Anders Tornberg, Lund; Käthe Kollwitz Preis 1996; Akademie der Künste, Berlin; Galerie Gisela Capitain, Köln; Metro Pictures, New York; Galerie 3, Klagenfurt **1996** L'Atelier Soardi, Nizza; Galerie Bleich Rossi, Groz; Galerie Mikael Andersen, Kopenhagen; Galerie Gisela Capitain, Köln; European ArtForum, Berlin; Galerie Samia Saouma, Paris; Villa Merkel, Esslingen; Turbine Halls, Kopenhagen; Konrad von Soest-Preis 1996, Münster **1995** Hirshhorn Museum and Sculpture Garden, Washington; Galerie Borgmann Capitain, Köln **1994** Metro Pictures, New York; Galerie Borgmann Capitain, Köln; Museum Boijmans Van Beuningen, Rotterdam; Nolan/Eckman Gallery, New York; Galerie Barbel Grässlin, Frankfurt; Galeria Juana de Aizpuru, Madrid

1993 Centre Georges Pompidou, Musée National d'Art Moderne, Paris; Forum for Contemporary Art, St Louis **1992** Metro Pictures, New York; Galerle Klein, Bonn; Galerie Max Hetzler, Köln **1991** Galerie Samia Saouma, Paris; Pace/MacCill Gallery New York; San Francisco Museum of Modern Art, San Francisco; David Nolan Gallery, New York; Kölnischer Kunstverein, Köln; AC & T Corporation, Tokyo; K-Raum Daxer, München **1990** Villa Arson, Nizza; Studio Marconi, Mailand; Anders Tornberg, Lund; Metro Pictures, New York; Galerie Grässlin-Ehrhardt, Frankfurt; Galerie Peter Pakesch, Wien; Galerie Gisela Capitain, Köln

SELECTED GROUP EXHIBITIONS SINCE 1990
1999 Apertutto La Biennale di Venezia; *Zoom, Ansichten zur deutschen Gegenwartskunst Sammlung Landesbank Baden-Wurttemberg* Städtisches Museum Abteiberg, Monchengladbach; *Malerei* , INIT Kunst-Halle, Berlin; Carnegie International, Carnegie museum of Art, Pittsburgh **1998** *Fast Forward*, Kunstverein Hamburg; *MAI 98*, Kunsthalle Köln **1997** *Home Sweet Home*, Deichtorhallen Hamburg; Skulptur Projekte in Münster; *documenta X*, Kassel; *deutschlandbilder*, Martin Gropius Bau, Berlin; *KölnSkulptur 1*, Skulpturenpark, Köln **1996** *Everything That's Interesting Is New*, The Dakis Joannou Collection, Athens School of Fine Arts, Athens; *Sammlung Speck*, Museum Ludwig, Köln; *a/drift: Scenes From the Penetrable Culture*, Center for Curatorial Studies Museum, Bard College **1995** Reinventing the Emblem; *Contemporary Artists Re-create the Renaissance Idea*, Yale University Art Gallery, New Haven; *Das Ende der Avant-garde; Kunst als Dienstleistung*, Kunsthalle der Hypo-Kulturstiftung, München **1994** *Welt-Moral Moralvorstellungen in der Kunst heute*, Kunsthalle Basel; *Return of the Hero*, Luhring Augustine, New York; *Temporary Translation(s)*, Deichtorhallen, Hamburg; *Cocido y Crudo*, Museo National Centro de Arte Reina Sofia, Madrid **1993** *Nachtschattengewächse/The Nightshade Family*, Museum Fridericianum, Kassel; Museum auf Zeit Kippenberger Kunstverein Kassel; Museum Fridericianum Kassel **1992** *Allegories of Modernism: Contemporary Drawings*,The Museum of Modern Art, New York; *Photography in Contemporary German Art: 1960 to the Present*, Walker Art Center, Minneapolis und Tour *Ars pro Domo Zeitgenossische Kunst aus Kölne Privatbesitz*, Museum Ludwig, Köln; *The Boundary Rider*, 9th Biennale of Sydney, Sydney; *Post Human*, FAE Museé d'Art Contemporain, Pully/Lausanne und Tour *Qui, quoi, ou? Un regard sur l'art en Allemagne en*, Museé d'art Moderne de la Ville de Paris **1991** *Fluxattitudes*, Hallwalls, Buffalo, New York und Tour *Obects for*

the Ideal Home, Serpentine Gallery, London **1990** *Artificial Nature*, The House of Cyprus, Athen

PUBLICATIONS
Has featured in numerous international journals and magazines SELECTED READING **1999** *The Happy End of Franz Kafka's Amerika*, Deichtorhallen, Hamburg **1998** *Martin Kippenberger: Die gesamten Plakate 1977-1997*, Kunsthaus Zurich; *Martin Kippenberger*, Kunsthalle Basel; *The Last Stop West*, MAK Center, Schindler House Cantz Verlag, Stuttgart **1997** *Martin Kippenberger: Der Eiermann und Seine*, Kollwitz-Preis, Akademie der Kunste, Berlin

Yayoi Kusama

Lives and works in Tokyo. Born in Matsumoto-shi, Nagano-ken, Japan in 1929, Kusama has been exhibiting since 1957.

SELECTED SOLO EXHIBITIONS SINCE 1990
1999 *Yayoi Kusama Now*, Kantor Gallery, Los Angeles; *Yayoi Kusama Retrospective*, Museum of Contemporary Art, Tokyo **1998** *Love Forever: Yayoi Kusama*, Los Angeles County Museum of Art, Los Angeles & Museum of Modern Art, New York & Walker Art Center, Minneapolis; *Yayoi Kusama Now*, Robert Miller Gallery, New York; *Yayoi Kusama: Works from the 1950s*, Blumarts Inc, New York; *Yayoi Kusama*, Chikugo Gallery, Fukuoka; *Yayoi Kusama 1967-1970: Cage Painting Women*, Media of Modern Art Contemporary, Fukuoka **1997** *Yayoi Kusama: Recent Works and Paintings from New York Years*, Baumgartner Galleries Inc, Washington; *Yayoi Kusama*, Kato Kyobundo, Osaka; *Yayoi Kusama: Obsessional Vision*, The Arts Club Chicago, Chicago; *Yayoi Kusama Prints*, Gallery Olive, Tokyo; *Kusama's Kusama*, Ota Fine Arts, Tokyo; *Yayoi Kusama: Recent Work*, Margo Leavin Gallery, Los Angeles; *Yayoi Kusama*, Gallery East **1996** *Yayoi Kusama*, Gallery Olive, Tokyo; *Yayoi Kusama*, Media of Modern Art Contemporary, Fukuoka; *Yayci Kusama: A Panorama of My Youth*; *Yayoi Kusama: Ten Paintings from the '60s to the present*, Ota Fine Arts, Tokyo; *Yayoi Kusama: The 1950s and 1969s*, Paula Cooper Gallery, New York; *Yayoi Kusama*, Ouka Shorin, Nagano; *Yayoi Kusama*, Robert Miller Gallery, New York **1995** *Yayoi Kusama*, Gallery Kura, Matsumoto; *Yayoi Kusama: I Who Committed Suicide*, Ota Fine Arts, Tokyo; *Yayoi Kusama Recent Prints*, Fuji Television Gallery, Tokyo; *Yayoi Kusama*, YU Contemporary Art, Yokohama; *Yayoi Kusama Etchings*, 77 Gallery, Tokyo **1994** *Yayoi Kusama*, Gallery Kura, Matsumoto; *Yayoi Kusama*, Atelier Kan Gallery, Tokyo; *Yayoi Kusama*, Komagane Kogen Art Museum, Nagano; *Yayoi Kusama*, Nagano Prefectural Shinano Art Museum, Nagano; *Yayoi Kusama*, Bunkamura Gallery, Tokyo; *Yayoi Kusama: My Solitary Way to Death*, Fuji Television Gallery, Tokyo; *Yayoi*

Kusama, Orient Gallery, Tokyo; *Yayoi Kusama*, Okayama Art Gallery, Takashimaya Department Store, Tokyo; *Yayoi Kusama*, Gallery Art Wing, Kanagawa; *Yayoi Kusama*, Chiyoda Gallery, Shizuoka*Yayoi Kusama: Recent Works*, Gallery Now, Toyama; *Yayoi Kusama*, Media of Modern Art Contemporary Gallery, Fukuoka **1993** *Yayoi Kusama*, Galleria Finarte, Nagoya; *Ham Collection: Yayoi Kusama*, Gallery Ham, Nagoya; *Yayoi Kusama*, Bunkamura Gallery, Tokyo; *Yayoi Kusama*, Galleria Valentina Moncada, Rome; *Yayoi Kusama*, Galleria Cardazzo, Venice; *Yayoi Kusama*, Gallerie d'Arte del Naviglio, Venice; The 45th Venice Biennale, Japanese Pavillion, Venice; *Yayoi Kusama*, Shuyu Gallery, Tokyo; *Yayoi Kusama*, Gallery Now, Toyama; *Yayoi Kusama*, Gallery Tomita, Hiroshima **1992** *Yayoi Kusama*, Art Gallery K2, Tokyo; *Yayoi Kusama*, Gallery Aries, Tokyo; *Yayoi Kusama*, Gallery Mominoki, Tochigi; *Yayoi Kusama*, Ouka Shorin, Nagano; *Yayoi Kusama*, Bunkamura Gallery, Tokyo; *Yayoi Kusama*, Gallery Takeuchi, Aichi; *Yayoi Kusama*, Art Gallery K2, Tokyo; *Yayoi Kusama*, Gallery Kura, Nagano; *Yayoi Kusama*, Gallery Esprit-Nouveau, Okayama; *Yayoi Kusama*, Gallery Toki, Hokkaido; *Yayoi Kusama*, Media of Modern Art Contemporary, Fukuoka; *Yayoi Kusama*, YU Contemporary Art, Kanagawa *Yayoi Kusama*, Gallery Lamia, Tokyo *Yayoi Kusama: Bursting Galaxies*, Sogetsu Museum of Art, Tokyo; Niigata City Art Museum, Niigata; *Yayoi Kusama*, Sho Art Gallery, Fukushima **1991** *Kusama's Collage 1953-86*, Nabis Gallery, Tokyo; *Yayoi Kusama 1953-*1990, Art Gallery K2, Tokyo; *Yayoi Kusama*, Media of Modern Art Contemporary, Fukuoka; *Self-Obliteration*, Tokyo Art Expo 1991, Pre-Event, Ginza Sony Building, Tokyo; *Yayoi Kusama*, Tokyo Art Expo 1991, The Tokyo International Trade Center at Harumi, Tokyo; *Yayoi Kusama*, YU Contemporary Art, Kanagawa; *Yayoi Kusama*, Bunkamura Gallery, Tokyo; *Between Heaven and Earth*, Fuji Television Gallery, Tokyo; *Yayoi Kusama*, Gallery Kura, Nagano; *Yayoi Kusama: Paintings Prints Objects*, Oka Shorin, Nagano; *Yayoi Kusama*, Gallery Lamia, Tokyo; *Yayoi Kusama*, YU Contemporary Art, Kanagawa; *Yayoi Kusama*, Gallery Ashibi-sha, Saitama **1990** *Yayoi Kusama*, Shinon Nishiwaki Gallery, Kanagawa; *Yayoi Kusama*, Gallery Kura, Nagano; *Yayoi Kusama*, Fine Art Hiiragi, Kagoshima; *Yayoi Kusama*, Kyouni Gallery, Tokyo; *Yayoi Kusama*, Chikugo Gallery, Tokyo; *Yayoi Kusama*, Kyouni Gallery, Tokyo; *Yayoi Kusama*, Gallery Kosai, Tokyo

SELECTED GROUP EXHIBITIONS SINCE 1990
1999 *Contemporary Classicism*, Neuberger Museum of Art, Purchase College, State University of New York, Purchase **1998** *Tension*, Robert Miller Gallery, New York; *Essence of the Orb*, Michael Rosenfeld Gallery, New York; *Painting: Now and Forever Part 1*, Pat Hearn Gallery, New York;

XXIV Bienal de São Paulo, Pavilhao Ciccillo Matarazzo, São Paulo **1997** *New Collections*, Museum of Modern Art, Saitama, Urawa; *Drawing the Line (and Crossing It)*, Peter Blum Gallery, New York; *The Maximal Sixties*, Museum of Modern Art, New York; *NHK Heart Exhibition*, Bunkamura Gallery, Tokyo; *De-Genderism*, Setagaya Art Museum, Tokyo; *Art Fashion*, Guggenheim Museum, Soho, New York; *Exhibition by Three Women Artists from Shinshu*, Suzaka Prints Museum, Nagano; *Exhibition of Works in Permanent Collection*, Museum of Modern Art, Saitama, Urawa; *Contemporary Art. How Can They Possibly Understand It?*, Itabashi Art Museum, Tokyo; *Floating Images of Women in Art History*, Tochigi Prefectural Art Museum, Tochigi; *Japanese Summer 1960-64*, Art Tower Mito, Ibaraki; Bunkamura Gallery, Tokyo; *Blue*, In Khan Gallery, New York; *No Small Feat: Investigations of the Shoe in Contemporary Art*, Rhona Hoffman Gallery, Chicago; Shoto Museum, Tokyo **1996** Ronald Feldman Gallery, New York; *Inside the Visible: An Elliptical Traverse Of 20th Century Art*, The Institute of Contemporary Art, Boston; *1964: A Turning Point in Japanese Art*, Museum of Contemporary Art, Tokyo; *Collection in Focus: Selected Drawing*, Museum of Contemporary Art, Tokyo; *An Exhibition of 50 Contemporary Japanese Artists*, Nabio Museum of Art, Osaka; Galerie A / Harry Ruhe, Amsterdam; *GEKI and GEKI: Art Then Art Now*, Hara Museum ARC, Gunma; *The 31st Artist Today Exhibition*, Yokohama Citizen's Gallery, Yokohama; *Inside of Works, Outside of Works*, Itabashi Art Museum, Tokyo; *Art at Home: Ideal Standard Life*, Spiral Garden, Tokyo; *Art of Postwar 1960s Avant-Garde*, Kurashiki Municipal Art Museum, Okayama; *Now Here*, Louisiana Museum of Modern Art, Humlebaek; *L'informe. Mode d'emploi*, Museé National d'art moderne, Centre Georges Pompidou, Paris; *A Decade of Avant-Garde Artists*, Itabashi, Art Museum, Tokyo; *Shedding Light on Art in Japan 1953*, Meguro Museum of Art, Tokyo; *Materials and Forms: Nine Artists'Attitudes*, Ibaraki Prefecture Museum of Modern Art, Ibaraki; *Art/Fashion*, Forte Belvedere, Florence; *Form Beyond Forms: 16 Abstract Paintings in Japan*, Fukushima Prefectual Museum of Art, Fukushima; *Art on a Diet*, JR Osaka Selvis Gallery, Osaka & Gallery Seira, Tokyo; *Exhibition of Portraits*, Ota Fine Arts, Tokyo **1995-1996** *Contemporary Art from the Museum Collection*, Museum of Contemporary Art, Tokyo **1995** *Narcissistic Disturbance*, Otis Gallery, Los Angeles; *Division of Labor: Women's Work in Contemporary Art*, Bronx Museum of the Arts, Bronx; *Ars 95 Helsinki*, Museum of Contemporary Art Finnish National Gallery, Helsinki; *Maux Faux*, Ronald Feldman Fine Art, New York; *Hyogo Aid '95 by Art*, Gallery Do ra

pe. Japan; *Auguries of the 21st Century: Prints*, Hillside Gallery, Tokyo; *View of Contemporary Prints, Part II*, Niigata City Art Museum, Niigata; *Japanese Culture: The Fifty Postwar Years*, Meguro Museum of Art, Tokyo; Hiroshima City Museum of Contemporary Art; Hyogo Prefectural Museum of Modern Art, Kobe; Fukouka Prefectural Museum of Art; *Human Figures*, Ota Fine Arts, Tokyo; *Minimal Form*, Fuji Television Gallery, Tokyo; *About Lines: Non-existing Modernism and Invisible Realism*, Itabashi Art Museum, Tokyo; *Revolution: Art of the Sixties From Warhol to Beuys*, Museum of Contemporary Art, Tokyo; *ARCADIA Group Show*, Gallery Isogaya, Tokyo; *Imagery Forest*, Inazawa City Ogisu Memorial Museum of Art, Aichi; Kanagawa International Prints Festival, Kanagawa Prefectual Hall, Yokohama; *50 Artists 50 Works*, Satani Gallery, Tokyo; *Hyogo Aid '95 by Art*, Ban Gallery, Osaka **1994** *Japanese Art After 1945: Scream Against the Sky*, Yokohama Museum of Art, Yokohama & Guggenheim Museum Soho, New York, San Francisco Museum of Modern Art, San Francisco; *Cross and Square Grids*, Museum of Modern Art, Saitama, Urawa; *When the Body Becomes Art*, Itabashi Art Museum, Tokyo; *Japanese Self-Portrait*, Mitaka City Gallery of Art, Tokyo; *Out of Bounds*, Benesse House Naoshima Contemporary Art Museum, Okayama; *Super Suburb*, Museum City Tenjin, Fukuoka **1993** *Highroads of the 60s*, Galerie Delta, Rotterdam; *Contemporary Art from the Museum Collection*, Niigata City Art Museum, Niigata; *Vision, Illusion and Anti-Illusion from the Museum Collection*, Tokyo Metropolitan Art Museum, Tokyo; *Abject Art: Repulsion and Desire in Contemporary Art*, Whitney Museum of American Art, New York; *Art from US*, Landmark Hall, Yokohama; *Parallel Visions: Modern Artists and Outsider Art*, Setagaya Art Museum, Tokyo **1992-1993** *10 Artists: Contemporary Japanese Art of the 1980s-90s*, Tokyo Metropolitan Museum of Art, Tokyo **1992** *Adam & Eve*, Museum of Modern Art, Saitama, Urawa; *Christmas Art Party by 200 Artists*, Guardian Garden, Tokyo **1991** Sumida Riverside Hall Gallery, Tokyo; *The World of Box*, ATM Contemporary Art Gallery, Mito Art, Ibaraki; *Monochrome to Monochrome*, Tokyo Metropolitan Museum of Art, Tokyo; *Nine Artists Today*, Jean Art Gallery, Tokyo **1990** *Still Life*, Shonan Prefectural Museum of Art; *Box Art '90*, Heineken Village, Tokyo; *The Art of Collage & Assemblage from the Museum Collection*, Tokyo Metropolitan Art Museum, Tokyo; *Pharmakon '90*, Nippon Convention Center, Makuhari Messe, Chiba; *Power of Vision*, Miyagi Museum of Art, Sendai, Miyagi; *Artists Gone to America*, Nagano Prefectural Shinano Art Museum, Nagano; *Multiplying Image*, Prefectural Museum of Modern Art Hyogo, Kobe

PUBLICATIONS
Has featured in numerous international journals and magazines
SELECTED READING **1998** *Love Forever: Yayoi Kusama 1958 – 1968*, exhibition catalogue, Los Angeles County Museum of Art, Los Angeles **1998** *Yayoi Kusama Now*, exhibition catalogue, Robert Miller Gallery, New York **1996** *Yayoi Kusama: Recent Works*, exhibition catalogue, Robert Miller Gallery, New York

---

John Mawurndjul

Kuninjku (Eastern Kunwinjku). Lives and works in Central Arnhem Land. Born in 1952, Mawurndjul has been exhibiting since 1982.

SELECTED SOLO EXHIBITIONS SINCE 1990
1999 Annandale Galleries, Sydney **1998** *John Mawurndjul: recent works from Milmilngkan*, Gallery Gabrielle Pizzi, Melbourne **1995** Gallery Gabrielle Pizzi, Melbourne **1994** Savode Gallery, Brisbane **1993** Gallery Gabrielle Pizzi, Melbourne

SELECTED GROUP EXHIBITIONS SINCE 1990
1999 *16th National Aboninal and Torres Strait Islander Art Award Exhibition*, Museum and Art Gallery of the Northern Territory, Darwin; *Fighting for Culture*, Indigenart, Perth **1998** Maningrida Group Show, Alliance Francaise, Canberra **1997** Pizzi Biennale exhibition, Venice; *Mawurndjul and Bulunbulun*, Annandale Gallery, Sydney; *Dreamings: Aboriginal Art from Australia*, Asia Society Galleries, New York **1996** *The Language of Place*, Framed Gallery, Darwin; *Marking Our Times*, National Gallery of Australia, Canberra; *Eye of the Storm*, National Gallery of Modern Art, New Delhi; National Gallery of Australia, Canberra **1995** *Stories my Parents Sang*, National Maritime Museum, Sydney; *12th National Aboriginal and Torres Strait Islander Art Award Exhibition*, Museum and Art Gallery of the Northern Territory, Darwin **1994** *Power of the Land: Masterpieces of Aboriginal Art*, National Gallery of Victoria, Melbourne; *An of the Rainbow Snake*, National Gallery of Victoria, Melbourne **1993-1994** *Aratyara: Art of the first Australians*, Kunstsammiung Nordrhein-Wesffalen, Dusseldorf & Hayward Gallery, London & Louisiana Museum, Humlebaek **1993** *The 10th National Aboriginal Art Award Exhibition*, Museum and Art Gallery of the Northem Territory, Darwin **1992** *The Ninth National Aboriginal Art Award Exhibition*, Museum and Art Gallery of the Northern Territory, Darwin; *1992 Crossroads – Towards a New Reality: Aboriginal Art from Australia*, National Museums of Modem Art, Kyoto and Tokyo **1991** *The Speaking Land and Sea Australian*, National Maritirne Museum, Sydney; *Flash Pictures*, National Gallery of Australia, Canberra, ACT; *Canvas and Bark*, South Australian Museum, Adelaide **1990** *Spirit in Land Bark*

Paintings from Arnhem Land, National Gallery of Victoria, Melbourne; *Painted Ship, Painted Oceans,* SH Ervin Gallery, Sydney; *l'ete Australien a' Montpellier*, Museé Fabre Gallery, Montpellier; *Keepers of the Secrets: Abonginal Art from Arnhemland*, Art Gallery of Western Australia, Perth; *Contemporary Aboriginal Art 1990 – From Australia*, Third Eye Centre, Glasgow

PUBLICATIONS
Has featured in numerous international journals and magazines
SELECTED READING **1999** *John Mawurndjul*, exhibition catalogue, M Garde & A Saulwick, Annandale Galleries, Sydney, Australia **1997** 'Ngalyon in My Head: The Art of John Mawurndjul', *Mawurndjul and Bulunbulun*, exhibition catalogue, M Garde, Annandale Galleries, Sydney **1993** *Aboriginal Art*, W. Caruana, Thames and Hudson, London; *Aratjara: Art of the First Australians*, exhibition catalogue, B. A. Luthi, Dumont Buchverlag, Köln

Maningrida Artists

England Banggala Gochan Jiny-Jirra, language: Gun-Nartpa
Jimmy Bungurru Kurrindin, language: Kunibidji/Kunbarla
James Iyuna Mumeka, language: Kuninjku
Willie Jolpa Gorronggorrong, language: Anbarra-Burarra
Mick Kubarkku Yikarrakkal, language: Kuninjku
Crusoe Kuningbal Minjilang, language: Kuninjku
Crusoe Kurddal Minjilang, language: Kuninjku
Jack Laranggai Babori, language: Myali
Jimmy Wood Maraluka Beswick, language: Rembarrnga
Jacky Maranbarra Yilan, language: Burarra
Les Midikurriya Bulman, language: Rembarrnga
Ivan Namirrkki Marrkolidjban, language: Kuninjku
Michael Ngalabiya Maningrida, language: Wurlaki
Alec Wurramala Ji-Marda, language: Burarra
Owen Yalandja Barrihdjowkkeng, language: Kuninjku
Lena Yarinkura Bolkdjam, language: Rembarrnga

Paul McCarthy

Lives and works in Los Angeles. Born in Salt Lake City in 1945, McCarthy has been exhibiting since 1991.

SELECTED SOLO EXHIBITIONS SINCE 1990
1999 *Tokyo Santa • Santa's Trees*, Blum & Poe Gallery, Los Angeles; *Dimensions of the Mind,* Sammlung Hauser and Wirth St Gallen, Switzerland; *Dead H and Early Performance Photographs*, Studio Guenzani Milan **1998** *Combination Vintage Performance Photographs, Table Photographs, Performance Video and Objects, 1969-1983,*

Luhring Augustine Gallery, New York & Patrick Painter, Los Angeles **1997** *Santa Chocolate Shop*, Galerie Hauser & Wirth, Zurich **1996** Paul McCarthy Tomio Koyama Gallery, Tokyo; *Yaa-Hoo*, Luhring Augustine Gallery, New York; *Video Works*, Galerie Drantmann, Brussels; *Videos and Drawings*, Galleri Nicolai Wallner, Copenhagen **1995** *5 Photographic Works, 1970-1974*, Blum & Poe, Santa Monica; *Painter*, Projects Room, Museum of Modern Art, New York; *Tomato Head*, Künstlerhaus Bethanien, Berlin; *Pinocchio Pipenose Householddilemma Tour*, Air de Paris, Paris & Galeria Antoni Estrany, Barcelona & Luhring Augustine, New York & Galleri Nicolai Wallner, Copenhagen & Esther Schipper Galerie, Koln & Studio Guenzani, Milan & McKinney Art Center, Dallas & Auckland City Art Gallery, Auckland & Ooe Landesmuseum, Linz **1994** Air de Paris, Paris; Le Fonds Regional d'Art Contemporain, Poitou-Charentz, Angouleme; Rosamund Felsen Gallery, Los Angeles; Galerie George-Philippe Vallois, Paris; Studio Guenzani, Milan **1993** *Video*, Ynglingagatan I, Sweden; Galerie Krinzinger, Vienna; *The Dead Viking*, Buchholz und Buchholz, Koln; Luhring Augustine Gallery, New York **1991** Rosamund Felsen Gallery, Los Angeles

SELECTED GROUP EXHIBITIONS SINCE 1990
1999 *Propposition Propposal*, collaboration with Jason Rhoades, Venice Biennale, Venice **1998** *Sod and Sodie Sock* collaboration with Mike Kelley, Secession, Vienna; *Out of Actions: Between Performance and the Object, 1949-1979*, Museum of Contemporary Art, Los Angeles & MAK, Vienna & Museu d'Art Contemporain, Barcelona & Museum of Contemporary Art, Tokyo **1997** *Display*, International Exhibition of Painting, collaboration Mike Kelley/Paul McCarthy, Charlottenborg Exhibition Hall, Copenhagen; *1997 Biennial Exhibition*, Whitney Museum of American Art, New York **1994** *Hors Limites*, Centre George Pompidou, Paris; *Cocido y Crudo*, Museo Nacional Centro de Arte Renia Sofic Madrid; *Sunshine & Noir* Louisiana Museum of Modern Art, Humlebaek; Kunstmuseum, Wolfsburg & Castello di Rivoli, Museo d'Arte Contemporanea, Torino, Italy; Armand Hammer Museum, Los Angeles **1992** *Post Human*, Museé d'art Contemporain Foundation Asher Edelman, Lausanne; Castello di Rivolo, Torino, Italy; Deste Foundation, Athens; Deichtorhallen, Hamburg

PUBLICATIONS
Has featured in numerous international journals and magazines
SELECTED READING **1999** 'Smells Like Teen Spirit', *Flash Art*, P. Ellis, Vol. XXXII No. 208 October, Milan; 'Visionary Violence, The Indelible Legacy of Paul McCarthy', *Juxtapoz* C. McCormick, No. 23 November/ December, San Francisco, CA;

'Sensitized', *SPIN*, D. Cooper, Vol. 15, No. 12 December, New York **1998** 'Shock Corridor', *Time Out New York*, H. Halle, Issue No. 136 April 30 – May 7, New York **1997** 'Mysterical Men', *Index – contemporary art and culture*, M. Lind, January, Stockholm **1996** 'Don't Try This At Home', *Dazed and Confused*, Mark Sanders, No. 22 July, London **1995** 'Paul McCarthy Alptraume Alpraume', *Kunstforum*, Johannes Lothar Schroder, January-April, Ruppichteroth, Germany **1994** 'Paul McCarthy', *The Los Angeles Cannibal*, Art Press, Eric Troncy, No. 187 January, Paris; 'Diaviations on a Theme', *Artforum*, Ralph Rugoff, XXXIII, No. 2 October, New York **1993** 'Leap Into The Void, Abjection and survival in the Work of Paul McCarthy', *Flash Art*, Michael Cohen, Vol XXVI No. 170 May/June, Milan

---

Boris Mikhailov

Lives and works in Berlin. Born in Charkow, Ukraine in 1938, Mikhailov has been exhibiting since 1988.

SELECTED SOLO EXHIBITIONS SINCE 1990
2000 The Photographers' Gallery, London; Stadt Fotomuseum, München; Sprengel Museum, Hannover **1999** Maison Européenne de la Photographie, Paris; DAAD-Galerie, Berlin; Galerie Scalo, Zürich; Museo Querini Stampalia, Venezia **1998** Center of Photography, Turku, Finnland; Gdanski Dom Kultury, Polen; Stedelijk Museum, Amsterdam; *Photo Biennal 98*, Moscow; Centro d'Arte Contemporanea, Castello di Rivera; *Les Misérables (Über dieWelt)*, Sprengel Museum, Hannover **1997** DAAD-Galerie, Berlin; Galerie in der Brotfabrik, Berlin; Galerij S 65, Aalst, Belgien; *Londonprojekt*, London; *Union of photographers in Fine Arts*, Helsinki; Galeria Manhattan, Lodz **1996** Kunsthalle Zürich; XL Gallery, Fotofestival, Moscow; Bard College Center for Curatorial Studies, Annadance-on-Hudson; Galerie Andreas Weiss, Berlin; Galerie Wohnmaschine, Berlin; SCCA, Soros Center Contemporary Art, Kiev; *Month of Photo*, Bratislava; Landeskulturzentrum, Salzau Bunny Yeager Gallery, Los Angeles **1995** Gelman Gallery, Moscow; The Institute of Contemporary Art, Philadelphia; Portikus, Frankfurt am Main **1994** Foto Fest, Bratislava; Hotel Europa, Photo Festival Rotterdam; Fotogalerie Friedrichshain, Berlin; Galerie in der Brotfabrik, Berlin; *By the Earth*, XL Gallery, Moscow; Perspektief Gallery, Photographic Center, Rotterdam **1993** *I am not I*, Photo-Postcriptum Gallery, St Petersburg **1992** *Boris Mikhailov: Works from 1970 to 1991*, Forum Stadtpark, Graz; Museum of Applied Art, Charkov; Galerie & Edition Koch, Kiel **1991** Army Museum, Stockholm; The Hasselblad Center, Göteborg **1990** National Bank Gallery, Helsinki; Central House of Cinematographers, Moscow; Museum of Contemporary Art,

Tel Aviv; *The Missing Picture: Alternative Contemporary Photography from the Soviet Union*, MIT List Visual Arts Center, Cambridge

SELECTED GROUP EXHIBITIONS SINCE 1990
1999 *Global Conceptualism*, Queens Museum of Art, New York; *under/expo*, metro, Stockholm; *Berlin Alexanderplatz – Konzepte*, NGBK, Berlin; *Stadt im Wandel*, NBK, Berlin **1998** *Nobuyoshi Araki & Boris Mikhailov*, Satani Gallery, Tokyo; Museum of Modern Art, New York; *Out of home*, Galerie Barbara Gross, München **1997** Palazzo Mocenigo, Venedig, Italien; SCCA, Tallinn **1996** *Jurassic Technologies Revenant*, 10th Biennale of Sydney, Sydney; *Acme*, Santa Monica; SCCA, Vilnius; *Russian Jewish Artists 1890-1990*, The Jewish Museum, New York **1995** *Multiple Exposures: Ukrainian Photography Today*, Rutgers Arts Center, New Brunswick; *Currents '95: Familiar Places*, The Institute of Contemporary Art, Boston; *Contemporary Russian Photography*, Akademie der Künste/Galerie im Marstall, Berlin **1994** *Art of Contemporary Photography: Russia, Ukrame, Belorus*, Central House of Artists, Moskau; *Photo-reclamation: New Art from Moscow and Saint Petersburg*, Photographers' Gallery, London; John Hansard Gallery, University of Southhampton; *2 x 2*, Contemporary Art Center, Moskau; *Rediscovered Europe: Project for Europe*, Kopenhagen; *Europa, Europa*, Kunst- und Ausstellungshalle der Bundesrepublik Deutschland, Bonn; *Contemporary Art Festival*, New Space Gallery, Odessa **1993** *New Photography 9*, Museum of Modern Art, New York **1992** *Herbarium: The Photographic Experience in Contemporary Russian Art*, Fotogalerie Wien/ Kunsthalle Exnergasse, Wien; Galerie Albrecht, Munchen; *2. Internationale FotoTriennale*, Galerie der Stadt Esslingen Perspektief Gallery, Rotterdam; *Litsa: Contemporary Portrait Photography from Russia, Belorussia and Ukraine*, Stichting CIRC, Amsterdam; *So Sein oder Nicht Sein*, Forum Stadtpark, Graz; *Foto Fest*, Georg R. Brown Convention Center, Houston **1991** *Carnegie International*, The Carnegie Museum, Pittsburgh; *Photo Manifesto*, Museum of Contemporary Arts, Baltimore; Fine Arts Center Long Island University, New York; *Erotica*, Amsterdam **1990** *Erosion*, Amos Anderson Art Museum, Helsinki; *Photography of Charkov and Ukraine*, Kunsthuset Stockholm; *Oppositions, commitment and identity in contemporary photography from Japan, Canada, Brazil, The Soviet Union and the Netherlands*, Photography Biennal, Rotterdam; *International Biennal of Photography 89*, Turin; *Contemporary Photography from the USSR*, Walker, Ursitti & McGinnis Gallery, New York

PUBLICATIONS
Has featured in numerous international journals and magazines

SELECTED READING **1999** *Boris Mikhailov: Case History*, Zurich **1998** *Boris Mikhailov – Les Miserables (Über die Welt/About the World)*, V. Tupitsyn, Die Liebe zum Negativen, Sprengel Museum, Hannover; *Boris Mikhailov, Unvollendete Dissertation*, Zurich **1996** *Boris Mikhailov: Die Dammerung*, B. Kolle, Koln; *Boris Mikhailov: Am Boden*, B. Kolle, Koln **1995** *Boris Mikhailov*, B. Kolle, Frankfurter Portikus und Kunsthalle Zurich, Stuttgart

Tracey Moffatt

Lives and works in Sydney and New York. Born in Brisbane in 1960, Moffatt has been exhibiting since 1984.

SELECTED SOLO EXHIBITIONS SINCE 1990
2000 *Laudanum*, Yerba Buena Center, San Francisco **1999** *Laudanum,* Roslyn Oxley9 Gallery, Sydney & LA Galerie, Frankfurt & Paul Morris Gallery, New York & Victoria Miro Gallery, London; *Tracey Moffatt,* Parco, Tokyo; *Tracey Moffatt,* Institute of Modern Art, Brisbane, & touring through Asia; *Tracey Moffatt,* Galerie Laage Salomon, Paris; *Tracey Moffatt,* Freiburger Kunstverein, Freiberg; *Tracey Moffatt,* Centre National de la Photographie, Paris; *Tracey Moffatt,* Galerie Schneider, Karlsruhe; *Tracey Moffatt,* Neueer Berliner Kunstverien, Berlin; *Laudanum,* Rupertinum, Salzburg; *Tracey Moffatt,* Centro Galego de Arte Contemporain, Santiago de Compostela; *Tracey Moffatt,* Ulmer Museum, Ulm; *Tracey Moffatt,* Six Freidrich, Lisa Ungar Gallery, Munich; *Tracey Moffatt,* Torch Gallery, Amsterdam; *Tracey Moffatt,* Lawing Gallery, Houston; *Tracey Moffatt, Up in the Sky,* Le Case D'Arte, Milan; *Tracey Moffatt,* Galeria Helgade Alvear, Madrid; *Tracey Moffatt,* Fundacio "la Caixa", Sala San Juan, Barcelona; *Free Falling*, ICA, Boston; *Tracey Moffatt,* Rena Bransten Gallery, San Francisco; *Tracey Moffatt*, Le Case D'Arte, Milano; *Tracey Moffatt,* Curtin University Gallery, Perth **1998** *Up in the Sky,* Roslyn Oxley9 Gallery, Sydney; *Tracey Moffatt,* Galleri Larsen, Stockholm; *Tracey Moffatt,* Arnolfini, Bristol; *Free Falling*, Renaissance Society, Chicago; *Tracey Moffatt,* Le Case D'Arte, Milano; *Tracey Moffatt,* Victoria Miro Gallery, London; *Tracey Moffatt,* Curtin University Gallery, Perth; *Tracey Moffatt,* LA Galerie, Frankfurt; *Tracey Moffatt,* Kunsthalle Vienna, Vienna; *Tracey Moffatt,* Wurtembergischer Kunstverein, Stuttgart; *Tracey Moffatt,* Il Ponte Contemporanea, Rome; *Tracey Moffatt,* Arte/GE Bozen/Bolzano; *Tracey Moffatt,* Voralberger Kunstverein, Bregenz; *Tracey Moffatt,* Australian Centre for Contemporary Art, Melbourne **1997** *Free Falling*, Dia Center for the Arts, New York; *Tracey Moffatt,* LA Galerie, Frankfurt; *Tracey Moffatt,* Galerie Andreas Weiss, Berlin; *Tracey Moffatt,* Galleri Faurschou, Copenhagen; *Tracey Moffatt*, Films, Museé d'Art Contemporain, Lyon **1995** GUAPA *(Goodlooking)*, Karyn Lovegrove Gallery, Melbourne & Mori Gallery, Sydney; *Short Takes*, ArtPace, San Antonio, Texas **1994** *Scarred for Life*, Karyn Lovegrove Gallery, Melbourne **1992** *Pet Thang*, Mori Gallery, Sydney; *Tracey Moffatt*, Centre for Contemporary Arts, Glasgow

SELECTED GROUP EXHIBITIONS SINCE 1990
1999 *The Promise of Photography: Selections from the DG Bank Collection*, PS1 Contemporary Art Centre, New York; *Full Exposure: Contemporary Photography*, New Jersey Center for Visual Arts, Summit; *Wohin kein Auge reichtl*, Deichtorhallen Hamburg; *In de Ban van de Ring*, Provencial Centrum voor beeldene Kunst, Hasselt; *Female*, Wessel + O'Connor Gallery, New York; *Wonderland: Fotomanifestatie Noorderlicht 1999*, Noorderlicht Fotogalerie, Groningen; *Violence*, Espai d'art Contempitani de Castello, Castellon; *Kunstwelden im Dialog*, Museum Ludwig, Cologne; Museé d'art contemporain de Bordeaux, Bordeaux; *Rosa für Jungs, Weiß für Mädchen*, Neue Gesellschaft für bildende Kunst, Berlin; *100 Meisterwerke aus Malerie, Fotographie*, Skulptur and Intallationskunst, Lehmbachhaus, Munich & Von der Heydt Museum, Wuppertal, Kunstsammlung Bötcherstraße, Bremen; *Signature Works*, Australian Centre for Photography, Sydney; *La Casa, Il Corpo, Il Cuore*, Museum für Moderne Kunst, Stiftung Kunst, Vienna; *Das Versprechen der Photographie. Die Sammlung der DG Bank*, Kestner Gesellschaft Hannover; Centre Nationale de la Photographie, Paris; Galerie Schneider, Ettlingen **1998** *Museum van Hedendaagse Kunst Gent*, Gent; *Family Viewing*, Museum of Contemporary Art, Los Angeles; *Portraits*, Paul Morris Gallery, New York; *Echolot*, Museum Fridericianum, Kassel; *Foto Triennale Esslingen*, Esslingen; Museé Departemantal d'Art Contemporain, Rochechouart; *Artenergie – Art in Jeans*, Palazzo Corsini, Florence; *Die Nerven enden an den Fingerspitzen, Die Sammlungen Wilhelm Schurmann*, Kunsthaus Hamburg; *Presumed Innocence*, Anderson Gallery, Richmond; *Strange Days: Guinness Contemporary Art Exhibition*, Art Gallery of New South Wales, Sydney; *Nature of Man*, Lund Konsthall, Lund; *Roteiros x 7 Bienal de São Paulo*, São Paulo; *Life is a bitch*, De Appel Foundation, Amsterdam; *Der Mensch (The Human Being)*, Kunstverein Schloß Plön; *Pusan International Contemporary Art Festival*, Pusan; *Horizont*, Brecht Haus am Weissensee, Berlin; *Fleeting Portraits*, Neue Gesellschaft für bildende Kunst, Berlin **1997** *Venice Biennale*, Venice; *Group Show*, Matthew Marks Gallery, New York; *Group Show*, Anthony Reynolds Gallery, London; *Group Show*, Roslyn Oxley9

Gallery, Sydney; *Printemps de Cahors*, Paris; *Steierischer herbst 97*, Graz; *Site Santa Fe*, Santa Fe, New Mexico; *Campo 6, The Spiral Village*, Bonnefanten Museum, Maastricht; *Subject to Representation*, Gallery 101, Ottawa **1996** *Fundacao Bienal de São Paulo*, São Paulo; *Campo 6, The Spiral Village*, Museum of Modern Art, Torino; *Jurassic Technologies Revenant*, 10th Biennale of Sydney; *Prospect 96*, Schirn Kunsthalle, Frankfurt **1995** *Antipodean Currents*, The Guggenheim Museum (Soho), New York; *Familiar Places*, ICA, Boston; *'95 Kwangju Biennale*, Kwangju; *New Works 95.2*, ArtPace, San Antonio; *Perspecta 95*, Art Gallery of New South Wales, Sydney **1994** *Antipodean Currents*, The Kennedy Center, Washington; *Power Works*, Govett Brewster Gallery; *Eidetic Experiences*, toured through regional galleries in Queensland **1993** *The Boundary Rider*, 9th Biennale of Sydney, Sydney **1992** *Artist's Projects*, Adelaide Festival of the Arts, Adelaide **1991** *From the Empire's End*, Circulo de Bellas Artes, Madrid **1990** *Satellite Cultures*, New Museum of Contemporary Art, New York

PUBLICATIONS
Has featured in numerous international journals and magazines
SELECTED READING **1999** *Tracey Moffatt*, exhibition catalogue, Fundacio la Caixa, Barcelona and Centre national de la photographie, Paris; *Tracey Moffatt: laudanum*, exhibition catalogue, Ulmer Museum & Neuer Berliner Kunstverein & Kunstverein Freiburg im Marienbad; *Tracey Moffatt*, J. Turner, MonteVideo/TBA, Netherlands Media Art Institute, Amsterdam **1998** *Strange Days*, exhibition catalogue, Art Gallery of New South Wales, Sydney, Australia; *Indigenous Australia – in the Nation's Parliament House*, Parliament House, Canberra, Australia; *Free Falling*, L. Cooke, Dia Center for the Arts, New York; *Echolot*, exhibition catalogue, Museum Fridericianum, Kassel; *Tracey Moffatt*, exhibition catalogue, Kunsthalle Wien, Vienna

Mariko Mori

Lives and works in New York. Born in Tokyo in 1968, Mori has been exhibiting since 1993.

SELECTED SOLO EXHIBITIONS SINCE 1990
1999 *Empty Dream*, The Brooklyn Museum of Art, Brooklyn; *Mariko Mori*, Kunstmuseum Wolfsburg, Wolfsburg; *Dream Temple*, Prada Foundation, Milan; *Voiceovers*, Art Gallery of New South Wales, Sydney **1998-1999** *Mariko Mori*, The Museum of Contemporary Art, Chicago **1998** *Contemporary Projects 2: Mariko Mori*, Los Angeles County Museum of Art, Los Angeles; *Mariko Mori*, The Andy Warhol Museum, Pittsburgh; *Mariko Mori*, The Serpentine Gallery, London **1997** *Play with Me*, Dallas Museum of Art,

Dallas; *Mirage*, Gallery Koyanagi, Tokyo **1996** Centre National D'Art Contemporain De Grenoble, Grenoble; Galerie Emmanuel Perrotin, Paris; MADE IN JAPAN, Deitch Projects, New York **1995** American Fine Arts Co, New York; MADE IN JAPAN, Shiseido Gallery, Tokyo **1993** *Art & Public*, Geneva; *Close-up*, Project Room, New York

SELECTED GROUP EXHIBITIONS SINCE 1990
1999 *Seeing Time*, San Francisco Museum of Art, San Francisco; *Tokyo 60/90 14 Photographers*, Metropolitan Museum of Photography, Tokyo; *Images: Festival of Independent Film and Video*, Toronto; *Centenary: Emergent Art in 1999*, University Art Gallery, University of California, San Diego; *Surrogate*, Henry Art Gallery, University of Washington, Seattle **1998** *Close Encounters*, Ottawa Art Gallery; *I Love New York*, Museum Ludwig, Koln; *Mariko Mori/Jana Sterback*, Museum of Contemporary art, Chicago; *Span*, Govett Brewster Art Gallery, New Plymouth, New Zealand & Shanghai Museum, Shanghai & Artspace, Auckland; *Spectacular Optical*, Thread Waxing Space; *View: One*, Mary Boone Gallery, New York **1997** Biennale de Lyon d'Art Contemporain, Lyon; *Cities On The Move*, Weiner Secession, Vienna; *Culturgest Project*, Lisbon, Portugal; *The Desire and the Void*, Kunsthalle zu Kiel; *The Desire and the Void*, Arken Museum of Modern Art, Ishoji, Finland; 5th International Istanbul Biennial, Istanbul, Turkey; Kwangju Biennale, Kwangju, South Korea; *Land Marks*, John Weber Gallery, New York; *Natural Habitat*, The Tannery, London; *Simon Says*, SoHo Arts Festival, New York; *Some Kind of Heaven*, Kunsthalle Nurnberg, Nurnberg & Cornerhouse, Manchester, South London Gallery, London; *La Biennale di Venezia, Past Present Future*, Venice; Johannesburg Biennale, Johannesburg **1996** *Body Capsule in Shibuya*, Postmasters Gallery, New York; *By Night*, Fondation Cartier Pour l'art Contemporain, Paris; *Departure Lounge*, Clocktower Gallery, New York; *Doug Aitken, Mariko Mori, Ricardo Zulueta*, Elga Wimmer Gallery, New York; *Ideal Standard Life*, Spiral Garden, Tokyo; *In the Shadows of Storms: Art of Postwar Era from the MCA Collection*, Museum of Contemporary Art, Chicago; *Intermission*, Basilico Fine Arts, New York; *Ironic Fantasy*, The Miyagi Museum of Art, Miyagi, Japan; *Nach Weimar*, Kunstsammlungen Zu Weimar, Weimar; *New Histories*, The Institute of Contemporary Art, Boston; *The Scream*, Arken Museum of Modern Art, Ishoji, Finland; *Show and Tell*, Lauren Wittels Gallery, New York; *Tokyo Pop*, Hiratsuka City Art Museum, Hiratsuka, Japan; *25th Anniversary: 25 Younger Artists Exhibition*, John Weber Gallery, New York; *The Scream*, Arken Museum of Modern Art, Ishoji, Finland **1995** *All*

Dressed Up, Apex Art, New York; American Fine Arts Co, New York; *Guys and Dolls*, Postmasters Gallery, New York; *Linking Worlds*, Nicole Klagsbrun Gallery, New York; *On Beauty*, Regina Gallery, Moscow; *Self Made*, Grazer Kunstverein, Graz, Austria **1994** American Fine Arts Co, New York **1993** *Fall from Fashion*, Aldrich Museum of Contemporary Art, Ridgefield, Connecticut

PUBLICATIONS
Has featured in numerous international journals and magazines
SELECTED READING **1999** *Mariko Mori: Dream Temple*, Fondazione Prada, Milan; *Mariko Mori – Esoteric Cosmos*, Kunstmuseum, Wolfsburg **1998** *Mariko Mori*, exhibition catalogue, Museum of Contemporary Art, Chicago & the Serpentine Gallery, London **1997** *Concentrations 30: Mariko Mori, Play with Me*, Dallas Museum of Art **1996** *Mariko Mori*, Centre National d'Art Contemporain de Grenoble, Grenoble, France

---

Juan Muñoz

Lives and works in Madrid. Born in 1953, Muñoz has been exhibiting since 1981.

SELECTED SOLO EXHIBITIONS SINCE 1990
2000 *Juan Muñoz*, The Louisiana Museum, Copenhagen **1999** *Crossroads*, Marian Goodman Gallery, New York; *Juan Muñoz* Bernier/Eliades, Athens **1998** *Juan Muñoz: Streetwise*, Site Santa Fé, Santa Fé; Moderna Museet, Stockholm, inaugural exhibition of new space Sala Robayera, Miengo, Spain **1997** 47th Biennale di Venezia, Venice; *Juan Muñoz: Mobiliario*, Marco Noire Contemporary Art, San Sebastiono, Turin; Smithsonian Institution, Washington; Museum für Gegenwartskunst, Zürich; *Directions*, Hirshhorn Museum & Sculpture Garden Washington, DC; Galleria Continua, San Gimignano **1996** Galerie Jean Bernier, Athens; Museo Nacional Centro de Arte Reina Sofia, Madrid; *A Place Called Abroad*, Dia Center for the Arts, New York; *Silence Please*, Stories after the works of Juan Muñoz, Irish Museum of Modern Art, Dublin **1995** Laura Carpenter, Sante Fé; Centro Galego de Arte Contemporaneo, Santiago de Compostela; Kunstverein Hamburg, Hamburg; Isabella Stuart Gardner Museum, Boston **1994** Musée d'Art Contemporain, Nîmes; Irish Museum of Modern Art, Dublin; Kasper König, Düsseldorf **1993** Galerie Konrad Fischer, Düsseldorf; Lisson Gallery, London; Galerie Jean Bernier, Athens; Marian Goodman Gallery, New York; Castello di Rivoli, Torino **1992** Frith Street Gallery, London; Centro del Carme, Instituto Valenciano de Arte Moderno, Valencia **1991** Stedelijk Van Abbemuseum, Eindhoven; Marian Goodman Gallery, New York; Galerie Konrad Fischer, Düsseldorf; Museum Haus Lange, Krefeld; Galerie

Ghislaine Hussenot, Paris; Centre d'art Contemporain, Geneva **1990** The Renaissance Society at the University of Chicago, Chicago; Centre d'Art Contemporain, Geneva; Galerie Jean Bernier, Athens; Arnolfini Gallery, Bristol

SELECTED GROUP EXHIBITIONS SINCE 1990
2000 *Inner Eye, Contemporary Art from the Marc and Livia Straus Collection*, Neuberger Museum of Art, New York; *0 to 60 in 10 Years*, Frith Street Gallery, London; 6th Istanbul Biennial, Istanbul; *A Summer Show*, Marian Goodman Gallery, New York; *Regards Croisés*, Forum Culturel du Blanc-Mesnil, Département e la Seine-Saint-Denis, France; *20 años de escultura española. Hacia un nuevo clasicismo*, Circulo de Bellas Artes, Madrid; *North-South. Transcultural Visions*, Mediterranean Foundation and the National Museum, Warsaw; *Nye Konstellationer*, Louisiana Museum of Modern Art, Humblebek, Denmark; *Grabados*, Centro Comunae d'Arte e Cultura, Cagliari, Italy; *Het Betoverde Plein*, Zeeuws Museum, Middleburg, The Netherlands; *Trace*, Liverpool Biennial of Contemporary Art, Liverpool; *Vergiss den Ball und spiel' weiter*, Nuremberg Kunsthalle, Nuremberg; *Collectors Collect Contemporary: 1990-1999*, ICA, Boston; *Zeitwenden*, Kunstmuseum Bonn **1998** *Breaking Ground*, Marian Goodman Gallery, New York; *Voice over*, Arnolfini, Bristol; *Louisiana at 40: The Collection Today*, Louisiana Museum of Modern Art, Humlebaek, Denmark; *Voor het verdwijnt en daarna*, SMAK in Watou, Watou; *II Trienal de Arte Gráfico: La Estampa Contemporánea*, Centro Cultural Caja de Asturias, Palacio Revillagigedo, Gijon, Spain; *Wounds Between Democracy and Redemption in Contemporary Art*, Moderna Museum, Stockholm; *Bienal de Pontevedra*, Pontevedra, Spain; *Dibujos Germinales*, Museo Nacional Centro de Arte Reina Sofia, Madrid; *United Enemies Mannerism and Synthesis*, Galerie Jiri Svestka, Prague; Margo Leavin Gallery, Los Angeles; *Tableaux*, Contemporary Arts Museum, Houston; *A man in a room, grambling*, The Gavin Bryars Ensemble with Juan Muñoz, BBC Studio, London **1996** *Everything That's Interesting is New*, The Dakis Joannou Collection, an Exhibition organized by the Deste Foundation in conjunction with the Museum of Modern Art, Copenhagen; Galerie Jean Bernier, Athens; *Marks*, The Israel Museum, Jerusalem; Marian Goodman Gallery, New York; *Cityscape*, City Space, Copenhagen; Crown Gallery, Knokke; *Collezioni di Francia: leopere dei Fondi Regionali d'Arte Contemporanea*, Castello di Rivoli, Museo d'arte contemporanea **1995** Le Nouveau Musée/Institut d'Art Contemporain, Villeurbanne; *Duck Not On A Pond*, Public Art Project on Rochdale Canal, Manchester; ars 95, Museum of

Contemporary Art/ Finnish National Gallery, Helsinki; *A summer show*, Marian Goodman Gallery, New York; *Trust*, Tramway, Glasgow; *Regards croisés*, ELAC, Lyon; *Le Domaine du diaphane*, Le Domaine de Kerguehennec, Centre d'Art Contemporain, Bignan; *Tutte la strade portano a Roma*? Palazzo delle Esposizioni, Rome; *Incidentes*, Casa da Parra, Santiago de Compostela; Galerie Jean Bernier, Athens; *Collectie Marlies en Jo Eyck*, Bonnefantenmuseum, Maastricht; *A collection of Sculptures*, Caldic Collection, Rotterdam; *Malpaís*, Galería Soledad Lorenzo, Madrid; *Everything that's Interesting is New*, Deste Foundation, Athens & Museum of Modern Art, Copenhagen **1994** *Drawings*, Frith Street Gallery, London; *The Little House on the Prairie*, Marc Jancou Gallery, London; Castello di Rivoli, Torino; *A Sculpture Show*, Marian Goodman Gallery, New York; *Selections From The Le Witt Collection*, Atrium Gallery; Museo Marugame, Hirai, Japan; *Fragmentis de un museo imaginario*, Fundaçao Serralves, Lisbon; *Entre la presencia y la representacion*, Centro Atlántico de Arte Moderno, Las Palmas de Gran Canaria, Spain; *Portfolio Lettre International*, Galerie Bernd Kluser, Munich; FRAC Aquitane, France; *Malpais: Grabados y monotipos 1994*, Galeria Soledad Lorenzo, Madrid; *Même si c'est la nuit*, Capc Musée d'Art Contemporain, Bordeaux; *Weltmoral*, Kunsthalle, Basel; *A Group Show*, Marian Goodman Gallery, New York; *Juxtaposition*, Charlottenburg, Copenhagen; *Doubletake*, Kunsthalle Wien, Vienna; *New Sculptures*, Park Middelheim, Antwerpen; *Accrochage*, Xavier Hufkens Gallery, Brussels; documenta 9, Kassel; *Los últimos días*, Galería del Arenal, Sevilla; *Tropismes*, Centre de Cultura Tecla Sala, Barcelona; *Artistas en Madrid: años 80*, Comunidad de Madrid, Madrid; *Jahresgaben '92*, Kunstverein Düsseldorf, Düsseldorf; *Contradictory Shapes of Truth*, Modern Galerija, Ljubljana **1991** *In anderen Räumen*, Museum Haus Lange and Haus Esters, Krefeld; *Carnegie International*, Carnegie Museum of Art, Pittsburgh; *Art in Inter cultural Limbo*, Rooseum Center for Contemporary Art, Malmö; *History as Fiction*, Meyers/Bloom Gallery, Santa Monica; *A Group Show*, Marian Goodman Gallery, New York **1990** *Possible Worlds, Sculpture from Europe*, Institute of Contemporary Arts, Serpentine Gallery, London; *Weitersehen*, Museum Haus Lange and Museum Haus Esters, Krefeld; Marian Goodman Gallery, New York; Galerie Joost Declercq, Gent; The Biennale of Sydney, Australia; *Objectives: The New Sculpture*, Newport Harbor Art Museum, Newport Beach; *X Salon de los 16*, Museo Español de Arte Contemporáneo, Madrid; *Le Spectaculaire*, Centre d'Histoire de l'Art Contemporain, Rennes; *Meeting*

Place, York University, Toronto & Nickle Arts Museum, Calgary & Vancouver Art Gallery, Vancouver; *Jardins de bagatelle*, Galerie Tanit, München

PUBLICATIONS
Has featured in numerous international journals and magazines
SELECTED READING **1997** *Juan Muñoz: monologues & dialogues*, exhibition catalogue, James Lingwood, Palacio de Velazquez, Museo Nacional Centro de Arte Reina Sofia, Madrid; *Juan Muñoz*, exhibition catalogue, Lynne Cooke, Dia Center for the Arts, New York

---

Bruce Nauman

Lives and works in Santa Fe, New Mexico. Born in Fort Wayne, Indiana in 1941, Nauman has been exhibiting since 1966.

SELECTED SOLO EXHIBITIONS SINCE 1990
1997-1999 *Bruce Nauman: Image/Text 1966-1996*, Kunstmuseum Wolfsburg; Centre George Pompidou, Paris; Mnam-Centre de Creation Industrielle, Paris; Hayward Gallery, London; Nykytaiteen Museo/Museum of Contemporary Art Kiasma, Helsinki **1993-1995** *Bruce Nauman* (Retroperspective), Museo Nacional Centro de Arte Reina Sofia, Madrid; The Walker Art Center, Minneapolis; Museum of Contemporary Art, Los Angeles; Hirshhorn Museum and Sculpture Garden, Smithsonian Institute, Washington; The Museum of Modern Art, New York **1990-1992** *Bruce Nauman: Skulpturen und Installationen, 1985-1990*, Museum fur Gegenwartskunst, Basel; Stadtische Galerie, Stadelsches Kunstinstitut, Frankfurt am Main; (combined with exhibition entitled *Bruce Nauman: Arbeiten auf Papier* and called *Bruce Nauman: Human Nature/Animal Nature: Skulpturen, Installationen und Arbeiten auf Papier*) Museé Cantonal des Beaux-Arts, Lausanne

SELECTED GROUP EXHIBITIONS SINCE 1990
2000 *Samuel Beckett/Bruce Nauman*, Kunsthalle Wien Karlsplatz, Vienna **1999** *Afterimage: Drawing Through Process*, The Museum of Contemporary Art and the Geffen Contemporary, Los Angeles; Contemporary Arts Museum, Houston; Henry Art Gallery, Seattle **1997-1998** *Sunshine and Noir: Art in LA 1960-1997*, Louisiana Museum of Modern Art, Humlebaek; Kunstmuseum, Wolfsburg; Armand Hammer Museum of Art, Los Angeles **1991-1992** *Carnegie International 1991*, The Carnegie Museum of Art, Pittsburgh; *Dislocations: Louise Bourgeois, Chris Burden, Sophie Calle, David Hammons, Ilya Kabakov, Bruce Nauman, Adrian Piper*, The Museum of Modern Art, New York **1990-1991** *The New Sculpture: 1965-1975 Between Geometry and Gesture*, Whitney Museum of American Art, New York; The Museum of Contemporary Art, Los Angeles

PUBLICATIONS
Has featured in numerous
international journals and magazines
SELECTED READING **1999** *House of
Sculpture*, M. Auping, Modern Art
Museum of Fort Worth **1998** 'Susan
Rothenberg and Bruce Nauman',
*Portraits: Talking with Artists at the
Met, the Modern, the Louvre and
Elsewhere*, M. Kimmelman, Random
House; *Bruce Nauman:
Versuchsanordnungen, Werke 1965-
1994*, U. M. Scheede, Hamburger
Kunsthalle. **1997** 'Bruce Nauman:
Work in Progress', *Beaux Arts*,
J. Simon, December; *Bruce Nauman:
Image/text, 1966-1996*, C. van
Assche

Shirin Neshat

Lives and works in New York. Born in
Qazvin, Iran in 1957, Neshat has
been exhibiting since 1993.

SELECTED SOLO EXHIBITIONS SINCE 1990
2000 Wexner Center, Columbus,
Ohio; Lia Rumma, Milan; Dallas
Museum of Art, Dallas; Matrix,
Berkeley Art Museum, Berkeley;
Kunsthalle Wien, Vienna **1999** Art
Institute of Chicago, Chicago; Patrick
Painter Gallery, Los Angeles;
D'Amelio Terras Gallery, New York;
Galerie Jerôme de Noirmont, Paris;
Henie Onstad Artsentre, Oslo; Lia
Rumma Gallery, Milan; Tensta
Konsthall, Spanga **1998** Tate Gallery,
London; Whitney Museum of
American Art, Philip Morris Branch,
New York; Maison Européenne de la
Photographie, Paris; Thomas Rehbein
Gallery, Koln; Bruce Nauman,
Greenwich **1997** Hosfelt Gallery, San
Francisco; Museum of Modern Art,
Ljubljana; Annina Nosei Gallery, New
York; Lumen Travo, Amsterdam;
Artspeak, Vancouver **1996** Centre
d'Art Contemporain Kunsthalle,
Fribourg; Marco Noire Contemporary
Arts, Turin; Lucio Amelio Gallery,
Naples; Haines Gallery, San Francisco
1995 Annina Nosei Gallery, New York
1993 Franklin Furnace, New York

SELECTED GROUP EXHIBITIONS SINCE 1990
2000 Lyon Biennial, Lyon; Biennale of
Sydney, Sydney; Kwangju Biennale,
Kwangju; Whitney Biennial, Whitney
Museum of American Art, New York;
Contact: A 90's Journal,
Contemporary Arts Museum,
Houston; Kunstsammlung Nordrhein-
Westfalen, Dusseldorf **1999** *Heaven:
An Exhibition That Will Break Your
Heart*, Tate Gallery Liverpool;
Zeitwenden: Rückblick und Ausblick,
Kunstmuseum Bonn, Bonn; Malmö
Konsthall, Malmö; *Shirin Neshat:
Rapture/ Pipilotti Rist: Sip My Ocean*,
The Fabric Workshop & Museum,
Philadelphia; *Voiceovers*, Art Gallery
of New South Wales, Sydney;
*Project 70: Shirin Neshat, Simon
Patterson, Xu Bing*, The Museum of
Modern Art, New York; Carnegie
International, Carnegie Museum of
Art, Pittsburgh; *My Culture – My
Self: Lee Friedlander, Gerhard Richter,
Christian Boltanski, Shirin Neshat*,
Ydessa Hendeles Art Foundation,

Toronto; *La Biennale di Venezia*,
Venice; *Exploding Cinema*, Rotterdam
Film Festival, Boijman Museum,
Rotterdam; *Unfinished History*,
Museum of Contemporary Art,
Chicago; *Video Cultures*,
ZKM/Museum of Contemporary Art,
Karlsruhe; *La Ville, Le Jardin, la
Memoire*, Villa Medici, Rome; *Global
Art Rheinland 2000*, Ludwig
Museum, Koln; SITE SANTA FE: *Looking
For A Place*, Santa Fe, New Mexico;
*Zeitwenden – outlook into the next
millennium*, Kunstmuseum Bonn,
Bonn; *Heavenly Figure*, Kunsthalle
Dusseldorf **1998** *Unfinished History*,
Walker Art Center, Minneapolis; *In
The Detail*, Barbara Gross Galerie,
Munich; *7th Summer of Photography*,
Museum van Hedendaagse Kunst,
Antwerp; *Mar de Fondo*, Roman
Theatre of Sagunto, Valencia;
Vanessa Beecroft & Shirin Neshat,
Galleria d'Arte Moderna, Bologna;
Maschile Femminile e oltre, Palazzo
Branciforte, Palermo; *Mostrato*,
Pescara; ECHOLOT, Museum
Fridericianum Kassel, Kassel;
Transatlantico, Centro Atlantico de
Arte Moderno, Canary Islands; *A
Noir*, Triennale di Milano, Milan;
Interference, Comunidad de Madrid,
Madrid; *Genders and Nations:
Reflections on Women in Revolution*,
Johnson Museum, Cornell University,
Ithaca **1997** *On Life, Beauty,
Translations and Other Difficulties*,
5Th International Istanbul Biennale
Istanbul; *Trade Routes: History and
Geography*, 2nd Johannesburg
Biennale 1997, Johannesburg;
Unbeschreiblich Weiblich,
Fotomanifestatie Noorderlicht,
Groningen; *Triple X: Contemporary
Investigating Arts*, International Art
Festival, Amsterdam; *Der Rest der
Welt*, Haus Der Kulturen Der Welt,
Berlin; *International Art Festival City
of Medellin*, Medellin; *Foto text/text
foto*, Museum of Modern Art,
Bolzano; Frankfurt Kunstverein; *Le
Masque et le Miroir*, Museum of
Contemporary Art of Barcelona,
Barcelona **1996** *Jurassic
Technologies Revenant*, 10th Biennial
of Sydney, Sydney; *Le Masque et le
Miroir*, Rencontres Internationales de
la Photographie, Arles;
Inclusion/Exclusion, Kunstlerhaus,
Graz; *Radical Images: Austrian
Triennal of Photography 1996*, Neue
Galerie & Kunstlerhause, Graz;
Kunsthalle, Szombathely; *Interzones*,
Kunstforeningen Gl. Strand,
Copenhagen; Uppsala Konstmuseum,
Uppsala; *Ghostwriter*, Mercer Union,
Toronto; *Group Exhibition*, Haines
Gallery, San Francisco; *Auf Den Leib*,
Kunsthalle, Vienna; *Gallery Artists*,
Galerie Lumen Travo, Amsterdam;
Imaginary Beings, Exit Art, New York;
Video Installation, Brooklyn Bridge,
New York **1995** *Orientation*, USA
participation, Istanbul Biennial 95,
Istanbul; *Transculture*, Venice Biennial
95; Contemporary Art Museum,
Okayama; *Campo '95*, Venice
Biennial 95, Venice; Fondazione
Sandretto Rebaudengo Per L'Arte,
Turin; *It's How You Play the Game*,
Exit Art, New York **1994** *Three New

Photographers*, Haines Gallery, San
Francisco; *Revolving Histories*, SF
Camerawork, San Francisco;
Selection from the Artists File, Artists
Space, New York; *Labyrinth of Exile:
Recent Works by Four Contemporary
Iranian Artists*, Fowler Museum of
Cultural History, UCLA, Los Angeles;
Fever, Wexner Center, Columbus;
*Beyond the Borders: Art By Recent
Immigrants*, The Bronx Museum of
the Arts, Bronx; *The Office: History,
Fantasy and Irregular Protocols*, The
Lower Manhattan Cultural Council,
New York **1993** *Fever*, Exit Art
Gallery, New York

PUBLICATIONS
Has been featured in numerous
international journals and magazines.

Chris Ofili

Lives and works in London. Born in
Manchester in 1968, Ofili has been
exhibiting since 1989.

SELECTED SOLO EXHIBITIONS SINCE 1990
1999 Gavin Brown's enterprise, New
York **1998-99** Whitworth Art Gallery,
Manchester **1998** Southampton City
Art Gallery, Southampton; Serpentine
Gallery, London **1997** *Pimpin ain't
easy but it sure is fun*, Contemporary
Fine Art, Berlin **1996** *Afrodizzia*,
Victoria Miro Gallery, London **1995**
Gavin Brown's enterprise, New York
1991 *Paintings and Drawings*, Kepler
Gallery, London

SELECTED GROUP EXHIBITIONS SINCE 1990
1999 *Le Casa d'Arte*, Milan; *Trouble
Spot: Painting*, NICC and MUHKA,
Antwerp; 6th International Istanbul
Biennial; *Carnegie International*,
Carnegie Museum of Art, Pittsburgh
1998 *About Vision: New British
Painting in the 1990's*, Laing Art
Gallery, Newcastle; *Pictura Britannica*,
Museum of New Zealand Te Papa
Tongarewa, Wellington; *A to Z*, The
approach, London; *Heads willl roll*,
Victoria Miro Gallery, London; *The
Jerwood Foundation Painting Prize*,
Jerwood Gallery, London; *Sensation:
Young British Artists from the Saatchi
Collection*, Hamburger Bahnhof, Berlin
& Royal Academy of Arts, London;
The Turner Prize, Tate Gallery, London
1997-1998 *Pictura Britannica*, Art
Gallery of South Australia, Adelaide;
Date with an artist, Northern Gallery
for Contemporary Art, Sunderland
1997 *Popoccultural*, Southampton
City Gallery; *Belladonna*, ICA, London;
*About Vision: New British Painting in
the 1990's*, The Fruitmarket Gallery
Edinburgh & Christchurch Mansion,
Ipswich; *Package Holiday*, New
British Art in the Ophiuchus Collection,
The Hydra Workshop, Hydra; *Pictura
Britannica*, Museum of Contemporary
Art, Sydney; *Minor Sensation*,
Victoria Miro Gallery, London; *20th
John Moores Liverpool Exhibition of
Contemporary Painting*, Walker Art
Gallery, Liverpool; *Dimensions
Variable*, Helsinki City Art Museum &
Stockholm Royal Academy of Free
Arts & Soros Centre for Contemporary
Art & Gallery Zacheta, Warsaw &

Städtische Kunstsammlungen
Chemnitz & Prague National Gallery of
Modern Art & Zagreb Union of
Croatian Artists & Magistrat der
Stradt Darmstadt & Vilnius
Contemporary Art Centre & Budapest
Museum of Contemporary Arts &
Ludwig Museum, Budapest & Slovak
National Gallery Bratislava &
Bucharest National Theatre Galleries
1996-1997 *Mothership Connection*,
Stedelijk Museum Bureau,
Amsterdam **1996** *About Vision: New
British Painting in the 1990's*,
Museum of Modern Art, Oxford;
Young British Artists, Roslyn Oxley9
Gallery, Paddington; *NowHere*,
Louisiana Museum of Modern Art;
Maps Elsewhere, Institute of
International Visual Arts, London;
Brilliant! New Art From London,
Museum of Contemporary Art,
Houston; *Wingate Young Artists
Award*, Art '96, Business Design
Centre, Islington, London; *British Art
Show 4*, toured in England;
Popoccultural, South London Gallery
1995 *Cocaine Orgasm*, Bank Space,
London; *Prints*, Brooke Alexander
Gallery, New York; *Im/Pure*,
Osterwalder's Art Office, Hamburg;
John Moore's Exhibition, Walker Art
Centre, Liverpool; *Contained*, Cultural
Instructions, London; *A Bonnie
Situation*, Contemporary Fine Art,
Berlin; *Brilliant! New Art from London*,
Walker Art Centre, Minneapolis;
Shoshana Wayne Gallery, LA
Invitational, Los Angeles; *Selections
Spring '95*, The Drawing Centre, New
York **1994** *Miniatures*, The Agency,
London; *Take Five*, Anthony Wilkinson
Fine Art, London; *Painting Show*,
Victoria Miro Gallery; **1993-1994** *BT
New Contemporaries*, Cornerhouse
Gallery, Manchester & Orchard
Gallery, Derry & Mappin Art Gallery,
Sheffield & Stoke-on-Trent Gallery,
CCA, Glasgow **1993** *Shit Sale*, Brick
Lane, London; *Shit Sale*, Strasse 17
Juni, Berlin; *Borderless Print*,
Rochdale Art Gallery, London; *To
Boldly Go*, Cubitt Street Gallery,
London; *Riverside Open*, Riverside
Gallery, London; *Tokyo Print Biennale*,
Manchida City Museum, Tokyo; *Lift*,
Atlantis Basement, London **1992-93**
Pachipamwe International artists'
workshop exhibition, Bulawayo Art
Gallery, Harare **1991** *Whitworth Young
Contemporaries*, Whitworth Art
Gallery, Manchester; *BP Portrait
Award*, National Portrait Gallery;
London; *Blauer Montag*, Raum für
Kunst, Basel **1990** *Whitworth Young
Contemporaries*, Whitworth Art
Gallery, Manchester; *BP Portrait
Award*, National Portrait Gallery,
London

PUBLICATIONS
Has been featured in numerous
international journals and magazines
SELECTED READING **2000** *High Art Lite*,
J. Stallabrass, Verso, London & New
York. **1999** *Trouble Spot: Painting*,
edited by K. Vanbelleghem and
T. Vermeulen, NICC and MUHKA,
Antwerp; VISION. *50 Years of British
Creativity*, Thames and Hudson,
London; *Young British Art: The

Saatchi Decade, Booth-Clibborn Editions, London **1998** *Chris Ofili*, exhibition catalogue, Southampton City Art Gallery and the Serpentine Gallery, London **1997** *Date with an artist*, K. Alexander and L. Wirz, BBC Education Production

Yoko Ono

Lives and works in New York. Born in Tokyo in 1933, Ono has been exhibiting and performing since 1960.

PERFORMANCE WORKS

1966 Africa Centre, London **1965** *Perpetual Fluxus Concert*, East End Theater, New York; *Cut Piece*, Yamachi Hall, Kyoto **1962** Sogetsu Art Center, Tokyo **1961** Carnegie Recital Hall, New York

FILMS

1970 *Fly* **1969** *Rape* **1968** *No. 5 Smile* **1966** *No. 4 Bottoms* **1964** *Six Film Scores*

MUSIC/SOUND RECORDINGS

1995 *Rising* **1992** *Onobox* **1981** *Season of Glass* **1980** *Double Fantasy 1* **1973** *Feeling the Space* **1972** *Approximately Infinite Universe* **1971** *Fly* **1968** *Two Virgins* **1962** *Cough Piece*

MUSIC PERFORMANCE

1996 Rising World Tour **1986** Starpeace World Tour **1974** Feeling the Space Tour, Japan

BILLBOARD/PUBLIC SPACE WORKS

1999 *Open Window* **1997** *Have You Seen the Horizon Lately?* **1996** *Fly* **1994** *In Celebration of Being Human* **1969-1970** *War is Over!*

PHOTOGRAPHY BASED WORKS

1998 *Memory Paintings* **1997** *Vertical Memory*; *Mommy Was Beautiful* **1992** *Portrait of Nora*

INSTALLATION WORKS

1997 *Morning Beams*; *Exlt* **1996** *Cleaning Piece*; *Wish Tree* **1992** *Endangered Species* **1990** *En Trance* **1967** *Half-A-Room* **1966** *Blue Room*

SELECTED SOLO EXHIBITIONS

2000 *Senses & Sensitivity* (tentative title) Placio de Sastago, Zaragosa **1999-2000** *Open Window* Um El Fahem **1999** *Impressions*, Bergen Kunstmuseum **1998-1999** *Wish Trees For Brazil*, Brazil **1997-2000** *Have You Seen the Horizon Lately?* Museum of Modern Art, Oxford & Israel Museum, Jerusalem **1996-1999** *Entrance-Ex It*, The Generalitat Valenciana, Spain & South America

BOOKS

1996 *Acorns*, Y. Ono, a book created specifically for the web **1995** *Instruction Paintings*, Y. Ono, Weatherhill NY; *Pennyviews*, Turkey Press, California **1971** *Grapefruit*, Y. Ono, Museum of Modern (F)Art 1971

Mike Parr

Lives and works in Sydney. Born in 1945, Parr has been exhibiting since 1969.

SELECTED SOLO EXHIBITIONS SINCE 1990

1999 *Deep Sleep [The Analytical Disabling of Mind and Matter]* Noxon/Parr, 72 hour performance, National Portrait Gallery, Canberra; *Wrong Face*, Anna Schwartz Gallery, Melbourne; *Three Collaborations*, Sarah Cottier Gallery, Sydney **1998** *Female Factory*, 7 hour performance, Australian Center for Contemporary Art, Melbourne; *Blood Box*, 24 hour performance, Artspace, Sydney; *Photo-Realism*, Anna Schwartz Gallery, Melbourne; *Mike Parr*, Shepparton Art Gallery; *Mike Parr*, Sherman Galleries Hargrave Sydney; *The Rest of Time*, Sherman Galleries Goodhope, Sydney; *Outrage 3*, Artspace, Sydney **1997** Anna Schwartz Gallery, Melbourne **1996** *The Infinity Machine*, Sherman Galleries Goodhope, Sydney; Anna Schwartz Gallery, Melbourne; *Head on a Plate*, New York Studio School, New York; *The White Hybrid (Fading)*, Artspace, Sydney; *Unword*, University of Western Australia, Nedlands **1995** *The Illusion of the End*, Sherman Galleries Goodhope and Hargrave, Sydney; *Day Break*, Scene Shop at the Cultural Centre of Manila, Manila **1994** *Mike Parr*, Anna Schwartz Gallery, Melbourne; *Works from the Self Portrait Project*, Brisbane City Hall Art Gallery and Museum, Brisbane; *Echolalia (the road): Prints from the Self Portrait Project: Mike Parr 1987-1994*, National Gallery of Victoria, Melbourne **1993** *100 Breaths* from (ALPHABET/HAEMORRHAGE) *Black Box of 100 Self Portrait Etchings, 2, 1992*, Royal Melbourne Institute of Technology, Melbourne; *Pinch*, Victorian College of the Arts, Melbourne; *Visiting Australian Artist*, Kunst, Sydney; *Mike Parr*, Roslyn Oxley9 Gallery, Sydney; *Black Mirror/Pale Fire, Various Routes, Whistle/White*, Ivan Dougherty Gallery, Sydney **1992** *Survey of Prints*, Delaney Gallery, Perth; *ALPHABET/HAEMORRHAGE*, Arthouse, Perth & Institute of Modern Art, Brisbane & City Gallery, Melbourne & Museum of Contemporary Art, Sydney; *Memory of a Monochrome (for John Nixon)*, A-Atrophy, Field/Feeled, School of Fine Arts, The University of New South Wales, Sydney; *100 Breaths* from (ALPHABET/HAEMORRHAGE) *Black Box of 100 Self Portrait Etchings*, Australian National Gallery, Canberra; *Memory of a Monochrome Part 1 (Belah/Belly), Memory of a Monochrome Part 2 (Bloodhouse/Blow), Introjection of a Chair (Block/Blood), Green Self Portrait (Bitzer/Black)*, from *Black Book*, The Gunnery, Sydney; *The Shelf*, Nixon/Parr 1972-1992, Art Gallery of New South Wales, Sydney **1991** *Mike Parr, Artist in Residence 1990-1991*, Ian Potter Gallery, The University of Melbourne Museum of Art, Melbourne;

3 Installations, City Gallery, Melbourne; *Mike Parr*, Roslyn Oxley9 Gallery, Sydney; *Survey of Recent Work*, Art Gallery of New South Wales, Sydney; Perth Institute of Contemporary Art, Perth **1990** *I think of Drypoint in terms of Braille and Excavation*, The Drill Hall Gallery, National Gallery of Australia, Canberra; *Drawings from the Self Portrait Project 1983-1990*, City Gallery, Melbourne; *Köln Art Fair*, Roslyn Oxley9 Gallery, Sydney

SELECTED GROUP EXHIBITIONS SINCE 1990

1999 *Other Stories: Five Australian Artists*, Hokkaido Museum of Modern Art, Sapporo; *Parr Sachs Tillers Young*, Orange Regional Gallery, Orange; *home and away*, Auckland Art Gallery, Auckland; *Five Continents and One City*, Mexico City Gallery; *Trace*, Liverpool Biennial of Contemporary Art, Liverpool **1998** *Wounds: Between Democracy and Redemption in Contemporary Art*, Moderna Museet, Stockholm; *Southern Reflections: An Exhibition of Contemporary Australian Art to Northern Europe*, Kulturhaus, Stockholm & Konathallen Götsberg, Gothenberg & Arhus Konstmuseum, Arhus & Museum Tamminiementle, Helsinki & Neues Museum, Bremen & Staatliche Sammlung fur Kunst, Chemnitz; *Telling Tales*, Ivan Dougherty Gallery, Sydney; *Red Field (Liquidation)*, Australian Centre for Contemporary Art, Melbourne **1997** *Anon*, Sherman Galleries Goodhope, Sydney; *Dead Sun*, Art Gallery of New South Wales, Sydney; *Body*, Art Gallery of New South Wales, Sydney; *Tokyo International Art Festival*, Tokyo International Forum, Tokyo; *In Place (Out of Time): Contemporary Art in Australia*, Museum of Modern Art, Oxford & Art Gallery of Western Australia, Perth; *Media and Human Body*, The Fukui Biennale 7, Fukui City Art Museum, Fukui; *Havana Biennale*, Havana; *The Real Thing*, Museum of Modern Art at Heide, Melbourne **1996** *Systems End: Contemporary Art in Australia*, OXY Gallery, Osaka & Hakone Open-Air Museum, Tokyo, Dong-Ah Gallery, Seoul; *Spirit & Place: Art in Australia 1861-1996*, Museum of Contemporary Art, Sydney; *No Exit: The Guinness Contemporary Art Project*, Art Gallery of New South Wales, Sydney **1995** *Antipodean Currents: 10 Contemporary Artists from Australia*, Guggenheim Museum SoHo, New York; *Kedumba Drawing Award 1995*, Fairmont Resort, Leura **1994** *25 Years of Performance Art in Australia*, Ivan Dougherty Gallery, Sydney & Institute of Modern Art, Brisbane & Perth Institute of Contemporary Arts, Perth & Experimental Art Foundation, Adelaide & Australian Centre for Contemporary Art, Melbourne; *Tell me a Story*, Plimsoll Gallery, Centre for the Arts, Hobart; *Adelaide Installations*, 1994 Adelaide Biennial of Australian Art, Adelaide **1993** *The Joan and Peter Clemenger Triennial*

Exhibition of Contemporary Australian Art, National Gallery of Victoria, Melbourne; *Identities: Art from Australia*, Taipei Fine Arts Museum, Taipei; Wollongong City Gallery, Wollongong; *The Black Show*, Geelong Art Gallery & Warrnambool Art Gallery & Waverley City Art Gallery & Mildura Arts Centre & La Trobe Regional Gallery & Orange Regional Gallery & Wollongong City Gallery & Nolan Gallery Canberra **1992** *Pages*, The Museum Collection, Museum of Contemporary Art, Sydney; *My Head is a Map – A Decade of Australian Prints*, National Gallery of Australia, Canberra **1991** *Early and Recent Work by 8 Contemporary Artists*, City Gallery, Melbourne; *The Corporeal Body*, The Drill Hall, Canberra; *Off the Wall / In the Air: A Seventies' Selection*, Monash University Gallery & Australian Centre for Contemporary Art, Melbourne; *Opening Transformations*, Museum of Contemporary Art, Sydney; *Contemporary Art Archive*, Museum of Contemporary Art, Sydney **1990** *EDGE 90: The New Work (Art & Life in the Nineties)*, Newcastle-upon-Tyne; *Group Show*, Roslyn Oxley9 Gallery, Sydney; *Acquisitions 1984-90: A Collection of Contemporary Australian Art*, Griffith University, Brisbane; *Inland*, Australian Centre for Contemporary Art, Melbourne

PUBLICATIONS

Has been featured in numerous international journals and magazines SELECTED READING **1999** 'Australia's 50 most collectable Artists', Australian Art Collector, Issue 7, Jan-Mar **1997** *In Relief: Australian Wood Engravings, Woodcuts and Lino*, J. Smith, National Gallery of Victoria, Melbourne; *Spirit and Place: Art in Australia 1861-1996*, exhibition catalogue, N. Waterlow, Museum of Contemporary Art, Sydney; 'A Conversation', *Body*, exhibition catalogue, A. Bond and M. Parr, Art Gallery of New South Wales, Bookman Schwartz, Melbourne; *In Place (Out of Time): Contemporary Art in Australia*, exhibition catalogue, H. Morphy and D. Elliott, Museum of Modern Art, Oxford; 'The Construction of Difference', *Media and Human Body*, exhibition catalogue, M. Parr, Fukui Biennale 7, Fukui City Art Museum, Fukui, Japan; *Dead Sun*, M. Parr and P. Ross, Art Gallery of New South Wales, Sydney **1991** *Identities: A Critical Study of the Work of Mike Parr 1970-1990*, David Bromfield, University of Western Australia, Perth

Lisa Reihana

Lives and works in Auckland. Born in 1964, Reihana has been exhibiting since 1990. Collaborations with the Pacific Sisters began in 1995.

SELECTED SOLO EXHIBITION SINCE 1990

1999 *Fluffy Fings*, Archill Gallery **1998** *Fluffy Fings*, Performance

Space, Sydney **1993** *Take*, Robert McDougall Art Annexe, Christchurch

SELECTED GROUP EXHIBITIONS SINCE 1990
1999 *Toi Toi Toi*, Museum Fridericianum, Kassal; Auckland Art Gallery, Auckland; *More Then Ever*, Fiat Lux Gallery, Auckland **1998** *Facing It – Art Now Looks Back*, Te Papa Tongarewa, Wellington; *Fisi – The Blossoming of the Waves*, Mori Gallery, Sydney **1997** *Inei/Konei*, Australian Centre for Photography, Sydney **1996** *Second Asia Pacific Triennial*, Brisbane; *Badge*, Fisher Gallery, Auckland; *Lapa*, Lopdell House, Auckland; *Monitor*, Physics Room, Christchurch; Dunedin Public Art Gallery, Dunedin; Wellington City Gallery, Wellington **1995** *Korurangi – Contemporary Maori Art*, New Gallery, Auckland **1992** *ARX – 3*, Perth Institute Contemporary Art, Perth; *Fourth Wind*, CSA Gallery, Christchurch; *Tales Untold*, South Island Arts Project, Christchurch **1990** *Choice* Artspace Gallery, Auckland

PUBLICATIONS
Has been featured in numerous international journals and magazines
SELECTED READING **1999** *Toi Toi Toi: Three Generations of Artists from New Zealand*, Museum Fridericianum, Kassal; Auckland Art Gallery, Auckland **1998** 'Lisa Reihana Native Portraits', *Photofile*, No. 55, Australian Centre for Photography; 'Lisa Reihana's Video Weavings', *Art Asia Pacific*, No. 21 **1997** 'Wooden Heart', *Log Illustrated*, Winter, Christchurch; *Inei/Konei*, Australian Centre for Photography, Sydney **1996** 'Wish you were here', *Art Asia Pacific*, Vol. 3 No. 1 **1993** *Disrupted Borders: Skinflicks*, Rivers Orams Press, London **1991** *Pleasures and Dangers*, Longman Paul, New Zealand

Lisa Reihana & The Pacific Sisters

Henry Ah-Foo Taripo born in Auckland in 1965. Lives and works in Manukau.
Ani O'Neil born in 1971 Lives and works in Auckland
James Pinker born in 1960 Lives and works in Auckland
Rosanna Raymond born in Auckland in 1967. Lives and works in London.
Suzanne Tamaki born in 1966 Lives and works in Wellington
Niwhai Tupaea born in Hawkes Bayin 1971. Lives and works in Sydney.

Gerhard Richter

Has lived and worked in Cologne since 1983. Born in Dresden in 1932, Richter has been exhibiting since 1963.

BIOGRAPHY
1998 Wexner Prize, Columbus/Ohio **1997** Golden Lion of the 47th Venice Biennial; Praemium Imperiale Prize, Tokyo **1995** Wolf Prize in Arts, Jerusalem **1993-1994** Extensive retrospective in Paris, Bonn, Stockholm & Madrid **1989-1995** The cycle of paintings '18. Oktober 1977' is shown in Krefeld, Frankfurt, London, Rotterdam, Saint Louis, New York, Los Angeles, Boston & Jerusalem **1988** Guest professorship at the Städelschule Frankfurt; *Kaiserring* of the city of Goslar; Retrospective in Chicago, Toronto, Washington & San Francisco **1986** Extensive retrospective in Düsseldorf, Berlin, Bern & Vienna **1985** Oskar Kokoschka Prize, Vienna **1981** Arnold Bode Prize, Kassel **1978** Guest professorship at the College of Art in Halifax, Canada **1972** Exhibition in the German Pavilion at the 36th Venice Biennale; First participation in *documenta*, Kassel **1971** Professorship at the Art Academy in Düsseldorf (until 1994) **1967** Guest professor at the College of Fine Arts in Hamburg; Art Prize *Junger Western* of the city of Recklinghausen **1963** Exhibition *Demonstation für den Kapitalistischen Realismus* in Düsseldorf together with Konrad Lueg and Sigmar Polke **1962** *Tisch*, an oil painting copied from a newspaper photograph, begins the index of works, that is continued up to this date, with the number 1 **1961** Moves to Düsseldorf and studies there for two years under K. O. Götz at the Art Academy. Here he meets Konrad Lueg, Sigmar Polke and Blinky Palermo **1952-1957** Studies at the Dresden Art Academy

Ginger Riley

Mara. Lives and works in South East Arnhem Land, Northern Territory. Born in 1937, Riley has been exhibiting since 1987.

SELECTED SOLO EXHIBITIONS SINCE 1990
1999 *Always at Home*, Alcaston Gallery, Melbourne **1998** *The same but different*, Alcaston Gallery, Melbourne **1997** *Ginger Riley – 10 Year Retrospective*, National Gallery of Victoria, Melbourne **1995** *Ginger Riley Munduwalawala – you can see for long way*, Alcaston House Gallery, Melbourne **1994** *Ginger Riley*, Alcaston House Gallery, Melbourne **1991** *Ginger Riley Munduwalawala – Limmen Bight Country South East Arnhem Land*, Tandanya National Aboriginal Cultural Institute, Adelaide (in conjunction with Alcaston House Gallery, Melbourne); *Ginger Riley Munduwalawala – My Mother's Country Limmen Bight Gulf of Carpentaria*, Hogarth Gallery, Sydney (in conjunction with Alcaston House Gallery, Melbourne); *Ginger Riley Munduwalawala*, The Australia Gallery, SoHo, New York (in conjunction with Alcaston House Gallery, Melbourne); *Ginger Riley Munduwalawala*, William Mora Galleries, Melbourne (in conjunction with Alcaston House Gallery, Melbourne) **1990** *Ginger Riley Munduwalawala – Limmen Bight Country*, William Mora Galleries, Melbourne (in conjunction with Alcaston House Gallery, Melbourne)

SELECTED GROUP EXHIBITIONS SINCE 1990
2000 *Beyond the Pale*, 2000 Adelaide Biennial, Art Gallery of South Australia, Adelaide **1999** *Spirit Country: Australia Aboriginal Art from the Gantner Myer Collection*, Fine Arts Museums of San Francisco, San Francisco; *All About Art*, Alcaston House Gallery, Melbourne **1998** *All About Art*, Alcaston House Gallery, Melbourne; *Australian Contemporary Art Fair*, Exhibition Buildings, Melbourne; *Christmas Show 1998*, Alcaston House Gallery, Melbourne **1997** *Ngundungunya: Art for Everyone*, National Gallery of Victoria, Melbourne; *Beat Strit – ten years on*, Alcaston House Gallery, Melbourne; *Brisbane V Essendon*, Fireworks Gallery, Brisbane (in conjunction with Alcaston House Gallery, Melbourne); *Imaging the Land*, National Gallery of Victoria, Melbourne **1996** *Hidden Treasures – Australian Football League Centennial Art Expo*, Melbourne Function Centre, Melbourne; *All about Art*, Alcaston House Gallery, Melbourne **1995-1996** *Aboriginal & Torres Strait Islander National Art Award*, MAGNT touring exhibition **1995** *Stories – A Journey Around Big Things*, The Holmes a Court Collection, Sprengel Museum, Hannover & Museum fur Volkerkunde zu Leipzig & Haus der Kulturen der Welt, Berlin & Ludwig-Forum fur Internationle Kunst, Aachen; *Interweave – Tapestry a Collaborative Art*, Museum of Modern Art at Heide, Melbourne; *Roper River*, Hogarth Galleries, Sydney (in conjunction with Alcaston House Gallery, Melbourne) **1994** *The John McCaughey Memorial Art Prize*, National Gallery of Victoria, Melbourne; *Tyerabarrbowaryaou II*, The Fifth Havana Biennial, Havana & Museum of Contemporary Art, Sydney; *Yiribana*, Art Gallery of New South Wales, Sydney **1993-1994** *Aratjara: Art of the First Australians*, Kunstsammlung Dusseldorf & Hayward Gallery, London & Louisiana Museum, Humlebaek; *National Bank River Collection*, travelling exhibition; **1992-1993** *Heritage of Namatjira*, travelling exhibition **1992** Hogarth Gallery, Sydney (in conjunction with Alcaston House Gallery, Melbourne); *The Alice Springs Prize*, Araluen, Alice Springs; National Museum of Modem Art, Kyoto (in conjunction with Art Gallery of Western Australia) **1991-1992** *Flash Pictures*, National Gallery of Australia, Canberra **1991** Austral Gallery St Louis, (in conjunction with Alcaston House Gallery, Melbourne); *Aboriginal Art and Spirituality*, The High Court of Australia, Canberra & Parliament House, Canberra & The Exhibitions Gallery, The Waverley Centre, Wheelers Hill & The Ballarat Fine Art Gallery, Ballarat **1990** *Contemporary Aboriginal Art from the Holmes à Court Collection*, Carpenter Centre for the Visual Arts, Harvard University & James Ford Bell

Country, William Mora Galleries, Melbourne (in conjunction with Alcaston House Gallery, Melbourne)

SELECTED GROUP EXHIBITIONS SINCE 1990
Museum, University of Minnesota & Lakewood Centre for the Visual Arts, Lake Oswego & Art Gallery of New South Wales, Sydney

PUBLICATIONS
Has been featured in numerous international journals and magazines
SELECTED READING **1999** *Spirit and Place: Source of the Sacred?* M. Griffith and J. Tulip, **1998** *Australian International Religion*, Literature and the Arts Conference Proceedings, Centre for Studies in Religion, Literature and the Arts, Australian Catholic University; *Spirit County*, J. Isaacs, Fine Arts Museums of San Francisco **1997** *Ginger Riley – Ten Year Retrospective*, J. Ryan, National Gallery of Victoria; *Stories: A Journey Around Big Things – work by 11 Aboriginal Artists*, The Holmes à Court Collection, A. M. Brody, Craftsman House **1994** *Tyerabarrbowaryaou II*, Museum of Contemporary Art, Sydney

Pipilotti Rist

Lives and works in Zurich. Born in The Swiss Rhyne Valley in 1962, Rist has been exhibiting and performing since 1984.

SELECTED PERFORMANCES SINCE 1990
1999 Galeria d'Arte Moderna di Torino, Turin; *Performing Generations: Classic and Contemporary Performative Video*, Art Gallery of Greater Victoria, Victoria; International Videoart Festival Videoarchelogy, Sofia; Metropolitan Museum of Contemporary Art, Tokyo; Public Art Fund, New York; Winterthurer Musikfestwochen, Winterthur; The Images Festival of Independent Film and Video, Toronto; MAMCO, Geneva; *Experimentalfilm im Klostergarten Land- und Leidenschaften*, Kunstmuseum des Kantons Thurgau, Warth; *Performing Generations: Classic and Contemporary Video*, Art Gallery of Missisauga, Mississauga; Medienkunst Festival, Communication Front, Plovdiv; *TABU – Erotischer Blick und dokumentarischer Film*, Haus des Dokumentarfilms, Stuttgart; Wacoal Art Center: SPIRAL TV, Tokyo; International Film Festival Rotterdam, Rotterdam; Moderna Museet, Stockholm **1998** Tate Gallery, London; Experimental Film Festival, Tirana/Albanien; Filmclub Xenix, Auswahl Schweizerfilme in Dharamsala, Dharamsala; Frauenmuseum Meran, Meran; Austauschprogramm Videokunst Kanada-Schweiz, Montréal, Québec-City, Toronto; *Grenzenlos Berlin a Barcelona*, Art club Berlin, Berlin; Kunstmuseum Bern, Bern; Impakt Festival, Utrecht; Sveriges Television, Malmö; PODEWIL, Berlin; 11th Annual Dallas Video Festival, Dallas; Visibilità Zero, Rome; *Frankfurt IV: Grenzübertretung (Neue Schweizer Filme)*, Frankfurt; Video Art Festival Locarno **1997** A *Scenic Detour through Commodity Culture* Jan van

Eyck Academy, Maastricht; *Never Mind the nineties*, HdK Berlin; *Sex und Traum*, Kunsthaus Zurich; *Women and the Art of Multimedia*, National Museum of Women in the Art, Washington; *1 minute scéenario*, printemps de cahors Kulturkreis Zollikon; *Transit Oeuvres du Fonds national dart contemporain*, Paris; *The Sixth New York Video Festival*, Lincoln Center; *Transcontinent*, London Film Makers Co-op; Art Club Berlin; *Three Video Stations: Pipilotti Rist, Yael Feldmann, Sylvie Fleury*, Herzliya Museum of Art; 1. Filmfestival Zurich; Centre dart contemporain de Basse-Normandie; Progetto Giovanni, Milano **1996** Looking Awry, Ambassade du Brésil, Paris; Fernsehen DRS; *Inside the Visible*, The Institute of Contemporary Art, Boston; *Hello World*, Museum für Gestaltung, Zurich; Centre George Pompidou Paris; The Winnipeg Women's International Film & Video Festival, Winnipeg; *Joined*, Kunstwerk Cologne; Landesgalerie Linz; Förderkreis der Leipziger Galerier für Zeitgenössische Kunst, Leipzig; Deutsche Film- & Fernsehakademie, Berlin; *Fuzzy Logic*, ICA, Boston; *Escape Attempts*, Fabrikken Christiania, Copenhagen; *Feminale*, Köln; *Surfing Systems*, Kassel; *Auto reverse 2*, Magazin, Grenoble; *Video Viewpoints*, Museum of Modern Art, New York & elbow room, Art Chicago **1995** *FrauenWoche*, Chaotikum, Zug; *New Media Logia*, Soros Center Contemporary Arts, Moscow; *8th Stuttgarter Filmwinter*, Stuttgart; Filmfest Bremen; Musée des Beaux Arts, Lausanne; Frauenwerkschau Filmtage Zofingen; Kadertagung Schweizerische Nationalbank, Davos; Fra nord e sud, compositrice italiane e svizzere, Rome; *Art Metropol: Money Talks ... Art Walks*, Linda Génereux Gallery, Toronto; Casino Knokke kine(kunst)95, Knokke; Cinéville Subsoil, Zurich; *Auktion für das Arbeitslosenkowithee*, Galerie Goetz, Basel; *Kurzfilmnacht*, Uster; *Stay or Go*, Galleri Bie & Vadstrup, Frederiksberg, Viper, Lucerne; *Naughty Girls*, Zaal de Unie & Nederland Filmmuseum, Rotterdam; Vorführung, Kunstschule Hertsogen Bosch; *True visions of nature*, reVisions Womens Film & Video Festivals, Winnipeg; Frauen-Film-Wochenende, Würzburg; *Show must go on*, Fondation Cartier pour l'art contemporain, Paris; Stichting Bellissima, Amsterdam **1994** Filmfest, Kassel; Film- und Videotage, Basel; *Videoausstellung*, Collège Marcel Duchamps, Chateauroux; *Festival Silence elles tournent*, Montréal; *No Mans Land*, Palazzo delle Esposizioni, Rome; *Discours Amoureux*, Saint Gervais Geneva; *Minima Media*, Medienbiennale Leipzig; *International Video Festival*, New York; *New Media Logia*, Soros Center for Contemporary Arts, Moscow; Institute of Contemporary Arts, Perth; Contemporary Art Center, Moscow **1993** Filmfestival Uppsala; *Femme Totale*, Dortmund;

Sinemafestival, Antwerp; *Carte Blanche der A BAO A QOU Paris* at Electronic Art Intermix, New York & Musée d'Art Moderne, Paris **1992** Medienkunstfest, Osnabrück; 38th Westdeutsche Kurzfilmtage, Oberhausen Fernsehen DRS; Int. Filmfestival, Locarno; 4th Int. Video-Biennale Museo d'arte Moderno, Mendellin; *New Visions*, Glasgow; Videoartfestival, Montbéliards **1991** Perlen vor die Säue, Festival Berlin 91 Viper, Lucerne; Bergen aan Zee, Stedelijk Museum, Amsterdam **1990** Kunstmesse, Frankfurt; Feminale, Köln; Festival Int. de Film et Video de Femmes, Montreal; Videozart, Zurich; Video Suico Contemperano, Lisbon; Filmfest, Kassel; Sound Basis Visual Art Festival, Warsaw

SELECTED GROUP EXHIBITIONS SINCE 1990
2000 *Wonderland*, The Saint Louis Art Museum, Saint-Louis; *Over the Edges*, Stedelijk Museum voor Actuele Kunst, Gent; *Snapshot*, Contemporary Museum, Baltimore; *Beauty Now: Evolving Esthetics and Contemporary Art*, Haus der Kunst, Munich **1999** *Quelques unes des récentes acquisition de la Collection Frac Rhône-Alpes*, Institut d'art contemporain, Villeurbanne; Galerija Likovnih Umetnosti Slovenj Gradec, Slovenja; Parkett Verlag, Vergriffene und Neue Parkett-Editionen, Zurich; Centre d'Art Contemporain, Geneva; Kunstmuseum St Gallen, St Gallen; *Video-Aus der Sammlung,* Kunsthaus Zürich, Zurich; *Blown Away*, 6th Caribbean Biennial, San Martin; Centraal Museum, Utrecht; Kunstmuseum Bonn, Bonn; *d'APERTutto*, Biennale di Venezia, Venice; *Beauty Now: Evolving Esthetics and Contemporary Art*, Hirshhorn Museum and Sculpture Garden, Washington; *The Passion and the Waves*, 6th International Istanbul Biennial, Istanbul; *Vision of the Body in Fashion*, Metropolitan Museum of Modern Art, Tokyo **1998** Luhring Augustine Gallery, New York; *Global Vision: New Art from the 90s*, Deste Foundation, Athens; *Trance*, Philadelphia Museum of Art, Philadelphia; *La coscienza luccicante: Arte nelletà elettronica*, Palazzo delle Esposizioni, Rome; *Nonchalance Revisited*, Akademie der Künste, Berlin; *Swiss Contemporary Art,* Sun Gok Museum, Seoul; *Divas,* Western Front, Center of the Arts, Vancouver; *Strange Days,* Art Gallery of New South Wales, Sydney; Guggenheim Museum Soho, New York; Berlin Biennale, Klaus Biesenbach, Hans-Ulrich Obrist, Berlin; ARKIPELAG, Stockholm European Capital of Culture, Seehistorisches Museum Stockholm, Stockholm **1997** *On Life, Beauty, Translations and other Difficulties,* 5th International Istanbul Biennale, Istanbul; *Unmapping the Earth,* Kwangju Biennale, Seoul; *Lautre,* 4e Biennale de Lyon, Lyon; *Rooms with a View: Environments for Video,* Guggenheim Museum Soho, New York; *Epicenter Ljubljana,* Moderna Galerija Ljubljijana, Ljubljijana; *Some Kind of Heaven / Ein Stück vom*

Himmel, Corner House Manchester, Manchester & John Hansard Gallery, Southampton & South London Gallery London, London & Kunsthalle Nürnberg, Nuremberg **1996** *The Scream,* Arken Museum of Modern Art, cur. Kim Levin, Ishoj; *Electronic Undercurrents,* Statens Museum for Kunst, Copenhagen; *Mirades,* Museo d'Arte Contemporanea, Barcelona; *fremd Körper,* Museum für Gegenwartskunst, Basel; *mässig und gefrässig,* Museum für Angewandte Kunst, Vienna; *Ich und Du,* Museum für Gestaltung, Zurich; *Wunderbar,* Kunstraum Wien, Vienna **1995** *Femininmasculin: Le sexe de l'art,* Centre Pompidou, Paris; *Wild Walls,* Stedelijk Museum, Amsterdam; *How is everything,* Kunstbunker Nürnberg, Vienna; *Video Visions Cairo,* Cairo University, Cairo; *I confess,* Nicolaj Contemporary Art Centre, Copenhagen; Public Bologna, Bologna; *Beyond Switzerland,* Hong Kong Museum of Art, Hong Kong **1994** *Use Your Allusion: Recent Video Art,* Museum of Contemporary Art Chicago, Chicago; *Oh Boy, its a Girl! !* Feminismen in der Kunst, Kunstraum Wien, Vienna & Kunstverein München, Munich; *Arte in Video,* Le Case d'Arte, Milan **1993** *No Audience,* Galerie Vera Vita Gioia, Naples; *Aperto,* Biennale di Venezia, Venice; *Body & Co,* Documentario 2, Milan **1992** *Projekt Schweiz,* Kunst-halle Basel, Basel; *Überlebenskunst*, Kunsthaus Oerlikon, Zurich; *The Metaphor of Light / Poliset,* Centro Video Arte, Ferrara **1991** Inter-nationales Videoartfestival Locarno, Locarno; Kulturzentrum Kammgarn, Schaffhausen; Chamer Räume Kunst an Ort, Cham

PUBLICATIONS
Has featured in numerous international journals and magazines.

Dieter Roth
Born in Hannover in 1930. Dieter Roth died in Basel in 1998. Roth began exhibiting in the 1950s. He is widely published in numerous international journals and magazines, and has published over 200 artists' books. For details contact Gallery Hauser & Wirth & Presenhuber, Zürich.

Sanggawa (1994-1998)

FOUNDING MEMBERS
Elmer Borlongan born in 1967 College of Fine Arts, University of the Philippines
Karen O. Flores born in 1966 (BFA 1988) College of Fine Arts, University of the Philippines
Mark Justiniani born in 1966 College of Fine Arts, University of the Philippines
Jocelyn Mallari born in 1966 College of Fine Arts, University of the Philippines
Fedrico Sievert born in 1961 (BFA 1983) College of Fine Arts, University of Santo Tomas

SELECTED EXHIBITIONS
1998-1999 *At Home and Abroad: 20 Contemporary Filipino Artists*, Asian Art Museum of San Francisco & Contemporary Arts Museum, Houston & Metropolitan Museum of Manila **1998** *Alab ng Puso*, Metropolitan Museum of Manila **1997** *Glimpses Into the Future: Art in Southeast Asia 1997*, Museum of Contemporary Art, Tokyo & Hiroshima Museum of Contemporary Art **1996-1998** *Traditions/Tensions: Contemporary Art in Asia*, Asia Society Galleries, New York **1996** *The Second Asia-Pacific Triennial* Queensland Art Gallery, Brisbane; *Container 96: Art in cargo containers,* Copenhagen, Denmark; *Memories of Overdevelopment: Philippine diaspora in contemporary art*, University of California, Irvine

SELECTED MURAL COMMISSIONS
1998 *Engaging Echoes*, Asian Art Museum, Fukuoka; *Kasaysayan (History)*, Heroes Hall, Malacanang Palace, Manila **1997** *Balud kag*, Studio 1, ABS-CBN Compound, Quezon City **1996** *Paglaom, Padayon*, Studio 1, ABS-CBN Compound, Quezon City **1995** *Getting Into the Out*, Central Lecture Block, University of New South Wales, Kensington

PUBLICATIONS
Has been featured in numerous international journals and magazines.

Mick Namarari Tjapaltjarri
Pintupi. Born in the Nyunmanu region c. 1930. Mick Namarari Tjapaltjarri died in 1998. Tjapaltjarri commenced painting in 1971 and exhibiting in 1974.

SELECTED SOLO EXHIBITIONS SINCE 1990
1998 *Mick Namarari Tjapaltjarri: A Survey 1972-1997*, Utopia Art, Sydney **1994** *Mick Namarai Tjapaltjarri: New Paintings*, Utopia Art, Sydney **1993** *Namarari Tjapaltjarri and Maxie Tjampitjinpa*, Utopia Art, Sydney **1992** *Mick Namarari Tjapaltjarri*, Gallery Gabrielle Pizzi, Melbourne **1991** *Mick Namarari Tjapaltjarri*, Gallery Gabrielle Pizzi, Melbourne

SELECTED GROUP EXHIBITIONS SINCE 1990
1997 *Pintupi Painters*, Papunya Tula Artists, Alice Springs; *Nineteenninetyseven*, Utopia Art, Sydney; *The Chartwell Collection: A Selection*, Auckland City Art Gallery **1996** *Voices of the Earth*, Jehangir Nicholson Museum National Centre for the Performing Arts, Mumbai; *Spirit + Place*, Museum of Contemporary Art, Sydney; *Group Show*, Papunya Tula Artists, Alice Springs; *Contemporary Abstract Aboriginal Art,* Sherman Galleries, Sydney; *Contemporary Australian Abstraction*, Niagara Galleries, Melbourne **1995** Papunya Tula Artists, Alice Springs; Utopia Art, Sydney **1994** Spazio Krizla, Milan; Fondazione Gorrardo, Lugano; Gallerie Australis, Adelaide;

Chapman Gallery, Manuka, Canberra **1993** *Aratjara: Art of the First Australians,* Kunstammlung Nordheim-Westfalen, Düsseldorf & Hayward Gallery, London & Louisiana Museum of Modern Art, Denmark & Museum of Man, San Diego & the Art Gallery of Western Australia, Perth; *After the Field,* Manly Art Gallery, Sydney & Utopia Art, Sydney **1992** *Crossroads Towards a New Reality,* National Museum of Modern Art Kyoto, Japan & Museum of Modern Art, Tokyo; Contemporary Art Centre of South Australia; Ballarat Fine Art Gallery, Ballarat **1991** *The Painted Dream,* Auckland City Art Gallery, Auckland & the National Art Gallery and Museum, Wellington; SH Erwin Gallery, Sydney; Marble Hall, St Pertersburg **1990** Gallery Gabrielle Pizzi, Melbourne; *I'Ete Australien a Montpellier,* Museé Fabre Galerie Saint Ravy, Montpellier

PUBLICATIONS
Has been featured in numerous international journals and magazines.
SELECTED READING **1996** *Nangara,* J. Maughn and J. Zimmer, The Aboriginal Gallery of Dreamings, Melbourne; *Dreamings of the Desert,* V. Johnson, Art Gallery of South Australia, Adelaide **1994** *Aboriginal Artists of the Western Desert: A Bibilographical Dictionary,* V. Johnson, Craftsman House, Sydney **1993** *Aboriginal Art,* W. Caruana, Thames and Hudson, London **1991** *Papunya Tula Art of the Western Desert,* G. Bardon, McPhee Gribble, Melbourne; *Aboriginal Art and Spirituality,* edited by R. Crumlin, Collins Dove, Melbourne; *Desert Dreamings,* Aboriginal Art from Central Australia, Art Gallery of Western Australia, Perth **1990** *Contemporary Aboriginal Art,* A. Brody, Heytesbury Holdings, Perth; *The Face of the Centre: Papunya Tula Painting 1971-1984,* A. Brody, National Gallery of Victoria, Melbourne

Luc Tuymans
Lives and works in Antwerp, Belgium. Born in Mortsel in 1958, Tuymans has been exhibiting since 1985.

SELECTED SOLO EXHIBITIONS SINCE 1990
2000 Zeno X Gallery, Antwerpen; Wako Works of Art, Tokyo; Tokyo Opera City Art Gallery, Tokyo **1999** *The Passion,* Zeno X Gallery, Antwerpen; The Douglas Hyde Gallery, Dublin; *Splendid Isolation,* White Cube, London; *The Purge, Schilderijen – Paintings 1991-1998,* Bonnefantenmuseum, Maastricht & Kunstmuseum Wolfsburg; *Luc Tuymans,* Salzburger Kunstverein, Salzburg **1998** *Premonition. Drawings,* CAPC Musée d'art contemporain de Bordeaux, Bordeaux; *Der Architekt,* Galerie Gebauer, Berlin; *Delayed,* Anders Tornberg Gallery, Lund; *Security,*

David Zwirner Gallery, New York **1997** *Premonition. Zeichnungen,* Kunstmuseum Bern; *Ons Geluk,* one-year's presentation of Luc Tuymans and Dany Devos, Breydelstraat 5, Antwerpen; *Premonition: Drawings,* University Art Museum, Berkeley; *Illegitimate,* Zeno X Gallery, Antwerpen **1996** *The Heritage,* David Zwirner Gallery, New York; *Necklace,* Zeno X Gallery, Antwerpen **1995** *Superstition,* The Renaissance Society, Chicago; *Superstition,* Institute of Contemporary Art, London; *Le Verdict,* Centre genevois de gravure contemporaine, Genève; *Blow Up: Luc Tuymans childerijen/paintings 1985-1995,* De Pont, Tilburg; *Luc Tuymans: Paintings, 1978-1993,* Goldie Paley Gallery, Moore College of Art, Philadelphia; *Heimat,* Zeno X Gallery, Antwerpen; *The Agony,* Galeria Foksal SBWA, Warszawa; *Heimat,* Musée des Beaux-Arts, Nantes **1994** *Indelible Evidence,* Galerie Erika + Otto Friedrich, Bern; *Superstition,* Portikus, Frankfurt am Main & Gallery David Zwirner, New York & Art Gallery of York University, Toronto; *At random,* Zeno X Gallery, Antwerpen **1993** Museum Haus Lange, Krefeld; Galerie Paul Andriesse, Amsterdam; *Intolerance,* Zeno X Gallery, Antwerpen; Kabinett für Aktuelle Kunst, Bremerhaven **1992** Kunsthalle, Bern; Zeno X Gallery, Antwerpen; *Repulsion,* Isabella Kacprzak, Köln **1991** *Disenchantment,* Zeno X Gallery, Antwerpen; *Le Creux de l'Enfer,* Centre d'Art Contemporain, Thiers **1990** Provinciaal Museum voor Moderne Kunst, Oostende; Vereniging voor het Museum van Hedendaagse Kunst, Gent; *Tekeningen,* Schouwburg Galerij, Rotterdam; *Suspended,* Zeno X Gallery, Antwerpen; *Schilderijen 1978-1989,* Plateau, Brussel

SELECTED GROUP EXHIBITIONS SINCE 1990
2000 Tuymans – De Keyser, SMAK, Gent; Biennale of Sydney **1999** *Examining Pictures,* Whitechapel Art Gallery, London & MOCA Chicago; *Trouble Spot: Painting* MuHKA/NICC, Antwerpen; *De Opening* SMAK, Stedelijk Museum voor Aktuele Kunst, Gent; *Carnegie International 1999/2000,* Carnegie Museum of Art, Pittsburgh; *Am Horizont,* Kaiser Wilhelm Museum, Krefeld **1998** *58/98 The fascinating faces of Flanders through art and society,* Centro Cultural de Belém, Lisbon; *Privacy Luc Tuymans, Miroslav Balka,* Fundacao de Serralves, Porto **1997** *10 Jahre Stiftung Kunsthalle Bern,* Kunsthalle Bern; *Painting – The extended field,* Magasin 3 Konsthall, Stockholm; *La pittura fiamminga e olandese,* Palazzo Grassi, Venezia; *Future, Present, Past,* 47th Venice Biennial, Venice; *John Currin, Elisabeth Peyton, Luc Tuymans,* MOMA Museum of Modern Art, New York; *4e Biennale de Lyon,* Halle Tony Garnier, Lyon **1996** *Painting – The extended field,* Rooseum – Center for Contemporary Art, Malmö

& Magasin 3 Konsthall, Stockholm; *4x1 im Albertinum* Gemäldegalerie, Dresden; *Face à l'Histoire,* Centre Georges Pompidou, Paris; *Some Recent Acquisitions,* MOMA Museum of Modern Art, New York **1995** *Change of Scene VII,* Museum für Moderne Kunst, Frankfurt am Main; *Ars 95,* Museum of Contemporary Art, Helsinki; *Positionen,* Museum Folkwang, Essen; *Des Limites du Tableau,* Musée départemental de Rochechouart; *Ripple across the water,* The Watari Museum of Contemporary Art, Tokyo **1994** *Unbound: Possibilities in painting,* Hayward Gallery, London; *Zeitgenossen,* Kunstmuseum, Bern **1993** *Der Zerbrochene Spiegel: Positionen zür Malerei,* Kunsthalle, Wien & Deichtorhallen, Hamburg; *Het sublieme Gemis,* Koninklijk Museum voor Schone Kunsten, Antwerpen; *Menschenwelt,* Portikus, Frankfurt am Main; *Backstage,* Kunstverein, Hamburg; *Andere Länder – ander Sitten: Zeichnungen aus dem Kunstmuseum Bern,* Nationalgalerie Praag, Palais Kinsky **1992** *documenta IX,* Kassel

PUBLICATIONS
Has been featured in numerous international journals and magazines
SELECTED READING **1999** *La Consolation Magasin,* exhibition catalogue, centre National d'Art Contemporain; *Trouble Spot: Painting,* exhibition catalogue, MuHKA/NICC, Antwerpen; *De verzameling,* exhibition catalogue, Stedelijk Museum voor Aktuele Kunst, Gent; *Negotiating Small Truths,* exhibition catalogue, J. S. Blanton Museum of Art, Austin, Texas, USA **1998** *Fascinating faces of Flanders.* exhibition catalogue, Centro Cultural de Belem. Lisboa, Portugal

Ken Unsworth
Lives and works in Sydney. Born in Melbourne in 1931, Unsworth has been exhibiting since 1967.

SELECTED SOLO EXHIBITIONS SINCE 1990
1998 *Survey Ken Unsworth,* Art Gallery of New South Wales, Sydney **1997** *So you shall reap,* Australian Centre for Contemporary Art, Melbourne **1995** *Fly by Night,* Ruine des Kunste, Berlin **1993** *Australian Rhino,* Kunst Gallery, Sydney **1991** *Self and Environment,* Galerie Lunami, Tokyo

SELECTED GROUP EXHIBITIONS SINCE 1990
1999 *Chronos und Kairos,* Museum Fridericianum, Kassel **1998** *Telling Tales,* Ivan Dougherty Gallery, Sydney **1997** *Contempora 5,* National Gallery of Victoria, Melbourne; *Body,* Art Gallery of New South Wales, Sydney **1996** *Spirit and Place,* Museum of Contemporary Art, Sydney **1995** *Through a Glass Darkly,* Art Gallery of New South Wales, Sydney; *Istanbul Biennale,* Istanbul **1994** *Off and On, On and Off,* 25 Years of Performance Art, Ivan Dougherty

Gallery **1993** *Luminaries,* Monash University, Melbourne; *Confrontations,* Ivan Dougherty Gallery, Sydney; *My Home is Your Home,* Lodz; *Inner Space,* Fifth Australian Sculpture Triennale, National Gallery of Victoria, Melbourne **1992** *Head Through the Wall,* Statens Museum for Kunst, Copenhagen & Helsinki, Reyjavik, Nuremberg; *Classical Modernism: The George Bell Circle,* National Gallery of Victoria, Melbourne; *Strangers in Paradise, Contemporary Australian Art to Korea,* National Museum of Contemporary Art, Seoul **1991** *Construction in Process, Return to Lodz,* Lodz **1990** *The Ready Made Boomerang,* 8th Biennale of Sydney, Art Gallery of New South Wales and Bond Store 4, Sydney

PUBLICATIONS
Has been featured in numerous international journals and magazines
SELECTED READING **1999** 'The Theatre of Life', *Sculpture,* K. Scarlett, Vol 18 No.5 **1996** 'Art Imitates Death', *Art Monthly,* G. Alexander **1994** 'My Home is Your Home', *Art & Text,* Gregory Volk, No. 47, January; 'Ken Unsworth', *Art & Text,* G. Forsyth, No.48 **1991** 'Ken Unsworth – The Moralising Moralist From Australia', *Arts by Australians Series 1,* E. Lynn, Australia Council **1988** 'Ken Unsworth at the DAAD Galerie', *Kunstforum,* T. Wulffen, February **1987** *Kunst und Elektronik,* D Galloway, Econ Verlag Dusseldorf **1978** 'Letter from Australia', *Art International,* E. Lynn, Vol XII5, July; 'The Performance Art of Ken Unsworth', *ICA Magazine,* P. McGillick, No. 9, January; *The Development of Australian Sculpture,* G. Sturgeon, Thames and Hudson

Adriana Varejão
Lives and works in Rio de Janeiro. Born in 1964, Varejão has been exhibiting since 1987.

SELECTED SOLO EXHIBITIONS SINCE 1990
2000 Lehmann Maupin Gallery, New York; Galeria Camargo Vilaça, São Paulo **1999** Museu Rufino Tamayo, Mexico; *Alegria,* Galeria Camargo Vilaça, São Paulo **1998** Galeria Soledad Lorenzo, Madrid; Pavilhão Branco, Instituto de Arte Contemporânea, Lisbon **1997** Galerie Ghislaine Hussenot, Paris; Museo de Arte Contemporaneo Sofia Imber, Caracas **1996** Galeria Camargo Vilaça, São Paulo; Galerie Barbara Farber, Amsterdam **1995** Annina Nosei Gallery, New York **1993** Thomas Cohn Arte Contemporânea, Rio de Janeiro **1992** Galerie Barbara Farber, Amsterdam; Galeria Luisa Strina, São Paulo **1991** Thomas Cohn Arte Contemporânea, Rio de Janeiro

SELECTED GROUP EXHIBITIONS SINCE 1990
1999 Liverpool Biennial, Liverpool; *Cinco Continentes e uma Cidade,* Museu da Cidade, Mexico; *Inconfidência Mineira-Imagens da Liberdade,* Secretaria de Estado da

Cultura, Governo de Minas Gerais, Belo Horizonte, Minas Gerais **1998** *Desde el cuerpo: alegorias de lo feminino*, Museu de Bellas Artes,Caracas; XXIV Bienal Internacional de São Paulo, São Paulo; *Situacionismo un grupo de fotografias*, Galeria OMR, Mexico; *Um Olhar Brasileiro*, Coleção Gilberto Gateaubriand, Haus der Kulturen der Welt, Berlin; *O Contemporaneo na Produção Artistica de Brasil e Portugal*, Centro Cultural São Paulo, São Paulo; *Fronteiras*, Itaú Cultural. São Paulo; *Camargo Vilaça BIS*, Galeria Camargo Vilaça, São Paulo **1997** *A Arte Contemporânea da Gravara Brasil – Reflexão 97*, MUMA, Museu Metropolitano de Arte de Curitiba, Curitiba; *Asi Esta La Cosa: Arte Objeto e Instalaciones de America Latina*, Centro Cultural Arte Contemporaneo, Mexico; Whitechapel Art Gallery, London **1996** *New Histories*, The Institute of Contemporary Art, Boston; *Excesso*, Paço das Artes, São Paulo; *96 Containers: Art Across the Oceans*, Copenhagen; Galerie Ghislaine Hussenot, Paris; *Avantpremière d'un muséeLe Musée d'Art Contemporain de Gand*, The Institut Néerlandais, Paris **1995** *Johannesburg Biennale*, Joannesburg; *Havanna / São Paulo*, Haus der Kulturen der Welt, Berlin; *TransCulture*, Venice Biennale, Palazzo Giustinian Lolin, Venice; Benesse Haouse Naoshima Contemporary Art Museum, Okayama City; *Mostra da Gravura*, Museu Municipal de Arte, Curitiba; Fundação Romulo Maiorana, Belem, Brazil; Museo Carrillo Gil, Mexico City; Galeria Camargo Vilaça, São Paulo **1994** V Bienal de la Habana, Havana; *Mapping*, Museum of Modern Art, New York; XXII Bienal Internacional de São Paulo, São Paulo **1993** *Panorama da Arte Brasileira Atual*, Museu de Arte Moderna, São Paulo; *De Rio a Rio*, Galeria OMR, Ciudad de Mexico **1991** *Viva Brasil Viva*, Liljevalchs Konsthall, Stockholm

PUBLICATIONS
Has been featured in numerous international journals and magazines
SELECTED READING **1997** *New Art*, M. Roxana, D. Murphy, & E. Sinaico, Harry N. Abrams Inc., New York; *Biblioteca Nacional, a história de uma coleção*, P. Herkenhoff, Editora Salamandra, Rio de Janeiro **1993** *Adriana Varejão: paginas de arte e teatro da historia*, P. Herkenhoff, Thomas Cohn Arte Contemporanea, Rio de Janeiro **1992** *Varejão A China within Brasil*, P. Herkenhoff, Galerie Barbara Farber, Amsterdam; *Terra Incognita*, A. Varejão, Galeria Luisa Strina, São Paulo

Jeff Wall
Lives and works in Vancouver. Born in 1946, Wall has been exhibiting since 1969.

SELECTED SOLO EXHIBITIONS SINCE 1990
1999 *Odradek*, Mies van der Rohe

Foundation, Barcelona; *Jeff Wall/Pepe Espaliu: Suspended Time*, EAC, Castellon; *Jeff Wall:Oeuvres 1990-1998*, Musée d'art contemporain de Montréal **1998** *Here and Now II: Jeff Wall* Henry Moore Institute, Leeds; *Jeff Wall: Photographs of Modern Life: Works from 1978 to 1997 in the Basel Public Art Collection and the Emanuel-Hoffmann-Foundation*, Museum für Gegenwartskunst, Basel; Marian Goodman Gallery, New York; Galerie Rüdiger Schöttle, Munich; Galerie Johnen & Schöttle, Cologne **1997** The Hirshhorn Museum and Sculpture Garden, Washington & The Museum of Contemporary Art, Los Angeles & Art Tower Mito, Mito **1996** Museum of Contemporary Art, Helsinki & Whitechapel Gallery, London & Chicago & Paris; *Jeff Wall: Landscapes and Other Pictures*, Kunstmuseum Wolfsburg, Wolfsburg; *Jeff Wall: Space and Vision*, Städtische Galerie im Lenbachhaus **1995** Museum of Contemporary Art, Chicago & the Museé Nationale du Jeu de Paume, Paris; Marian Goodman Gallery, New York **1994** The White Cube, London; Deichtorhallen, Hamburg; Stadtische Kunsthalle Dusseldorf; Galerie Rüdiger Schöttle, Munich; Neue Gesellschaft fur Bildende Kunst, Berlin; Centro d'Arte Reina Sofia, Madrid; Galerie Johnen & Schottle, Cologne; De Pont Foundation for Contemporary Art, Tilburg **1993** Kunstmuseum Luzern, Lucerne & The Irish Museum of Modern Art, Dublin; Galerie Roger Pailhas, Marseille; Fondation Cartier pour l'art contemporain, Jouy-en-Josas **1992** Louisiana Museum, Humlebaek; Palais des Beaux-Arts, Brussels; Marian Goodman Gallery, New York **1991** San Diego Museum of Contemporary Art, San Diego; Galerie Meert-Rihoux, Brussels; Galerie Christian Stein, Milan; Galerie Johnen & Schottle, Cologne **1990** *Jeff Wall 1990*, Vancouver Art Gallery, Vancouver & Art Gallery of Ontario, Toronto; The Carnegie Museum of Art, Pittsburgh; The Ydessa Hendeles Art Foundation, Toronto

SELECTED GROUP EXHIBITIONS SINCE 1990
2000 *Architecture without Shadow*, CAAC, Seville; Art Gallery of Western Australia, Perth **1999** Kaiser Wilhelm Museum, Krefeld, *Carnegie International 1999*, Carnegie Museum of Art, Pittsburgh; *Seeing Time: Selections from the Pamela and Richard Kramlich Collection of Media Art*, San Francisco Museum of Modern Art; *Foul Play*, Thread Waxing Space, New York; *Warten*, Kunst – Werke, Berlin; *The Time of Our Lives*, New Museum of Contemporary Art, New York; *Gesammelte Werke 1: Zeitgenössiche Kunst seit 1968*, Kunstmuseum Wolfsburg; *Plain Air*, Barbara Gladstone Gallery, New York; *Flashes: Collection Fondation Cartier pour l'art contemporain*, Centro

Cultural de Belem; *From Beuys to Cindy Sherman: the Lothar Schirmer Collection*, Kunsthalle Bremen, Bremen & Staatliche Galerie im Lenbachhaus, Munich; *The Museum as Muse: Artists Reflect*, The Museum of Modern Art, New York; *August Sander: Landschafts-photografien/ Jeff Wall: Bilder von Landschaften*, Die Photografische Sammlung/SK Stiftung Kultur, Cologne & Nederlands Foto Instituut, Rotterdam; *Art at Work: Forty Years of the Chase Manhattan Collection*, Museum of Fine Arts & Museum of Contemporary Art, Houston **1998** *Under/Exposed: The World's Greatest Photo Exhibition, in the Underground of Stockholm*, Stockholm Metro, Stockholm; Aspen Museum of Art; *The Parkett Artists' Editions at the Museum Ludwig*, Museum Ludwig, Cologne; *Auf der Spur: Kunst der 90er Jahre im Spiegel von Schweizer Sammlungen*, Kunsthalle, Zurich; *Breaking Ground*, Marian Goodman Gallery, New York; Bienal de Sal Paulo, São Paulo; *Odradek*, Center for Curatorial Studies, Bard College, Annandale-on-Hudson; Museum of Contemporary Art, Helsinki; *The Art of the 80s, exhibition of contemporary art for the Lisbon World Expostion 1998*, Culturgest, Lisbon; *Inner Eye: Contemporary Art from the Marc and Livia Straus Collection*, The Harn Museum of Art, University of Florida, Gainesville & Neuberger Museum of Art; *Tuning Up #5: Selections from the Permanent Collection*, Kunstmuseum Wolfsburg, Wolfsburg **1997** Marian Goodman Gallery, New York; *La Collection de la Fondation Cartier pour l'art contemporain Fondation Cartier*, Paris; *Deslocaçõs/From Here to There*, Fundação Calouste Gulbenkian, Lisbon; *documenta x*, Museum Fridericianum, Kassel; *Framed Area: site-specific works in Haalemmermeer, Hoofdorp, and Schiphol Airport*, Framed Area Foundation, Amsterdam; *Veronica's Revenge*, Centre d'Art Contemporain, Geneva; *At the Edge of the Landscape*, Galeria Estrany – De La Mota, Barcelona; *Photography 1: Absolute Landscape: Between Illusion and Reality*, Yokohama Museum of Art, Yokohama **1996** *Face à l'Histoire 1933-1996: L'artiste moderne face à lévénement historique*, Musée nationale d'art moderne, Centre Georges Pompidou, Paris; Marian Goodman Gallery, New York; *a/drift*, Center for Curatorial Studies, Bard College, Annandale-on-Hudson; Sammlung Goetz, Munich; *Portrait of the Artist*, Anthony d'Offay Gallery, London; *Arrêt sur Images*, Casino Luxembourg, Forum d'art contemporain, Luxembourg; *Prospect 96: Photographie in der Gegenwartskunst*, Frankfurter Kunstverein & Schirn Kunsthalle, Frankfurt; *Consommation/ Contemplation*, Le Carré-Musée Bonnat & the FRAC Collection Aquitaine, Bayonne **1995** *Public Information: Desire, Disaster, Document*, San Francisco Museum of

Modern Art; *Spirits on the Crossing Travellers to/from Nowhere: Contemporary Art in Canada 1980-1994*, Setagaya Museum, Tokyo & National Museum of Modern Art, Kyoto & Hokkaido Museum of Modern Art, Sapporo; *About Place: Recent Art of the Americas*, Art Institute of Chicago; *Micromegas*, The American Center, Paris & Israel Museum, Jerusalem; *Biennial Exhibition*, Whitney Museum of American Art, New York; *Prato, l'immagine riflessa: a selection of contemporary photography from the LAC Collection*, Centro per l'Arte Contemporanea Luigi Pecci; *Projections: Alfred Stieglitz, Walker Evans, Brassaï, Weegee, Cindy Sherman, Jeff Wall*, Ydessa Hendeles Art Foundation, Toronto; *Notion of Conflict: A Selection of Contemporary Canadian Art*, Stedelijk Museum, Amsterdam; *Kwangju Biennale*, Kwangju Museum of Contemporary Art, Kwangju; *Le Domaine du Diaphane*, Le Domaine de Kerguéhennec, Centre d'art contemporain, Kerguéhennec; *L'Effet Cinéma*, Musée d'art contemporain de Montréal; Musée du Luxembourg, Paris; *fémininmasculin: le sexe de l'art*, Musée nationale d'art moderne, Centre Georges Pompidou, Paris; *4 x 1 im Albertinum: Golub, Huber, Julius, Wall*, Gemäldegalerie Neue Meister, Albertinum, Dresden; *Passions Privées: Collections particulières d'art moderne et contemporain en France*, Musée d'Art Moderne de la Ville de Paris **1994** Angles Gallery, Los Angeles; Institute of Contemporary Arts, London; *Foundation Cartier: a Collection*, National Museum of Contemporary Art, Seoul & Fine Art Museum of Taipei; Institut Français de Madrid; *Los Generos de la Pintura*, Centro Nacional de Exposiciones, Madrid; Nicole Klagsbrun Gallery, New York; *Prospect/Retrospect: Contemporary Art from the Collection*, Kunstmuseum, Lucerne; *The Ghost in the Machine*, MIT List Visual Arts Center, Cambridge; *The Century of the Multiple: from Duchamp to the Present*, Deichtorhallen, Hamburg; Gimpel Fils, London; *The Epic and the Everyday: Contemporary Photographic Art*, Hayward Gallery, London; The Artimo Foundation / The Netherlands Red Cross, Amsterdam; Marian Goodman Gallery, New York; *Urban Paradise: Gardens in the City*, Public Art Fund / Paine Webber Art Gallery, New York; Arteleku, Bilbao & the Frac Aquitaine, Bordeaux; *Pictures of the Real World (In Real Time)*, Paula Cooper Gallery, New York **1993** *Beneath the Paving Stones: Art, Architecture, City*, Charles H. Scott Gallery, Emily Carr College of Art & Design, Vancouver; Foundation Still / Archipel Apeldoorn, Rotterdam; *Widerstand: Denkbilder fur die Zukunft*, Bayerische Staatsgemaldesammlungen, Munich; Museum Boymans-van

Beuningen, Rotterdam; *Strange Hotel: International Art*, Aarhus Kunstmuseum, Aarhus; *Le Magasin*, Centre Nationale d'Art Contemporain, Grenoble; *Photoplay: Works from the Chase Manhattan Collection*, Center for the Fine Arts, Miami; *Post-Human*, Deichtorhallen, Hamburg; *Renegotiations: Class, Modernity, Photography*, Norwich Gallery, Norfolk Institute of Art & Design, Norfolk; *The Sublime Void: An Exhibition on the Memory of the Imagination*, Palais Royale des Beaux-Arts, Antwerp **1992** *Queues, Rendezvous and Riots: Questioning the Public*, Walter Phillips Gallery, Banff Centre for the Arts, Banff; *Avantgarde & Kampagne*, Stadtische Kunsthalle, Dusseldorf; *Images Metisses*, Institut du Monde Arabe, Paris; *Territorium*, Kunst-und Austellungshalle der Bundesrepublik Deutschland, Bonn; *The Binary Era*, Museé d'Ixelles, Brussels & Kunsthalle Wien, Vienna; *What Is Political Anyway?* Konstmuseum, Boras; *Pour la Suite du Monde*, Museé d'art contemporain de Montreal; *The Last Days*, Salas del Arenal, Seville; Centre d'Art Santa Monica, Barcelona & Circulo de Bellas Artes, Madrid **1991** Museum Haus Lange and Haus Esters, Krefeld; *La Revanche de l'Image*, Galerie Pierre Huber, Geneva; Marian Goodman Gallery, New York; *Metropolis*, Martin-Gropius Bau, Berlin; Centre internationale d'art contemporain de Montreal; *Squardo di Medusa*, Castello di Rivoli, Museo d'arte contemporanea; Sala de Arte La Recova, Santa Cruz de Tenerife, Centro de Fotografía Isla de Tenerife **1990** *Life Size: A Sense of the Real in Recent Art*, The Israel Museum, Jerusalem; Krefelder Kunstmuseen, Krefeld; *Passages de l'Image*, Centre Georges Pompidou, Paris & Fundacio Caixa de Pensions, Barcelona, Wexner Center for the Visual Arts, Ohio & State University, Columbus & San Francisco Museum of Modern Art, San Francisco; *Culture and Commentary: An Eighties Perspective*, Hirshhorn Museum and Sculpture Garden, Washington; National Garden Festival, Gateshead, Newcastle; *Le Territoire de l'Art 1910-1990*, Musée Russe, Leningrad

PUBLICATIONS
Has been featured in numerous international journals and magazines SELECTED READING **1998** *The Art of Interruption: Realism, Photography and the Everyday*, Manchester University Press, Manchester and New York **1997** 'Vorwart', *Jeff Wall, Szenarien in Bildraum der Wirklichkeit: Essays und Interviews*, G. Stemmrich, Verlag der Kunst, Fundus Books **1996** *Jeff Wall*, Phaidon Books, London **1995** *Jeff Wall*, la lettre volée, Singularités, F. Migayrou, Brussels **1992** *Jeff Wall: The Storyteller*, R Linsley, Schriften zur Sammlung des Museums für Moderne Kunst, Frankfurt

Gillian Wearing
Lives and works in London. Born in Birmingham in 1963, Wearing has been exhibiting since 1991.

SELECTED SOLO EXHIBITIONS SINCE 1990
2000 Gomey Bravin + Lee, New York **1999** *Drunk*, De Vleeshal, Middelburg; *I Love You*, Maureen Paley Interim Art, London; *A Woman Called Theresa*, The Hydra Workshop, Hydra **1998** Gallery Koyanagi, Tokyo; Centre d'Art Contemporain, Geneva **1997** Galerie Drantmann, Brussels; Jay Gomey Modem Art, New York; Wiener Secession, Vienna; *10-16*, Chisenhale Gallery, London; Kunsthaus Zurich; *Gillian Wearing/Barbara Visser*, Bloom Gallery, Amsterdam; Emi Fontana, Milan **1996-1997** Maureen Paley Interim Art, London **1996** *Wish You Were Here* (Video Evenings at De Appel), Amsterdam; Le Consortium, Dijon, France; *Gillian Wearing, City Projects – Prague, Part II*, The British Council, Prague; Valentina Moncada, Rome; Maureen Paley Interim Art, London **1995** *Western Security*, Hayward Gallery, London **1994** Maureen Paley Interim Art, London **1993** City Racing, London

SELECTED GROUP EXHIBITIONS SINCE 1990
2000 *Let's Entertain*, Walker Art Center, Minneapolis **1999** *21*, Spacex Gallery, Exeter; *Hundstage*, Gesellschaft fur Aktuelle Kunst, Bremen; *The History of the Turner Prize*, ArtSway, Sway, Hampshire; *This Other World of Ours*, TV Gallery, Moscow; *Rewind to the Future*, Bonner Kustverein, Bonn; *Very Private*, Art Gallery Slovenj Gradec; *Rattling the Frame: The Photographic Space 1974-1999*, SF Camerawork, San Francisco; *6th International Istanbul Biennial*, Istanbul, Turkey; *Garden of Eros*, Centre Cultural Tecla Sala, Barcelona; *Common People*, Fondazione Sandretto re Rebaudengo per l'Arte, Turin; *Sweetie: Female Identity in British Video*, The British School at Rome; *Searchlight: Consciousness at the Millennium*, CCAC Institute, Oakland/San Francisco; *Private Room / Public Space*, Almeers Centrum Hedendaagse Kunst, Al Almere **1998** *La Concienza Luccicante*, Palazzo delle Esposizioni, Rome; *In Visible Light*, Moderna Museet, Stockholm; *Fast Forward Body Check*, Kunstverein, Hamburg; *Sensation – Young British Artists from the Sautchi Collection*, Museum fur Gegenwart, Berlin; *Contemporary British Art*, The Museum of Contemporary Art, Seoul, Korea; Galerija Dante Marino Cettina, Umag, Croatia; *UK Maximum Diversity*, Galerie Krinzinger, Bregenz & Kunste Wein, Vienna; *A Collection in the Making*, The Irish Museum of Modern Art, Dublin; *Internationale Foto Triennale/Photography as Concept*, Galerien der Stadt Esslingen, Esslingen; *Made in London*, Musea de Electricidade, Lisbon; *La Sphere de L'Intime*, Le Printemps de Cahors, Saint-Cloud; *Real/Life: New British Art*, Tochigi Prefectural & Museum of Fine Arts & Fukuoka City Art Museum & Hiroshima Museum of Contemporary Art & Tokyo Museum of Contemporary Art; Musée du Rochechouart; Rochechouart; *Videorama*, Depot, Kunst und Diskussion, Vienna; *White Noise*, Kunsthalle Berne; ENGLISH ROSE *in Japan*, The Ginza Artspace, Tokyo **1997** *The Turner Prize 1997*, Tate Gallery, London; *Private Face – Urban Space*, Hellenic Art Galleries Association, Athens & The Rethymnon Centre for Contemporary Art, Rethymnon; *Tales from the City*, Stills Gallery, Edinburgh; *Sensation*, Sautchi Collection, Royal Academy of Art, London; *Pictura Britannica: Art from Britain*, Museum of Contemporary Art, Sydney & Adelaide & Wellington; *Projects*, The Irish Museum of Modern Art, Dublin; *I.D.*, Nouveau Museé, Villeurbanne; Galerie Anne de Villepoix, Paris; S.L. Simpson Gallery, Toronto; *In Visible Light: Photography and Classification in Art, Science and the Everyday*, Museum of Modem Art, Oxford **1996** *I.D.*, Van Abbe Museum, Eindhoven; *Life / Live*, Museé d'Art Modeme de la Ville de Paris, Paris; *Full House – Young British Art*, Kunstmuseum Wolfsburg; *Playpen – Corpus Delirium*, Kunsthalle Zurich; *a/drift: Scenes From the Penetrable Culture*, Center for Curatorial Studies, Bard College, New York; *The Aggression of Beauty*, Galerie Arndt + Partner, Berlin; *Private View*, Contemporary Art in the Bowes Museum, Barnard Castle, County Durham; *The Fifth New York Video Festival*, The Film Society of Lincoln Center, New York; *Toyama Now '96*, The Museum of Modern Art, Toyama; *The Cauldron*, Henry Moore Institute, Leeds; *NowHere*, Louisiana Museum of Modem Art, Humlebaek, Denmark; *Auto-reverse 2*, Centre National D'Art Contemporain Grenoble; *Traffic*, CAPC Museé Contemporain Bordeaux; *Imagined Communities*, Oldham Art Gallery; John Hansard Gallery, Southampton; Firstsite, Colchester; Walsall Museum and Art Gallery; Royal Festival Hall, London; Gallery of Modern Art, Glasgow; *Pandaemonium; London Festival of Moving Images*, ICA London **1995** *X/Y*, Centre Georges Pompidou, Paris; *Campo*, Venice Biennale; *Sage*, Galerie Michel Rien, Tours; *It's not a picture*, Galleria Emi Fontana, Milan; *Brilliant! New Art from London*, Walker Art Center, Minneapolis; *Brill: Works on Paper by Brilliant Artists*, Montgomerie Glasgoe Fine Art, Minneapolis; *British Art Show 4*, touring Great Britain; *Mysterium Alltag*, Kampnagel, Hamburg; *Aperto '95*, Nouveau Museé, Institut d'Art Contemporam, Villeurbanne; *Make Believe*, Royal College of Art, London; *Moblus Strip*, Basilico Fine Arts, New York; *Gone, Blum & Poe*, Los Angeles **1994** *Le Shuttle*, Kunstlerhaus Bethanien, Berlin; *3.016.026.*, Theoretical Events, Naples; *Uncertain Identity*, Galerie Analix B + L Polla, Geneva; *Fuori Fase*, Via Farini, Milan; *Domestic Violence*, Gio Marconi's House, Milan; *RAS* Galerie Analix B + L. Polla, Geneva; *Not Self-Portrait*, Karsten Schubert, London **1993** *BT Young Contemporaries*, Comerhouse, Manchester; Orchard Gallery, Derry; The Mappin Art Gallery, Sheffield; City Museum and Art Gallery, Stoke-on-Trent; Centre for Contemporary Art, Glasgow; *Okay Behaviour*, 303 Gallery, New York; *Mandy Loves Declan 100%*, Mark Boote Gallery, New York; *2 into 1*, Centre 181 Gallery, London; *Vox Pop*, Laure Genillard Gallery, London **1992** *Instruction*, Marconi Gallery, Milan; *British Art Group Show*, Le Museé des Beaux Arts dans Le Havre **1991** *Piece Talks*, Diorama Art Centre, London; *Clove 1*, The Clove Building, London; *Empty Gestures*, Diorama Art Centre, London

PUBLICATIONS
Has been featured in numerous international journals and magazines SELECTED READING **1999** *Gillian Wearing*, Phaidon Press; *Gillian Wearing, Art at the End of the Millennium*, S. Titz, Taschen, Cologne; *Gillian Wearing, The Museum as Muse: Artists Reflect*, exhibition catalogue, L. Tone, Museum of Modern Art, New York **1997** *Signs that say what you want them to say and not Signs that say what someone else wants you to say*, exhibition catalogue, Maureen Paley Interim Art; *Projects Wiener Secession 1997*, Stedelijk Van Abbemuseum, Eindhoven **1996** *Artisti britannici a Roma*, Umberto Allemandi & C, Torino, Italy; *The Cauldron*, The Henry Moore Institute, Leeds

Franz West
Lives and works in Vienna. Born in 1947, West has been exhibiting since 1977.

SELECTED SOLO EXHIBITIONS SINCE 1990
2000 Mies Van der Rohe Pavillion, Barcelona; Palacio Velazquez, Reina Sofia, Madrid; The Renaissance Society at the University of Chicago, Chicago **1999** *Mike Kelley/ Franz West*, Hôtel Empain, Brussels; *Franz West*, David Zwirner, New York & Rooseum Center for Contemporary Art, Malmö **1998** *Franz West*, Middelheim Open Air Museum & Akira Ikeda Gallery, Tokyo **1997** *Recyclages*, FRAC Champagne-Ardenne, Reims; *Projects*, Museum of Modern Art, New York; *Franz West*, Fundação de Serralves, Oporto (cat) **1996** *Franz West. Gelegentliches*, Städtisches Museum Abteiberg, Mönchengladbach (cat); *Franz West: Proforma*, Museum Moderner Kunst, Stiftung Ludwig Wien, 20er Haus, Vienna & Kunsthalle Basel, Basel & Rijksmuseum Kröller-Müller, Otterlo (cat); *Franz West and Hans Arp*, Kunstverein Hamburg, Hamburg; *Franz West: Leviten*, Bonnefanten Museum, Maastricht **1995** Villa Arson, Nice **1994** *Franz West: Rest*, DIA Center For The Arts, New York;

Franz West: Test, Museum of Contemporary Art, Los Angeles; **1991** Galerie Max Hetzler, Cologne **1990** Stichting de Appel Museum, Amsterdam (cat)

SELECTED GROUP EXHIBITIONS SINCE 1990
2000 *Expo 2000*, Hannover; *Sammlung (1)*, Sammlung Hauser und Wirth in der Lokremise St Gallen, St Gallen; *12th Biennial of Sydney*, Sydney; *Open Air Exhibition*, Schlosspark Ambrass, Innsbruck **1999** *Zeitwenden-Rückblick und Ausblick*, Kunstmuseum, Bonn & Museum moderner Kunst Stiftung Ludwig Wien, Vienna; *Melbourne International Biennial*, The Ian Potter Museum of Art, Melbourne **1998** *Biennale* São Paulo, São Paulo; *Köln Skulptur 1*, Skulpturenpark Köln, Köln; *Ethno-Antics,* (Arkipelag) Nordiska Museet, Stockholm; *Pink Fluid* (Arkipelag), Sjohistoriska Museet, Stockholm; *Nine Artists From Europe*, Museum of Modern Art Gunma, Gunma; *Das Jahrhundert der kuenstlerischen Freiheit*, Wiener Secession, Vienna & Helsinki Art Museum, Helsinki; *Wounds: Between democracy and redemption in contemporary art*, Moderna Museet, Stockholm; *Out of Actions: Between Performance and the Object*, 1949-1979, Museum of Contemporary Art, Los Angeles & MAK, Vienna & MAC Barcelona & MOCA, Tokyo & NMA, Osaka; *Austria im Rosennetz*, Palais des Beaux Arts, Brussels **1997** *Lyon Biennale*, Lyon; *Munster Skulptur Projekte*, Munster; *Venice Biennale*, Venice; *documenta X*, Kassel **1996** *Jurassic Technologies Revenant*, 10th Biennale of Sydney, Sydney; *Art at Home, Ideal Standard Life*, Spiral Garden, Tokyo; *Model Home*, PS 1 Museum Clocktower Gallery, New York; *Austria im Rosennetz*, Museum für Angewandte Kunst, Vienna **1995** *1995 Carnegie International*, The Carnegie Museum of Art, Philadelphia; *Das Ende der Avant Garde: Kunst als Dienstleistung*, Sammlung Schürmann, Hypobank Galleries, Munich; *Take Me (I'm Yours)*, Serpentine Gallery, London **1994** *Hors Limites: L'Art et la Vie 1952-1994*, Centre Georges Pompidou, Paris; *Jetztzeit*, Kunsthalle Wien, Vienna **1993** *The sublime void*, Koninklijk Museum voor Schone Kunsten, Antwerp **1992** *documenta IX*, Kassel; *Beelden Buiten '92*, Tielt; *Dirty Data – Sammlung Schürmann*, Ludwig Forum für internationnale Kunst, Aachen; *Ars Pro Domo*, Museum Ludwig, Cologne **1991** *Metropolis*, Martin Gropius Bau, Berlin **1990** Musée de l'Art Moderne de la Ville de Paris. Paris & The Renaissance Society at the University of Chicago, Chicago; *Possible Worlds*, The Institute of Contemporary Art & the Serpentine Gallery, London

PUBLICATIONS
Has been featured in numerous international journals and magazines SELECTED READING **1999** *Franz West*, R Fleck, Phaidon Press Limited London; *Franz West*, Rooseum. Malmö, Sweden **1998** *Franz West*, exhibition catalogue, Meewis Openluchtmuseum voor Beedlhouwkunst Middelheim, Antwerp, Belgium; *Eight People from Europe*, exhibition catalogue, K. König, The Museum of Modern Art, Gunma, Japan; *Out of Actions: Between performance and the object 1949-1979*, exhibition catalogue, Museum of Contemporary Art Los Angeles, CA **1997** *Home Sweet Home*, Oktagon, Hamburg, Germany; *Franz West*, exhibition catalogue, J. Fernandes and L. Cooke, Fundação de Serralves Porto, Portugal

---

Xu Bing
Lives and works in New York. Born in Chongqing, China in 1955, Xu Bing has been exhibiting since 1986.

SELECTED SOLO EXHIBITIONS SINCE 1990
1999 *Xu Bing*, Bates College Museum of Art, Maine **1998** *Xu Bing*, New Museum of Contemporary Art, New York; *Xu Bing*, Jack Tilton Gallery, New York; *Xu Bing*, The Wood Street Gallery, Pittsburgh; *Xu Bing: Recent Projects*, California Institute for the Arts, Valencia; *Xu Bing*, Gallery of University of Wisconsin-Oshkosh, Wisconsin **1997** *Classroom Calligraphy*, Joan Miro's Foundation at Mallorca; *Installation by Xu Bing*, Institute of Contemporary Arts, London; *Xu Bing*, Tokyo Gallery, Tokyo; Charpa Gallery, Valencia; *Xu Bing: Lost Letters*, Asian Fine Arts Factory, Berlin; *The Net: A Collaborative Installation by Xu Bing*, December Art Center, Eastern Illinois University, Charleston **1996** *Xu Bing: A Book from the Sky*, University Art Museum, Albany **1995** *Xu Bing: Language Lost*, Massachusetts College of Art, Boston; *Xu Bing Series Exhibition 2*, North Dakota Museum of Art, Grand Forks; *Xu Bing*, Randolph Street Gallery, Chicago; *Xu Bing*, Dille Center for the Arts, Moorhead State University, Minnesota; *Xu Bing: Recent Projects*, University Gallery, University of South Dakota **1994** *Xu Bing: Recent Work*, The Bronx Museum of the Arts, New York; *Xu Bing: Negotiation Table*, Art Center College of Design, Pasadena; *Xu Bing: Experimental Exhibit*, Han Mo Art Center, Beijing **1993** *Xu Bing: A Case Study of Transference*, Ethan Cohen Fine Art, New York **1992** *Xu Bing Series Exhibition 1*, North Dakota Museum of Art, Grand Forks **1991** *Three Installations by Xu Bing*, Elvehjem Museum of Art, Madison-Wisconsin **1990** *Xu Bing: A Book from the Sky*, Tokyo Gallery, Tokyo

SELECTED GROUP EXHIBITIONS SINCE 1990
1999 *Banner Project*, MOMA, New York; *Half A Century Of Chinese Woodblock Prints*, The Museum of Art Ein Harod, Israel; *Art Worlds in Dialogue – Global Art Rhineland 2000*, Museum Ludwig, Koln; *Global Conceptualism: Points of Origin*, Queens Museum of Art, New York; *Animal:Anima:Animus*, PS 1, New York; *Ist Fukuoka Asian Art Triennale*, Fukuoka Asian Art Museum; *Inside Out – Chinese New Art*, SFMOMA & the Asian Art Museum; *The Third Asia-Pacific Triennial of Contemporary Art*, Queensland Art Gallery, Brisbane; *Zeitwenden-Looking Back and Looking Forward through the Fine Arts*, Kunstmuseum, Bonn; *The 3rd Art Life 21*, Spiral/Wacoal Art Center, Tokyo; *CON(TEXT)*, The Bronx Museum of the Arts, New York; *Transience: Chinese Experimental Art at the End of the Twentieth Century*, University of Chicago Museum, Chicago; *Concerning Truth*, Gallery 400, The School of the Art Institute of Chicago; *Text Project*, Ikon Gallery, Birmingham; *The Art of Artist's Books*, Mexico City; University of Oregon Museum of Art, Eugene, Oregon; Hood Museum of Art, Dartmouth College, New Hampshire; *Chinese Woodblock Prints*, Mishkan Le'Omanut Museum of Art, Israel; *Contemporary East Asian Letter Arts*, Seoul Arts Center, Seoul **1998** *Crossings*, The National Gallery of Canada, Ottawa; *Animal: Anima: Animus*, Museum voor Moderne Kunst, Arnhem; *The Library of Babel*, ICC-Intercommunication Center, Tokyo; *Transatlantic*, Centro Atlantico de Arte Moderno Museum, Las Palmas de Gran Canaria; *Site of Desire*, 1998 Taipei Biennial, Taipei Fine Art Museum, Taipei; *Unreadable Books: New Letters*, The Mitaka City Art Center. Mitaka; *Animal: Anima: Animus*, Pori Art Museum; *Inside-out*, Gallerie of Asia Society; PS 1, New York; *Where Heaven and Earth Meet: Xu Bing and Cai Guo-Qiang*, Museum of Center for Curatorial Studies, Bard College, New York; *New Installations by Xu Bing & Hong Yong Ping (Modern and Contemporary Art from South of the Yangzi River)*, Art beatus, Vancouver; *Beyond the Form: The Transformation and the Symbolic of Chinese Character in the Arts*, New York Lincoln Center, Cork Gallery, New York; *Freedom of Art Project*, The Stedelijk Museum of Amsterdam; *Exhibition of Contemporary Chinese Art and The Fin de Siecle*, Lehman College Art Gallery, New York; *5 Continentes y Una Cuidad*, Mexico City Museum; *Autonomous Action: New Chinese Performance Art on Video*, Artspace, Auckland; *Plural Speech*, White Box Gallery, New York **1997** *power*, 2nd Kwangju Biennale, Kwangju; *Transversions*, 2nd Johannesburg Biennale, Johannesburg; *Around Us, Inside Us – Continents*, Boras Konsmuseet Museum, Broas; *The other Modernities*, House of World Cultures, Berlin; *4 New China*, Jack Tilton Gallery, New York; *An Aspect of Chinese Contemporary Art: In Between Limits*, Sonje Museum of Contemporary Art, Kyongju; *New Art in China: Post 1989*, Chicago Cultural Center, Chicago **1996** *Interzones*, Kunstforeningen, Copenhagen; *Fractured Fairy Tales: Art in the Age of Categorical Disintegration*, Duke University Museum of Art, Durham; *Origins and Myths of Fire*, The Museum of Modern Art, Saitama; *New Works: 96.3*, The International Artist in Residence program, ArtPace Foundation for Contemporary Art, San Antonio; *Installation/ Performances*, Marstall Performance Centre, Munchen; *New Art in China, Post 1989*, University of Oregon Museum of Art, Oregon & Fort Wayne Museum of Art, Denver **1995** *China Avant-Garde Art*, Santa Monica Art Center, Barcelona; *New Art in China, 1989-1994*, Vancouver Art Gallery, Vancouver **1994** *Cocido y Crudo*, Reina Sofia Museum of Art, Madrid; *Jumping Typography*, 0 Art Museum, Tokyo; *Flesh & Ciphers*, Here Foundation, New York **1993** *45th Venice Biennale*, Venice; *Fragmented Memory: The Chinese Avant-Garde in Exile*, Wexner Center for the Visual Arts, Columbus; *Mao Goes Pop: China Post 1989*, Museum of Contemporary Art, Sydney **1992** *Desire for Words*, Hong Kong Arts Centre, Hong Kong; *New Art From China*, Queensland Art Museum, Brisbane; City of Ballarat Art Museum, Ballarat; Canberra School of Art, Canberra; Museum of New South Wales, Sydney; *Looking for Tree of Life: A Journey to Asian contemporary Art*, Museum of Modern Art, Saitama; International Art Project: FAX-ART, Venice; Manchester; Tokyo; Vienna **1991** *The Book as an Object d' art*, Hong Kong Arts Centre, Hong Kong; *Don't Want to Play Cards With Cezanne and Other Works*, Pacific Asia Museum, California

PUBLICATIONS
Has been featured in numerous international journals and magazines SELECTED READING **1999** *Beyond the Future: The Third Asia-Pacific Triennial of Contemporary Art*, exhibition catalogue, Queensland Art Gallery, Brisbane; *Xu Bing*, exhibition catalogue, The Ist Fukuoka Asian Art Triennale, Fukuoka, Japan **1998**. *Xu Bing: Introduction to New English Calligraphy*, exhibition catalogue, D. Cameron, New Museum of Contemporary Art, New York; *The Library of Babel*, exhibition catalogue, ICC-NTT Inter Communication Center, Tokyo **1997** *Xu Bing: Classroom Calligraphy*, exhibition catalogue, The Joan Miro Foundation, Mallorca, Spain

---

Yun Suknam
Lives and works in Seoul. Born in Manchuria in 1939, Yun Suknam has been exhibiting since 1982.

SELECTED SOLO EXHIBITIONS SINCE 1990
1998 *The Seeding of Lights*, Kamakura Gallery, Tokyo **1997** *The Seeding of Lights*, Chosun Daily News Art Gallery; Art Space Seoul; Hakgojee, Seoul **1996** *Yun, Suk Nam*, Kamakura Gallery, Tokyo; *Yun, Suk Nam*, Johyun Gallery, Pusan **1993** *The Eyes of Mother*, Kumho Art Museum, Seoul

SELECTED GROUP EXHIBITIONS SINCE 1990
1999 *Exhibition for 50th Anniversary of the Universal Declaration of Human Rights*, Art Center, Seoul; *Art, People and Event in the Park*, Youido Park, Seoul; *Exhibition for 5th Anniversary of Woong-Jeon Gallery: Facing up to the Reality*, Uloong-Jeon Gallery, Seoul; *Art of Kum Gang (Diamond Mountain) from 18th Century to 20th Century in Korean Art*, Museum of Art Seoul; *Self-Portrait of 1999*, Art M&C Gallery Fusion, Seoul; *The Sculptures in the Theater*, The National Theater of Korea **1998** *Taipei Biennial: Site of Desire*, Taipei Fine Art Museum, Taipei; *Kim's Outlet Off-Museum: Displacement Replacement*, Kim's outlet, Sumgnam; *Ancient Traditions New Forms: Contemporary Art from Korea*, Joseloff Gallery, University of Hartford; *Seoul Olympic 10th Anniversary Sculpture Symposium: Nature + Environment + Human*, '88 Olympic Park, Seoul **1997** *Portraits of Our Times*, Sumgkog Museum, Seoul; *River – Minjoong Art*, Seoul City Museum, Seoul; *VERSUS III*, Velan, Torino; *'97 MANIF*, Seoul Art Center, Seoul; *'97*

Apartment, Gallery Art-Beam, Seoul **1996** *Art 27 '96,* Basel Art Fair, Basel; *'96 Seoul Art Fair*, Seoul Art Center, Seoul; *'96 Korean Art: New Sensation*, USA & Mexico & Sweden; *Exhibition of Environment Art: The 200th Anniversary of Suwon Fortification*, Suwon; *An Aspect of Korean Art in the 1990s*, National Museum of Modern Art, Tokyo; National Museum of Art, Osaka; *The Second Triennial Asia-Pacific of Contemporary Art*, Queensland Art Gallery, Brisbane; *Traditions / Tensions*, Asia Society, New York; *Development of Korean Modernism, Conquest of Modern Art 1970-1990*, Kumho Art Museum, Seoul; *Interpretation of Human*, Gallery Savina, Seoul; *Minioong Art Exhibition*, Seoul City Museum, Seoul; *The Korean Historical Portraits of 20th Century in Art*, Rho Gallery, Seoul **1995** *Tiger's Tail*, Venice Biennial Special Exhibition for Korean Contemporary Art: Venice; *6 Triennale Kleinplastik: Europa-Ostasien*, Stuttgart; *Korea, 100 Self-Portraits: From Yi Dynasty to Contemporary*, Museé de Seoul, Seoul; *Seeds Exhibition*, Sonje Seoul

Art Center, Seoul; *Woman, History*, Garam Gallery, Pusan; *Korean Art '95: Quality, Quantity, Sensation*, National Museum of Contemporary Art, Kwachun; *Where We Are? 1945-1995*, Seoul Art Centre, Seoul; *The Exhibition of Primitivism 1995*, Moran Open Air Museum, Masuk; *Korean Women Artists' Festival 1995*, Seoul City Museum, Seoul; *Korean Modern Art*, Art Museum of Peking, Peking; *Korean Sculpture Now*, Jongro Gallery, Seoul; *Looking Mirror in Our Time*, Dong-A Gallery, Seoul; *The Road of Self Respect*, Kumho Art Museum, Seoul **1994** *Technology, Environment & Information Expo*, Daejon; *Commemoration for Centennial Donghak Revolution*, Seoul Art Center, Seoul; *15 Years of Minjoong Art*, National Museum of Contemporary Art, Kwachun; *Women, the Difference and the Power*, Hankook Gallery, Seoul **1993** *Across the Pacific*, The Queens Museum of Art, New York; Kumho Art Museum, Seoul; *Open Show*, Gallery Bhak, Seoul; *Re-Open Show*, Koart Gallery, Seoul; *Peak of Contemporary Korean Art*, Min Art

Gallery, Seoul; *Herstory II*, Batanggol Gallery, Seoul **1992** *Women and Reality*, Min Art Gallery, Seoul

PUBLICATIONS
Has been featured in numerous international journals and magazines
SELECTED READING **1998** *Ancient Traditions New Forms*, exhibition catalogue, National Museum of Contemporary Art Seoul, Korea **1997** *Yun Suknam's Eyes and Light*, exhibition catalogue, Back Ji-Sook, Art Space Seoul, Korea **1996** *An Aspect of Korean Art in the 1990s*, exhibition catalogue, National Museum of Modern Art, Tokyo, Japan; *Contemporary Art, Traditions/ Tensions in Asia*, exhibition catalogue, New York, USA
1995 *Triennale Kleinplastik 1995, Europe-Ostasien*, exhibition catalogue, Stuttgart, Germany; *The Tiger's Tail*, National Museum of Contemporary Art, Seoul, Korea; *Korean Women Artists' Festival 1995*, exhibition catalogue, Seoul City Museum, Seoul, Korea

Ramingining artists
Aboriginal Memorial 1988
200 burial poles
installed at Pier 2/3
7th Biennale of Sydney
collection: National Gallery
of Australia, Canberra

Looking Back
The Biennale of Sydney 1973-1998
Paula Latos-Valier

The Biennale of Sydney was created in 1973 as an international showcase for contemporary art. Conceived, invented and financially supported by Franco Belgiorno-Nettis, it grew out of the Transfield Art Prize for contemporary Australian art, an acquisitive prize which reached its peak in the 1960s. It operated for about a dozen years before Transfield decided to transform what was a local initiative into an international exhibition.

From the beginning of his association with contemporary art Belgiorno-Nettis aimed to encourage creativity, as well as change the attitudes of Australians towards recent art. He felt that the inventiveness in new art would energise the broader community and encourage innovation and creativity. The Biennale of Sydney, which he modelled on the successful Venice Biennale, was a way of opening up Australia to the world at a time when it remained relatively unknown. His aims were to encourage communication and dialogue as well as build links between Australia and other countries.

In 1973 the Biennale of Sydney held its first, modest exhibition of thirty-seven artists in the exhibition hall of the new Sydney Opera House, an event opened with fanfare by the Prime Minister, Gough Whitlam. Taking part were artists from fifteen countries, over half being from nations in the Asia Pacific region. This recognition of the links between Asia and Australia, and the showcasing of Asian contemporary art within a wider western context, was quite visionary for that time.

After a three year interval the second Biennale exhibition was held in 1976. Titled *Recent International Forms in Art* it took place against a backdrop of heated political debate concerning the dismissal of the Whitlam government. The opening ceremonies, presided over by the new Prime Minister, Malcolm Fraser, met with an artists' walkout. This was the first Biennale held at the Art Gallery of New South Wales, which was to become the primary venue for the exhibition over the next two decades. The 1976 exhibition was also the first with a clearly articulated curatorial theme developed by one artistic director. The decision to allow a single curator to determine the theme and the selection of artists became the hallmark of the Sydney Biennale and is perceived to be one of its enduring strengths.

The work in the 1976 exhibition explored new forms in sculpture including video, performance and mail art, each of which tested the basic definition of sculptural form. Much of the work selected by Thomas McCullough caused considerable debate in the community. People were confronted by the non traditional mediums of Stelarc, an artist who suspended his body from hooks piercing his skin, to Fujiko Nakaya whose fog piece which filled the Domain Park at the entrance to the Art Gallery of New South Wales, was literally a sculpture with no substance. In all, eighty artists from ten countries participated in the second Biennale, which was strongly focused on recent work from the Pacific Rim. The exhibition also included a small number of European countries such as Italy, Germany, France, Holland and Britain.

The third Biennale in 1979, *European Dialogue*, was substantially larger, involving over one hundred and thirty artists from nineteen countries, and including special exhibitions of recent European drawing and uses of photography which toured nationally. Nick Waterlow's concept was to explore the influences and links between Europe and Australia, and questioned the predominance of New York as the international art centre. Many major European artists were seen in Australia for the first time, and made an enormous impact on local audiences. The late 1970s was a period of considerable political debate and polarisation, on issues such as equality of women's representation and the percentage of Australian art required in international exhibitions. Public demonstrations and street marches coincided with the opening of the third Biennale and the exhibition became a backdrop for sometimes heated discussion. A small grass roots publication, *Biennale of Sydney: Red Herring or White Elephant* captured the essence of the debate and today gives considerable insight into the spirit of that time.

In 1982, the largest of all Biennale exhibitions involved over two hundred and twenty groups and individuals and seventeen countries took part. Bill Wright's *Vision in Disbelief* was an inclusive event which featured separate sections devoted to performance, video and sound, the latter being presented in part at a new venue, ABC Radio. Memorable performances included Min Tanaka, Anthony Howell and Terry Allen. The video section presented at the University of Technology drew enormous interest and the video works of Laurie Anderson and Brian Eno were particularly popular. A pivotal exhibit was the creation of the largest Aboriginal sand painting ever presented indoors. It was an enormous undertaking. Truckloads of red earth were delivered and packed down to create a smooth surface which filled one entire gallery of the Art Gallery of New South Wales, over a number of days the white patterns taking shape. Other memorable works included the enormous projections of Krzyzstof Wodiczko's anonymous corporate persona which gave the high rise facades of the city skyline an unsettling presence.

This Biennale was also distinguished by a vibrant six week program of lectures, performances, and international panel discussions, as well as a broad based program of satellite exhibitions. An ambitious national outreach program took international visiting artists to many cities around Australia for lectures and workshops, and provided direct contact in a way which had never happened before. This program left a legacy of friendships and professional relationships which subsequent Biennales would continue.

Enormous controversy erupted over a painting by Juan Davila, and its seizure by the vice squad fuelled heated media coverage. The Premier of New South Wales and Minister for the Arts, Neville Wran, rose to the occasion and defended freedom of expression in the face of police censorship of an art exhibition. The resulting media frenzy, as well as threatening references by the extreme right to confiscate the exhibition catalogue which illustrated the work, kept the exhibition on the front pages for weeks.

In 1984 *Private Symbol: Social Metaphor*, the fifth Biennale of Sydney, brought together the work of sixty-six artists from twenty countries and spanned several generations. It took as its theme the expression of personal and public political issues and explored the metaphors and symbols used by artists to express their beliefs. There was a strong figurative thread running through the exhibition, and an intensity of imagery as well as conceptual belief. Leon Paroissien selected works with clear political references and powerful images

Magdalena Jetelová – *Houses* 1984 – installation – Pier2/3

invited viewers to contemplate their own positions on issues as varied as sexual politics and economic rationalism. A new approach to photo-based media by artists like Barbara Kruger, Cindy Sherman, Hans Haacke and Gilbert & George — who displayed one of their largest works ever — communicated powerfully to a broad cross section of society.

The 1986 and 1988 Biennale exhibitions were directed by Nick Waterlow and both made use of a major new venue, Pier 2/3. It was also used as a major venue in the 1998 Biennale. This huge timber wharf provided rough, industrial space of enormous proportions for large installations and site specific work. It is remembered for such captivating pieces as Wolfgang Laib's sifted flower pollen, and the massive rough hewn structures of Magdalena Jetelová. Pier 2/3 made it possible to bring to the public work of a scale hitherto difficult to house, and inspired many artists to make new work specifically for Sydney. Its dramatic, cathedral-like ambience transformed many unforgettable installations, including the two hundred Ramingining burial posts in 1988.

The theme of the exhibition in 1986, *Origins Originality + Beyond*, questioned the concept of what constitutes originality in the work of artists as diverse as Malcolm McLaren, Eric Fischl, Carlo Maria Mariani and Glen Baxter. Baxter

created a memorable and eloquent image for the catalogue and poster, *It was Tom's first brush with Modernism* which playfully engaged some of the serious undercurrents of the theme, as did McLaren's spray painted framing of his album cover image for Bow Wow Wow's *Go Wild in the Country*. At a time when the transition between modernism and postmodernism was at its height, the sixth exhibition explored the origins of form and imagery as well as the nature of quotation and appropriation in the art of one hundred and twenty three artists from twenty one countries.

In 1988, the year of Australia's Bicentennial celebrations, the Biennale of Sydney toured for the first and only time to Melbourne making it a national event for that year. The theme presented a particular Australian perspective on world art from 1940 onwards and featured key early works by artists such as Léger, Duchamp, Klein, Balthus, Bonnard, Beckmann and de Kooning. Pier 2/3 was chosen to house the moving Aboriginal memorial, a work made of two hundred hollow log coffins from Ramingining, one burial post standing for each year of white settlement in Australia. Also at the Pier was a large installation by Hermann Nitsch whose video tapes provoked a second visit and confiscation by the vice squad. Simulated blood proved equally controversial and Arnulf Rainer's crucified teddy bear provoked demonstrations by local teddy bear societies.

Specially programmed to mark this Bicentennial exhibition, a Japanese art and performance festival, *Close Up of Japan*, was presented in Australia for the first time. It featured traditional drummers, butoh dancers and the Suzuki Company of Toga, as well as an enormous outdoor installation by Imai. The 1988 event brought one hundred and twenty seven artists from fifteen countries together in an exhibition whose works spanned nearly fifty years.

In the eighth Biennale in 1990, René Block demonstrated the distinctive historical connections of the 'ready-made' as it spirals conceptually through twentieth century art. 'Art is Easy' was splashed across the cover of the catalogue, a deceptive statement given the complexity and subtlety of Block's curatorial concept. Titled *The Readymade Boomerang*, the exhibition centred on three key figures at the start of the century, Duchamp, Man Ray and Picabia, and the distinctive historical connections with their work throughout the century. Artists of the sixties such as Warhol, Hamilton, Beuys and Cage, and conceptual artists such as On Kawara, Manzoni and Nauman were positioned surrounding these three. Artists of the seventies and eighties such as Koons, Gober, Mucha and Polke formed a second circle. This configuration revealed a mainstream of aesthetic innovation based around the idea of the readymade.

The 1990 Biennale spilled into a new and immense venue, the Bond Store, where site specific works by artists like Olaf Metzel and Simone Mangos were created. The exhibition was also marked by performances and special events including pianist Carlos Santos, who played as his piano was pulled on a barge under the Sydney Harbour Bridge. In all one hundred and forty-eight artists from twenty-eight countries participated. Due to the strength of its art historical references this Biennale had a particular resonance for artists and educators.

The 1992/3 Biennale reflected a shift away from Europe and the USA, and over ninety per cent of the artists chosen by Anthony Bond had not been exhibited before in

Wolfgang Laib – *63 Rice Meals for a Stone* 1983 – rice, brass plates, buttercup pollen, a stone – Pier 2/3

Australia. Titled *The Boundary Rider*, its theme explored conceptual and cultural boundaries. It examined their transgression through the work of such controversial artists as Orlan, whose surgical manipulation of her own body captured the imagination of both the public and the media. This was an expansive international event with some thirty-six countries participating, many not traditionally included in previous Sydney Biennales, such as Benin, Cameroon, Haiti, Ghana and South Africa.

An extensive lecture, film and public program marked this Biennale, and a special course on contemporary art was offered to broaden audience awareness, as well as intensify debate. In addition to the traditional venues of the Art Gallery of New South Wales and others such as the Ivan Dougherty Gallery, which housed an overwhelming painting installation by Igor Kopystiansky, the Bond Store once again provided a dramatic location for installations and site specific works. These included the Border Art Workshop, a group based around the US/Mexico border, who worked in the outer suburbs of Sydney with young, disenfranchised, immigrant communities, in ways that changed the lives of some of the young participants. This interaction with the local community and its legacy are emblematic of many Biennale exhibitions and programs, which expose people to new ideas and experiences. Perhaps more than anything else the Biennale's real strength has been to act as a catalyst.

The tenth Biennale in 1996 was the most tightly focused and smallest held. Titled *Jurassic Technologies Revenant*, it featured forty-eight artists from twenty four countries. Lynne Cooke's exhibition re-appraised older reproductive technologies including photography, video, film and print media. It compared artists' various uses of technology to comment on the world, and revealed how some issues transcend generational, gender, ethnic and national boundaries. Themes which ran through the exhibition included identity, memory versus history, the fantastic and the Gothic. The section of the exhibition presented at Artspace is remembered for a number of powerful works including a large Franz West installation.

In 1996 satellite exhibitions and programs were hosted in Sydney as well as Canberra and Melbourne, and a dynamic nationwide outreach program for the visiting artists and curators took the art and artists, as well as the current debate about contemporary art, to many cities and regional centres. The Biennale of Sydney outreach program, which began in the first decade of the exhibition, has consistently fulfilled one of the longstanding aims of the organisation, that is to increase dialogue, interest and participation in the visual arts and to foster new relationships and professional networks.

Jonathan Watkins' 1998 exhibition, *every day*, was one of the largest and most expansive Biennales in recent years. It exhibited one hundred and one artists in ten venues. The Museum of Contemporary Art participated for the first time, showing interactive works like Ann Veronica Janssens' fog room and Patrick Killoran's observation deck which allowed people to lie down on a sliding platform with their heads outside the third floor window. Martin Creed's balloons filled an entire house on Goat Island, a new location reached only by a special Biennale ferry. Other heritage architecture on Goat Island housed work by artists such as David Cunningham, whose interactive sound installation transformed the old powder magazine. Pier 2/3 exhibited large scale works by artists including Thomas Struth, Ernesto Neto and Beat Streuli as well as Perry Roberts' enormous outdoor painting, which could be viewed from the Biennale ferry against the Sydney skyline.

The 1998 exhibition was distinguished by a large outdoor component of site specific work which transformed the city's parks and gardens. Particularly memorable and controversial were Tadashi Kawamata's corrugated garden sheds which were scattered throughout the Royal Botanic Gardens. Gereon Lepper's floating and submerging discs, located in one of the Gardens' ponds, became as amusing to the local birds as they were to visitors. Rasheed Araeen created an enormous pyramid sculpture constructed of industrial scaffolding which was set in the lush gardens of Government House.

The theme of the eleventh exhibition explored the simpler materials of everday life and showed how artists from many different cultures draw inspiration from the domestic and everyday environment. Simpler processes and materials, the small repetitive gestures of everyday life, the passage of time and the integration of art and life were sub themes.

As we look back over a quarter century of intense activity a few things emerge clearly. Since 1973 eleven Biennale of Sydney exhibitions have been presented and more than 1000 artists from some sixty countries have participated. Most of the artists were brought to Australia by the

Biennale, which also facilitated their travel and coordinated their professional engagements in many art schools and universities across Australia.

From the beginning the Biennale has acted as a catalyst for cultural development and discussion. It has created unique opportunities for direct contact between foreign artists, writers, and curators — as well as collectors and dealers — with their counterparts in Australia. This outreach program has involved hundreds of educational and cultural institutions over the past quarter century and invigorated artists, students and educators alike.

Over the years many important works imported for exhibition in the Biennale have remained in the permanent collections of state galleries and art museums. A listing of only a few examples more than illustrates the point. Fujiko Nakaya's fog sculpture (1976 Biennale) was acquired by the National Gallery of Australia. Works by Rebecca Horn and Miriam Schapiro (1982 Biennale) were acquired by the Art Gallery of New South Wales. From the 1984 exhibition a massive canvas by Jorg Immendorf entered the collection of the Museum of Contemporary Art, along with photographic works by Cindy Sherman. Enormous works by Jannis Kounellis and

Richard Deacon (1988 Biennale) and works by Haim Steinbach, Gerhard Richter, Perejaume and Svetlana Kopystiansky (1992/93 Biennale) were all acquired for the Art Gallery of New South Wales.

For two decades the Biennale of Sydney's regular importation of works of art by major artists has offered rare collecting opportunities to many public institutions across Australia. Works of substantial scale by artists of international renown, which would otherwise have remained out of the reach of local collections, became accessible. The cumulative impact on the holdings in public collections, though probably little known, is another example of the Biennale of Sydney's enduring contribution to Australian art and culture.

The following texts are based on my interviews with the artistic directors of the past eleven exhibitions. I have had the pleasure and the challenge of working alongside many of them during my involvement in six Biennale exhibitions. The interviews provide insight into their curatorial thinking, and how the concept for each Biennale developed. Some reminiscences and descriptions of memorable artists and events as well as the political environment of the time are quite extraordinary.

Tadashi Kawamata – *Garden Sheds* 1998 – prefabricated garden sheds – Royal Botanic Gardens, Sydney – photography: Sarah Blee

The Biennale
of Sydney
Opera House
Nov 23, 1973

1973
The Biennale of Sydney
November – December

Franco Belgiorno-Nettis AC CBE
Founding Governor

Since 1973, and for more than a quarter century, the Biennale of Sydney has been an event of great importance for contemporary art in Australia. Over the years it has contributed to changing audience attitudes, influencing art, fashion, design, and contemporary culture. There is a new maturity making Australia part of the globalisation process in a much wider context.

I am an engineer. Transfield is a company with an Italian connection, engaged in all aspects of construction. From a local competition — the Transfield Art Prize early in the 60s — the Biennale has grown to become one of the great festivals that contribute to the quality of life we enjoy every day.

My love affair with Venice, where I have been a frequent visitor for years, is the source of inspiration for the Biennale. How do you break the isolation of Australia, which I felt strongly myself in the early 50s? How do you inject that flavour of international extravaganza, originality and explosive vision that you see at gatherings in Venice, in the Giardini, in the Corderia, in the Arsenale, with their centuries of tradition? With the concept of an event such as the Biennale in a city so vibrant, so eclectic and now so multicultural as this great city, the city of Sydney.

Italy was very much alive in the early 1970s — there were many parts to the Venice Biennale, not only the avant-garde in art but also in furniture and design. Such an event was exactly what Australia needed, a link to the world. To break the tyranny of distance, Australia needed some sort of connection. I felt it was important do something about opening up Australia and that is why I felt a Sydney Biennale could follow on the example of Venice. That was my great inspiration.

You have to start somewhere — and so I began with the Transfield Art Prize for contemporary Australian art which had already played an important role in the 60s. I now made it into an international event, making Sydney part of the avant-garde art movement which so much influenced our life. I had the chance of meeting young artists in that period — prolific, rebellious artists — and I was intrigued by their originality. I saw the possibility of a dialogue to open the door to a much wider audience. The artists of many countries became ambassadors in a two-way traffic between distant and far away places.

The first Biennale of Sydney started with a modest trial at the Sydney Opera House, in the Exhibition Hall, and already then we had artists not only from Europe and America but a large representation from the closer area of South East Asia. It is often said that Australia is part of Asia but the distance was much greater then.

Thinking back on the first Biennale with which I was closely involved, there were about 37 artists and, without really planning it, a link with Asia was established. Over half the countries represented in the 1973 Biennale were Asian countries, including Japan, Thailand and the Philippines. The second Biennale, three years later in 1976, also focused on the Asia-Pacific region. In this respect, in forging new links, we were ahead of our time and I think we really opened new ways of seeing Australia.

I see the first Biennale with nostalgia — the poster of John Coburn on the first catalogue and the presence of the Prime Minister, Gough Whitlam, with his wife Margaret on the opening night. "Yes", he said, "this is another first — the first Biennale of Sydney".

We opened the gate for a new chapter in the history of art in this country, as we do with every new Biennale — so many nations, so many artists from distant lands, critics, visitors, all breaking the distance of these shores, forging new ties and bringing Australia closer to the rest of the world. This is a great continent with few inhabitants and one of the oldest civilisations, and now Aboriginal art is exported and well known outside Australia.

Aboriginal art has been a powerful presence in our Biennales and some very important pieces were seen for the first time in our exhibitions. In 1982 the largest indoor sand painting ever created covered the floor of one entire gallery at the Art Gallery of New South Wales. And in the Bicentennial Biennale in 1988 we brought together 200 burial posts, the *Aboriginal Memorial*, a moving tribute and the highlight of the Biennale at Pier 2/3.

Many people ask how a company that is involved in civil engineering came to link itself to contemporary art. But the fact is, as an engineer with a keen interest in science, I have always seen a clear link between science and art. They may appear on opposite sides of the fence, but they are very much a continuum. One of the world's greatest inspirations is Leonardo, a man of unlimited versatility. He was a great scientist and a great artist. Leonardo is at the apex of human endeavour and represents the best of human genius, art and design, engineering and construction. I like to believe that the Biennale of Sydney, like every biennale in the world, links all these elements, introducing innovative technology and communication, as well as new ways of seeing the world.

Engineering is science and art is also engineering. There is no doubt in my mind, when I talk about invention and inventors, that the greatest progress has been in engineering. Today our standard of living — and I include in this communication, exploration and technology — reflects the inventiveness of engineering. But in all aspects of human creativity the artist is the greatest wellspring. Therefore, we should give artists the maximum chance and latitude to express their ideas. This is for me the heart of every biennale.

Art has no boundary and we should not put up fences. The Biennale of Sydney should always open the gates to newcomers, to the experimental and to innovative technologies. Originality remains the distinctive power of the human race.

1976
Recent International Forms in Art
13 November – 19 December

Thomas G. McCullough
Artistic Director

When I was invited to do the 1976 Biennale exhibition it was an opportunity to get away from the earlier emphasis on painting. The first Biennale had taken place at the Opera House three years before and the Board wanted the 1976 exhibition to be a curated exhibition and to happen in the state art gallery. I was known for the innovative Mildura Sculpture Triennials of the 1970s, so in this sense the theme was already set. There was an expectation of a shift away from formalist object-sculptures, because the Mildura

events had already moved well away from the formal, romantic works of the 1960s. Artists who were extending three-dimensional ideas beyond the pedestal into installations, earth-works and performance art were regularly showing in Mildura by the 1975 Triennial, and I consulted them on new concepts, contacts and ideas for the upcoming Biennale.

In 1976 I visited only two countries while preparing for the Biennale, as we didn't have much money. I was only allowed two weeks overseas so I decided to focus on a Pacific triangle (the first Biennale had quite an emphasis on Asia). New Zealand, California and Japan were selected for their ambience of experimentation that would suit Australian attitudes to sculpture and art generally.

One of the pieces that still resonates over 20 years later is Fujiko Nakaya's *Fog Sculpture* which was installed in the Domain (and later acquired by the National Gallery in Canberra). I found Fujiko a most engaging person and a very thorough planner. The fog sculpture was a difficult proposal with great engineering requirements. High-pressure water was pumped through very, very fine nozzles to create mist. The hydraulic problems were tremendous as Sydney water required metal gauze filters that would not break up (we couldn't use paper filters because of the water pressure). This piece took a great deal of planning and expertise, yet it was such a simple concept — water pumped through pipes in a park. It was a pivotal concept and questioned the whole idea of sculpture being a set, static form. *Fog Sculpture* was kinetic; it changed form. It was temporal; it only happened for a certain length of time. And it was attractive to the public as well as to other artists! This was noticeable when a non-exhibitor, Ellis D Fog (a psychedelic nom-de-plume), put on a light show at night playing colours through Fujiko's sculpture, using laser beams — possibly for the first time in the visual arts.

We also had a representation of Joseph Beuys' work in the 1976 exhibition (for the first time in Australia). Beuys' attitude to art was liberating; that everybody is capable of being an artist ... that one *lives* art ... that even speaking

can be a form of sculpture. Art is not just for dealers, connoisseurs and curators, but must touch the people as a whole. His idea of breaking those barriers down was a very central one in the 1970s.

Many other artists incorporated this socio-political aspect too — for instance, the British artist Stuart Brisley. He worked with very accessible, common materials — pine framing, a saw, hammer and nails — and he built this fantastic-looking cage in nearby Hyde Park. He tapped and hammered and sawed. Everybody loves to watch somebody working. But all the time he was talking to passers-by who became increasingly curious. So his wooden structure was not an end in itself: it was the performance ... the making of sculpture.

Stuart had already worked in English mining towns and involved ordinary, working class people in the art-making process. In Sydney he 'educated' office workers coming down for their lunch ... he even slept inside his sculpture at night. You have to be a little bit mad to do things like that. There were drunks around, and times when he was threatened, but he stuck it out.

The day Stuart eventually caged himself in completely, people still brought him food but talked less to him, and aggression appeared — though there was great sympathy for him among some. Why would an artist do this? It raised the question: what is art about and why do people do it? Then at the nominated hour we all went down to see him break out of the cage. After nailing himself into the metaphorical 'art corner' he then broke free and stood up on top of his shattered cage as a throng of people cheered.

It was a great, glorious moment in that Biennale. As an avid photographer of sculpture I visited Stuart often and took a lot of photographs. Some of that documentation was very pleasing and I have since donated all my slides and papers to the La Trobe Library, Melbourne. Going back 25 years, my main criticism of the 1976 Biennale of Sydney is the lack of documentation. I didn't have many essays published or artists' statements printed in the catalogue which I'm looking at now ... it even smells awful!

Fujiko Nakaya – *Fog Sculpture* 1976 – The Domain, Sydney – courtesy Experiments in Art and Technology, New York

Unfortunately I did what I thought was pretty groovy in 1976, using one-colour ink on a cheap cardboard cover and spirex-bound pages of brown paper inside. I felt it was more in keeping with the *arte povera* spirit of the exhibition, but it meant that all of the illustrations are a dull monochrome, printed on cheap, sepia paper. I did a great dis-service to the 1976 Biennale by not putting together a big, glossy book on the exhibition (even though I really did not have the time, money or resources to do so). The exhibition deserved commemorating, the artists deserved better representation, but at the time this poor publication seemed adequate and it saved a lot of money.

Of course in those days, there were no computers; I had to have eighty individual biographies manually typed out, catalogue pages separately typeset and there was also endless proof-reading at each stage. If only we could have e-mailed the artists around the world instead of putting letters in the mail and waiting for replies. Months and months often went past in silence — Italy seemed to go up in smoke at one stage and it was very difficult contacting Europe, apart from Germany. The British and Americans were fast, the Japanese were great, and the New Zealanders were falling over themselves to get into the exhibition, making it seem good fun. The trouble with the Europeans began because of

the lack of communication, so it seems ironic that the next Biennale was called *European Dialogue!*

Thinking about changing attitudes, themes and the presentation of contemporary art, I have just one other broad observation. I felt that the 1976 Biennale was a great apex of achievement for those visual artists who were not painters. Leaving Mildura after the 1978 Sculpture Triennial, I went on to do the first Australian Sculpture Triennial in Melbourne in 1981, so it really looked as though sculpture was going to continue receiving the attention it deserved into the 1980s. However, subsequent Biennales were differently selected and both of those Sculpture Triennials were eventually abandoned, so the swing back to the usual interest in two-dimensional artforms was obvious. I would like to see a built-in guarantee that there is a fair slab of every Biennale that deals with other aspects of the visual arts than painting and drawing. Other important surveys also should take this oversight into account if they use 'art' in their title.

When I think further about the relevance today of the Biennales, there are a number of interesting points. First, even back in 1976, we were trying to address the idea of people going *to* art in galleries, etc. Getting art to people via the postal service was one of the exhibits that Terry Reid presented in his *Art In*

The Mail project. He was posting stuff all over the place from Sydney, like the movement originating in Europe called 'Fluxus' where art-in-the-mail suggested an alternative to mounting complicated art exhibitions. The concept was that ideas could be put down on a postcard or into a letter. Now that's an appropriate tool for a certain kind of art and certain ideas work well that way — and the same applies to the electronic media of the 2000s. They're just other palettes for the creative mind to use. As a museum man I believe that 'the original' needs to be shown, and needs to be interpreted. The problem with e-mail and the web — and I love them for their convenience — is that you're experiencing them effectively *on your own*. That's an advantage of the new communications, but that's also their problem. I'm a great believer in festivals and live activities, and the Biennale is like an international meeting place or living conference of artists and critics. Every time you bring people together a new chemistry comes into being ... the activity changes in itself making the whole greater than the sum of the individual parts.

Twenty-five years ago the Art Gallery of New South Wales was a different place to what it is today. In the mid-1970s it also had very exciting curators working there: Daniel Thomas, Frances McCarthy,

Bernice Murphy and Robert Lindsay. They were talented individuals but I think their employers placed too much emphasis on traditional things like the Archibald Prize to give them the scope to experiment. On the other hand, I was appointed as a youngish 'Guest Director' in his 39th year, and felt very much like a country hick from Mildura. But I had a concept for that old building coming to life with international forms of art that would go beyond the walls of the Art Gallery and into Hyde Park and the Domain for the first time ever. I had these little drawings for illustrating my talks with the AGNSW Trustees, when I needed to persuade them that there weren't going to be blocks of stone just sitting around. There would be 'happenings' for the people, and performance artists would do extraordinary things that would attract the great international arts audience …

I also needed to involve their curators as much as possible because I had virtually no staff. It was Tom McCullough, full stop, for most of 1976 and one really had to get on with the professional staff of the gallery. Luckily, my colleague Peter Laverty, who was their director, was quite happy to step back quietly — he did not interfere one bit throughout the whole exhibition and I was able to build great bridges with the staff and designate areas in which to install specific works that I believed related to each other. The AGNSW curators then got in touch with the artists I nominated to present work, and they jointly organised the final installations according to my overall plans. Really, this laid foundations for the ongoing Biennale project, which began virtually in 1976, as far as the Art Gallery of New South Wales is concerned.

One memorable moment in 1976 wasn't about the art at all: it was the Official Opening, which triggered the artists' walkout. Gough Whitlam, a Prime Minister we all loved, had opened the first Biennale in 1973. The political scene had changed dramatically since the 'coup' took place on the 11th of November, 1975. Gough's Labor Government with its generosity towards the Visual Arts Board (which was one of the Biennale's sponsors) fell, and Malcolm Fraser's conservatives took over Australia …

These were fiery times. Artists felt very strongly about politics and the dismissal of the Whitlam Government. It split some families, but the 1976 Biennale of Sydney itself went off like a rocket and shook the art world. It caused great divisions and certain people never forgave me for putting together an exhibition called *Recent International Forms In Art*. The formalists somehow assumed that the word 'sculpture' was being tampered with and that "this performance stuff really isn't art and it certainly isn't sculpture". It caused a great schism and I guess by the end of the 70s you were in either of two camps: the formalists (aligned with the conservative English school and Anthony Caro's followers) and the other camp which some sculptors referred to as 'the lunatic fringe'. The strange thing is that the lunatic fringe didn't die out or get lost. Performance and video, for instance, are very much part of the whole art scene today.

Contemporary art has not changed all that much, I suppose, and certainly not nearly as much as it changed in the 25 years before 1976. I thought the decade of the 70s in Australia was really very revolutionary. I thought that we were on a wave of invention and if you look at the 50s and the 60s, they bear almost no relation to the 70s. There are lots of things happening now that I see simply as 'swings and roundabouts' … the post-modernist attitude of recycling

Stelarc – *Event for Stretched Skin* 1976 – performance – photography: Shigeo Anzai; courtesy the artist & Sherman Galleries

or re-inventing, rather than inventing. At that time things were ripe for experimentation and the great works of 1976 were groundbreaking. Think of an artist like Stelarc. When I went to Tokyo and first met this friendly, helpful Greek-Australian he was working in Japan because they wouldn't let him legally investigate his own body in Australia. The Biennale photographs of his *Suspension* still make my blood run cold. Later he came to Melbourne quietly, and I saw him actually suspend himself in an old lift-shaft, using only his skin for supporting points for small hooks. I then realised how transforming and cathartic his work could be.

One of the sad things about revisiting the 1976 Biennale is to remember some of the artists who are my age (some are now dead) and to think of how rich that whole 70's era was. The affection which I felt for lots of those artists is still very real to me, and I like to visit a few of them — Marr Grounds for instance, who made an instructive and amusing *Art Bit Installation* under some stairs inside the Art Gallery of New South Wales. How the hell he talked the guards into letting him bring his dog into the building each day is still a mystery!

I think that most artists are very valuable members of their society. They're ordinary people basically, but I do believe there is occasionally magic in what they can achieve. The truly creative artist helps less gifted people, like myself, to learn more about everything in life, and even a little about the future as well.

PARTICIPATING ARTISTS – 1976
William Robert Allen, Giovanni Anselmo, Ant Farm, John Armstrong, Robert Arneson, Lynda Benglis, Joseph Beuys, Stuart Brisley, Tony Coleing, Gianni Colombo, Michael Craig-Martin, Marleen Creaser, John Davis, Agnes Denes, Mark Di Suvero, Jan Dibbets, Koji Enokura, Robert Grosvenor, Marr Grounds, Nigel Hall, Noriyuki Haraguchi, Julian Hawkes, Noel Hutchison, Tony Ingram, Robert Janz, Tatsuo Kawaguchi, Robert Kinmont, Gloria Kisch, Les Kossatz, Kyubei Kiyomizu, Lee Kang-So, Lee U-Fan, John Lethbridge, Les Levine, Loren Madsen, Yutaka Matsuzawa, Michael McMillen, James Melchert, Shigeo Miura, Maurizio Mochetti, Kevin Mortensen, Clive Murray-White, Tsuneo Nakai, Natsuyuki Nakanishi, Fujiko Nakaya, Manuel Neri, Michael Nicholson, Minoru Nishiki, Bernard Pages, Ti Parks, Philip Pasquini, Jonh Penny, Guiseppi Penone, Carl

Plackman, James Pomeroy, Terry Powell, Insik Quac, Terry Reid, Jock Reynolds, Ron Robertson Swann, Fred Sandback, Joel Shapiro, Noel Sheridan, Shim Moon-Seup, Morio Shinoda, Robert Smithson, Stelarc, John Sturgeon, Kishio Suga, Noburu Takayama, Kakuzo Tatehata, Kenji Togami, David Troostwyk, William Tucker, Greer Twiss, Ken Unsworth, William Wiley, David Wilson, Elyn Zimmerman, Gilberto Zorio

1979
European Dialogue
12 April – 27 May

Nick Waterlow
Artistic Director

The concept and themes of the 1979 exhibition evolved from the range of new work that was coming out of Europe, that hadn't been seen in Australia, which I knew about before moving to Australia in 1977.

There had also been a couple of major American exhibitions here so there existed more of a need to show the European avant-garde in relation to Australia. The exhibition did bring a lot of post-object work that hadn't been seen before as well as artists like Marcel Broodthaers, Gerhard Richter, Hanne Darboven, Mario Merz, A R Penck, Valie Export, Daniel Buren and Armand Arman. There was also some terrific performance work from Marina Abramovic and Ulay, Jürgen Klauke, Ulrike Rosenbach and others.

The 1979 Biennale caused quite a stir and it made people sit up; there were even demonstrations. Contemporary art became a very hot item. There were great expectations then, because not

much work from the rest of the world was seen in Australia, and the anticipation was extraordinary. But in 1979, the feminist movement and the Left united and they wanted greater Australian representation, and in particular more women in the exhibition ... 50% Australian representation and 50% female representation. I had to walk a tightrope, and they were a very persuasive bunch.

In the end there was a very sizeable Australian representation, but it was not possible in the whole Biennale to include as many women as men. The Australian representation however did achieve this and I remember very well the impact. One work for example, *Feathered Fence* by Rosalie Gascoigne, epitomised for the visiting Europeans the psyche of the Australian landscape and it helped them understand it more effectively. There were people, however, who didn't see it as purely educational. The exhibition became very controversial.

Over time the 1979 Biennale has been an extraordinary catalyst. For instance the struggle surrounding it accelerated the formation of the Artworkers Union, an organisation for artworkers intent on protecting artists' rights. Many critics visited Australia for the first time, Giancarlo Politi and Helena Kontova for instance, which resulted in much coverage over the years in Flash Art. The controversy surrounding the exhibition reached the whole art community and really got

Jurgen Klauke – *The Harder they come (Architecture of a City)* 1979 (detail) – photograph – part of performance

Philip Dadson – *Triad 3* 1979 – performance

people discussing future needs. Partly as a result of all this, a year later in 1980 the first national survey of recent Australian art, *Perspecta,* took place.

There were many memorable moments in that 1979 exhibition and, for me, many projects have stood the test of time. It included Aboriginal artists, which was the first time they had been shown in an international contemporary context. Mario Merz was unforgettable, in every way. When he arrived in Sydney the first thing he wanted was a python for his work, so we had to dissuade him from that. There are many hilarious stories of Mario: when he was in Melbourne he was taken to a theatre-restaurant and he got up on the stage and had the audience in convulsions; he mimicked the actors who didn't know how to handle it at all. In Sydney he created an extraordinary piece, *Objet cache toi,* that dominated the whole of the entrance court of the Art Gallery of New South Wales. There was also Tadeusz Kantor, a remarkable Polish artist and dramatist, who ran the Cricot Theatre, some of whose sculptural work was also part of his theatrical piece *The Dead Class.*

Other highlights included Daniel Buren, who had never been to this country before; Marina Abramovic

and Ulay and their remarkable performance work, and a film loop with them both naked — Ulay with an erection; provocative performance pieces by Jürgen Klauke and Ulrike Rosenbach; paintings by Stephen Buckley, Louis Cane, Howard Hodgkin, Laszlo Lakner and Gerhard Richter; and terrific work by Mike Parr, Peter Kennedy, Tom Arthur and Rosalie Gascoigne, among others. Another very particular piece was that by Nikolaus Lang, which combined Aboriginal ochres from South Australia with European pigments — literally a bringing together of two cultures, a real dialogue. This work is now in the collection of the National Gallery of Australia.

Casting my mind back over the eleven exhibitions over twenty five years — three of which I did — I can say that each Biennale has been a particular and different achievement. Joseph Beuys, for example, appeared for the first time in Australia in Tom McCullough's Biennale in 1976 with that wonderful piece *Eurasia*, the work with the dead hare. And the first major showing for Anselm Kiefer was in a Sydney Biennale. Bill Wright's Biennale in 1982 introduced people to extraordinary Aboriginal sand painting for the first time.

Since 1979 the themes, attitudes

and presentation of contemporary art have changed greatly. One of the factors, of course, has been the development of technology and many exhibitions of contemporary art around the world now include electronic and digitally manipulated work. The resulting experience is quite different. But strong painting continues to be created and performance has been an extra-ordinarily energetic element in the history of the Biennale, and it still flourishes.

In the early years of the Biennale, artists were very concerned with certain social and political issues but that's changed a bit too. The post-modernist movement and the appropriation of existing images changed the focus of many artists, but now the modernist/post-modernist nexus has broken open again.

In spite of the amount of travel, electronic communication of images and information transfer that is so much part of today's world, I still think the important thing about these events is the way the art world is brought together. It is the experience of sharing that people from all over the world want. The Venice Biennale is such a beautiful place to meet, as indeed is Sydney. There is also always work that wouldn't come to the fore

Peter Kennedy – *November Eleven* 1978-1979 (detail) – painted banner with needlework & video installation 274 x 305 cm – photography: Jim Fairbairn – collection: Art Gallery of Western Australia

if it wasn't for this or that particular event. In 1999 in Venice, for example, it was the work of Doug Aitken. It is also important to be able to see the work of artists from countries you don't hear that much about.

Now that there is a proliferation of biennales, it is crucial to consider what another Biennale of Sydney can offer: how will it be different to others? You need to keep ahead of the game and be very clear-headed. At some point one could focus on performance or on painting, or one could look at using artists as curators. You need to be constantly inventive and not work in the same old way. Biennales have a place, but directors and organisers need to be aware of what's happening in the entire field. It's essential to ensure an event like the Sydney Biennale retains its pre-eminence and that it makes people want to visit Sydney which, after all, is an extraordinary location. It is very important that it continues as there is still relatively little opportunity to see recent work from the rest of the world regularly in Australia.

Another necessary thing about this event is that it grows out of Australian soil. There must also always be a significant range of indigenous Australian work in it. Rather than creating an exhibition that might have been put together

from any other part of the world, I think people coming to Australia expect to see work that they wouldn't otherwise be confronted by; it also gives artists and the Australian public the chance to see the culture of their own country in a broader context.

The Biennale of Sydney is distinct in many ways from similar events around the world. For a start, the use of Pier 2/3 as a venue has given it a very close relationship with the harbour setting. It is also the event responsible for showing Aboriginal art for the first time in a contemporary international context. Many parts of the world still experience relatively little art from Australia and other parts of Asia, so it is essential that Australia corrects the imbalance. It is fair to say that the Biennale of Sydney has helped with this and it has created memorable exhibitions that have

uniquely showcased artists from this part of the world with their international peers.

PARTICIPATING ARTISTS – 1979
Marina Abramovic & Ulay, Hermann Albert, Pierre Alechinsky, Carlo Alfano, Gisela Andersch, Armand P. Arman, Eduardo Arroyo, W. Thomas Arthur, Joannis Avramidis, Bruce Barber, Gianfranco Baruchello, Bernd & Hilla Becher, Laszlo Beke, Joseph Beuys, Olive Bishop, Christian Boltanski, Peter Booth, Bernard Borgeaud, Mark Boyle, George Brecht, Marcel Broodthaers, Stanley Brouwn, Anatol Brusilowsky, Stephen Buckley, Bungawuy, Daniel Buren, Victor Burgin, Tim Burns, Louis Cane, Barbara Chase-Riboud, Eduardo Chillida, Virginia Coventry, Philip Dadson, Aleksander Danko, Hanne Darboven, John Davies, Janet Dawson, Jan Dibbets, Braco Dimitrijevic, Rita Donagh, Richard Dunn, Valie Export, Hamish Fulton, Wolfgang Gäfgen, Rosalie Gascoigne, Jochen Gerz, Paul Armand Gette, Raimund Girke, Zbigniew Gostomski, Elizabeth Gower, Gotthard Graubner, Alan Green, Joan Grounds, Hetum Gruber, Sigurdur Gudmundsson, Renato Guttuso, Erich Hauser, Tim Head, David Hockney, Howard Hodgkin, Alfred Hofkunst, Rudolph Hoflehner, Horst Janssen, Tadeusz Kantor, Peter Kennedy, Michael Kenny, Ronald B Kitaj, Jurgen Klauke, Jiri Kolár, Laszlo Lakner, Nikolaus Lang, Maria Lassnig, Jean Le Gac, Alun Leach-Jones, Kerrie Lester, Bernhard Luginbühl, Urs Luthi, Heinz Mack, Robert MacPherson, Bea Maddock, Malangi, Kenneth Martin, Mario Merz, Annette Messager, Henri Michaux, Milpurrurr, Bernard Moninot, Marcello Morandini, Francois Morellet, Ugo Mulas, Ann Newmarch, Hermann Nitsch, John Nixon, Robert Owen, Panamarenko, Giulio Paolini, Mike Parr, A. R. Penck, Wolfgang Petrick, Anne and Patrick Poirier, Arnulf Rainer, Martial Raysse, Gerhard Richter, Bridget Riley, Klaus Rinke, Ulrike Rosenbach, Dieter Roth, Leszek Rózga, Antonio Saura, Sam Schoenbaum, Jan J Schoonhoven, Bernard Schultze, Ursula Schultze-Bluhm, Helmut Schweizer, Daniel Spoerri, Antoni Starczewski, Madonna Staunton, Feliks Szyszko, Antoni Tapies, Sandra Taylor, André Thomkins, Imants Tillers, Jean Tinguely, Gérard Titus-Carmel, Günther Uecker, Ger van Elk, Ben Vautier, Carel Visser, Klaus Vogelgesang, Krzysztof Wodiczko, Zoran Music, Alberto Porta Zush

W. Thomas Arthur
Sameness amidst Flux, Private amidst Public 1979 (detail) mixed media installation

1982
Vision in Disbelief
7 April – 23 May

William Wright
Artistic Director

Earlier this year I was interviewed by Paula Latos-Valier. We spent a little over two hours in an enjoyable ramble across the craggy terrain of the 4th Biennale, its successes and failings, and what follows is a liberal encapsulation of my responses to my own and Paula's reminiscences and questions.

My involvement with the Biennale of Sydney was unexpected and of unexpected duration. It began in 1980 when I accepted the director-ship and continued well beyond this when, immediately following, I became a member of the Biennale Board of Directors — a position I held in varying capacities for the next seventeen years.

It all began in mid-1980. I had just returned home to East 20th Street in Manhattan from the State University of New York at Purchase, entering the city as usual via the whispering arch at Grand Central with a requisite readjustive stopover at its renowned oyster bar: a dozen bluepoints apiece and a bottle of best white (co-enjoyed by Hilarie Mais, my then as now companion). Upon arrival at our 8th floor loft I was greeted by a pile of mail including an alarming number of telegrams: four, each from a different member of the Biennale Board and each inviting me to consider returning to Australia to take up the directorship of the next Biennale. I was bemused as to the motivation behind this mysterious

collective invitation, especially so given that, while known for my exploits in the art educational sphere, I had up to that time only organised exhibitions of incommensurably small scale and scope as part of my various college programmes. However all became apparent when later the same evening I received a phone call from my old friend, the artist Robert Owen, who was — requisite in those days — an artist member of the Board and who, it emerged, had been the instigator. His arguments as to my suitability to undertake the onerous task were detailed and persuasive and upon reflection I became increasingly convinced that the project would relate cogently to the focus of my interests in contemporary art practice; the prospect of a period of extensive revision and research

into the emerging visual arts also engaged my imagination.

Australia Council had provided a grant enabling me to spend time in Europe on my way back to Sydney, and I used this as a lead-in to Biennale selection, making and renewing contact with European artists and curators, as in similar consultation I had spent the months prior to leaving New York. It was a process of informing, updating and cross-referencing, a kind of no stone unturned mosaic approach precursive to determining the event's form and spheres of content. As then, I still regard the Biennale as being central in a greater sphere of informational and educational enrichment, for creative development as much as informing the population at large. It follows, if it is to enmesh with local perception

Walpiri Sand Painting 1982 – performance – courtesy Lajamanu Community, Northern Territory

and imagination, that it should, as in most biennales, include adequate representation from the host culture. From the outset I had favoured the notion of an inclusive, of necessity large biennale, one that would meaningfully contextualise a plurality of diverse creative forms in a way that would engage the creative attention of Australian artists, students and public alike. I had not lived in Australia for over twenty-two years but had kept in touch, making numerous visits linked to educational programs and exchanges for Australian artists and students I had initiated and run during the two previous decades. But while my knowledge of Australian art infrastructure was extensive, my awareness of

compose a biennale that would encompass a wide range of current practice and interconnections between various visual and aural modalities; innovation in both new and reinvested fields of application. The thing that gave me the most gratification was the way the Biennale 82 intersected with and enriched the diverse terrain of art practice in Australia.

It is difficult to talk of individual works that stand out retrospectively from the vantage of eighteen years hence but I might nominate the large earth painting/performance work of the Walpiri group (Lajamanu) in the central void at The Art Gallery of New South Wales. Beside its sheer mesmeric

performances of the Japanese Bhutto master Min Tanaka, and Krzysztof Wodiczko's sardonic projections onto various strategically chosen buildings across central Sydney, including the facade of the Art Gallery of New South Wales. With over 220 artists included it is inevitable that I will fail to mention most, but I would cite the works by Laurie Anderson, Katharina Sieverding, Rebecca Horn, Susan Rothenberg, Bill Henson, Lucas Samaras, Fiona Hall, Bernhard Blume, Ken Unsworth, Miriam Schapiro, Philip Guston, Michael Snow, General Idea, Terry Allen, Jorg Immendorff, Georg Baselitz, Francesco Clemente, to name a few among an equally deserving cast of many.

Bill Woodrow – *Twin Tub with Chainsaw* 1981 – installation

current developments and issues was fragmentary.

Given the intention to represent Australian art as a focal component of the 4th Biennale, I engaged in a program of research and travel immediately upon my return, to familiarise myself with the state of activity in the various regions around Australia. I was naturally more aware of the art of the northern hemisphere than Australia at the time and my desire was to

presence it had the effect of interposing the dimension of cultural time, with an impact on the many artists who came from other countries; the experience of exhibiting alongside tribally integrated artists of such deep and extensive cultural memory was profound. Others which come to mind are Mary Kelly's *Post Partum Document*, John Baldessari's *Blasted Allegories*, Mike Parr's *Parapraxis III*, Brian Eno's *Memories of Medieval Manhattan*, the

Another feature which distinguished the 4th Biennale was the way we opened it out, into and across both Sydney and Australia, via an extensive, well orchestrated outreach program of forums, lectures and events. In Sydney alone there were six full weeks of external events beyond the eight venue exhibition and soundwork programs, and visiting artists and critics were contracted to visit other cities and towns across Australia. The rebound energy resulted in an unprecedented level of attendance and involvement at the events and forums. It is vital to its ongoing success to fully comprehend that the Biennale is not just an exhibition; its scope and diversity are critical factors for nourishing artistic development as much as wider audience engagement. I have listened recently with some dismay to people reiterating the view that small is beautiful, a show tailored only to engage the enthusiasm of the culturally committed few. I daresay one of the most satisfying aspects of the Biennale 82 was its scale/scope, its energy, its public engagement, and its flow-on of debate and conjecture.

When I arrived back in Sydney in late 1980 there was a palpable sense of both expectation and healthy suspicion surrounding the Biennale. The artist community was alive and energised, with more fervent discussion between artists and factions in Sydney than exists now. The reasons for the present complacency may be that we no longer live in a bipolar system of world power but exist in a less resistant, overtly corporatised social

John Ahearn – *Steve Brown* – NYC 1980
polymer paint on cast plaster 37.4 x 41.5 x 23.2 cm

environment, blanketed by a pall of accommodating conservatism. Nearer home — for art — this is characterised by career-option negativism on the part of many of our more prominent art critics who fail to account for the fact that the critical core of any period's artistic endeavour is distinguished by radicalism and innovation. This is compounded editorially in our public media by an unwillingness to embrace society's counter views, which are usually not published when offered, resulting in a general aura of futility.

Apart from Transfield's continuing sponsorship throughout its 27 years of existence, the Biennale of Sydney has been consistently restricted due to inadequate local support. For years it was bolstered by support from the participating countries (often up to 60%) and consistently it had to survive on below 5%, now nearer 10%, of the operating budgets of Venice, São Paulo, Kwangjiu and other peer events abroad. What at this juncture does the Biennale need? It is always well managed so, apart from more enlightened and courageous art critics in the public media, it needs money.

It may be considered remiss if I fail to mention the abortive arrest, by the NSW vice squad, of Juan Davila's now legendary work *Stupid as a Painter,* an event in itself which became an autonomous *cause célèbre*, briefly railroading everyone's attention away from the work of every other artist. Fortunately — for the exhibitions — we had at the time a culturally engaged and courageous Premier, Neville Wran, who saw through the whole charade at a glance and ordered it returned with the now legendary declamation: "the police have no business meddling in matters of

art, give it back". Another fortuitous occurrence, of a more optimistic tenor, came in the form of a radio station 2JJJ and its presenter Graham Bartlett, who provided a unique and far reaching sonic venue for our contemporary sound/music component, additionally providing a program of historic sound works from the time of the Futurists to the (then) present.

Unquestionably the Biennale of Sydney has been pivotally influential in the development of contemporary art practice in our country, intrinsically so, while spawning a number of other seminally important events in its wake such as Australian Perspecta, the Adelaide Biennial, the Asia Pacific Triennial and, recently, the all too briefly extant Melbourne Biennial. The Biennale has brought more important artists, curators and critics to Australia than otherwise ventured here throughout our entire post-1778 history, and (largely) because of this event, begun in the isolation of 1973, our own artists are better known and increasingly included in the programs of art museums and galleries world-wide, no longer victims of cultural seclusion to the great extent that we once were.

PARTICIPATING ARTISTS – 1982
Marina Abramovic, Mac Adams, John Ahearn, Davida Allen, Terry Allen, Frederic Amat, Laurie Anderson, Anti-Music, Billy Apple, Jacki Apple, Robert Ashley, Christian L Attersee, Frank Auerbach, John Baldessari, Sydney Ball, Ray Barrie, Judith Barry, Georg Baselitz, Didier Bay, Yann Beauvais, Frank Bendinelli, Luis F. Benedit, Vivienne Binns, Skip Blumberg, Bernhard J Blume, Claus Bohmler, Marion Borgelt, Ed Bowes, Ian Breakwell, Bill Brown, Ronald Brownson, Gunter Brus, Wojciech Bruszewski, Barbara Buckner, Bungawuy, Michael Buthe, James Byrne, Peter Callas, Colin Campbell, Michel Cardena, John Carson, David Chesworth, Sandro Chia, Gunter Christmann, Shirley Clarke, Francesco Clemente, Norman Cohn, James Coleman, Alan Cote, Enzo Cucchi, Roger Cutforth, Radomir Damnjanovic-Damnjan, Juan Davila, Philipe de Montaut, Juan Downey, Russell Dumas, Jean Dupuy, Ed Emshwiller, Brian Eno, Sue Ford, Dale Frank, Alphons Freijmuth, William Furlong, General Idea, Harry Georgeson, Paul Armand Gette, Dan Graham, Philip Guston, Sakumi Hagiwara, Adrian Hall, Fiona Hall, Goji Hamada, Nanette Hassall, Christine Hellyar, Bill Henson, Alberto Heredia, Gary Hill, Susan Hiller, Leigh Hobba, Charlie Hooker, Madelon Hooykaas, Rebecca Horn,

Anthony Howell, HP, Alexis Hunter, Mako Idemitsu, Norio Imai, Jörg Immendorff, Mitsutaka Ishii, Joan Jonas, Lyndal Jones, Stephen Jones, Just Another Asshole, Shinichiro Kato, Mary Kelly, Roger Kemp, David Kerr, Ken Kiff, Richard Killeen, Per Kirkeby, Hakudo Kobayashi, Christine F Koenigs, Maria Kozic, Derek Kreckler, Yoshinobu Kurokawa, Robert Kushner, Vineta Lagzdina, Olavi Lanu, Gilbert Lascaut, Laughing Hands, Micha Laury, Bertrand Lavier, F. Uwe Laysiepen, Jean Le Gac, Christopher LeBrun, John Lethbridge, Dianne Lloyd, Annea Lockwood, Chip Lord, Markus Lupertz, MAG Magazin, Liz Magor, Leopoldo Maler, Anne Marsh, Toshio Matsumoto, John McEwen, Bruce McLean, Michael Moon, Ian Murray, Kou Nakajima, Fujiko Nakaya, Maurizio Nannucci, David Nash, New Wilderness Foundation, Gerald Newman, Nancy Nicol, Keisuke Oki, Jorge Ortiz, Hannah O'Shea, Tony Oursler, Nam June Paik, Mimmo Paladino, Mike Parr, Peter Peryer, Lutz Presser, Hilary Radner, Robert Randall, Susan Rankine, Dean Richards, Josef Robakowski, Clive Robertson, Miguel Rojas, Martha Rosler, Susan Rothenberg, Ulrich Ruckriem, Claude Rutault, Hiroya Sakurai, Andraz Salamun, Salome, Lucas Samaras, Dan Sandin, Sankaijuku, Gareth Sansom, Sarkis, Miriam Schapiro, Eva Schramm, Edita Schubert, Jill Scott, Ilene Segalove, Kathleen Seltzer, Peter Sengl, Terry Setch, Severed Heads, Kevin J Sheehan, Kuniichi Shima, Yasuo Shinohara, Katharina Sieverding, Signals, Tony Sinden, Slave Guitars, Michael Snow, Eve Sonneman, Miriam Stannage, Elsa Stansfield, Lisa Steele, Kishio Suga, Rod and VEC Summers, Min Tanaka, Clorindo Testa, The Connotations, Claude Torey, Niele Toroni, David Troostwyk, Philip Trusttum, Tsk Tsk Tsk, Katsushi Tsumara, Shotaro Uchiyama, Ken Unsworth, Luis Fernando Valencia, Paul van Dijk, John van't Slot, Steina & Woody Vasulka, Jacques Vieille, Jean-Luc Vilmouth, Bill Viola, John

Min Tanaka – performance – 1982

173

Walker, Ryszard Wasko, Jenny Watson, John Watt, Boyd Webb, William Wegman, Rodney Werden, Gary Willis, Krzysztof Wodiczko, Bill Woodrow, Gary Wragg, Katsuhiro Yamaguchi, Keigo Yamamoto

FIFTH BIENNALE OF SYDNEY

1984
Private Symbol: Social Metaphor
11 April – 17 June

Leon Paroissien
Artistic Director

The theme of the Fifth Biennale of Sydney was my response to a succession of international exhibitions I had seen in Europe: The 'Aperto' section of the 1980 Venice Biennale (shown in the Magazzini del Sale), *Westkunst* in Köln in 1981, and in 1982, the Venice Biennale, *documenta*, and *Zeitgeist*, a major international survey shown in the recently restored Martin Gropius Bau in Berlin, in the same year. Common to these exhibitions was a focus on the resurgence of figuration, with an emphasis especially on so-called Neo-expressionist painting. Bill Wright's 1982 Biennale of Sydney surveyed for Australian audiences many of the newly prominent artists spanning expressionist and other figurative tendencies, and I found myself questioning the category labels being applied to work that was quite dissimilar in its intent.

I became interested in the interaction between context, form and content in some of this work, in the continuing issue of the socialisation of images, and in the work of other artists not included in these shows. Artists whose work had figurative motifs, but was informed by a tradition of abstraction, were bracketed together with artists whose work drew on aspects of conceptual and political art that had evolved in the 1960s and 1970s. Such work displayed a newly intense vibration between images and signs, whether in traditional media such as painting, or in photography,

installation and video. Often similar concerns could be found in the work of three generations of artists: social issues expressed through an evolved personal language of signs.

It was also apparent that such work had appeared spontaneously in non-metropolitan art centres. While I knew a little of what was happening in countries outside Western Europe and North America, travelling to research the exhibition, especially in Asia, Latin America and Eastern Europe, amplified my interpretation of the theme.

Some of the most significant moments in working on the exhibition occurred in discussions with young artists who had never been in a major international show, and with artists in countries such as Poland, Japan and Chile where, for different reasons, the opportunity of exhibiting abroad was an infrequently provided opportunity to intervene in the mainstream of contemporary art activities internationally.

I was equally fascinated by an emerging generation of American artists whose work embraced social themes, but using media such as photography, text and installation in new ways — artists such as Cindy Sherman, Barbara Kruger and Mike Kelley (who was at that time yet to show in New York, and whose visit

René Block planting one of Joseph Beuys' trees at the Art Gallery of New South Wales 1984

174

to Australia instigated the next phase of his work).

The Biennale of Sydney has established a reputation for being selected by curators who exercise great control and who are given freedom by the governing body and the institutions in which the exhibition is exhibited. There is also an absence of pressures from dealers to include artists currently prominent in the art market. This freedom to include young artists, possibly projecting them into a more international arena, has become one of the hallmarks of the Biennale of Sydney.

The 1979 Biennale took Australia back into a strong relationship with Europe, exposing Australian audiences to what had been happening in Europe during the previous decade, when artists and their audiences had focused on New York. René Block's 1990 Biennale also, in part, revealed multiple historical paths in putting the ready-made in context. However that Biennale, and every other exhibition, has brought to Sydney an exceptional range of work by young artists.

Over the years of the Biennale of Sydney's life, information about international contemporary art has become more and more accessible. Audiences have travelled much more, and are relatively well informed. In an age when Internet imagery spans every conceivable form — literal and virtual — contemporary art is seldom likely to engage purely through its ability to confront. Competing interests (even non-art museums show contemporary art), and the great number of biennial exhibitions in Australia and abroad, now put far greater pressure on curators to justify the rationale for mounting such massive exhibitions. Unlike Europe, Australia does not have a potentially huge audience for contemporary art within easy travelling time of its main venues, and Biennale of Sydney attendances — although high on a per capita basis — are still small compared with the numbers attending major historical shows in Australian museums.

However, there is no substitute for the physical presence or material form of the works of art, and even people familiar with international contemporary art through travel may enjoy extending their experience if the concept and realisation of an exhibition are challenging and engaging.

Major exhibitions, historical as well as contemporary, must now acknowledge the presence of generally informed audiences, but ones that may be unfamiliar with the work of preceding decades or with the contemporary context in which the work was created, and respond with appropriate strategies, without suffocating contemporary art's fundamentally resistant spirit.

The idea of an exhibition spreading throughout a city was initially a very exciting concept. The first Melbourne International Biennial in 1999 adopted and modified the model of the Venice Biennale by establishing 'national pavilions' in various art institutions throughout the city. While the central exhibition was vigorous and achieved considerable critical approval, the attempt to capture the whole city with 'pavilions' was generally found to be the weakest aspect of the event. Similarly, the city-wide spread of the 1999 Australian Perspecta exhibition of Australian art dissipated much energy that such exhibitions are capable of discharging. Such a geographic spread depends on a strong core exhibition, with a meaningful theme behind the juxtaposition of works.

PARTICIPATING ARTISTS – 1984
Davida Allen, Armando, Art & Language, Terry Atkinson, Breda Beban, Frank Bendinelli, Joseph Beuys, Tony Bevan, Annette Bezor, François Boisrond, Peter Booth, Tomasz Ciecierski, Tony Cragg, Juan Davila, Antonio Dias, Gonzalo Díaz, Eugenio Dittborn, Felix Droese, Marlene Dumas, Edward Dwurnik, Mimmo Germana, Gilbert & George, Mike Glier, Hans Haacke, Jenny Holzer, Ralph

Anna Oppermann – *Ensemble on the Economic Aspect* (detail) 1978-84 – mixed media installation

Gilbert & George – *Drunk with God* 1983 – picture 482 x 1103 cm – courtesy the artists & Ludwig Museum, Köln

175

Hotere, Jörg Immendorff, Berit Jensen, Birgit Jürgenssen, Mike Kelley, Peter Kennedy, Anselm Kiefer, Karen Knorr, Barbara Kruger, Robert Longo, Syoko Maemoto, Colin McCahon, Sandra Meigs, Cildo Meireles, Gianni Melotti, Annette Messager, Olaf Metzel, Sara Modiano, Josef Felix Müller, Christa Näher, Annick Nozati, Anna Oppermann, Andy Patton, A R Penck, Robert Randall, Jytte Rex, Georges Rousse, Klaudia Schifferle, Hubert Schmalix, Cindy Sherman, Vincent Tangredi, Peter Taylor, Dragoljub Raša Todosijević, Vicki Varvaressos, Jenny Watson, Michiko Yano, Eva Man-Wah Yuen

ORIGINS ORIGINALITY + BEYOND

20 The Biennale of Sydney 1986

1986
Origins Originality + Beyond
16 May – 6 July

Nick Waterlow
Artistic Director

In the first Biennale in 1973, nine or so of the 15 countries were Asian, so more than half the participation in national terms was Asian. Looking back, this now seems visionary. Tom McCullough's Biennale in 1976 focused on the Pacific Rim. Ten years later in 1986, with postmodernism rampant, the premise was to ask the question, the death or resurrection of originality? At the time appropriation was overly dominant, and the intention was to look at the nature of the postmodern world and a reliance on preceding imagery, as well as at related and supportive thought structures. Alongside this was work that was not based on appropriation, but that was closer to certain modernist ideals. So, essentially, it presented a critical survey of postmodernism in its many guises. Naturally you can only critique something if the work itself is present. Some of the most memorable works for me were by

Eric Fischl, Bruce McLean, Stuart Sherman and Rosemarie Trockel; but there were many many others too.

Stuart Sherman's performances at the Performance Space were extraordinary. And there was a Japanese artist Hiroshi Hori, who did astonishing work at the same venue. Also part of that country's New Generation, Katsuhiko Hibino looked at images from all over the world and brought them together in a very dynamic way. Kuniko Kisanuki's remarkable Butoh dancing, in front of Magdalena Abakanowicz's strange burlap figures based on the female form, was utterly memorable. And it was wonderful to have the very rare opportunity to show Cy Twombly in

Australia. There was amazing sculptural work by Magdalena Jetelova, both at the Pier and at the Art Gallery of New South Wales, and there were wonderful woven mythical figure pieces by Indian artist Mrinalini Mukherjee.

Australian artists made memorable contributions, amongst them Colin Lanceley, Tony Coleing, Richard Dunn, Tim Johnson, Hilarie Mais, Ramingining Performance Group, William Robinson and Michael Nelson Tjakamarra.

The extraordinary thing still about the Biennale of Sydney is that it always brings to Australia remarkable artists who have yet to be seen in this country. There is not that continuity of exhibitions that

Malcom McLaren – *Go Wild in the Country* 1981 – mixed media installation

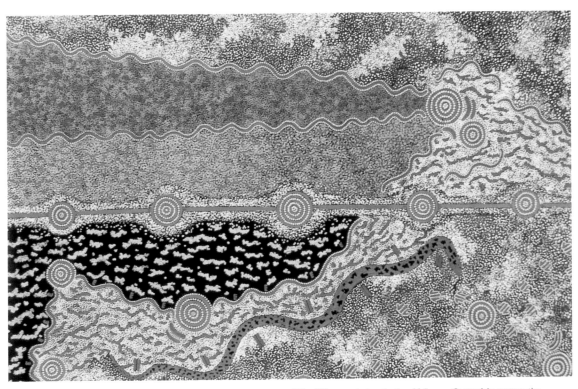

Michael Nelson Tjakamarra – *Possum Dreaming* 1985 – polymer paint on canvas 122 x 182 cm – private collection, Melbourne © copyright courtesy the Aboriginal Artists Agency, Sydney

you have in London, Tokyo and other large, metropolitan art centres in the western world. In 1986 artists like David Salle and Eric Fistula were represented and they had not been seen here before the Biennale exhibition. Kounellis was in the 1986 Biennale and had hardly been seen here. Kiefer also had some terrific painting and Miriam Cahn presented a remarkable installation of her drawings and books.

Glen Baxter was a godsend; his image used on the cover of the catalogue, *It was Tom's first brush with Modernism*, encapsulated the meaning of the exhibition for me and the general public. Likewise, Malcolm McLaren's version of Manet's *Déjeuner sur l'herbe* for the pop group Bow Wow Wow seemed to cause as much controversy as the original! Works such as these attracted a totally different audience to the

Glen Baxter – *Agnes was perturbed* 1986 crayon and ink on paper 57 x 80 cm

Biennale and to the artists' talks as well.

It is worth remembering that Biennales have often brought work to this country, which subsequently entered public collections, that probably wouldn't have happened otherwise. This has been another long-term contribution. Works by Richard Deacon and Jannis Kounellis were purchased by the Art Gallery of New South Wales, and William Tucker by the National Gallery of Victoria, and their inclusion in the Biennale assisted their purchase; these are just a few examples.

I do think the Biennale has had a major impact on the community as it has enabled people to see work that otherwise they would not; it has helped develop an understanding of what is happening around the world in every arena from painting to new technologies. I also believe the public has become better informed not only about contemporary art generally, but how effective and varied Australian art looks in an international setting. This has been one of the most significant benefits. It helps to appreciate the qualities of work from your own country when it can be seen alongside peers from elsewhere and I think that the Biennale has given both the public and artists greater

understanding and therefore confidence about what has been happening in Australia.

Origins, Originality + Beyond provided the opportunity, through texts by Rosalind Krauss, Jean-François Lyotard, Hal Foster, Thomas McEvilley and Thomas Lawson amongst others, to examine comprehensively the postmodern arena, forcefully represented by so many of the aforementioned artists in the Biennale itself, as well as through the related forums and other public programs, reinforced by the presence in Sydney of many of the artists such as Bruce McLean, Laurie Anderson, Malcolm McLaren, Wolfgang Laib and Thomas Lawson, and writers such as McEvilley.

PARTICIPATING ARTISTS – 1986
Magdalena Abakanowicz, Robert Adrian, Laurie Anderson, John Armleder, Miguel Barceló, Glen Baxter, Joseph Beuys, Peter Booth, Joan Brassil, Julie Brown-Rrap, Bazile Bustamante, James Lee Byars, Miriam Cahn, Bruno Ceccobelli, Marek Chlanda, Tony Clark, Tony Coleing, Stephen Cox, Nicola De Maria, Stefano Di Stasio, Braco Dimitrijevic, Jiri Georg Dokoupil, John Dunkley-Smith, Richard Dunn, Eric Fischl, From Scratch, Flavio Garciandia, Gerard Garouste, Naoko Goto, Anne Graham, Bill Henson, Katsuhiko Hibino, Hiroshi Hori, Neil Jenney, Magdalena Jetelovà, Tim Johnson, Lyndal Jones, Junji

Kawashima, Niek Kemps, Richard Killeen, Kuniko Kisanuki, R. B. Kitaj, Astrid Klein, Robert Klippel, Pierre Klossowski, Komar & Melamid, Gickmai Kundun, Wolfgang Laib, Colin Lanceley, Bertrand Lavier, Thomas Lawson, Lindy Lee, Francisco Leiro, Carlos Leppe, Sherrie Levine, Hilarie Mais, Rainer Mang, Carlo Maria Mariani, Agnes Martin, Malcom McLaren, Bruce McLean, Lisa Milroy, Marta Minujin, Pieter Laurens Mol, Malcolm Morley, Reinhard Mucha, Mrinalini Mukherjee, Avis Newman, John Nixon, Susan Norrie, Nunzio, Luigi Ontani, Eric Orr, Therese Oulton, Robert Owen, Mimmo Paladino, Mike Parr, Piero Pizzi Cannella, Sigmar Polke, Norbert Prangenberg, Richard Prince, Ramingining Performance Group, Jacky Redgate, Ad Reinhardt, William Robinson, Gerwald Rockenschaub, Carol Rudyard, David Salle, Gareth Sansom, Thomas Schütte, Vivienne Shark LeWitt, Stuart Sherman, Jose Maria Sicilia, Laurie Simmons, James Simon, Nancy Spero, Yumiko Sugano, Philip Taaffe, Masami Teraoka, Imants Tillers, Michael Nelson Tjakamarra, Rosemarie Trockel, Cy Twombly, Peter Tyndall, Ken Unsworth, Hans Van Hoek, Dick Watkins, Robin White, Joel-Peter Witkin, Alberto Porta Zush

1988

From the Southern Cross:
A View of World Art
c1940–1988
18 May – 3 July, Sydney
4 August – 18 September, Melbourne

Nick Waterlow
Artistic Director

The 1988 Sydney Biennale was special in that it took place in the year of Australia's Bicentennial celebrations and was able to travel to Melbourne; it also offered a natural yet rare opportunity to display a rich range of Australian art over half a century. It looked thematically

at the historical context for the development of a number of key Australian modernist artists whose work was presented alongside their peers or inspirations from around the world. It was therefore possible to show seminal artists like Sidney Nolan alongside Lèger, who had so positively influenced him, Nolan having seen Lèger's work in the 1939 *Herald* exhibition that Rupert Murdoch's father Sir Keith had brought to Australia. Fred Williams was shown in relation to the extraordinary late flowering of Georges Braque, when he contradicted Cubism and created those remarkable landscapes with a horizon line reminiscent of Williams. The Biennale also provided the opportunity to look at Balthus, for example, in relation to images by a younger generation artist Julie Brown-Rrap, who had referenced his work. So it was possible to weave together the work of many artists and generations under the exhibition title, *From the Southern Cross, a view of world art c.1940-1988*.

It was also exciting to be able to show a Matisse collage *Polynésie la mer* that related to the southern hemisphere and the Pacific in particular, to show Peter Booth in relation to Francis Bacon and Max Beckmann, Rosalie Gascoigne in relation to Colin McCahon, Mike Parr to Arnulf Rainer, and so on and so forth. There were also two remarkable Australian-based modernist pioneers in the exhibition, Ian Fairweather and Tony Tuckson, who developed an uncanny understanding of the

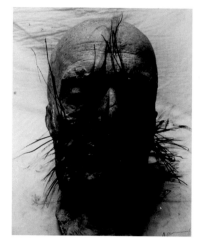

Arnulf Rainer – *Death Mask* 1984 – oil on photograph 80 x 60 cm – © Arnulf Rainer, Vienna

cultures of the region, not to mention Ralph Balson, Joy Hester and Arthur Boyd.

Perhaps the most remarkable single work in 1988 was the *Aboriginal Memorial*. This piece originated through Djon Mundine, then art advisor at Ramingining. It consisted of one memorial for each year of white occupation of Australia. Each took the form of a traditional hollow log coffin. The 200 burial poles have been on display since then at the National Gallery in Canberra, their permanent home. This year they have also been exhibited, to considerable acclaim, in Germany and Russia.

This Biennale, with the support of the Australian Bicentennial Authority, travelled to the National Gallery of Victoria and thus brought to a very large audience a coherently structured and broad view of unique developments in

Julie Rrap – *Thief's Journal* 1988 (detail) – mixed media installation

Australian art, from the ground breaking moment of Margaret Preston to the postmodern generation of Vivienne Shark LeWitt and Jacky Redgate. Coherent relationships between ideas expressed in this part of the world, with corresponding ones from artists of similar generations in Asia, Europe and the Americas, allowed the creation of a rich exhibition. It expanded the meaning and understanding of the present by clearly articulating, through the inclusion of remarkable precursors and their work, the way ideas from so many parts of the world connect.

Catalogue essays by authors such as Ian Burn, Jürgen Habermas and Terence Maloon, with a vibrant series of forums and lectures in both Sydney and Melbourne involving artists and writers, gave sustained, informed and informative meaning to the project.

PARTICIPATING ARTISTS – 1988
Renate Anger, W. Thomas Arthur, Richard Artschwager, Gianni Asdrubali, Francis Bacon, Ralph Balson, Balthus, Max Beckmann, Michael Biberstein, Ross Bleckner, Christian Boltanski, Pierre Bonnard, Peter Booth, Marie Bourget, Arthur Boyd, Georges Braque, Julie Brown-Rrap, Günter Brus, Michael Buthe, Geneviève Cadieux, Sarah Charlesworth, Hannah Collins, Robert Combas, Neil Dawson, Willem De Kooning, Richard Deacon, Marcel Duchamp, Lili Dujourie, Lesley Dumbrell, Richard Dunn, Brian Eno, Luciano Fabro, Ian Fairweather, Helmut Federle, Bill Fontana, Katharina Fritsch, Gérard Garouste, Rosalie Gascoigne, Isa Genzken, Godbold & Wood, Franz Graf, Peter Halley, Eitetsu Hayashi, Joy Hester, Roger Hilton, Taishi Hirokawa, Jenny Holzer, Rebecca Horn, Robert Hunter, Toshimitsu Imai, Irwin, Michael Johnson, Anselm Kiefer, Yves Klein, Robert Klippel, Jannis Kounellis, Barbara Kruger, Nikolaus Lang, Maria Lassnig, Fernand Léger, Ingeborg Lüscher, Len Lye, Hilarie Mais, Henri Matisse, Colin McCahon, Victor Meertens, Gerhard Merz, François Morellet, Robert Morris, Olivier Mosset, Natsu Nakajima, Hermann Nitsch, John Nixon, Sidney Nolan, Gianfranco Notargiacomo, Maria Olsen, Tatsumi Orimoto, Sonja Oudendijk, Guilio Paolini, Mike Parr, Guiseppe Penone, Pablo Picasso, Margaret Preston, Martin Puryear, Arnulf Rainer, Ramingining Artists Community, Edward and Nancy Reddin-Keinholz, Jacky Redgate, Gerhard Richter, Mark Rothko, Gareth Sansom, Anna Maria Santolini, Eva Schlegel, Richard Serra, Severed Heads, Vivienne Shark LeWitt, David Smith, Henryk Stazewski, Gary Stevens & Caroline Wilkinson, Andrzej Szewczyk, Imants Tillers, William Tucker, Tony Tuckson, Bill Viola, Jeff Wall, Andy Warhol, Caroline Williams, Fred Williams

1990
The Readymade Boomerang: Certain Relations in 20th Century Art
11 April – 3 June

René Block
Artistic Director

The development of western art has often been regarded as a linear process. In my opinion, it takes place in cycles, in rings. When you take a look at the art of the last century, this becomes very clear. The developments are like the annual rings on a tree trunk which differ according to colour. The colours reflect different styles in art. And just as the colours repeat themselves after a few years, so

Richard Deacon – *Listening to Reason* 1988 – laminated timber 226 x 609 x 579 cm

Carle Santos – piano performance, 1990 – photography: Heidrun Lohr

Ange Leccia – *Arrangement* 1990 – installation, Art Gallery of New South Wales, Sydney

artists constantly return to earlier developments. One series of rings reflects emotionally intensive painting from Expressionism to the present day. Other rings represent Constructive art movements. Still others, Object and Concept Art. These cycles became the theme of my Biennale — for example, the Ready-made from its invention and pure use by Duchamp, to its resurgence in Nouveau Realism, Pop Art, and Fluxus of the 60s, all the way to new versions by young contemporary artists.

I got the idea in 1988, on a train trip lasting several days from Sydney to Perth, after the Board of the Biennale had asked whether I wanted to direct the 8th Biennale in 1990. The idea crystallised in the following months after several encounters with artists and art historians. Lynne Cooke, the author of the catalogue text, was particularly encouraging. I view a biennale as a workshop, a specific place where artists from different countries come together, show their works, and find out about the works of fellow artists. Something like a fair of ideas. Originally, this workshop atmosphere was to be supplemented by a well-curated historical exhibition on the topic of the ready-made. However, constant budget cuts forced me to merge the two into a single exhibition, which turned out okay in the end.

I had a wonderful team, and we developed very creative ways of ignoring the constraints imposed by the then Biennale Board and the manager appointed by it. With the help of the chairman, Franco Belgiorno Nettis, we managed to put on the Biennale despite the Board. That made us incredibly close. And when the artists came along, it became a weeks-long party. Ten years later, I still have fond memories of it. A highlight was the piano concert given by Carlos Santos, on a timber raft in the harbour in front of the opera house — but I don't want to talk about individual works. The *Ready-made* Biennale has stood the test of time well. It has remained current.

I didn't see all the Biennales, but Nick Waterlow's *European Dialogue* in 1979 made a strong impression on me. It had a good atmosphere and was clear and easy to grasp. I was a fan of the Sydney Biennale

after that. The Biennale's greatest achievement is doubtless the great effect it has had on young artists in Australia. The art scene underwent an enormous transformation. Artists, galleries, collectors, and international exchange turned Sydney into a lively art centre. This makes me very happy, and I invite Australian artists to my projects whenever I can.

The mobility brought about by faster means of travel, on the one hand, and the flood of electronic images, on the other, have made exhibitions such as biennales more necessary than ever. This is evident in their great resonance with the media and with the public. In an age where everything can be reproduced, encounters with originals are of the utmost importance. This applies to all works created by artists. Virtual artworks, some media art, and audio and video art reach audiences through the media in their original form too. This is just another kind of original. It is wonderful that everything is side by side and is being developed side by side — paintings, sculptures, objects, installations, photographs, video art and computer art — and is to be seen in biennale exhibitions side by side. And the Sydney Biennale is now the most important exhibition of contemporary art, both national and international, in Australia.

PARTICIPATING ARTISTS – 1990
Dennis Adams, Arman, Mrdan Bajic, Joseph Beuys, Ernst Billgren, Barbara Bloom, Anna Blume, Bernhard Blume, Jennifer Bolande, Christian Boltanski, Peter Bonde, Montein Boonma, Jonathon Borofsky, George Brecht, KP Brehmer, Marcel Broodthaers, Stanley Brouwn, Janet Burchill, Ian Burn, James Lee Byars, Geneviève Cadieux, John Cage, Sophie Calle, Ernst Caramelle, Ian Carr-Harris, César, Ouhi Cha, Giuseppe Chiari, Tony Cragg, Michael Craig-Martin, Peter Cripps, Bill Culbert, Hanne Darboven, Stan Douglas, Marija Dragojlovic, Marcel Duchamp, Richard Dunn, Lauren Ewing, Öyvind Fahlström, Robert Filliou, Fischli & Weiss, Alain Fleischer, Terry Fox, Dale Frank, György Galántai, Rosalie Gascoigne, Robert Gober, Zvi Goldstein, Angela Grauerholz, Asta Gröting, Kristjan Gudmundsson, Federico Guzman, Hans Haacke, Raymond Hains, Hulda Hakon, Richard Hamilton, Ian Hamilton Finlay, Bill Henson, Rut Himmelsbach, Jenny Holzer, Rebecca Horn, Christina Iglesias, Alfredo Jaar, Megan Jenkinson, Ilya Kabakov, Allan Kaprow, On Kawara, Milan Knizák, Alison Knowles, Jeff Koons, Arthur Køpcke,

Brigitte Kowanz, Jaroslaw Kozlowski, Derek Kreckler, Christina Kubisch, Shigeko Kubota, Raimund Kummer, Marie Jo Lafontaine, Ange Leccia, John Lethbridge, Sonja Lixl, Joan Logue, George Maciunas, Robert MacPherson, Simone Mangos, Piero Manzoni, Helmut Mark, Allan McCollum, Cildo Meireles, Truls Melin, Annette Messager, Olaf Metzel, Tatsuo Miyajima, Joo Moon, Juan Muñoz, Maurizio Nannucci, Bruce Nauman, John Nixon, Bjørn Nørgaard, Julian Opie, Ingrid Orfali, Nam June Paik, Panamarenko, Francis Picabia, Hermann Pitz, Sigmar Polke, Stephen Prina, Rober Racine, Markus Raetz, Fritz Rahmann, Mel Ramsden, Man Ray, Jacky Redgate, Robert Rooney, Mimmo Rotella, Dieter Roth, Carol Rudyard, Ilona Ruegg, Ed Ruscha, Reiner Ruthenbeck, Sarkis, Julian Schnabel, Jill Scott, Servaas, Cindy Sherman, Michael Snow, Wolfgang Staehle, Barbara Steinman, Bent Stokke, Ilkka-Juhani Takalo-Eskola, Rosemarie Trockel, Merylyn Tweedie, Peter Tyndall, Ken Unsworth, Ger van Elk, Ben Vautier, Andy Warhol, Robert Watts, Boyd Webb, Lawrence Weiner, Richard Wentworth, Arthur Wicks, Emmett Williams, Anne Zahalka, Rémy Zaugg

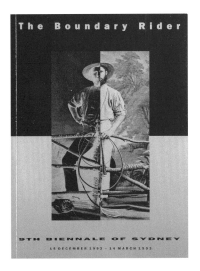

1992/93
The Boundary Rider
15 December – 14 March

Anthony Bond
Artistic Director

When I started working on *The Boundary Rider* in 1990, two years before the exhibition, it was a very interesting time: boundaries were collapsing, the Iron Curtain was coming down, and there was a shift in the economic balance away from Wall Street towards South East Asia. 'Shifting boundaries' was the current theory. It was the buzzword that included physical borders as well as those to do with gender and

Igor Kopystiansky – *Interior* 1992 – installation

difference and also psychological boundaries. A previous proposal for a biennale that I made in the mid-1980s had concerned itself with materials as signifiers in modern art with an emphasis on artists working with the forms of design, furniture, architectural models and so on. I wanted to pick up on some of those 'boundaries' between art and life and conflate them with current theoretical issues. It seemed like a good idea at the time, but it became unmanageable. I'm older and wiser now, and I don't think I'd attempt to conflate so many ideas again.

I think I included the largest number of countries to date in the 1992-93 Biennale, about 35, many of which had never been represented before in Australia. I included mainstream figures alongside emerging artists from beyond the traditional centres. If you're dealing with 'breaking boundaries', you need to expand the understanding of Internationalism. One of the pleasing aspects was that, a long time afterwards, the New York based curator Dan Cameron wrote asking for a catalogue; he just happened to see one in an artist's studio and wanted a copy. He saw it as a precursor for a show he was working on called *Raw and Cooked*.

The research trips took me to some

fascinating places that are not on the routine curatorial rounds. Michael Schnorr from Border Art Workshop took me along the Mexican border. It was an extraordinary thing to be meeting people and experiencing life on 'the border'. It was no longer a kind of artistic rhetoric; it was actual. These situations shift your perceptions and so the show evolved as a response to the things that I saw.

A memorable aspect of the Biennale was the chance to work with an artist like Doris Salcedo. It was very moving to witness the actual process of producing the work and to see the impact it had on those young Australian artists who worked with her. I've had an opportunity to observe that again on two subsequent occasions. When you work with Doris you actually change your whole conception of materiality and come to realise the importance of specific tactile qualities that give the work its resonance. This is not about image or reading the text. It's about a body language, about specificity of labour and of touch.

Working closely with artists and selecting stimulating spaces for site specific work are effective ways to get really strong new work from the artists. In 1992-93 I did a video walk-around of the sites and sent

tapes to artists such as Melanie Counsell and Richard Wilson describing the spaces I was suggesting. As I walked round the space with the camera I would say, "I'm pointing up to the ceiling now ... you can see it's probably a bit dark up there, a bit dingy, strong smell of the old lanoline ..." giving them a complete run-through of the location. When Richard Wilson came, he made a work that inscribed my text onto the fire doors that he removed and suspended in the space. He was talking about this disembodied description and how different it is when you are in the actual space.

There were others things that evolved like that. When I had a dialogue with Dolly Nampijimpa Daniels I said, "Now I don't want to show dot pictures of the desert because in the context of this International theme people will think you're just the token dot-picture-painter. The show is about people showing their place and their life by using objects that they use everyday." She came back after three months and said, "I'm going to bring my place ... all I need is a truck" and so she brought her humpy. She brought it lock, stock and barrel ... oil barrel and tarpaulin and old sticks, and blankets, the works ... and she set up camp in the gallery. It was extraordinary:

she didn't go for any mimetic effects either, so when we wanted to put poles in the ground to erect the humpy and we were going to drill holes in the concrete, she said, "No, no, no, if the ground's too hard you fill a bucket with sand and stick the pole in that." She was very matter-of-fact ... there were going to be no illusions here!

And there was the Border Art Workshop, a wonderfully scruffy bunch who had come from the USA and who ended up working with the kids in western Sydney. They were out working with a group at Cabramatta getting them to talk about their experience as boatpeople. Then they went up to Darwin and actually saw people come off the boats and got video footage of one of these boats being burned on the beach at Darwin. When they brought it back and showed it to the kids at Cabramatta it turned out that it was the boat one of them had arrived on. She was born on board and had been named after the boat. It became a real emotion loop for them. The children then made an exhibition at Cabramatta shopping centre, including videos and oral histories. Nobody had been able to get stories out of these people before, but the kids had a way of instilling confidence. Since that time I've had these youngsters ringing me up and asking for help to tour the exhibition. They wanted it to be seen nationally and get other children involved ... and I've helped as much as I can.

It's spin-offs like these that make the Biennale of Sydney experience worthwhile. And these can happen long after the event. For instance, young artists who have assisted visiting artists have since gone abroad to study with them. These relationships endure and are enormously important. In 1992-93 we tried to match volunteers and skills with artists' needs to make up dedicated teams and this worked really well.

It is important, then, that the Biennale exhibition is not bound within the museum model and it's not just a matter of diversifying venues. Rather, it is about bringing people here to work. In the visual arts there's a real sense of community and while Australia seems to be at a distance, this is not insurmountable. For instance,

if you're able to work with 40 or 50 artists, you should be able to bring them all to Sydney twice, first to research the site and local context then to install or even produce the work. Ideally you would have three or four artists here for residential periods of a couple of months; this is the sort of thing that really breathes life into the Biennale and it is something that can be incorporated into the marketing of the exhibition.

Themes, attitudes and presentations of contemporary art have changed over the 27 years of Biennale exhibitions. Interestingly, some of the exhibitions captured a particular Zeitgeist. In 1982 the new image painting was very much on everybody's lips. The 1979 Biennale was a kind of summation of the pluralism of the 1970s when people were moving from an American to a European focus. And then in 1986 there was the origins and originality debate that attempted to capture the debates about appropriation at the time.

In 1992 I tried to capture a certain spirit, but conflated too many 'zeit-geisty' things in one show. It was more like three shows ... interestingly, my more recent exhibition *Body* was a response to this.

Thinking about the proliferation of biennales around the world and the future of the Biennale of Sydney, I don't think Sydney should settle for any set model. The crucial point, I would have thought, is to 're-invent' it every time. I think a higher

level of site specificity would be invaluable ... having artists coming here to work.

What has distinguished the Sydney Biennale until now has been having a single curatorial vision. It doesn't always work, but the strength of a singular vision and the capacity of a curator to work closely with artists they believe in are the best ways to get great art happening. Increasingly, Sydney got control of the Biennale by getting rid of the commissioners and the imperatives associated with foreign funding agencies and so on. I think that has become a great strength; it would be a pity to walk away from that now. Other countries are picking up on the Sydney model just as we are losing confidence in it, which is ironic. For once, we got there first and we must have the courage of our convictions.

The Biennale also gets energy from the community. In the late 1970s, for instance, you had the anger after Whitlam's dismissal, you had the new energy of the Art Workers Union and the impact of feminism in Australia. There was a context for all the arguments raging against 'fine art', 'high art', and within this an international exhibition of the 'great artists' was something of an anathema. That kind of anxiety produced a lot of tension around the exhibition and created fierce debate, something that has lapsed a bit since. That is not the Biennale's fault but reflects a degree of cultural lethargy in Sydney. In 1992 I tried to get a

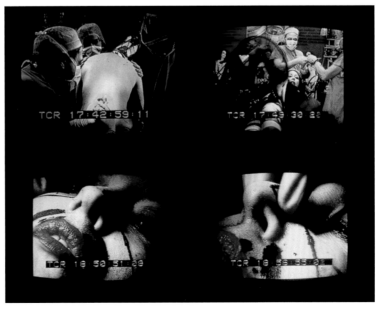

Orlan – *Untitled* 1992 – video installation

different kind of public access by arranging a symposium that would have significant academic relevance. The symposium should be an important part of the Biennale. There is an enormous hunger here in Sydney for conferences on visual arts and there are at least a dozen conferences a year, but this is a special context for contemporary art.

There has been some loss of confidence in contemporary art in recent years that has been a direct result of negative publicity in the popular press. We have had critics who have adopted editorial policies to debunk new ideas and to destabilise the institutions who strive to facilitate and promote contemporary practice. We are in a new millennium now. It seems to me we only need a small trigger to completely overturn the current dire situation. The MCA and the Biennale appear to be so fragile in the face of community indifference but Sydney is one place that should embrace the new, the stimulating, the difficult and take risks. It's just a matter of finding the switch that could persuade people to take a chance with new ideas. Unfortunately, the media are encouraging a deadly, backward-looking, boring and negative view. Somebody has got to put a bomb under them ... there is something wrong with the editorial policies here, horribly wrong, when a lust for failure replaces fresh optimism and curiosity.

PARTICIPATING ARTISTS – 1992/93
Aladins neue Lamp, Charles Anderson, Hany Armanious, L. C. Armstrong, Miroslaw

Balka, Cécile Bart, Bizhan Bassiri, Marcel Beifer & Beat Zgraggen, Gordon Bennett, Joseph Beuys, Ashley Bickerton, Guillaume Bijl, Dominique Blain, Border Art Workshop / Taller de Arte Frontizerio, BP, Kate Brennan, Imelda Cajipe-Endaya, Campfire Group, Eugene Carchesio, Claus Carstensen, Helen Chadwick, Sarah Charlesworth, Melanie Counsell, Walter Dahn, Cathy de Monchaux, Wim Delvoye, Maria Anne Dewes, Sarah Diamond, Jiri Georg Dokoupil, Michiel Dolk, Milena Dopitová, Orshi Drozdik, Katsura Funakoshi, Diena Georgetti, Jochen Gerz, Guillermo Gómez-Pena & Coco Fusco, Rainer Görß, Jörg Herold, Joyce Hinterding, Martin Honert, Lucero Isaac, Zuzanna (Baranowska) Janin, Tim Johnson, Narelle Jubelin, Jon Kessler, Anselm Kiefer, Martin Kippenberger, Igor Kopystiansky, Svetlana Kopystiansky, Kane Kwei, Janet Laurence, Bertrand Lavier, Annette Lemieux, Kamin Lertchaiprasert, Romero de Andrade Lima, Ken Lum, Fiona MacDonald, Per Maning, Claudia Matzko, Tony McGregor Nigel Helger, Lázaro Garciá Medina, Yechiel (Hilik) Mirankar, Tracey Moffatt, Joey Morgan, Julia Morison, Anne Mosey & Dolly Nampijimpa Daniels, Juan Muñoz, Jean-Baptiste Ngnetchopa, Hitoshi Nomura, Antoine Oleyant, Orlan, Guilio Paolini, Perejaume, Kamol Phaosavasdi, Adrian Piper, Post Arrivalists, Marc Quinn, Charles Ray, Philippe Thomas readymades belong to everyone®, Gerhard Richter, Julie Rrap, Eva Schlegel, Michael Scholz, Bill Seaman, Jeffrey Shaw, Claude Simard, Lorna Simpson, Vasan Sitthiket, Pia Stadtbäumer, Haim Steinbach, Mladen Stilinovic, Peter Stitt, Annelies Strba, Tibor Szalai, Richard Kelly Tipping, Cyprien Tokoudagba, Lidwien van de Ven, Jan Vercruysse, Patrick Vilaire, Vuyile Cameron Voyiya, Ruth Watson, Rachel Whiteread, Martin Wickström, Sue Williamson, Richard Wilson, Dan Wolgers, Erwin Wurm

1996
Jurassic Technologies Revenant
27 July – 22 September

Dr Lynne Cooke
Artistic Director

The concept for *Jurassic Technologies Revenant* evolved in response to issues that were being addressed by contemporary artists, and in relation to the exhibition being presented in Sydney where a lot of contemporary art isn't frequently seen. I thought the audience might find the theme interesting given that, historically, Australian culture has been very dependent on reproductive technology, for information, for entertainment, and for a view of contemporary developments elsewhere.

Restricting the Biennale to 40-plus artists was a very deliberate decision for two reasons. Firstly, there are literally hundreds of contemporary artists currently discussed in magazines and seen in a wide range of shows, both nationally and internationally. What is needed at the moment — as it was then — is interpretation. Rather than simply providing yet more information, curators do a greater service by attempting to find issues, thematics and areas that provide a focus for their exhibitions. Secondly, it's more satisfying to have a substantial statement rather than a sample.
By restricting the number of artists, each could be given more space. In addition, if there are one hundred or more artists the viewer is overwhelmed; it is difficult to remember anything.

Haim Steinbach – *Untitled (graters, Victorian iron banks)* 1990 – aluminium laminated wood shelf with glass display case and objects 150 x 150 x 62 cm – Mervyn Horton Bequest Fund 1993, collection: Art Gallery of New South Wales, Sydney

One interesting thing in the exhibition was the linking of textiles and technology, and thinking about how textiles involve reproductions in one form or another. I wanted to bring together artists not normally seen in close conjunction, for example, artists as diverse as Emily Kngwarreye, Alighiero Boetti and Philip Taaffe in the one room. It produced a very revealing dialogue. Other memorable moments were certain talks that artists gave, sitting in galleries, surrounded by their own work — Araya Rasdjarmrearnsook and Willie Doherty spring to mind. Willie was talking about an Irish diaspora that doesn't know Ireland directly and how that related to representations of the Irish situation. I found that very moving and illuminating.

Reflecting back on previous Biennales, I think Nick Waterlow's 1986 exhibition was very considered and brought more Australian art into an international context. René Block had a very different perspective; he was very intuitive in the way he made decisions. He seemed interested in the unexpected.

I think exhibitions like the Biennale of Sydney are still necessary. There is no substitute for a direct encounter with a work of art; even a virtual work has to be encountered at some level. In terms of a material object no reproduction can substitute for a direct experience of it as a work of art. I don't think electronic technology has obviated the need for physical, phenomenologically based engagement. Although a lot of work now is electronically based, and there is a lot of discussion and exploration in that field, I find it a somewhat immature area. For me, much of the most exciting work is still physically grounded. Despite the fact that many people are travelling more, the art market remains a great determinant of where work is sent. There still isn't a huge amount that is brought to Australia, so I think that the Biennale of Sydney will continue to play a very important role.

Another important aspect is the educational outreach, both in terms of what goes on in the exhibition proper, as well as the travel for individual participants that is organised after the opening. *Jurassic* brought foreign artists to schools, universities and museums elsewhere in the country. That seemed important both for the visiting artists, as it gave them a sense of the country at large, and also for local artists and others who were able to interact directly with these visitors.

Sydney's Biennale is distinguished by its Australasian audience. Very few people from abroad see the exhibition, so it can be honed and focused towards local audiences. This gives it a particularity that differentiates it from a show like the Carnegie International, which brings a whole stew of international art world travellers to Pittsburgh. The positive side of this situation is that it permits the Biennale of Sydney to function as a more focused concentration on specific sites and their audiences.

Inevitably and necessarily, contemporary art has changed a lot.

Ann Hamilton – *bearings* 1996 – DC motor, video projection and silk organza – photography: Jenni Carter, courtesy Sean Kelly Gallery, New York

More importantly the pool from which artists are drawn for exhibitions today is genuinely broader, more global. On the other hand, real issues have arisen from trying to bring together art made in wildly different situations and circumstances. The question becomes how well does this work travel. What happens when it is lifted out of one context and placed in a very different one? This makes the choreographing of an exhibition increasingly difficult. In the past works that came from a more homogeneous situation could be more readily placed together.

One of the consequences of this development is that exhibitions need to be more self-reflexive. They have to look at their own internal histories and the fact that they belong to a specific genre or typology, and how that relates to a history of exhibition-making. Reflexivity should be part of the exhibition. The exhibition should not be read as transparent, as simply opening up a series of thematic issues that are embedded in the work on display. It has to be understood as an exhibition *tout court*, rather than merely a conjunction of works of art.

Peter Peryer – *Dead Steer* 1987 – gelatin silver print 24 x 24 cm

There's a lot to be said for the single artistic director and a particular vision or interpretation. The more partisan and partial the better, because no exhibition is definitive. Any one vision will be replaced or succeeded by another with a totally different perspective. I feel a series of strong but different positions is much more challenging and, ultimately, more productive than consensus mentality. Curating a biennale is an enormous responsibility, undertaken with a sense of commitment. Selection by committee is a different matter. Working on a team that occupies a tiny segment of one's total activity is very different to directing a biennale as one's primary occupation for a couple of years. The most interesting work in the 21st Century is bound to be heading in directions we don't yet know about: it will take us by surprise.

PARTICIPATING ARTISTS – 1996
Chantal Akerman, Matthew Barney, Alighiero e Boetti, Frédéric Bruly Bouabré, Francesco Clemente, Claude Closky, Willie Doherty, Heri Dono, Stan Douglas, Jeanne Dunning, Nia Fliam & Agus Ismoyo, Nan Goldin, Felix Gonzalez-Torres, Douglas Gordon, Silvia Gruner, Andreas Gursky, Ann Hamilton, Jaques Herzog & Pierre de Meuron, Susan Hiller, Rebecca Horn, Lyndal Jones, William Kentridge, Emily Kame Kngwarreye, Louise Lawler, Matts Leiderstam, Glenn Ligon, Esko Männikkö, John Massey, Boris Michailov, Tracey Moffatt, Yasumasa Morimura, Jean-Luc Mylayne, Shirin Neshat, Ruben Ortiz-Torres, Tony Oursler, Peter Peryer, Araya Rasdjarmrearnsook, Thomas Ruff, Yinka Shonibare, Hiroshi Sugimoto, Philip Taaffe, Diana Thater, Rosemarie Trockel, Eulàlia Valldosera, Mark Wallinger, Franz West

William Kentridge – *Private Ward* (detail) 1996 – charcoal and pastel on paper 120 x 160 cm

Margaret Robyn Djunginy – *Untitled* 1998
woven bottles from pandanus palms

1998
every day
18 September – 8 November

Jonathan Watkins
Artistic Director

When I started planning the 1998 Biennale of Sydney, what I did was draw up a list of artists whose work I liked, who I felt were communicating something poignant or new. It was from that core list that I began to articulate a more global view of current art practice.

The idea for my exhibition was derived very much from artists' work. It was not so much an idea that I developed out of an extensive cultural theory, to be exemplified through contemporary visual art — rather, the content of the exhibition evolved from conversations I had with artists. The very first ideas occurred to me as I was organising a Fischli & Weiss exhibition for the Serpentine Gallery, London, and talking with these two artists a lot about the nature of ordinariness and the 'everyday'. This certainly catalysed the concept for my Biennale.

I was concerned not to be too literal in my interpretation of the exhibition's concept ... I wanted to consider work that not only depicted the everyday — or represented everyday activity — but also work that actually embodied the everyday. I wanted to get away from the idea that 'everyday' was necessarily synonymous with what was on-the-street, abject, tough or culturally under-privileged. I wanted to suggest something more abstract, philosophically speaking, and thus encourage the audience to look beyond surface appearances.

My initial ideas for the Biennale were like a kind of block-sketch ... or a hunch, and then it was a question of going out to test it in an international context. It was important to have Nikos Papastergiadis' essay in the catalogue, concerned particularly with the current British scene, because that was the context from which the concept sprang. However I had to see whether or not the idea had correspondence in other artistic communities. Was it as true in Japan ... in Brazil ... in Africa ... in New Zealand? That was, of course, the fundamental point of my research for the Biennale.

Very interesting ideas, from my point of view, developed as I moved from country to country — ideas that I would not necessarily have predicted — with a strong emphasis on ecology, the continuing need for inventiveness, an assertion of domesticity and to some extent a recapturing of child-like perception. These relate very much to the idea of directness as a virtue, a desire for direct communication which, again, was one of the keys to the proposition of *every day*.

Rasheed Araeen – *Where there's a will there's a way* 1998 – outdoor installation at Government House, Sydney

Perry Roberts – *Untitled (outside Wharf, Pier 2/3)* 1998 – outdoor installation, computer generated colour on perforated acrylic fabric – photography: Sarah Blee
courtesy the artist

My ideas for this exhibition were very informed by the fact that it was going to be in Sydney and it was the Biennale just before the millennium. I wanted to play off the idea of the millennium — referring to it but not mentioning it. Significantly, I think, a lot of work in the show embodied the passage of time, sometimes by making explicit the processes by which the work was made ... I am thinking here of work by artists such as Bernard Frize or Germaine Koh which consists essentially of the process by which it was made and thus enables the viewer to apprehend the passage of time.

Many of the artists included in my Biennale expressed what it's like to be in the real world. I think this corresponds to a reassertion of a kind of realism ... a desire to communicate what it really feels like 'to be here now'.

When I think back on the exhibition, there were so many things I loved and they were not necessarily the most spectacular pieces on show. Something I'll always cherish is the On Kawara installation *Pure Consciousness* in a local kindergarten. I felt it was at the heart of my Biennale ... an invisible, perversely inaccessible part of the show, but absolutely available for the children who could see it, who lived with it. Here were seven paintings by one of the most uncompromising and stringent conceptual artists located in a situation which was as poetic as it was non-specialist.

The part played by Goat Island in the Biennale I'll also never forget. The experience of that trip on the ferry, which shuttled between the shore and the island, watching Perry Robert's work fit into the backdrop of the city ... listening to the music that Shimabuku had composed with an Aboriginal performance artist and then seeing Goat Island in the light of work by other Biennale artists.

From my point of view, the 'everyday' Biennale worked quite well. I had hoped that the environment within which the exhibition was taking place would become part of the exhibition. I would like to think that the Biennale succeeded in that respect. As one moved between the Art Gallery of New South Wales and the Museum of Contemporary

Art, through the Botanic Gardens, a lot of non-art experience could be taken in. The idea of art work no longer being discrete or self-contained but fused with its environment, for me, is crucial. Goat Island epitomised that idea — the idea that one's experience of a work of art doesn't equate with the perception of a self-contained object. Rather, it is an environmental experience.

Another memorable moment for me was Rirkrit Tiravanija's work outside the MCA on the opening night. There in all the confusion about admission — who could or couldn't be let in to this venue — was Rirkrit on the lawn with a tent and cases of beer, screening films

Beatriz Milhazes – *A Lua e o Mundo* 1996 – acrylic on canvas 244 x 275 cm – private collection, São Paulo – courtesy the artist & Galeria Camargo Vilaça, São Paulo

... and absolutely anybody could go in. There was a wonderful, informal feeling — and relief! — making this project very special.

It is interesting to me how many people in Australia refer to René Block's 1990 Biennale as particularly seminal. My impression is that he really got it right in terms of what local audiences needed at that time — to some extent it constituted a required modern art history lesson. From my point of view it's great that that exhibition had happened. I think there was a lot of overlap between the 1998 Biennale and René's, in terms of some of the artists included. The

idea that 'Art Is Easy', emblazoned on the cover of the 1990 Biennale catalogue perhaps wasn't so far from my 'every day' proposition.

It's fascinating how certain biennales have become lodged in a more popular imagination. There are reverberations, often years later ... biennales undeniably have an effect on local artistic communities but it is not necessarily an immediate one.

One important thing, I think, is to get as many artists as possible from abroad to come to Sydney because working alongside Australian artists means that significant relationships are formed. Artists leave and news about

what's going on in Australia then filters through, but in more informal ways. This is one very important role that the Biennale plays — far more effective than the most strategic Australia Council marketing campaign. It's because exhibitions like the Biennale of Sydney happen on a personal level ... the dialogue may be informal but chances are it's more authentic.

It is impressive the degree to which, over the years, the Biennale of Sydney has engaged with what's happening elsewhere in the world. It has been very relevant. For instance, Leon Paroissien's exhibition in 1984 captured the mood of a new spirit in painting, until then a very European phenomenon. I think Nick Waterlow's exhibition in 1986 was also very much a lightning rod through obfuscating conversations about appropriation and early post-modern culture. These were good things for local audiences, even if they weren't appreciated at the time.

Of late there has been an idea that exhibitions such as biennales are redundant. I don't think that's true — the fact that many more biennales are being invented would suggest otherwise. The fact that people are travelling more, and there is more communication and things are more immediate, doesn't necessarily work against the idea of such exhibitions, but it may change their nature. And consistent with the proposition of *every day*, there is nothing like confronting the real thing, nothing like having that physical experience of objects in space and the opportunity to see one work of art juxtaposed with another. The opportunity for artists to come together in a particular city and respond to it in a particular way is still very exciting. There's no reason why this shouldn't continue to happen in Sydney, as it does lately in Yokohama or Johannesburg. The proliferation of biennales is a healthy sign.

The Biennale of Sydney, like many exhibitions, acknowledges its context. The fact that it happens in Sydney immediately makes it different. I think this difference should be capitalised on. Rather than pretending that a Biennale of Sydney could happen anywhere, I think one has to make the most of the fact that the exhibition is happening in a very distinct landscape.

That said, it's hard to say where the Biennale of Sydney might be heading in the new century. To a large extent it's character will be determined by the Board: they will ultimately decide. I do think that the changing relationship between the artist, audience and curators is increasingly important. In a sense, they are all parts of the same machine ... collaborators if you like, and the changing relationships must be acknowledged. Audiences, too, see themselves as less passive, as freer, and curators are no longer simply 'selectors' ... just as artists can no longer be characterised as being especially sensitive creatures, a breed apart. Large exhibitions such as the Biennale of Sydney inevitably must reflect these changes.

PARTICIPATING ARTISTS – 1998
Ignasi Aballi, Absalon, Georges Adéagbo, Pep Agut, Carl Andre, Polly Apfelbaum, Chumpon Apisuk, Rasheed Araeen, Roy Arden, Vladimir Arkhipov, Howard Arkley, Elisabeth Ballet, Guy Bar-Amotz, Joël Bartoloméo, Rebecca Belmore, Frédéric Bruly Bouabré, Joyce Campbell, Martin Creed, David Cunningham, Thomas Demand, Margaret Robyn Djunginy, Elizabeth Djuttara, Colin Duncan, Olafur Eliasson, Ariane Epars, Fischli & Weiss, Ceal Floyer, Bernard Frize, Giuseppe Gabellone, Fernanda Gomes, Joseph Grigely, Katharina Grosse, Maria Hedlund, Henriette Heise, Gavin Hipkins, Roni Horn, Robert Hunter, Pierre Huyghe, Ann Veronica Janssens, Tadashi Kawamata, On Kawara, Kcho, Clay Ketter, Dieter Kiessling, Patrick Killoran, Kim Soo-Ja, Kim Young-Ji, Suchan Kinoshita, Germaine Koh, Udomsak Krisanamis, Denise Kum, Desmond Kum Chi-Keung, Surasi Kusolwong, Henrietta Lehtonen, Yuri Leiderman, Gereon Lepper, Robert MacPherson, Lani Maestro, Kelly Mark, Mike Marshall, Beatriz Milhazes, Lisa Milroy, Ernesto Neto, Ani O'Neill, Julian Opie, Owada, Platten/ Clarke/ Rodenrys, Khalil Rabah, Navin Rawanchaikul, José Resende, Perry Roberts, Peter Robinson, Manuel Rocha Iturbide, Lev Rubenshtein, Paul Saint, Joe Scanlan, Jean-Frédéric Schnyder, William Seeto, Shimabuku, Jim Speers, Beat Streuli, Thomas Struth, Yoshihiro Suda, Pascale-Marthine Tayou, Rover Thomas, Rirkrit Tiravanija, Grazia Toderi, Pekka Turunen, Marijke van Warmerdam, Richard Venlet, Franco Vimercati, Virginia Ward, Jimmy Wululu, Ding Yi, Noa Zait, Zhang Peili, Zhao Bandi, Zhu Jia, Ximena Zomosa

Julian Opie – *My Aunt's Sheep* 1997 – outdoor installation Royal Botanic Gardens, Sydney – photography: Sarah Blee – courtesy the artist & Lisson Gallery, London
opposite – England Banggala – *Wangarra Spirit Being* 1985 – natural pigments on wood – 288.5 x 24.5 x 20 cm – collection: Art Gallery of New South Wales, Sydney – photography: Ray Woodbury for AGNSW

12th Biennale of Sydney Sponsors and Supporters

Principal and Founding Sponsor:
Transfield Pty Ltd

Principal Sponsors:
Tempo Services Limited
Australia Council for the Arts
New South Wales Government –
Ministry for the Arts
City of Sydney

Major Sponsors:
ABN AMRO
Accor
A T Kearney
Beyond Online
The Daily Telegraph
Issues & Images
JCDecaux Australia
Lowndes Lambert Australia
Singapore Airlines

Supporters:
David Coe
Ann Lewis AM
Gene & Brian Sherman
Sydney Airport

The exhibition could not have been
realised without the assistance and
cooperation of our major venues,
the Museum of Contemporary Art
and the Art Gallery of New South
Wales, and the professional
collaboration of their staff. The
Biennale of Sydney is also grateful
for the support of all participating
organisations including Artspace,
Object Galleries, Customs House,
Government House and the Historic
Houses Trust of New South Wales,
the Sydney Opera House Trust and
the Sydney Film Festival. The
Biennale of Sydney would also like
to thank The University of New
South Wales, College of Fine Arts,
the New South Wales Government
Exhibitions Indemnification Scheme
and International Art Services for
their assistance. We would also like
to acknowledge the supporters and
volunteers who generously
contributed to the 12th Biennale of
Sydney after time of publication.

TRANSFIELD

A leading Australian company in
the construction, development
and maintenance of
infrastructure

TeMPO

Australia's leading
multi-service organisation

Australia Council
for the Arts

The Biennale of Sydney is
assisted by the Australia
Council, the Commonwealth
Government's arts funding and
advisory body

The Biennale of Sydney is assisted by
the New South Wales Government
through the Ministry for the Arts

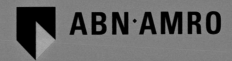

World's leading hotel and tourism
services group. Managers of Sofitel,
Novotel, Mercure, All Seasons, Ibis and
Formule 1 hotels.

*AT***KEARNEY**
an EDS company

BEYOND ONLINE

THE
Daily Telegraph
The word on Sydney

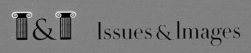

I & I Issues & Images

JCDecaux Australia

 **LOWNDES LAMBERT**

International insurance brokers and risk managers

A great way to fly

SINGAPORE AIRLINES

Participating Countries

Funding

Australia

Austria

Belgium

Brazil

Britain

Canada

China

The Democratic Republic of Congo

France

Germany

Iran

Italy

Japan

Korea

Mali

The Netherlands

New Zealand

The Philippines

Russia

Spain

Switzerland

Ukraine

The United States of America

The Biennale of Sydney is pleased to acknowledge the generous support of the following participating governments and cultural organisations that have assisted in the presentation of the exhibition.

Australia
Australia Council for the Arts – Visual Arts and Craft Fund Audience & Market Development Division

New South Wales Government – Ministry for the Arts

City of Sydney

Northern Territory Government – the Northern Territory Department of Arts and Museums

Austria
Kunst Bundeskanzleramt

Belgium
Ministry of Flemish Culture

Brazil
Ministry of Culture – Secretariat of Patrimony, Museums and Plastic Arts

Britain
The British Council, London & Sydney

Canada
Department of Foreign Affairs and International Trade/ Ministère des Affaires étrangères et Commerce International du Canada

The Canada Council/ Le Conseil des Arts du Canada

The British Columbia Arts Council

France
Association Francaise d'Action Artistque

Ministry of Foreign Affairs

Embassy of France, Canberra

Germany
Auswärtiges Amt

Institut for Foreign Cultural Relations

Goethe Institut, Sydney

Japan
The Japan Foundation

Shiseido Co. Ltd

Toshiba International Foundation

Korea
The Australia-Korea Foundation

Netherlands
The Mondriaan Foundation

New Zealand
Creative New Zealand, Arts Council of New Zealand Toi Aotearoa

Philippines
National Commission for Culture and the Arts

Spain
Ministerio de Asuntos Exteriores

Acción Cultural Exterior

Switzerland
Pro Helvetia, the Arts Council of Switzerland

USA
The Fund for U.S Artists at International Festivals and Exhibitions, a partnership of the Department of State United States

The National Endowment for the Arts

The Rockefeller Foundation

The Pew Charitable Trusts with support from Arts International

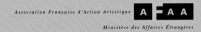

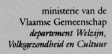

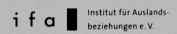

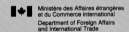

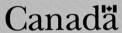

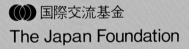

Participation by US artists in the Biennale of Sydney has been made possible, in part, by the Fund for US Artists at International Festivals and Exhibitions, a public/private partnership of the United States Department of State, the National Endowment for the Arts, the Rockefeller Foundation and the Pew Charitable Trusts with administrative assistance from Arts International.

Board and Staff of the
12th Biennale of Sydney

Franco Belgiorno-Nettis, AC CBE
Founding Governor

**Board members of the
Biennale of Sydney**

Guido Belgiorno-Nettis, *Chairman*

Edmund Capon AM

David Coe

Penelope Coombes

Ari Droga

John Kaldor AM

Ann Lewis AM

Frank Sartor

represented by Graham Jahn

Nick Waterlow OAM

Evan Williams

Staff of the Biennale of Sydney

Paula Latos-Valier
General Manager

Lesley Brown
Public Programs Manager
(until December 1999)

Michelle Culpitt
Administrator

Jane Gillespie
Office Assistant

Craig Judd
Education Manager

Dolla S Merrillees
Exhibition Manager

Rilka Oakley
Publications / Venue Manager

Akky van Ogtrop
*Public Programs
& Marketing Manager*

Anders Pleass
Special Projects Officer

Euan Upston
Finance & Administration Manager

Project Staff

Carola Akindele-Obe
Exhibition Assistant

Emma Collison
Publicity

Robert Herbert
Film Program

Peter Jackson
Technical Consultant

Ewen McDonald
Catalogue Editor

Tina Waring
Web-site Coordinator

Geoff Miller
(until December 1999)

Interns / Volunteers

Nicholas Bouf, Amanda Cachia,
Nathalie Caminada, Emily Dobbs,
Vasili Kaliman, Katherine Lea,
Kate Milner, Gia-Nghi Phung,
Alycia Sheppard, Georgina Smith

Education Focus Group

Diedre Armstrong, Chris Bates,
Katy Batha, Rhonda Clarke,
Aida Fulstone, Sam Gerardi,
Louise Guest, Glen Israel,
Karen King, Craig Malyon,
Karen Marass, Rhonda McFarlane,
Merle Olvet, Sandra Ristway,
Kerry Thomas

International selection panel

Fumio Nanjo
Independent curator and writer,
Tokyo

Louise Neri
Independent curator and former
senior editor, *Parkett* Magazine,
New York

Hetti Perkins
Curator, Aboriginal and
Torres Strait Islander Art,
Art Gallery of New South Wales,
Sydney

Sir Nicholas Serota
Director, Tate Gallery,
London

Robert Storr
Senior Curator,
Museum of Modern Art,
New York

Harald Szeemann
Director, Venice Biennale 1999
based in Zurich

Nick Waterlow
Director of three Sydney Biennales,
Senior Lecturer, The University of
New South Wales, College of Fine
Arts, Chairman of the panel

Lenders to the Exhibition

Alcaston Gallery, Melbourne

Alec O'Halloran and Helen Zimmerman, Sydney

Amanda Love, Sydney

André Magnin, Paris

Annandale Galleries, Sydney

Art Gallery of New South Wales, Sydney

Art Gallery of South Australia, Adelaide

Art Gallery of Western Australia, Perth

Astrup Fearnley Museum of Modern Art, Oslo

Australian Heritage Commission, Canberra

Barbara Gladstone Gallery, New York

Bonnefanten Museum, Maastricht

Bret Walker Collection, Sydney

Brondesbury Holdings Ltd, Caracas

Chartwell Trust Collection, Waikato Museum of Art and History, Hamilton

Cheim & Read Gallery, New York

Christine Abrahams Gallery, Melbourne

David Zwirner, New York

Deitch Projects, New York

Donald Young Gallery, Chicago

Dr Stephen Freiberg Collection, Sydney

Estate of Martin Kippenberger, Cologne

Fondation Cartier pour l'art contemporain, Paris

Frances and José Roberto Marinho, Rio de Janeiro

Galeria Gisela Capitain, Cologne

Galerie Hauser & Wirth & Presenhuber, Zurich

Galerie Hauser & Wirth, Zurich

Galerie Johnen & Schöttle, Cologne

Galerie Rüdger Schöttle, Munich

Gallerie Australis, Adelaide

Gallery Gabrielle Pizzi, Melbourne

Hocken Library, University of Otago, Dunedin

Irish Museum of Modern Art, Dublin

Isabella Prata and Idel Arcuschin, São Paulo

John Kaldor, Sydney

K. de Goede and P. Ruck, Amsterdam

Kunsthalle zu Kiel, Kiel

Laverty Collection, Sydney

Maureen Paley / Interim Art, London

Ministerie van de Vlaamse Gemeenschap, Ghent

Monika Sprüth Gallery, Cologne

Museum and Art Gallery of the Northern Territory, Darwin

Museum für Moderne Kunst, Frankfurt am Main

Museum of Contemporary Art, Sydney

Museum of New Zealand Te Papa Tongarewa, Wellington

Museum voor Moderne Kunst, Arnhem

National Gallery of Australia, Canberra

National Gallery of Victoria, Melbourne

Philip Bacon Galleries, Brisbane

Powerhouse Museum, Sydney

Queensland Art Gallery, Brisbane

Ray Hughes Gallery, Sydney

Ray Hughes, Sydney

Ron and Ann Pizzuti, Columbus

Roslyn Oxley9 Gallery, Sydney

Rubell Family Collection, Miami

Sanggawa, Manila

Setagaya Art Museum, Tokyo

Sperone Westwater, New York

Stedelijk van Abbemuseum, Eindhoven

The Buhl Foundation, New York

The Holmes à Court Collection, Heytesbury, Perth

The Marc and Livia Straus Family Collection

The Montreal Museum of Fine Arts, Montreal

The Paul Eliadis Collection of Contemporary Art, Brisbane

The University of Melbourne Art Collection

The University of Queensland, Brisbane

UNSW Art Collection, The University of New South Wales, Sydney

Utopia Art, Sydney

Victoria and Warren Miro, London

Victoria Miro Gallery, London

William and Maria Bell

Zeno X Gallery, Antwerp

The Biennale of Sydney also wishes to thank the artists who have lent works and the private collectors who do not wish to be named.

Supporting Galleries

303 Gallery, New York

Anna Schwartz Gallery, Melbourne

Barbara Gross Galerie, Munich

Bellas Gallery, Brisbane

Christopher Moore Gallery, Wellington

Frith Street Gallery, London

Galeria Camargo Vilaça, São Paulo

Luhring Augustine, New York

Maningrida Arts & Culture, Winnellie

Ota Fine Arts, Tokyo

Peter McLeavey Art Dealer, Wellington

Rex Irwin Art Dealer, Sydney

Sherman Galleries, Sydney

Sutton Gallery, Melbourne

List of works

Doug Aitken
eraser 1998
film transfer to laser disc
installed size variable
Collection: Astrup Fearnley Museum
of Modern Art, Oslo
Courtesy 303 Gallery, New York and
Victoria Miro Gallery, London
eraser Credits Doug Aitken,
Director/Camera; Eric Matthies,
Producer; David Levine, *Sound and
Logistics;* Wing Ko, *Camera
Technician;* Haines Hall, *Editor;*
Jon Huck, *Sound Design;* Jenny Liu,
Production Support; Joe Phillips,
Driver; Winston Telesford, *Police-
Montserrat;* Andre Caron, *Pilot;*
Susan Edgecombe, *Lodging;* Geo
Film Group, Pogocam; Tricia Todd,
Production Coordinator; Djahid
Elhami, *Camtec;* Kaywon Elhami,
Camera Support/Camtec; Needra
Kudrow, *Travel Agent;* Leticia Torres,
Equipment Transport
Post Production
Spotwelders, David Glean
Mastering
Neysa Horsburg, *Post Executive
Producer;* Gino Panaro, *Colorist;* Scott
Burrows, *Henry Editor*
Music and Sound
Original music composed by Steve
Roden. Composed from field
recordings in Montserrat by David
Levine. Courtesy of New Plastic
Music 1998
Additional Music
Low - *will the night* and *be right
there,* Porter Ricks; *beat sample,*
Louis Armstrong; *we have all the
time in the world,* Faust, *der Pfad*
Additional Music and Sounds
Doug Aitken; David Levine; Jon Huck
Generous Support By
Museum Ludwig, Köln
Pamela and Richard Kramlich
Jerome Foundation
Special Thanks
Lisa Spellman & 303 Gallery, New York
Thea Westreich; Neville Wakefield
Thank You
Brian Doyle, Nora Tobbe, Jenny Liu,
Montserrat Volcano Observatory and
Staff, Dr Alan Spira and the Travel
Medicine Centre, Oil Factory – Billy,
Heidi and Jay, Francesco Bonami,
Carmen Zita, Michael Black, Phillipe
Perrino, Seung-Duk Kim, Julia
Mascova, Michael Paradinas, Dean
Kuipers, Betsy Smith, Jim Toth,
Marilyn Aitken, Robert Aitken, Tom
Cugliani, Victoria Miro Gallery,
London

Matthew Barney
CREMASTER 2 1999
35mm film, colour, sound
Duration: 20 min 39 sec
Courtesy the artist and Barbara
Gladstone Gallery, New York

Vanessa Beecroft
vb40.067.vb.pol
**VB 40 Museum of Contemporary
Art, Sydney, Australia** 1999
digital type c print
63.5 x 81.3 cm inc. borders;
unframed
Photo: Vanessa Beecroft
Courtesy the artist and Deitch
Projects, New York
vb40.070.vb.pol.tiff
**VB 40 Museum of Contemporary
Art, Sydney, Australia** 1999
digital type c print
63.5 x 81.3 cm inc. borders;
unframed
Photo: Vanessa Beecroft
Courtesy the artist and Deitch
Projects, New York
vb37.342.vb
**Spiral Wacoal Art Center,
Tokyo, Japan** 1999
digital type c print
63.5 x 81.3 cm inc. borders;
unframed
Photo: Vanessa Beecroft
Courtesy the artist and Deitch
Projects, New York
vb35.079.vb
**VB 35 Show, Guggenheim
Museum, New York, NY** 1998
digital type c print
63.5 x 81.3 cm inc. borders;
unframed
Photo: Vanessa Beecroft
Courtesy the artist and Deitch
Projects, New York
vb34.030.al.vst
**VB 34 Moderna Museet,
Stockholm, Sweden** 1998
digital type c print
63.5 x 81.3 cm inc. borders;
unframed
Photo: Annia Larsson
Courtesy the artist and Deitch
Projects, New York
vb36.059.vb
**VB 36 Galerie für Zeitgenossische
Kunst, Leipzig, Germany** 1998
digital type c print
63.5 x 81.3 cm inc. borders;
unframed
Photo: Vanessa Beecroft
Courtesy the artist and Deitch
Projects, New York

vb36.344.ali.sld
**VB 36 Galerie für Zeitgenossische
Kunst, Leipzig, Germany** 1998
digital type c print
63.5 x 81.3 cm inc. borders;
unframed
Photo: Armin Linke
Courtesy the artist and Deitch
Projects, New York
vb25.022.ali
Liu Rumma, Naples, Italy 1997
digital type c print
63.5 x 81.3 cm inc. borders;
unframed
Photo: Armin Linke
Courtesy the artist and Deitch
Projects, New York
vb27.034.vb
**Galerie Analix, Geneva,
Switzerland** 1997
digital type c print
63.5 x 81.3 cm inc. borders;
unframed
Photo: Vanessa Beecroft
Courtesy the artist and Deitch
Projects, New York
vb29.009.vb.vst
**Le Nouveau Musée,
Lyon, France** 1997
digital type c print
63.5 x 81.3 cm inc. borders;
unframed
Photo: Vanessa Beecroft
Courtesy the artist and Deitch
Projects, New York
vb30.230.vb.vst
**Site Santa Fe,
Santa Fe, New Mexico** 1997
digital type c print
63.5 x 81.3cm inc. borders;
unframed
Photo: Vanessa Beecroft
Courtesy the artist and Deitch
Projects, New York
vb31.083.vb
**ICA Boston,
Boston, Massachusetts** 1997
digital type c print
63.5 x 81.3 cm inc. borders;
unframed
Photo: Vanessa Beecroft
Courtesy the artist and Deitch
Projects, New York
vb16.070.ali
**VB 16 Deitch Projects,
New York, NY** 1996
digital type c print
63.5 x 81.3 cm inc. borders;
unframed
Photo: Armin Linke
Courtesy the artist and Deitch
Projects, New York

vb20.011.vb.sld
**ICA Philadelphia,
Philadelphia, Pennsylvania** 1996
digital type c print
63.5 x 81.3 cm inc. borders;
unframed
Photo: Vanessa Beecroft
Courtesy the artist and Deitch
Projects, New York
vb25.062.vb.pol
**VB 25 Van AbbeMUSEUM,
Eindhoven, The Netherlands** 1996
digital type c print
63.5 x 81.3 cm inc. borders;
unframed
Photo: Vanessa Beecroft
Courtesy the artist and Deitch
Projects, New York
vb11.026.ali
**Galerie Analix - B & L Polla,
Geneva, Switzerland** 1995
digital type c print
63.5 x 81.3 cm inc. borders;
unframed
Photo: Armin Linke
Courtesy the artist and Deitch
Projects, New York
vb11.030.ali
**Galerie Analix - B & L Polla,
Geneva, Switzerland** 1995
digital type c print
63.5 x 81.3 cm inc. borders;
unframed
Photo: Armin Linke
Courtesy the artist and Deitch
Projects, New York
vb12.005.vb
**Caravanserraglio Arte Contem-
poranca, Pescara, Italy** 1995
digital type c print
63.5 x 81.3 cm inc. borders;
unframed
Photo: Vanessa Beecroft
Courtesy the artist and Deitch
Projects, New York
vb08.035.vb
**VB 08 PS 1 Museum,
Long Island City, New York** 1994
digital type c print
63.5 x 81.3 cm inc. borders;
unframed
Photo: Vanessa Beecroft
Courtesy the artist and Deitch
Projects, New York
vb09.014.vb.sld
**Schipper and Krome,
Cologne, Germany** 1994
digital type c print
63.5 x 81.3 cm inc. borders;
unframed
Photo: Vanessa Beecroft
Courtesy the artist and Deitch
Projects, New York

Gordon Bennett
Notes to Basquiat (In the Future Art will not be Boring) 1999
acrylic on linen
182.5 x 182.5 cm
Collection: the artist
Courtesy the artist, Bellas Gallery, Brisbane, Sherman Galleries, Sydney & Sutton Gallery, Melbourne
Home Decor (Preston + De Stijl = Citizen) Then & Now 1997
acrylic on linen
182.5 x 365 cm
The Paul Eliadus Collection of Contemporary Art, Brisbane
Big Romantic Painting (Apotheosis of Captain Cook) 1993
synthetic polymer paint on unprimed cotton canvas
182 x 400.5 cm
Collection: The University of Melbourne Art Collection, Ian Potter Museum of Art, University of Melbourne
Self Portrait (Schism) 1992
(recreated 2000)
antique dressing table, mirror, 2 painted panels (see *History Paintings* below)
installed size variable
Courtesy the artist and The Holmes à Court Collection, Heytesbury, Perth
History Painting (Burn + Scatter) 1992
acrylic and flashe on canvas
92 x 65 cm
Collection: The Holmes à Court Collection, Heytesbury, Perth
History Painting (Excuse my Language) 1992
acrylic and flashe on canvas
92 x 65 cm
Collection: The Holmes à Court Collection, Heytesbury, Perth
Culture bag 1992
suitcase, plaster, broken bottles, text
installed size variable
Courtesy the artist, Bellas Gallery, Brisbane, Sherman Galleries, Sydney & Sutton Gallery, Melbourne
Ancestor Figures 1989
oil on canvas
148 x 236 cm
Private collection, Brisbane
Courtesy Bellas Gallery, Brisbane
Outsider 1988
oil and acrylic on canvas
290 x 180 cm
Collection: The University of Queensland, Brisbane
The Coming of the Light 1987
acrylic on canvas
152 x 374 cm
Collection: the artist
Courtesy the artist, Bellas Gallery, Brisbane, Sherman Galleries, Sydney & Sutton Gallery, Melbourne

Louise Bourgeois
Cell VIII 1998
various media
254.3 x 335.3 x 254 cm
Courtesy Cheim & Read, New York
Untitled 1996
cloth, rubber, steel and mixed media
283.2 x 297.1 x 254 cm
Courtesy Cheim & Read, New York

He disappeared into complete silence 1947
10 engravings of which 9 are accompanied by text, introduction by Marius Bewley
25.5 x 35.5 cm
Collection: National Gallery of Australia, Canberra
C.O.Y.O.T.E 1941-48
painted wood
137 x 214 x 28 cm
Collection: National Gallery of Australia, Canberra

Cai Guo-Qiang
Still life performance 2000
horse, horseman, model, 3 painters, paints, canvas, brushes, easels, drapes
installed size variable
Courtesy the artist and Gene & Brian Sherman, Sydney

Sophie Calle
B, C, & W 1998
1 book, 4 black and white photographic texts, 4 colour photographs, 8 framed parts
67 x 67 cm each
installed size variable
Collection: the artist
Suite Vénitienne 1980
1 presentation text, 55 black and white photographs, 23 texts and 3 maps (edition of three in English)
installed size variable
Courtesy the artist and Donald Young Gallery, Chicago

Destiny Deacon
Sad and Bad 2000
series of photographs
installed size variable
Collection: the artist
I seen myself 2 from Blak Like MI series 1991
polaroids x 2
11 x 9cm each
Private collection, Melbourne
Venus half caste, series I 1990
polaroids x 2
11 x 9cm each
Collection: the artist
Brown skin babies on the menu, Blak Like MI series 1990
polaroids x 3
11 x 9cm each
Collection: the artist
Blak lik mi 1990
polaroids x 2
11 x 9cm each
Collection: the artist
Blak like mi 1990
polaroids x 3
11 x 9cm each
Private collection, Melbourne
The Men are Coming Home 1990
polaroids x 4
11 x 9cm each
Collection: the artist

Stan Douglas
Win, Place or Show 1998
two-channel video projection four-channel soundtrack (edition of two)
installed size variable
Courtesy the artist and David Zwirner, New York

Marlene Dumas
Pretty White Guy 1999
oil on canvas
100 x 56 cm
Private collection, Netanya
Shrimp 1998
ink on paper
125 x 70 cm
Collection: Museum für Moderne Kunst, Frankfurt am Main
Dorothy D-Lite 1998
ink on paper
125 x 70 cm
Collection: the artist
Young Boy 1996/98
ink on paper
125 x 70 cm
Collection: Museum für Moderne Kunst, Frankfurt am Main
No more One-liners 1993
ink on paper
6 parts, 34.7 x 31 cm each
Collection: Ron and Ann Pizzuti, Columbus, Ohio
Lovesick 1994
oil on canvas
60 x 50 cm
Private collection, London
Courtesy Frith Street Gallery, London
The blonde, the brunette and the black woman 1992
oil on canvas
3 parts, 2 parts 25 x 30 cm; 1 part 30 x 40 cm
Collection: Ministerie van de Vlaamse Gemeenschap, Ghent
A dead man 1988
oil on canvas
50 x 60 cm
Collection: K. de Goede and P. Ruck, Amsterdam
Waiting (for meaning) 1988
oil on canvas
50 x 70 cm
Collection: Kunsthalle zu Kiel, Kiel
Het Kwaad is banaal 1984
oil on canvas
125 x 105 cm
Collection: Stedelijk Van AbbeMUSEUM, Eindhoven
Emily 1984
oil on canvas
130 x 110 cm
Collection: Museum voor Moderne Kunst, Arnhem

Rosalie Gascoigne
Metropolis 1999
retro-reflective road signs on plywood
232 x 320 cm
Collection: Art Gallery of New South Wales, Sydney
Construction 1999
corrugated iron, brown & black wood
82 x 84 cm
Collection: the artist's estate, Canberra
Courtesy Roslyn Oxley9 Gallery, Sydney

Overland 1996
25 painted plywood panels
430 x 340 cm
Collection: the artist's estate, Canberra
Courtesy Roslyn Oxley9 Gallery, Sydney
Afternoon 1996
wood and paint
117 x 288 cm
Private collection, Melbourne
Courtesy Roslyn Oxley9 Gallery, Sydney
Loopholes 1996
reflective road signs on plywood
121 x 119 cm
Collection: the artist's estate, Canberra
Courtesy Roslyn Oxley9 Gallery, Sydney
White Garden 1995
synthetic polymer paint on corrugated iron on wood
177 x 184 cm
Private collection, Sydney
Courtesy Roslyn Oxley9 Gallery, Sydney
Compound 1994
timber and masonite
102.5 x 92.5 cm
Private collection, Coffs Harbour
Courtesy Roslyn Oxley9 Gallery, Sydney
Steel Magnolias 1994
corrugated iron on plywood
104.5 x 98.5 cm
Collection: Amanda Love, Sydney
Courtesy Roslyn Oxley9 Gallery, Sydney
White City 1993-94
synthetic polymer paint on sawn wood on composition board
110.5 x 108 cm
Collection: the artist's estate, Canberra
Courtesy Roslyn Oxley9 Gallery, Sydney
Fool's Gold 1992
retro-reflective road signs on plywood
158.7 x 161 cm
Collection: National Gallery of Australia, Canberra
Love Apples 1992
retro-reflective road signs on plywood
128 x 107 cm
Private collection, Sydney
Courtesy Roslyn Oxley9 Gallery, Sydney
Far View 1990
sawn soft drink crates on wood, polyptych
3 panels, 89 x 221 cm
Private collection, Melbourne
Courtesy Roslyn Oxley9 Gallery, Sydney
Monaro 1989
synthetic polymer paint on sawn soft drinks crates on plywood
four panels 129.5 x 114 cm each, overall size 130.8 x 457.4 cm
Collection: Art Gallery of Western Australia, Perth
Piece to Walk Around 1981
saffron thistle sticks
20 squares 80 x 80 cm each square, overall size 380 x 480 cm
Collection: the artist's estate, Canberra
Courtesy Roslyn Oxley9 Gallery, Sydney

Andreas Gursky

Klitschko 1999
type c photograph
207 x 261 cm
Courtesy the artist and Monika
Sprüth Galerie, Cologne

o.T.V (Nike) 1997
type c photograph
186 x 443 cm
Private collection, Melbourne

Chicago Mercantile Exchange
1997
type c photograph
186 x 249 cm
Collection: John Kaldor, Sydney
Courtesy Museum of Contemporary
Art, Sydney

Times Square, New York 1997
type c photograph
186 x 250.5 cm
Collection: John Kaldor, Sydney
Courtesy Museum of Contemporary
Art, Sydney

Paris, Centre Pompidou 1995
type c photograph
166 x 254 cm
Collection: John Kaldor, Sydney
Courtesy Museum of Contemporary
Art, Sydney

Ofenpass 1994
type c photograph
186 x 226 cm
Collection: John Kaldor, Sydney
Courtesy Museum of Contemporary
Art, Sydney

Fiona Hall

Gene Pool 2000
garden installation composed of
native flora
installed size variable
Courtesy the artist and Government
House, Historic Houses Trust of New
South Wales, Sydney

Dead in the Water 1999
pvc pipe, glass beads, silver wire,
vitrine (timber and perspex)
vitrine size 106.5 x 128 x 128 cm
Collection: National Gallery of
Victoria, Melbourne

Drift Net 1998
pvc pipe, glass beads, mother-of-
pearl buttons, wire, engraved bottle,
compass, vitrine (timber and
perspex)
vitrine size 129 x 160 x 76 cm
Courtesy the artist and Roslyn Oxley9
Gallery, Sydney

Paradisus Terrestris Entitled
1996
aluminium & tin, 21 component parts
installed size variable
Courtesy the artist
Collection: National Gallery of
Victoria, Melbourne

Bill Hammond

Hokey Pokey 1998
paint on canvas on stretchers
4 panels, overall size 200 x 500 cm
Private collection, Auckland
Courtesy Peter McLeavey Art Dealer,
Wellington

Living Large 6 1995
paint on loose canvas
300 x 200 cm
Private collection, Wellington

Courtesy Peter McLeavey Art Dealer,
Wellington

Watching for Buller 2 1993
acrylic on canvas
100 x 120 cm
Collection: the artist

Knocking on the Locker 1991
acrylic on kauri panel
89 x 98 cm
Private collection, Auckland

Passover 1989
acrylic and varnish on aluminium
120 x 61.5 cm
Chartwell Collection, Auckland Art
Gallery Toi o Tamaki Courtesy of
Waikato Museum of Art and History
Te Whare Taonga o Waikato

I Heat Up, I Can't Cool Down 1985
paint on loose canvas
56 x 76.3 cm
Collection: The Hocken Library,
University of Otago, Dunedin

It's Only Words 1984
oil on loose canvas
200 x 208 cm
Collection: Museum of New Zealand
Te Papa Tongarewa, Wellington

Gwyn Hanssen Pigott

Breath 1999
Limoges porcelain
24 pieces
Courtesy the artist and Philip Bacon
Galleries, Brisbane

Pair of bowls 1998
Limoges porcelain
Private collection, Melbourne
Courtesy Christine Abrahams Gallery,
Melbourne

Procession 1998
wheelthrown & woodfired porcelain
7 pieces
Private collection, Melbourne.
Courtesy Christine Abrahams Gallery,
Melbourne

Exodus II 1996
wheelthrown & woodfired porcelain
23 pieces
Private collection, Melbourne
Courtesy Christine Abrahams Gallery,
Melbourne

Black Mountain still life 1995
wheelthrown & woodfired porcelain
11 pieces
Collection: Bret Walker, Sydney
Courtesy Rex Irwin Art Dealer,
Sydney

Still life with blue bowls 1995
wheelthrown & woodfired porcelain
7 pieces
Collection: UNSW Art Collection,
The University of New South Wales,
Sydney

Still life with two jugs 1994
wheelthrown & woodfired porcelain
5 pieces
Private collection, Sydney
Courtesy Rex Irwin Art Dealer,
Sydney

Sombre still life 1993
wheelthrown & woodfired porcelain
5 pieces
Collection: Powerhouse Museum,
Sydney

Bill Henson

Untitled 1998/1999/2000
type c colour photographs (edition
of five)
127 x 180 cm (paper size)
Courtesy the artist and Roslyn Oxley9
Gallery, Sydney

Untitled 1997/98
type c colour photographs
127 x 180cm (paper size)
Courtesy the artist and Roslyn Oxley9
Gallery, Sydney

Untitled 1983/84
type c colour photographs
100 x 80cm (paper size)
Courtesy the artist and Roslyn Oxley9
Gallery, Sydney

Gary Hill

Viewer 1996
five-channel video installation
installed size variable
Courtesy the artist and Donald Young
Gallery, Chicago

Ilya & Emilia Kabakov

Monument To A Lost Civilization
1998/99
various media
installed size variable
Collection: the artists

Seydou Keïta

Untitled (series of 26) 1948-62
black and white photographs
50 x 60 cm
Courtesy André Magnin, Paris and
Ray Hughes Gallery, Sydney

Bodys Isek Kingelez

**Projet pour le Kinshasa du
troisième millénaire**
1997
wood, paper, cardboard, found
materials
100 x 332 diam cm
Collection: Fondation Cartier pour
l'art contemporain, Paris

Liège Belgique c1980
pens, pencils, biro on paper, plastic
card and plywood
54 x 50 x 50 cm
Collection: Ray Hughes, Sydney

Swissair c1980
pens, pencils, biro on paper, plastic
card and plywood
53 x 71 x 45 cm
Courtesy Ray Hughes Gallery, Sydney

Place de la Ville c1980
pens, pencils, biro on paper, plastic
card and plywood
40 x 75.5 x 85 cm
Courtesy Ray Hughes Gallery, Sydney

Miami City c1980
pens, pencils, biro on paper, plastic
card and plywood
58 x 50 x 50 cm
Courtesy Ray Hughes Gallery, Sydney

Martin Kippenberger

**I am going into the birch forest
as my pills will be taking effect
soon** 1990
artificial and real birch trees and
carved wooden pills
installed size variable
Collection: Estate of Martin
Kippenberger, Cologne
Courtesy Galerie Gisela Capitain,
Cologne

Yayoi Kusama

Dots, Obsession 1999
red balloons with white polka dots
filled with helium
installed size variable
Collection: the artist
Courtesy Ota Fine Arts, Tokyo

**Infinity Mirror Room - Phalli's
Field** 1965
(re-created room 2000)
sewn stuffed fabric, plywood, glass
mirrors
installed size variable
Collection: the artist
Courtesy Ota Fine Arts, Tokyo

John Mawurndjul

Untitled 2000
natural pigments, eucalyptus
tetradonta
dimensions unknown
Courtesy the artist and Maningrida
Arts and Culture, Winnellie

Mardayin at Mukkamukka 1999
natural pigments, eucalyptus
tetradonta
168 x 95 cm
Collection: Museum and Art Gallery
of the Northern Territory, Darwin

Mardayin Ceremony 1999
natural pigments, eucalyptus
tetradonta
153 x 88 cm
Laverty Collection, Sydney

Ngalyod 1999
natural pigments, eucalyptus
tetradonta
163 x 88 cm
Collection: Annandale Galleries,
Sydney

Mardayin Ceremony Theme 1 1997
natural pigments, eucalyptus
tetradonta
134.5 x 73.5 cm
Courtesy Annandale Galleries,
Sydney

Mardayin Burrk-dorreng
(Mumeka, Northern Territory) 1990
natural pigments, eucalyptus
tetradonta
160.3 x 73.4 cm (irreg)
Collection: National Gallery of
Victoria, Melbourne

**Mardayin ceremonial designs
from Kakodbebuldi** (Mumeka,
Northern Territory) 1990
natural pigments, eucalyptus
tetradonta
179.3 x 91.8 cm (irreg)
Collection: National Gallery of
Victoria, Melbourne

**Ngalyod (Female rainbow
serpent)** 1988
natural pigments, eucalyptus
tetradonta
230 x 90.5 cm (irreg)

Collection: Museum of Contemporary Art, Sydney
Nawurndjul (shooting star spirit) 1988
natural pigments, synthetic polymer paint, eucalyptus tetradonta
219.4 x 95.0 cm (irreg)
Collection: Museum of Contemporary Art, Sydney

Maningrida Sculpture

England Banggala
Wangarra spirit 1991
natural pigments, wood
235.6 x 20.5 x 23 cm
Collection: National Gallery of Victoria, Melbourne
Wangarra spirit being c1986
natural pigments, wood
267 x 15 x 11 cm
Collection: Art Gallery of New South Wales, Sydney
Wangarra spirit being 1985
natural pigments, wood
236 cm
Collection: Art Gallery of New South Wales, Sydney

Jimmy Bungurru
Double-Headed Mimih spirit at Kurrudin 1996
natural pigments, bombax ceiba
149 cm
Courtesy Gallery Gabrielle Pizzi, Melbourne

James Iyuna
Mimih spirit 1991
natural pigments, wood
250 x 19 x 14 cm
Collection: National Gallery of Victoria, Melbourne

Willie Jolpa
Wangarra spirit 1991
natural pigments, wood
193.6 x 19.2 x 14 cm
Collection: National Gallery of Victoria, Melbourne

Mick Kubarkku
Mimih spirit from Yikarrakkal 1995
natural pigments, bombax ceiba
269 cm
Courtesy Gallery Gabrielle Pizzi, Melbourne
Mimih spirit from Yirrakkal 1995
natural pigments, bombax ceiba
270 cm
Courtesy Gallery Gabrielle Pizzi, Melbourne
Mimih spirit 1992
natural pigments, wood
254 cm
Collection: National Gallery of Victoria, Melbourne
Mimih spirit 1992
natural pigments, wood
265 cm
Collection: National Gallery of Victoria, Melbourne
Mimih spirit 1992
natural pigments, wood
243 cm
Collection: National Gallery of Victoria, Melbourne

Crusoe Kuningbal
Mimih spirit 1984
natural pigments, wood
304.2 x 40 x 32.2 cm
Collection: National Gallery of Victoria, Melbourne
Mimih spirit 1984
natural pigments, wood
209.6 x 16.6 x 26.5 cm
Collection: National Gallery of Victoria, Melbourne

Crusoe Kurddal
Yawk Yawk Fresh Water Mermaid spirit 1996
natural pigments, bombax ceiba
328 cm
Courtesy Gallery Gabrielle Pizzi, Melbourne
Mimih spirit 1990
natural pigments, wood
294.5 x 27.8 x 24.1 cm
Collection: National Gallery of Victoria, Melbourne

Jack Laranggai
Balinjarngarlang spirit 1991
natural pigments, wood, fibre, feathers
215.2 x 27 x 28.3 cm
Collection: National Gallery of Victoria, Melbourne

Jimmy Wood Maraluka
Balinjarngarlang spirit 1991
natural pigments, wood
206 x 15.8 x 14 cm
Collection: National Gallery of Victoria, Melbourne

Jacky Maranbarra
Wangarra spirit 1991
natural pigments, wood
248 x 26.3 x 19.7 cm
Collection: National Gallery of Victoria, Melbourne

John Mawurndjul
Mimih 1998
natural pigments, wood, synthetic polymer paint
196 x 21 cm
Collection: National Gallery of Victoria, Melbourne

Les Midikkurriya and Lena Yarinkura
Ngorkorr spirit carrying woven bags 1991
natural pigments, wood, fibre
208.1 x 60.2 x 80.4 cm
Collection: National Gallery of Victoria, Melbourne

Ivan Namirrkki
Nakidjkidj spirit 1991
natural pigments, wood
259 x 21.5 x 17 cm
Collection: National Gallery of Victoria, Melbourne

Michael Ngalabiya
Warrabunbun spirit 1990-91
natural pigments, wood
200 x 23 x 23.9 cm
Collection: National Gallery of Victoria, Melbourne
Warrabunbun spirit 1990-91
natural pigments, wood
232.8 x 26.1 x 8 cm

Collection: National Gallery of Victoria, Melbourne

Alec Wurramala
Galabarrbarra Male/Female spirit from Jinamarda 1995
natural pigments, bombax ceiba
264 cm
Courtesy Gallery Gabrielle Pizzi, Melbourne
Galabarrbarra/Ganawarrna spirit 1991
natural pigments, wood, fibre
256.0 x 24 x 18 cm
Collection: National Gallery of Victoria, Melbourne
Galabarrbarra/Ganawarrna spirit 1991
natural pigments, wood, fibre
270 x 22 x 17.3 cm
Collection: National Gallery of Victoria, Melbourne

Owen Yalandja
Yawk Yawk 1999
natural pigments, kurrajong
264 x 14 x 13 cm
Collection: Art Gallery of New South Wales, Sydney
Yawk Yawk 1999
natural pigments, kurrajong
230 x 18 x 10 cm
Collection: Art Gallery of New South Wales, Sydney
Yawk Yawk Fresh Water Mermaid spirit at Barrhidjowkeng 1993
natural pigments, bombax ceiba
266 cm
Courtesy Gallery Gabrielle Pizzi, Melbourne

Paul McCarthy
Painter 1995
various media installation
installed size variable
Rubell Family Collection, Miami

Boris Mikhailov
"The Snowy People" from **Case History** series (1-7) 1998
gelatin silver prints
125 x 185 cm
Collection: the artist
"By the Ground" from the **Brown** series (1-20) 1991
sepia toned gelatin silver prints
11.5 x 29.5 cm each
Collection: the artist

Tracey Moffatt
Artist 1999-2000
video with stereo surround, playing time 10 min
Courtesy the artist and Roslyn Oxley9 Gallery, Sydney
Scarred for Life II 1999
off set print, series of 10 framed images, edition of 60
80 x 60 cm
Collection: Amanda Love, Sydney
Courtesy Roslyn Oxley9 Gallery, Sydney
Scarred for Life 1994
off set print, series of 9 images, edition of 50

80 x 60 cm
Courtesy the artist and Roslyn Oxley9 Gallery, Sydney
Something More 1989
photographs, series of 9 images, edition of 30
90 x 150 cm each
Courtesy Roslyn Oxley9 Gallery, Sydney

Mariko Mori
Pure Land 1996-98
glass with photointerlayer
5 panels, 305 x 610 x 2.2 cm overall
Collection: William & Maria Bell
Courtesy Deitch Projects, New York
Burning Desire 1996-98
glass with photointerlayer
5 panels, 305 x 610 x 2.2 cm overall
Collection: William & Maria Bell
Courtesy Deitch Projects, New York
Mirror of Water 1996-98
glass with photointerlayer
5 panels, 305 x 610 x 2.2 cm overall
Collection: William & Maria Bell
Courtesy Deitch Projects, New York
Entropy of Love 1996
glass with photointerlayer
5 panels, 305 x 610 x 2.2 cm overall
Collection: William & Maria Bell
Courtesy Deitch Projects, New York

Juan Muñoz
Conversation piece (Dublin) 1994
22 figures in resin, sand and cloth
installed size variable
Courtesy the artist and the Irish Museum of Modern Art, Dublin

Bruce Nauman
No, No, New Museum 1987
colour video tape,
playing time 60 minutes
The Marc and Livia Straus Family Collection
Left or Standing, Standing or Left Standing 1971/99
wallboard, yellow fluorescent lights, 2 monitors, 1 videodisc player, videodisc, text, video text "Standing"
installed size variable
Courtesy Sperone Westwater, New York
Window or wall sign 1967
fluorescent tubes
149.9 x 139.7 cm
Collection: National Gallery of Australia, Canberra

Shirin Neshat
Rapture 1999
video installation
installed size variable
Courtesy the artist and Barbara Gladstone Gallery, New York

Chris Ofili
He 1999
acrylic, oil, resin, paper collage, glitter, map pins & elephant dung on canvas
200 x 270 cm
Courtesy Victoria and Warren Miro, London

Set of 9 male and female double portraits 1999
watercolour
55 x 40 cm each
Courtesy the artist and Victoria Miro Gallery, London
The Adoration of Captain Shit and the Legend of the Black Stars 1998
acrylic, oil, resin, paper collage, glitter, map pins & elephant dung on canvas
243.8 x 182.8 cm
Courtesy Victoria and Warren Miro, London
She 1997
acrylic, oil, resin, paper collage, glitter, map pins & elephant dung on canvas
243.8 x 182.8 cm
Private collection, Puerto Rico
Courtesy Victoria Miro Gallery, London
Afrodizzia (2nd version) 1996
acrylic, oil, resin, paper collage, glitter, map pins & elephant dung on canvas
243.8 x 182.8 cm
Courtesy Victoria and Warren Miro, London
Black Flowerheads 1996
acrylic, oil, resin, paper collage, glitter, map pins & elephant dung on canvas
243.8 x 182.8 cm
Courtesy Victoria and Warren Miro, London

Yoko Ono
Scream 2000
banner installation
installed size variable
Collection: the artist
Ex It 1997
100 wooden coffins, 100 native trees
installed size variable
Collection: the artist
Imagine 1971
colour film, in collaboration with John Lennon, 70 min
Collection: the artist
Freedom 1970
colour film, playing time 1 min
Collection: the artist
Film No 5 (Smile) 1968
colour film, playing time 51 min
Collection: the artist
Lecture
Sydney Opera House
26 May 2000

Mike Parr
Shallow Grave 2000
14 sheets double hung woodblock prints
216 x 560 cm
Courtesy the artist and Sherman Galleries, Sydney
See Saw of the Either Or 2000
14 sheets double hung woodblock, drypoint & softground prints
216 x 560 cm
Courtesy the artist and Sherman Galleries, Sydney
Shallow Grave 2000
3 day performance, photographs
3000-4000
dimensions variable
Photographer: Felizitas Parr
Courtesy the artist and Sherman Galleries, Sydney

Wrong Face 1999
35 bronzes, table
100 x 400 x 120 cm table
Courtesy the artist and Anna Schwartz Gallery, Melbourne
Jesus' Orange Blood [for John Nixon] 1999
14 sheets double hung woodblock & liftground etching prints
216 x 560 cm
Courtesy the artist and Anna Schwartz Gallery, Melbourne
Wax Bride 1998
steel, wax casting of Parr as the Bride, table
100 x 200 x 90 cm table
Courtesy the artist and Anna Schwartz Gallery, Melbourne

Lisa Reihana & The Pacific Sisters
Andeertilopinae *feveris rod* 2000
deer antler
14 cm x 42 cm
Collection: the artist
'under cover of night: she shall be there' 2000
lambskin
300 x 180 cm
Collection: the artist
thingamybobs 1999
ceramic, cotton, bugle beads, feathers
2 parts, 17 x 6 x 60 cm each
Collection: the artist
Discomedusae *jellydialus* 1998
crystal, feathers
2 parts, 145 x 28 cm; 2 18 x 26 cm
Collection: the artist
Thalamophora furisish *love tusks* 1998
cow horns, fox fur tails
2 parts, 24 x 20 cm each
Collection: the artist
Tetracoralla vulvuelush *plush tusks* 1998
crystal, feathers
2 parts, 24 x 14 cm each
Collection: the artist
Pennatulida bruden *bloodline [furled]* 1998
cotton, feathers
10 cm x 5.6m
Collection: the artist
Ostraciontes *shellfish* 1998
shell, feathers
3 parts, 5 x 6 x 20 cm each
Collection: the artist
Lintosongiae *cleenus* 1998
dryer lint, feathers
22 cm (c) x 3 cm (h)
Collection: the artist
Te Wao O Tane 1997
cotton velvet, lingerie satin, feathers
300 x 180 cm
Private collection, Auckland
'native portraits n.19897' 1997
various media
installed dimensions variable
Collection: Museum of New Zealand Te Papa Tongarewa, Wellington

Gerhard Richter
Abstract Painting (812) 1994
oil on canvas
250 x 200 cm
Collection: Art Gallery of New South Wales, Sydney
Abstract Painting (797-2) 1993
oil on canvas
240 x 240 cm
Private collection, Sydney
Ema 1992
cibachrome photograph
227.5 x 153.5 cm
Collection: Art Gallery of New South Wales, Sydney
Abstract Painting (769-4) 1992
oil on canvas
200 x 180 cm
Private collection, Sydney
Abstract Painting (725-3) 1990
oil on canvas
225.8 x 200.6 cm
Collection: National Gallery of Victoria, Melbourne.
Landschaft bei Koblenz (640) 1987
oil on canvas
140 x 200 cm
Collection: The Montreal Museum of Fine Arts
Apfelbäume (650-1) 1987
oil on canvas
67 x 92 cm
Private collection, Cologne
Schädel (548/1) 1983
oil on canvas
55 x 50 cm
Private collection, Cologne
Gilbert and George 1975
oil on canvas
80.4 x 100.4 cm
Collection: National Gallery of Australia, Canberra

Ginger Riley
Ngak Ngak and the Ruined City 1998
synthetic polymer paint on canvas
193 x 249.3 cm
Collection: Art Gallery of New South Wales, Sydney
Ngak Ngak and the Owl at Night 1997
synthetic polymer paint on canvas
57 x 123 cm
Courtesy the artist and Alcaston Gallery, Melbourne
The Four Archers 1994
synthetic polymer paint on canvas
186.2 x 233 cm
Courtesy the artist and Alcaston Gallery, Melbourne
Ngak Ngak and the Four Archers 1993
synthetic polymer paint on canvas
171.0 x 288.7 cm
Collection: National Gallery of Victoria, Melbourne
Limmen Bight Country 1993
synthetic polymer paint on canvas
59.8 x 119.3 cm
Private collection, Melbourne
Courtesy Alcaston Gallery, Melbourne
Ngak Ngak in Flight 1993
synthetic polymer paint on canvas
59.8 x 119.3 cm
Courtesy the artist and Alcaston Gallery, Melbourne

Four Archers - Limmen Bight Country 1993
synthetic polymer paint on canvas
185 x 302 cm
Collection: Australian Heritage Commission, Canberra
Limmen Bight River Country 1992
synthetic polymer paint on canvas
244 x 244 cm
Collection: Art Gallery of New South Wales, Sydney
The Limmen Bight River 1990
synthetic polymer paint on canvas
156 x 202 cm
Collection: National Gallery of Australia, Canberra
Ngak Ngak and the Four Archers 1989
synthetic polymer paint on canvas
123.5 x 146 cm
Private collection, Melbourne
Courtesy Alcaston Gallery, Melbourne

Pipilotti Rist
SIP MY OCEAN 1996
video installation
installed size variable
Courtesy the artist, Galerie Hauser & Wirth, Zurich and Luhring Augustine, New York

Dieter Roth
SURTSEY 1973/74
18 prints in cassette, hyalographic print (callotype), 1-8 colours on white paper, on cardboard; (edition of 70; numbered and signed)
50 x 70 cm
Courtesy Galerie Hauser & Wirth & Presenhuber, Zurich
Now 1973
11 prints in cassette, with label (polaroid), intaglio prints (etching, from 4 zinc plate), on whitehandmade paper; (edition of 90; numbered and signed)
plate 30 x 42 cm
paper 39 x 54 cm
Courtesy Galerie Hauser & Wirth & Presenhuber, Zurich
Interrupted Breakfast 1972/79
11 prints in cassette, with label (polaroid), intaglio prints (copper engraving, all prints from the same plate), on white handmade paper; (edition of 18; numbered and signed)
plate 39.5 x 39.5 cm
paper 60 x 60 cm
Courtesy Galerie Hauser & Wirth & Presenhuber, Zurich
Containers 1971/73
33 prints and 3 watermarks
dimensions variable
Courtesy Galerie Hauser & Wirth & Presenhuber, Zurich
thomkinspatent 1968
screen print, 6 colours, vegetable juice on white card in plastic cover; (edition of 50; numbered and signed)
3 prints 72 x 102 cm each
Courtesy Galerie Hauser & Wirth & Presenhuber, Zurich

Sanggawa
Epilogo 1998
oil on canvas
162.88 x 548.64 cm
Private collection, Manila
The Second Coming 1995
oil on canvas
203 x 607 cm
Private collection, Manila
Palo-sebo 1995
oil on canvas
197 x 305 cm
Collection: Queensland Art Gallery,
Brisbane
Salubong 1994
oil on canvas
252 x 300 cm
Private collection, Manila
House of Sin 1994
oil on canvas
198 x 291 cm
Private collection, Manila

Mick Namarari Tjapaltjarri
Mouse Dreaming 1997
synthetic polymer paint on canvas
183 x 153 cm
Private collection, Darwin
*Untitled (Mala Hare-Wallaby
Dreaming at Marnpi)*
1997
synthetic polymer paint on canvas
183 x 153 cm
Private collection, Sydney
Untitled 1997
acrylic on linen
153 x 122 cm
Private collection, Sydney.
Courtesy Utopia Art, Sydney
Untitled 1994
synthetic polymer paint on canvas
152 x 183 cm
Laverty Collection, Sydney
*Tjuningpa (Desert Mouse)
Dreaming at Tjiterulpa*
1994
synthetic polymer paint on Belgian
linen
181 x 121 cm
Courtesy Gallerie Australis, Adelaide
Ninu (Bandicoot) Dreaming 1993
synthetic polymer paint on canvas
183 x 153 cm
Private collection, Darwin
Untitled 1989
acrylic on linen
149 x 35 cm
Courtesy Alcaston Gallery,
Melbourne
*Kangaroo and Bush Wallaby
Dreaming* 1989
acrylic on canvas
152 x 182 cm
Courtesy Gallery Gabrielle Pizzi,
Melbourne
Untitled (Papunya, NT) 1987
synthetic polymer paint on canvas
200.5 x 183 cm
Collection: Queensland Art Gallery,
Brisbane
Wallaby Dreaming (Kintore, South
Australia) 1982

synthetic polymer paint on canvas
101.7 x 102.4 cm
Collection: Art Gallery of South
Australia, Adelaide

Luc Tuymans
Gold 1999
oil on canvas
187.5 x 90.5 cm
Courtesy Zeno X Gallery, Antwerp
Illegitimate II 1997
oil on canvas
113 x 77.5 cm
Private collection, Brussels
Courtesy Zeno X Gallery, Antwerp
Belly 1996
oil on canvas
76.5 x 43.5 cm
Collection: Bonnefanten Museum,
Maastricht
Blessing 1996
oil on canvas
143 x 187 cm
Collection: Bonnefanten Museum,
Maastricht
The Flag 1995
oil on canvas
138 x 78 cm
Private collection, Oostende
Courtesy Zeno X Gallery, Antwerp
Recherches (x 3) 1989
oil on canvas
40 x 42 cm; 40 x 40 cm; 40 x 45 cm
Private collection, Ghent
Courtesy Zeno X Gallery, Antwerp
Schwarzheide 1986
oil on canvas
60 x 70 cm
Private collection, Ghent
Courtesy Zeno X Gallery, Antwerp

Ken Unsworth
The Skidderump 2000
bricks, steel, glass, timber, slide
projectors, sound tape, motorized
components
320 x 1034 diam cm
Collection: the artist

Adriana Varejão
Tilework in Live Flesh 1999
wood, aluminium, polyurethane,
oil paint
220 x 160 x 50 cm
Collection: Isabella Prata and Idel
Arcuschin, São Paulo
Courtesy Galeria Camargo Vilaça,
São Paulo
Tilework with Vertical Incision
1999
wood, aluminium, polyurethane,
oil paint
220 x 160 x 50 cm
Private collection, São Paulo
Courtesy Galeria Camargo Vilaça,
São Paulo
Tongue with Winding Pattern
1998
wood, aluminium, canvas,
polyurethane, oil paint

220 x 170 x 57 cm
Collection: Frances and Jose Roberto
Marinho, Rio de Janeiro
Courtesy Galeria Camargo Vilaça,
São Paulo
Kitchen's Tiles with Varied Game
1998
oil on canvas
140 x 160 cm
Private collection, São Paulo
Courtesy Galeria Camargo Vilaça,
São Paulo
Carne a Moda de Franz Post
1996
oil on canvas, porcelain
canvas 60 x 80 cm, 4 porcelain
pieces, 25 cm diam each
Collection: Brondesbury Holdings Ltd,
Caracas
Courtesy Galeria Camargo Vilaça,
São Paulo
Map of Lopo Homem 1992
oil, wood, cat-gut
110 x 140 cm
Collection: Brondesbury Holdings Ltd,
Caracas
Courtesy Galeria Camargo Vilaça,
São Paulo

Jeff Wall
Polishing 1998
cibachrome transparency in
aluminium display case, backlit with
flourescent tubes
198.1 x 243.8 x 21 cm
Collection: Art Gallery of Western
Australia, Perth
*Rear, 304 East 25 Ave.,
Vancouver, 9 May 1997,
1.14 & 1.17pm* 1997
cibachrome transparency in
aluminium display case, backlit with
flourescent tubes
246.4 x 363.2 cm
Collection: Buhl Foundation,
New York
Courtesy Marian Goodman Gallery,
New York
Just Washed 1997
cibachrome transparency in
aluminium display case, backlit with
flourescent tubes
47 x 51.8 cm
Courtesy the artist
*A Partial Account (of events
taking place between the hours
of 9:35am & 3:22pm, Tuesday,
21 January 1997)* 1997
cibachrome transparency in
aluminium display case, backlit with
flourescent tubes
56 x 402.4 cm
Courtesy of Galerie Johnen
& Schöttle, Cologne and Galerie
Rüdiger Schöttle, Munich
Private collection, Madrid
Volunteer 1996
cibachrome transparency in
aluminium display case, backlit with
flourescent tubes
207 x 274 cm
Courtesy the artist and Marian
Goodman Gallery, New York

Jell-O 1995
cibachrome transparency in
aluminium display case, backlit with
flourescent tubes
170 x 220 cm
Collection: Setagaya Art Museum,
Tokyo
Diagonal Composition 1993
cibachrome transparency in
aluminium display case, backlit with
flourescent tubes
40 x 46 cm
Courtesy the artist

Gillian Wearing
Sacha and Mum 1996
video projection
playing time 4 min 30 sec
Courtesy Maureen Paley /
Interim Art, London
Take Your Top Off 1993
type c prints mounted on aluminium
prints x 3, 73.5 x 99.5 cm each
Courtesy Maureen Paley / Interim
Art, London

Franz West
Symbol 1999
paper mache, paint, plastic,
gauze, wood
3 parts, part 1: 63 x 35 x 26 cm
part 2: 51 x 23 x 51 cm
part 3: 62 x 25 x 62 cm
Courtesy David Zwirner, New York
Three times the same 1998
paper mache, paint, plastic,
gauze, wood
3 parts, part 1: 83 x 26 x 33 cm
part 2: 57 x 39 x 43 cm
part 3: 62 x 42 x 33 cm
Courtesy David Zwirner, New York
L'Art pour l'Art 1975/97
23 framed works on paper
installed size variable
Courtesy David Zwirner, New York

Xu Bing
Picture Window 2000
window installation
installed size variable
Courtesy the artist
*Introduction to new English
calligraphy* 1994-96
installation comprising mixed
media/classroom, study materials,
monitor
installed size variable
Collection: the artist

Yun Suknam
Pink Room III 2000
Sofa A (wood, clothes); Sofa C
(wood, clothes); Figurative D (wood,
acrylic, colour); still nails; acrylic
beads
installed size variable
Collection: the artist

The list of works has been compiled from material received from each artist or artist's representative.
Every effort has been made to ensure that the information is accurate at time of printing.